Using OpenMP

Scientific and Engineering Computation
William Gropp and Ewing Lusk, editors; Janusz Kowalik, founding editor

Using OpenMP
Portable Shared Memory Parallel Programming

Barbara Chapman, Gabriele Jost, Ruud van der Pas

The MIT Press
Cambridge, Massachusetts
London, England

This book was set in LATEX by the authors and was printed and bound in the United States of America.

Library of Congress Cataloging-in-Publication Data

Chapman, Barbara, 1954-
  Using OpenMP : portable shared memory parallel programming / Barbara Chapman, Gabriele Jost, Ruud van der Pas.
      p. cm. – (Scientific and engineering computation)
  Includes bibliographical references and index.
  ISBN-13: 978-0-262-53302-7 (paperback : alk. paper)
  1. Parallel programming (Computer science) 2. Application program interfaces (Computer software) I. Jost, Gabriele. II. Pas, Ruud van der. III. Title.
QA76.642.C49 2007
005.2'75–dc22

                                2007026656

Dedicated to the memory of Ken Kennedy, who inspired in so many of us a passion for High Performance Computing

Contents

Series Foreword

The Scientific and Engineering Computation Series from MIT Press aims to provide practical and immediately usable information to scientists and engineers engaged at the leading edge of modern computing. Aspects of modern computing first presented in research papers and at computer science conferences are presented here with the intention of accelerating the adoption and impact of these ideas in scientific and engineering applications. Such aspects include parallelism, language design and implementation, systems software, numerical libraries, and scientific visualization.

This book is a tutorial on OpenMP, an approach to writing parallel programs for the shared-memory model of parallel computation. Now that all commodity processors are becoming multicore, OpenMP provides one of the few programming models that allows computational scientists to easily take advantage of the parallelism offered by these processors. This book includes a complete description of how to use OpenMP in both C and Fortran for real-world programs, provides suggestions for achieving high performance with OpenMP, and discusses how OpenMP-enabled compilers work. The book concludes with a discussion of future directions for OpenMP.

William Gropp and Ewing Lusk, Editors

Foreword

Programming languages evolve just as natural languages do, driven by human desires to express thoughts more cleverly, succinctly, or elegantly than in the past. A big difference is the fact that one key receiver of programs is nonhuman. These nonhumans evolve faster than humans do, helping drive language mutation after mutation, and—together with the human program writers and readers—naturally selecting among the mutations.

In the 1970s, vector and parallel computer evolution was on the move. Programming assistance was provided by language extensions—first to Fortran and then to C—in the form of directives and pragmas, respectively. Vendors differentiated themselves by providing "better" extensions than did their competitors; and by the mid-1980s things had gotten out of hand for software vendors. At Kuck and Associates (KAI), we had the problem of dealing with the whole industry, so Bruce Leasure and I set out to fix things by forming an industrywide committee, the Parallel Computing Forum (PCF). PCF struck a nerve and became very active. In a few years we had a draft standard that we took through ANSI, and after a few more years it became the ANSI X3.H5 draft. Our stamina gave out before it became an official ANSI standard, but the industry paid attention, and extensions evolved more uniformly.

This situation lasted for a few years, but the 1980s were a golden era for parallel architectural evolution, with many people writing parallel programs, so extensions again diverged, and programming needs grew. KAI took on the challenge of rethinking things and defining parallel profiling and correctness-checking tools at the same time, with the goal of innovative software development products. By the mid-1990s we had made a lot of progress and had discussed it a bit with some hardware vendors. When SGI bought Cray in April 1996, they had an immediate directive problem (two distinct extensions) and approached us about working with them. Together we refined what we had, opened up to the industry, and formed the Architecture Review Board (ARB). OpenMP was born 18 months later, as the *New York Times* reported:

NEW STANDARD FOR PARALLEL PROCESSING WORKSTATIONS

Compaq, Digital, Intel, IBM and Silicon Graphics have agreed to
support OpenMP, a new standard developed by Silicon Graphics and
Kuck & Associates to allow programmers to write a single version
of their software that will run on parallel processor computers
using Unix or Windows NT operating systems. The new standard will

```
hasten the trend in which scientists and engineers choose high-end
workstations rather than supercomputers for complex computational
applications.
```
(NYT 28 Oct. 1997)

OpenMP has been adopted by many software developers in the past decade, but it
has competed with traditional hand threading at the one extreme and MPI at the
other. These alternatives are much lower-level expressions of parallelism: threading
allows more control, MPI more scalability. Both usually require much more initial
effort to think through the details of program control, data decomposition, and
expressing thoughts with assembly-language-style calls. The multicore revolution
now demands simple parallel application development, which OpenMP provides
with language extensions and tools. While OpenMP has limitations rooted in its
technical origins, the ARB continues to drive the standard forward.

The supercomputing needs of the *New York Times* article have now been largely
replaced by scalable clusters of commodity multicore processors. What was a work-
station is now a desktop or laptop multicore system. The need for effective parallel
software development continues to grow in importance.

This book provides an excellent introduction to parallel programming and Open-
MP. It covers the language, the performance of OpenMP programs (with one hun-
dred pages of details about Fortran and C), common sources of errors, scalability
via nested parallelism and combined OpenMP/MPI programs, OpenMP implementation issues, and future ideas. Few books cover the topics in this much detail; it
includes the new OpenMP 2.5 specification, as well as hints about OpenMP 3.0
discussions and issues.

The book should be welcomed by academia, where there is rising interest in undergraduate parallel programming courses. Today, parallel programming is taught
in most universities, but only as a graduate course. With multicore processors now
used everywhere, introductory courses need to add parallel programming. Because
performance is little discussed in any undergraduate programming courses today,
parallel programming for performance is hard to incorporate. OpenMP helps to
bridge this gap because it can be added simply to sequential programs and comes
with multiple scheduling algorithms that can easily provide an experimental approach to parallel performance tuning.

OpenMP has some deceptive simplicities, both good and bad. It is easy to start
using, placing substantial burden on the system implementers. In that sense, it puts
off some experienced users and beginners with preconceived ideas about POSIX or
WinThreads, who decide that parallel programming can't be that simple and who
want to indicate on which processor each thread is going to run (and other unnec-

essary details). OpenMP also allows for very strong correctness checking versus the correctness of the sequential program to which OpenMP directives are added. Intel Thread Checker and other tools can dynamically pinpoint, to the line number, most OpenMP parallel programming bugs. Thus, OpenMP implementations indeed remove annoying burdens from developers. This book will help educate the community about such benefits.

On the other hand, the simplicity of getting started with OpenMP can lead one to believing that any sequential program can be made into a high-performance parallel program, which is not true. Architectural and program constraints must be considered in scaling up any parallel program. MPI forces one to think about this immediately and in that sense is less seductive than OpenMP. However, OpenMP scalability is being extended with nested parallelism and by Intel's ClusterOpenMP with new directives to distinguish shared- and distributed-memory variables. In the end, a high-performance OpenMP or OpenMP/MPI program may need a lot of work, but getting started with OpenMP remains quite easy, and this book treats the intricacies of scaling via nesting and hybrid OpenMP/MPI.

OpenMP is supported by thriving organizations. The ARB membership now includes most of the world's leading computer manufacturers and software providers. The ARB is a technical body that works to define new features and fix problems. Any interested programmer can join cOMPunity, a forum of academic and industrial researchers and developers who help drive the standard forward.

I am pleased that the authors asked me to write this foreword, and I hope that readers learn to use the full expressibility and power of OpenMP. This book should provide an excellent introduction to beginners, and the performance section should help those with some experience who want to push OpenMP to its limits.

David J. Kuck
Intel Fellow, Software and Solutions Group
Director, Parallel and Distributed Solutions
Intel Corporation
Urbana, IL, USA
March 14, 2007

Preface

At Supercomputing 1997, a major conference on High Performance Computing, Networking, and Storage held in San Jose, California, a group of High Performance Computing experts from industry and research laboratories used an informal "Birds of a Feather" session to unveil a new, portable programming interface for shared-memory parallel computers. They called it OpenMP. The proposers included representatives from several hardware companies and from the software house Kuck and Associates, as well as scientists from the Department of Energy who wanted a way to write programs that could exploit the parallelism in shared memory machines provided by several major hardware manufacturers.

This initiative could not have been more timely. A diversity of programming models for those early shared-memory systems were in use. They were all different enough to inhibit an easy port between them. It was good to end this undesirable situation and propose a unified model.

A company was set up to own and maintain the new informal standard. It was named the OpenMP Architecture Review Board (ARB). Since that time, the number of vendors involved in the specification and maintenance of OpenMP has steadily grown. There has been increased involvement of application developers, compiler experts, and language specialists in the ARB too.

The original proposal provided directives, a user-level library, and several environment variables that could be used to turn Fortran 77 programs into shared-memory parallel programs with minimal effort. Fairly soon after the first release, the specification was further developed to enable its use with C/C++ programs and to take features of Fortran 90 more fully into account. Since then, the bindings for Fortran and C/C++ have been merged, both for simplicity and to ensure that they are as similar as possible. Over time, support for OpenMP has been added to more and more compilers. So we can safely say that today OpenMP provides a compact, yet flexible shared-memory programming model for Fortran, C, and C++ that is widely available to application developers.

Many people collaborated in order to produce the first specification of OpenMP. Since that time, many more have worked hard in the committees set up by the ARB to clarify certain features of the language, to consider extensions, and to make their implementations more compatible with each other. Proposals for a standard means to support interactions between implementations and external tools have been intensively debated. Ideas for new features have been implemented in research prototypes. Other people have put considerable effort into promoting the use of OpenMP and in teaching novices and experts alike how to utilize its features to solve a variety of programming needs. One of the authors founded a not-for-profit company called cOMPunity to help researchers participate more fully in the evolution of OpenMP and to promote interactions between vendors, researchers, and users. Many volunteers helped cOMPunity achieve its goals.

At the time of writing, hardware companies are poised to introduce a whole new generation of computers. They are designing and building multicore platforms capable of supporting the simultaneous execution of a growing number of threads in a shared-memory system. Even laptops are already small parallel computers. The question is when and how the software will be adapted to take advantage of this trend. For a while, improved throughput is going to be the main benefit of multicore technology. It is quite typical to deploy multiple independent activities on a laptop or PC, but how many cores are needed for this? At some point, users will expect individual applications to take advantage of the additional processing power. To do so, a parallel programming model is required. We think OpenMP is in a perfect position to satisfy this need — not only today, but also in the future.

Why a book on OpenMP? After all, the OpenMP specification can be downloaded from the web. The answer lies in the fact that, although the specification has been written in a relatively informal style and has numerous examples, it is still not a particularly suitable starting point for learning how to write real programs. Moreover, some of the factors that may influence a program's performance are not mentioned anywhere in that document. Despite its apparent simplicity, then, additional information is needed. This book fills in those gaps.

Chapter 1 provides background information and explains where OpenMP is applicable, as well as how it differs from other programming interfaces.

Chapter 2 gives a brief overview of the features of OpenMP. It is intended as a high-level introduction that can be read either before or after trying out OpenMP. Among other topics, it explains how OpenMP deals with problems arising from the complex memory hierarchy present on most modern computers.

Chapter 3 is an essential chapter for novice parallel programmers. It discusses a complete OpenMP program (in both Fortran and C versions) that exploits a couple of the most widely used features, and it explains the basics of the OpenMP syntax.

Chapter 4 provides an extensive overview of the OpenMP programming model, with many examples. First, the most widely used features are introduced, with a focus on those that enable work to be shared among multiple threads. Then, some important additional elements of the API are presented. Finally, we describe some of OpenMP's lesser-used parts. In the early sections, our examples are straightforward. Later, we give solutions to some more challenging programming problems.

Chapters 5 and 6 discuss how to get good performance with OpenMP. We include a number of programming tips, along with an extended example that gives insight into the process of investigating performance problems. With the growing number of threads available on new platforms, the strategies given in Chapter 6 for achieving higher levels of scalability are likely to be important for many application developers.

Chapter 7 discusses problems of program correctness. Troubleshooting any application can be hard, but shared-memory parallel programming adds another dimension to this effort. In particular, certain kinds of bugs are nondeterministic. Whether they manifest themselves may depend on one or more external factors, such as the number of threads used, the load on the system, the compiler, and the OpenMP library implementation.

Chapter 8 shows how the compiler translates an OpenMP program to turn it into an application capable of parallel execution. Since OpenMP provides a fairly high level programming model, knowledge of what happens behind the scenes may help the reader understand the impact of its translation and the workings of OpenMP-aware compilers, performance tools, and debuggers. It may also give deeper insight into techniques and strategies for obtaining high levels of performance.

Chapter 9 describes some of the trends that are likely to influence extensions to the OpenMP specification. Included are comments on language features we expect to be included in the reasonably near future.

Acknowledgments

A number of people have worked very hard to help maintain OpenMP, provide feedback to users, debate and develop syntax for new language features, implement those features, and teach others how to use them. It is their work that we present here. We also acknowledge here the continuous efforts of many colleagues on the various committees of the OpenMP Architecture Review Board. We particularly mention Mark Bull, from the University of Edinburgh, without whom progress on the language front is difficult to conceive.

We thank our colleagues who have contributed to the activities of cOMPunity, which enables the participation of researchers and application developers in the work of the ARB. These include Eduard Ayguade, Rudi Eigenmann, Dieter an Mey, Mark Bull, Guy Robinson, and Mitsuhisa Sato.

We thank Michael Resch and colleagues at the High Performance Computing Center (HLRS) of the University of Stuttgart, Germany, for providing logisitical support for the creation of this manuscript and for offering a pleasant working environment and good company for one of us during a part of the writing phase. We particularly thank Matthias Müller, originally from HLRS, but now at the Dresden University of Technology, for his comments, encouragement, and support and for getting us started with the publisher's software.

Our sincere gratitude goes to the following organizations and individuals that have helped us throughout the writing of this book: Lei Huang, Chunhua Liao, and students in the HPC Tools lab at the University of Houston provided material for some examples and criticized our efforts. We benefited from many helpful discussions on OpenMP scalability issues with the staff of NASA Ames Research Center. In particular, we thank Michael Aftosmis and Marsha Berger for the flow-Cart example and Henry Jin for many interesting discussions of the NAS Parallel Benchmarks and OpenMP in general. Our thanks go to colleagues at CEPBA (European Center for Parallelism of Barcelona) and UPC (Universitat Politecnica de Catalunya), especially Judit Gimenez and Jesus Labarta for fruitful collaborations in performance analysis of large-scale OpenMP applications, and Eduard Ayguade, Marc Gonzalez, and Xavier Martorell for sharing their experience in OpenMP compiler technology.

Nawal Copty, Eric Duncan, and Yuan Lin at Sun Microsystems gave their help in answering a variety of questions on OpenMP in general and also on compiler and library implementation issues.

We gratefully acknowledge copious feedback on draft versions of this book from Tim Mattson (Intel Corporation) and Nawal Copty and Richard Friedman (both at Sun Microsystems). They helped us find a number of mistakes and made many suggestions for modifications and improvements. Remaining errors are, of course, entirely our responsibility.

Last but not least, our gratitude goes to our families for their continued patience and encouragement. Special thanks go to Dave Barker (a husband) for tolerating awakening to the sound of a popcorn popper (the keyboard) in the wee hours and for providing helpful feedback throughout the project; to Carola and Jonathan (two children) for cheerfully putting up with drafts of book chapters lying around in many likely, and some unlikely, places; and to Marion, Vincent, Stéphanie, and Juliette, who never complained and who provided loving support throughout this journey.

Using OpenMP

1 Introduction

OpenMP enables the creation of shared-memory parallel programs. In this chapter, we describe the evolution of computers that has led to the specification of OpenMP and that has made it relevant to mainstream computing. We put our subject matter into a broader context by giving a brief overview of parallel computing and the main approaches taken to create parallel programs. Our discussion of these topics is not intended to be comprehensive.

1.1 Why Parallel Computers Are Here to Stay

No matter how fast computers are, technology is being developed to make them even faster. Our appetite for compute power and memory seems insatiable. A more powerful machine leads to new kinds of applications, which in turn fuel our demand for yet more powerful systems. The result of this continued technological progress is nothing short of breathtaking: the laptops a couple of us are using to type this script would have been among the fastest machines on the planet just a decade ago, if they had been around at the time.

In order to achieve their breakneck speed, today's computer systems are highly complex [85]. They are made up of multiple components, or functional units, that may be able to operate simultaneously and have specific tasks, such as adding two integer numbers or determining whether a value is greater than zero. As a result, a computer might be able to fetch a datum from memory, multiply two floating-point numbers, and evaluate a branch condition all at the same time. This is a very low level of parallel processing and is often referred to as "instruction-level parallelism," or ILP. A processor that supports this is said to have a superscalar architecture. Nowadays it is a common feature in general-purpose microprocessors, even those used in laptops and PCs.

Careful reordering of these operations may keep the machine's components busy. The lion's share of the work of finding such a suitable ordering of operations is performed by the compiler (although it can be supported in hardware). To accomplish this, compiler writers developed techniques to determine dependences between operations and to find an ordering that efficiently utilizes the instruction-level parallelism and keeps many functional units and paths to memory busy with useful work. Modern compilers put considerable effort into this kind of instruction-level optimization. For instance, software pipelining may modify the sequence of instructions in a loop nest, often overlapping instructions from different iterations to ensure that as many instructions as possible complete every clock cycle. Unfortunately, several studies [95] showed that typical applications are not likely to contain more than three or four different instructions that can be fed to the computer at a time in this way. Thus, there is limited payoff for extending the hardware support for this kind of instruction-level parallelism.

Back in the 1980s, several vendors produced computers that exploited another kind of architectural parallelism.[1] They built machines consisting of multiple complete processors with a common shared memory. These shared-memory parallel, or multiprocessor, machines could work on several jobs at once, simply by parceling them out to the different processors. They could process programs with a variety of memory needs, too, and were thus suitable for many different workloads. As a result, they became popular in the server market, where they have remained important ever since. Both small and large shared-memory parallel computers (in terms of number of processors) have been built: at the time of writing, many of them have two or four CPUs, but there also exist shared-memory systems with more than a thousand CPUs in use, and the number that can be configured is growing. The technology used to connect the processors and memory has improved significantly since the early days [44]. Recent developments in hardware technology have made architectural parallelism of this kind important for mainstream computing.

In the past few decades, the components used to build both high-end and desktop machines have continually decreased in size. Shortly before 1990, Intel announced that the company had put a million transistors onto a single chip (the i860). A few years later, several companies had fit 10 million onto a chip. In the meantime, technological progress has made it possible to put billions of transistors on a single chip. As data paths became shorter, the rate at which instructions were issued could be increased. Raising the clock speed became a major source of advances in processor performance. This approach has inherent limitations, however, particularly with respect to power consumption and heat emission, which is increasingly hard to dissipate.

Recently, therefore, computer architects have begun to emphasize other strategies for increasing hardware performance and making better use of the available space on the chip. Given the limited usefulness of adding functional units, they have returned to the ideas of the 1980s: multiple processors that share memory are configured in a single machine and, increasingly, on a chip. This new generation of shared-memory parallel computers is inexpensive and is intended for general-purpose usage.

Some recent computer designs permit a single processor to execute multiple instruction streams in an interleaved way. Simultaneous multithreading, for example, interleaves instructions from multiple applications in an attempt to use more of the

---

[1] Actually, the idea was older than that, but it didn't take off until the 1980s.

hardware components at any given time. For instance, the computer might add two values from one set of instructions and, *at the same time*, fetch a value from memory that is needed to perform an operation in a different set of instructions. An example is Intel's hyperthreading^{TM} technology. Other recent platforms (e.g., IBM's Power5, AMD's Opteron and Sun's UltraSPARC IV, IV+, and T1 processors) go even further, replicating substantial parts of a processor's logic on a single chip and behaving much like shared-memory parallel machines. This approach is known as *multicore*. Simultaneous multithreading platforms, multicore machines, and shared-memory parallel computers all provide system support for the execution of multiple independent instruction streams, or *threads*. Moreover, these technologies may be combined to create computers that can execute high numbers of threads.

Given the limitations of alternative strategies for creating more powerful computers, the use of parallelism in general-purpose hardware is likely to be more pronounced in the near future. Some PCs and laptops are already multicore or multithreaded. Soon, processors will routinely have many cores and possibly the ability to execute multiple instruction streams within each core. In other words, multicore technology is going mainstream [159]. It is vital that application software be able to make effective use of the parallelism that is present in our hardware [171]. But despite major strides in compiler technology, the programmer will need to help, by describing the concurrency that is contained in application codes. In this book, we will discuss one of the easiest ways in which this can be done.

1.2 Shared-Memory Parallel Computers

Throughout this book, we will refer to shared-memory parallel computers as SMPs. Early SMPs included computers produced by Alliant, Convex, Sequent [146], Encore, and Synapse [10] in the 1980s. Larger shared-memory machines included IBM's RP3 research computer [149] and commercial systems such as the BBN Butterfly [23]. Later SGI's Power Challenge [65] and Sun Microsystem's Enterprise servers entered the market, followed by a variety of desktop SMPs.

The term SMP was originally coined to designate a symmetric multiprocessor system, a shared-memory parallel computer whose individual processors share memory (and I/O) in such a way that each of them can access any memory location with the same speed; that is, they have a *uniform memory access* (UMA) time. Many small shared-memory machines are symmetric in this sense. Larger shared-memory machines, however, usually do not satisfy this definition; even though the difference may be relatively small, some memory may be "nearer to" one or more of the processors and thus accessed faster by them. We say that such machines have *cache-coherent non-uniform memory access* (cc-NUMA). Early innovative attempts to build cc-NUMA shared-memory machines were undertaken by Kendall Square Research (KSR1 [62]) and Denelcor (the Denelcor HEP). More recent examples of large NUMA platforms with cache coherency are SGI's Origin and Altix series, HP's Exemplar, and Sun Fire E25K.

Today, the major hardware vendors all offer some form of shared-memory parallel computer, with sizes ranging from two to hundreds – and, in a few cases, thousands – of processors.

Conveniently, the acronym SMP can also stand for "shared-memory parallel computer," and we will use it to refer to *all* shared-memory systems, including cc-NUMA platforms. By and large, the programmer can ignore this difference, although techniques that we will explore in later parts of the book can help take cc-NUMA characteristics into account.

1.2.1   Cache Memory Is Not Shared

Somewhat confusing is the fact that even SMPs have some memory that is not shared. To explain why this is the case and what the implications for applications programming are, we present some background information. One of the major challenges facing computer architects today is the growing discrepancy in processor and memory speed. Processors have been consistently getting faster. But the more rapidly they can perform instructions, the quicker they need to receive the values of operands from memory. Unfortunately, the speed with which data can be read from and written to memory has not increased at the same rate. In response, the vendors have built computers with hierarchical memory systems, in which a small, expensive, and very fast memory called cache memory, or "cache" for short, supplies the processor with data and instructions at high rates [74]. Each processor of an SMP needs its own private cache if it is to be fed quickly; hence, not all memory is shared.

Figure 1.1 shows an example of a generic, cache-based dual-core processor. There are two levels of cache. The term *level* is used to denote how far away (in terms of access time) a cache is from the CPU, or core. The higher the level, the longer it takes to access the cache(s) at that level. At level 1 we distinguish a cache for data ("Data Cache"), one for instructions ("Instr. Cache"), and the "Translation-Lookaside Buffer" (or TLB for short). The last of these is an address cache. It is discussed in Section 5.2.2. These three caches are all private to a core: other core(s) cannot access them. Our figure shows only one cache at the second level. It is most likely bigger than each of the level-1 caches, and it is shared by both cores. It is also unified, which means that it contains instructions as well as data.

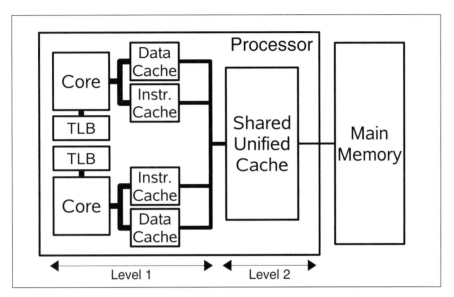

Figure 1.1: **Block diagram of a generic, cache-based dual core processor** – In this imaginary processor, there are two levels of cache. Those closest to the core are called "level 1." The higher the level, the farther away from the CPU (measured in access time) the cache is. The level-1 cache is private to the core, but the cache at the second level is shared. Both cores can use it to store and retrieve instructions, as well as data.

Data is copied into cache from main memory: blocks of consecutive memory locations are transferred at a time. Since the cache is very small in comparison to main memory, a new block may displace data that was previously copied in. An operation can be (almost) immediately performed if the values it needs are available in cache. But if they are not, there will be a delay while the corresponding data is retrieved from main memory. Hence, it is important to manage cache carefully. Since neither the programmer nor the compiler can directly put data into—or remove data from—cache, it is useful to learn how to structure program code to indirectly make sure that cache is utilized well.[2]

---

[2]The techniques developed to accomplish this task are useful for sequential programming, too. They are briefly covered in Section 5.2.3

1.2.2   Implications of Private Cache Memory

In a uniprocessor system, new values computed by the processor are written back
to cache, where they remain until their space is required for other data. At that
point, any new values that have not already been copied back to main memory are
stored back there. This strategy does not work for SMP systems. When a processor
of an SMP stores results of local computations in its private cache, the new values
are accessible only to code executing on that processor. If no extra precautions are
taken, they will not be available to instructions executing elsewhere on an SMP
machine until after the corresponding block of data is displaced from cache. But it
may not be clear when this will happen. In fact, since the old values might still be
in other private caches, code executing on other processors might continue to use
them even then.

This is known as the *memory consistency problem*. A number of strategies have
been developed to help overcome it. Their purpose is to ensure that updates to data
that have taken place on one processor are made known to the program running on
other processors, and to make the modified values available to them if needed. A
system that provides this functionality transparently is said to be *cache coherent*.

Fortunately, the OpenMP application developer does not need to understand how
cache coherency works on a given computer. Indeed, OpenMP can be implemented
on a computer that does not provide cache coherency, since it has its own set of rules
on how data is shared among the threads running on different processors. Instead,
the programmer must be aware of the *OpenMP memory model*, which provides for
shared and private data and specifies when updated shared values are guaranteed
to be available to all of the code in an OpenMP program.

1.3   Programming SMPs and the Origin of OpenMP

Once the vendors had the technology to build moderately priced SMPs, they needed
to ensure that their compute power could be exploited by individual applications.
This is where things got sticky. Compilers had always been responsible for adapting
a program to make best use of a machine's internal parallelism. Unfortunately, it is
very hard for them to do so for a computer with multiple processors or cores. The
reason is that the compilers must then identify independent streams of instructions
that can be executed in parallel. Techniques to extract such instruction streams
from a sequential program do exist; and, for simple programs, it may be worthwhile
trying out a compiler's automatic (shared-memory) parallelization options. However, the compiler often does not have enough information to decide whether it is

possible to split up a program in this way. It also cannot make large-scale changes to code, such as replacing an algorithm that is not suitable for parallelization. Thus, most of the time the compiler will need some help from the user.

1.3.1 What Are the Needs?

To understand how programmers might express a code's parallelism, the hardware manufacturers looked carefully at existing technology. Beginning in the 1980s, scientists engaged in solving particularly tough computational problems attempted to exploit the SMPs of the day to speed up their code and to perform much larger computations than were possible on a uniprocessor. To get the multiple processors to collaborate to execute a *single* application, they looked for regions of code whose instructions could be shared among the processors. Much of the time, they focused on distributing the work in loop nests to the processors.

In most programs, code executed on one processor required results that had been calculated on another one. In principle, this was not a problem because a value produced by one processor could be stored in main memory and retrieved from there by code running on other processors as needed. However, the programmer needed to ensure that the value was retrieved after it had been produced, that is, that the accesses occurred in the required order. Since the processors operated independently of one another, this was a nontrivial difficulty: their clocks were not synchronized, and they could and did execute their portions of the code at slightly different speeds.

Accordingly, the vendors of SMPs in the 1980s provided special notation to specify how the work of a program was to be parceled out to the individual processors of an SMP, as well as to enforce an ordering of accesses by different threads to shared data. The notation mainly took the form of special instructions, or *directives*, that could be added to programs written in sequential languages, especially Fortran. The compiler used this information to create the actual code for execution by each processor. Although this strategy worked, it had the obvious deficiency that a program written for one SMP did not necessarily execute on another one.

1.3.2 A Brief History of Saving Time

Toward the end of the 1980s, vendors began to collaborate to improve this state of affairs. An informal industry group called the Parallel Computing Forum (PCF) agreed on a set of directives for specifying loop parallelism in Fortran programs; their work was published in 1991 [59]. An official ANSI subcommittee called X3H5 was set up to develop an ANSI standard based on PCF. A document for the new

standard was drafted in 1994 [19], but it was never formally adopted. Interest in
PCF and X3H5 had dwindled with the rise of other kinds of parallel computers that
promised a scalable and more cost-effective approach to parallel programming. The
X3H5 standardization effort had missed its window of opportunity.

But this proved to be a temporary setback. OpenMP was defined by the *OpenMP*
Architecture Review Board (ARB), a group of vendors who joined forces during the
latter half of the 1990s to provide a common means for programming a broad
range of SMP architectures. OpenMP was based on the earlier PCF work. The
first version, consisting of a set of directives that could be used with Fortran, was
introduced to the public in late 1997. OpenMP compilers began to appear shortly
thereafter. Since that time, bindings for C and C++ have been introduced, and the
set of features has been extended. Compilers are now available for virtually all SMP
platforms. The number of vendors involved in maintaining and further developing
its features has grown. Today, almost all the major computer manufacturers, major
compiler companies, several government laboratories, and groups of researchers
belong to the ARB.

One of the biggest advantages of OpenMP is that the ARB continues to work to
ensure that OpenMP remains relevant as computer technology evolves. OpenMP
is under cautious, but active, development; and features continue to be proposed
for inclusion into the application programming interface. Applications live vastly
longer than computer architectures and hardware technologies; and, in general, application developers are careful to use programming languages that they believe will
be supported for many years to come. The same is true for parallel programming
interfaces.

1.4   What Is OpenMP?

OpenMP is a shared-memory application programming interface (API) whose features, as we have just seen, are based on prior efforts to facilitate shared-memory
parallel programming. Rather than an officially sanctioned standard, it is an
agreement reached between the members of the ARB, who share an interest in a
portable, user-friendly, and efficient approach to shared-memory parallel programming. OpenMP is intended to be suitable for implementation on a broad range of
SMP architectures. As multicore machines and multithreading processors spread in
the marketplace, it might be increasingly used to create programs for uniprocessor
computers also.

Like its predecessors, OpenMP is not a new programming language. Rather, it
is notation that can be added to a sequential program in Fortran, C, or C++ to

describe how the work is to be shared among threads that will execute on different processors or cores and to order accesses to shared data as needed. The appropriate insertion of OpenMP features into a sequential program will allow many, perhaps most, applications to benefit from shared-memory parallel architectures—often with minimal modification to the code. In practice, many applications have considerable parallelism that can be exploited.

The success of OpenMP can be attributed to a number of factors. One is its strong emphasis on structured parallel programming. Another is that OpenMP is comparatively simple to use, since the burden of working out the details of the parallel program is up to the compiler. It has the major advantage of being widely adopted, so that an OpenMP application will run on many different platforms.

But above all, OpenMP is timely. With the strong growth in deployment of both small and large SMPs and other multithreading hardware, the need for a shared-memory programming standard that is easy to learn and apply is accepted throughout the industry. The vendors behind OpenMP collectively deliver a large fraction of the SMPs in use today. Their involvement with this de facto standard ensures its continued applicability to their architectures.

1.5 Creating an OpenMP Program

OpenMP's *directives* let the user tell the compiler which instructions to execute in parallel and how to distribute them among the threads that will run the code. An OpenMP directive is an instruction in a special format that is understood by OpenMP compilers only. In fact, it looks like a comment to a regular Fortran compiler or a pragma to a C/C++ compiler, so that the program may run just as it did beforehand if a compiler is not OpenMP-aware. The API does not have many different directives, but they are powerful enough to cover a variety of needs. In the chapters that follow, we will introduce the basic idea of OpenMP and then each of the directives in turn, giving examples and discussing their main uses.

The first step in creating an OpenMP program from a sequential one is to identify the parallelism it contains. Basically, this means finding instructions, sequences of instructions, or even large regions of code that may be executed concurrently by different processors.

Sometimes, this is an easy task. Sometimes, however, the developer must reorganize portions of a code to obtain independent instruction sequences. It may even be necessary to replace an algorithm with an alternative one that accomplishes the same task but offers more exploitable parallelism. This can be a challenging problem. Fortunately, there are some typical kinds of parallelism in programs, and a variety of strategies for exploiting them have been developed. A good deal of knowledge also exists about algorithms and their suitability for parallel execution. A growing body of literature is being devoted to this topic [102, 60] and to the design of parallel programs [123, 152, 72, 34]. In this book, we will introduce some of these strategies by way of examples and will describe typical approaches to creating parallel code using OpenMP.

The second step in creating an OpenMP program is to express, using OpenMP, the parallelism that has been identified. A huge practical benefit of OpenMP is that it can be applied to *incrementally* create a parallel program from an existing sequential code. The developer can insert directives into a portion of the program and leave the rest in its sequential form. Once the resulting program version has been successfully compiled and tested, another portion of the code can be parallelized. The programmer can terminate this process once the desired speedup has been obtained.

Although creating an OpenMP program in this way can be easy, sometimes simply inserting directives is not enough. The resulting code may not deliver the expected level of performance, and it may not be obvious how to remedy the situation. Later, we will introduce techniques that may help improve a parallel program, and we will give insight into how to investigate performance problems. Armed with this information, one may be able to take a simple OpenMP program and make it run better, maybe even significantly better. It is essential that the resulting code be correct, and thus we also discuss the perils and pitfalls of the process. Finding certain kinds of bugs in parallel programs can be difficult, so an application developer should endeavor to prevent them by adopting best practices from the start.

Generally, one can quickly and easily create parallel programs by relying on the implementation to work out the details of parallel execution. This is how OpenMP directives work. Unfortunately, however, it is not always possible to obtain high performance by a straightforward, incremental insertion of OpenMP directives into a sequential program. To address this situation, OpenMP designers included several features that enable the programmer to specify more details of the parallel code. Later in the book, we will describe a completely different way of using OpenMP to take advantage of these features. Although it requires quite a bit more work, users may find that getting their hands downright dirty by creating the code for each thread can be a lot of fun. And, this may be the ticket to getting OpenMP to solve some very large problems on a very big machine.

1.6   The Bigger Picture

Many kinds of computer architectures have been built that exploit parallelism [55]. In fact, parallel computing has been an indispensable technology in many cutting-edge disciplines for several decades. One of the earliest kinds of parallel systems were the powerful and expensive vector computers that used the idea of pipelining instructions to apply the same operation to many data objects in turn (e.g., Cyber-205 [114], CRAY-1 [155], Fujitsu Facom VP-200 [135]). These systems dominated the high end of computing for several decades, and machines of this kind are still deployed. Other platforms were built that simultaneously applied the same operation to many data objects (e.g. CM2 [80], MasPar [140]). Many systems have been produced that connect multiple independent computers via a network; both proprietary and off-the-shelf networks have been deployed. Early products based on this approach include Intel's iPSC series [28] and machines built by nCUBE and Meiko [22]. Memory is associated with each of the individual computers in the network and is thus distributed across the machine. These distributed-memory parallel systems are often referred to as *massively parallel computers* (MPPs) because very large systems can be put together this way. Information on some of the fastest machines built during the past decade and the technology used to build them can be found at `http://www.top500.org`.

Many MPPs are in use today, especially for scientific computing. If distributed-memory computers are designed with additional support that enables memory to be shared between all the processors, they are also SMPs according to our definition. Such platforms are often called distributed shared-memory computers (DSMs) to emphasize the distinctive nature of this architecture (e.g., SGI Origin [106]). When distributed-memory computers are constructed by using standard workstations or PCs and an off-the-shelf network, they are usually called clusters [169]. Clusters, which are often composed of SMPs, are much cheaper to build than proprietary MPPs. This technology has matured in recent years, so that clusters are common in universities and laboratories as well as in some companies. Thus, although SMPs are the most widespread kind of parallel computer in use, there are many other kinds of parallel machines in the marketplace, particularly for high-end applications.

Figure 1.2 shows the difference in these architectures: in (a) we see a shared-memory system where processors share main memory but have their own private cache; (b) depicts an MPP in which memory is distributed among the processors, or nodes, of the system. The platform in (c) is identical to (b) except for the fact that the distributed memories are accessible to all processors. The cluster in (d) consists of a set of independent computers linked by a network.

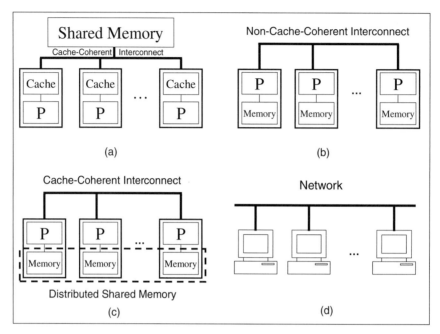

Figure 1.2: **Distributed- and shared-memory computers** – The machine in
(a) has physically shared memory, whereas the others have distributed memory. However,
the memory in (c) is accessible to all processors.

An equally broad range of applications makes use of parallel computers [61].
Very early adopters of this technology came from such disciplines as aeronautics,
aerospace, and chemistry, where vehicles were designed, materials tested, and their
properties evaluated long before they were constructed. Scientists in many disciplines have achieved monumental insights into our universe by running parallel
programs that model real-world phenomena with high levels of accuracy. Theoretical results were confirmed in ways that could not be done via experimentation.
Parallel computers have been used to improve the design and production of goods
from automobiles to packaging for refrigerators and to ensure that the designs com-
ply with pricing and behavioral constraints, including regulations. They have been
used to study natural phenomena that we are unable to fully observe, such as the
formation of galaxies and the interactions of molecules. But they are also routinely used in weather forecasting, and improvements in the accuracy of our daily
forecasts are mainly the result of deploying increasingly fast (and large) parallel
computers. More recently, they have been widely used in Hollywood and elsewhere

to generate highly realistic film sequences and special effects. In this context, too, the ability to build bigger parallel computers has led to higher-quality results, here in the form of more realistic imagery. Of course, parallel computers are also used to digitally remaster old film and to perform many other tasks involving image processing. Other areas using substantial parallel computing include drug design, financial and economic forecasting, climate modeling, surveillance, and medical imaging. It is routine in many areas of engineering, chemistry, and physics, and almost all commercial databases are able to exploit parallel machines.

1.7   Parallel Programming Models

Just as there are several different classes of parallel hardware, so too are there several distinct models of parallel programming. Each of them has a number of concrete realizations. OpenMP realizes a shared-memory (or shared address space) programming model. This model assumes, as its name implies, that programs will be executed on one or more processors that share some or all of the available memory. Shared-memory programs are typically executed by multiple independent threads (execution states that are able to process an instruction stream); the threads share data but may also have some additional, private data. Shared-memory approaches to parallel programming must provide, in addition to a normal range of instructions, a means for starting up threads, assigning work to them, and coordinating their accesses to shared data, including ensuring that certain operations are performed by only one thread at a time [15].

A different programming model has been proposed for distributed-memory systems. Generically referred to as "message passing," this model assumes that programs will be executed by one or more processes, each of which has its own private address space [69]. Message-passing approaches to parallel programming must provide a means to initiate and manage the participating processes, along with operations for sending and receiving messages, and possibly for performing special operations across data distributed among the different processes. The pure message-passing model assumes that processes cooperate to exchange messages whenever one of them needs data produced by another one. However, some recent models are based on "single-sided communication." These assume that a process may interact directly with memory across a network to read and write data anywhere on a machine.

Various realizations of both shared- and distributed-memory programming models have been defined and deployed. An ideal API for parallel programming is expressive enough to permit the specification of many parallel algorithms, is easy to use, and leads to efficient programs. Moreover, the more transparent its implementation is, the easier it is likely to be for the programmer to understand how to obtain good performance. Unfortunately, there are trade-offs between these goals and parallel programming APIs differ in the features provided and in the manner and complexity of their implementation. Some are a collection of library routines with which the programmer may specify some or all of the details of parallel execution (e.g., GA [141] and Pthreads [108] for shared-memory programming and MPI for MPPs), while others such as OpenMP and HPF [101] take the form of additional instructions to the compiler, which is expected to utilize them to generate the parallel code.

1.7.1 Realization of Shared- and Distributed-Memory Models

Initially, vendors of both MPPs and SMPs provided their own custom sets of instructions for exploiting the parallelism in their machines. Application developers had to work hard to modify their codes when they were ported from one machine to another. As the number of parallel machines grew and as more and more parallel programs were written, developers began to demand standards for parallel programming. Fortunately, such standards now exist.

MPI, or the Message Passing Interface, was defined in the early 1990s by a group of researchers and vendors who based their work on existing vendor APIs [69, 137, 147]. It provides a comprehensive set of library routines for managing processes and exchanging messages. MPI is widely used in high-end computing, where problems are so large that many computers are needed to attack them. It is comparatively easy to implement on a broad variety of platforms and therefore provides excellent portability. However, the portability comes at a cost. Creating a parallel program based on this API typically requires a major reorganization of the original sequential code. The development effort can be large and complex compared to a compiler-supported approach such as that offered by OpenMP.

One can also combine some programming APIs. In particular, MPI and OpenMP may be used together in a program, which may be useful if a program is to be executed on MPPs that consist of multiple SMPs (possibly with multiple cores each). Reasons for doing so include exploiting a finer granularity of parallelism than possible with MPI, reducing memory usage, or reducing network communication. Various commercial codes have been programmed using both MPI and OpenMP. Combining MPI and OpenMP effectively is nontrivial, however, and in Chapter 6 we return to this topic and to the challenge of creating OpenMP codes that will work well on large systems.

1.8   Ways to Create Parallel Programs

In this section, we briefly compare OpenMP with the most important alternatives for programming shared-memory machines. Some vendors also provide custom APIs on their platforms. Although such APIs may be fast (this is, after all, the purpose of a custom API), programs written using them may have to be substantially rewritten to function on a different machine. We do not consider APIs that were not designed for broad use.

Automatic parallelization: Many compilers provide a flag, or option, for automatic program parallelization. When this is selected, the compiler analyzes the program, searching for independent sets of instructions, and in particular for loops whose iterations are independent of one another. It then uses this information to generate explicitly parallel code. One of the ways in which this could be realized is to generate OpenMP directives, which would enable the programmer to view and possibly improve the resulting code. The difficulty with relying on the compiler to detect and exploit parallelism in an application is that it may lack the necessary information to do a good job. For instance, it may need to know the values that will be assumed by loop bounds or the range of values of array subscripts: but this is often unknown ahead of run time. In order to preserve correctness, the compiler has to conservatively assume that a loop is not parallel whenever it cannot prove the contrary. Needless to say, the more complex the code, the more likely it is that this will occur. Moreover, it will in general not attempt to parallelize regions larger than loop nests. For programs with a simple structure, it may be worth trying this option.

MPI: The Message Passing Interface [137] was developed to facilitate portable programming for distributed-memory architectures (MPPs), where multiple processes execute independently and communicate data as needed by exchanging messages. The API was designed to be highly expressive and to enable the creation of efficient parallel code, as well as to be broadly implementable. As a result of its success in these respects, it is the most widely used API for parallel programming in the high-end technical computing community, where MPPs and clusters are common. Since most vendors of shared-memory systems also provide MPI implementations that leverage the shared address space, we include it here.

Creating an MPI program can be tricky. The programmer must create the code that will be executed by each process, and this implies a good deal of reprogramming. The need to restructure the entire program does not allow for incremental parallelization as does OpenMP. It can be difficult to create a single program version that will run efficiently on many different systems, since the relative cost of communicating data and performing computations varies from one system to another and may suggest different approaches to extracting parallelism. Care must be taken to avoid certain programming errors, particularly deadlock where two or more processes each wait in perpetuity for the other to send a message. A good introduction to MPI programming is provided in [69] and [147].

Since many MPPs consist of a collection of SMPs, MPI is increasingly mixed with OpenMP to create a program that directly matches the hardware. A recent revision of the standard, MPI-2 ([58]), facilitates their integration.

Pthreads: This is a set of threading interfaces developed by the IEEE (Institute of Electrical and Electronics Engineers) committees in charge of specifying a Portable Operating System Interface (POSIX). It realizes the shared-memory programming model via a collection of routines for creating, managing and coordinating a collection of threads. Thus, like MPI, it is a library. Some features were primarily designed for uniprocessors, where context switching enables a time-sliced execution of multiple threads, but it is also suitable for programming small SMPs. The Pthreads library aims to be expressive as well as portable, and it provides a fairly comprehensive set of features to create, terminate, and synchronize threads and to prevent different threads from trying to modify the same values at the same time: it includes mutexes, locks, condition variables, and semaphores. However, programming with Pthreads is much more complex than with OpenMP, and the resulting code is likely to differ substantially from a prior sequential program (if there is one). Even simple tasks are performed via multiple steps, and thus a typical program will contain many calls to the Pthreads library. For example, to execute a simple loop in parallel, the programmer must declare threading structures, create and terminate the threads individually, and compute the loop bounds for each thread. If interactions occur within loop iterations, the amount of thread-specific code can increase substantially. Compared to Pthreads, the OpenMP API directives make it easy to specify parallel loop execution, to synchronize threads, and to specify whether or not data is to be shared. For many applications, this is sufficient.

1.8.1   A Simple Comparison

The code snippets below demonstrate the implementation of a *dot product* in each of the programming APIs MPI, Pthreads, and OpenMP. We do not explain in detail the features used here, as our goal is simply to illustrate the flavor of each, although we will introduce those used in the OpenMP code in later chapters.

Sequential Dot-Product

```
int main(argc,argv)
int argc;
char *argv[];
{
 double sum;
 double a [256], b [256];
 int n;
 n = 256;
 for (i = 0; i < n; i++) {
     a [i] = i * 0.5;
     b [i] = i * 2.0;
 }
 sum = 0;
 for (i = 1; i <= n; i++ ) {
     sum = sum + a[i]*b[i];
 }
 printf ("sum = %f", sum);
}
```

The sequential program multiplies the individual elements of two arrays and saves the result in the variable sum; sum is a so-called reduction variable.

Dot-Product in MPI

```
int main(argc,argv)
int argc;
char *argv[];
{
 double sum, sum_local;
 double a [256], b [256];
 int n, numprocs, myid, my_first, my_last;

 n = 256;

 MPI_Init(&argc,&argv);
 MPI_Comm_size(MPI_COMM_WORLD,&numprocs);
 MPI_Comm_rank(MPI_COMM_WORLD,&myid);
```

```
my_first = myid *  n/numprocs;
my_last = (myid + 1) *  n/numprocs;

for (i = 0; i < n; i++) {
   a [i] = i * 0.5;
   b [i] = i * 2.0;
}
sum_local = 0;
for (i = my_first; i < my_last; i++) {
    sum_local = sum_local + a[i]*b[i];
}
MPI_Allreduce(&sum_local, &sum, 1, MPI_DOUBLE, MPI_SUM,
                                MPI_COMM_WORLD);
 if (iam==0) printf ("sum = %f", sum);
}
```

Under MPI, all data is local. To implement the dot-product, each process builds
a partial sum, the sum of its local data. To do so, each executes a portion of the
original loop. Data and loop iterations are accordingly manually shared among
processors by the programmer. In a subsequent step, the partial sums have to be
communicated and combined to obtain the global result. MPI provides the global
communication routine MPI_Allreduce for this purpose.

Dot-Product in Pthreads

```
#define NUMTHRDS 4
double sum;
double a [256], b [256];
int status;
int n=256;
pthread_t thd[NUMTHRDS];
pthread_mutex_t mutexsum;

int main(argc,argv)
int argc;
char *argv[];
{

 pthread_attr_t attr;
```

```
for (i = 0;  i < n;  i++) {
   a [i] = i * 0.5;
   b [i] = i * 2.0;
}

thread_mutex_init(&mutexsum, NULL);
pthread_attr_init(&attr);
pthread_attr_setdetachstate(&attr, PTHREAD_CREATE_JOINABLE);

for(i=0;i<NUMTHRDS;i++)
{
  pthread_create( &thds[i], &attr, dotprod, (void *)i);
}

pthread_attr_destroy(&attr);

for(i=0;i<NUMTHRDS;i++) {
  pthread_join( thds[i], (void **)&status);
}

printf ("sum =  %f \n", sum);
pthread_mutex_destroy(&mutexsum);
pthread_exit(NULL);
}


void *dotprod(void *arg)
{
  int myid, i, my_first, my_last;
  double sum_local;

  myid = (int)arg;
  my_first = myid *  n/NUMTHRDS;
  my_last = (myid + 1) *  n/NUMTHRDS;

  sum_local = 0;
  for (i = my_first; i <= my_last; i++) {
```

```
    sum_local = sum_local + a [i]*b[i];
  }
  pthread_mutex_lock (&mutex_sum);
  sum = sum + sum_local;
  pthread_mutex_unlock (&mutex_sum);

  pthread_exit((void*) 0);
}
```

In the Pthreads programming API, all data is shared but logically distributed among the threads. Access to globally shared data needs to be explicitly synchronized by the user. In the dot-product implementation shown, each thread builds a partial sum and then adds its contribution to the global sum. Access to the global sum is protected by a lock so that only one thread at a time updates this variable. We note that the implementation effort in Pthreads is as high as, if not higher than, in MPI.

Dot-Product in OpenMP

```
int main(argc,argv)
int argc; char *argv[];
{
 double sum;
 double a [256], b [256];
 int status;
 int n=256;

 for (i = 0; i < n; i++) {
    a [i] = i * 0.5;
    b [i] = i * 2.0;
 }

 sum = 0;
 #pragma omp for reduction(+:sum)
 for (i = 1; i <= n; i++ ) {
    sum = sum + a[i]*b[i];
 }
 printf ("sum =  %f \n", sum);
}
```

Under OpenMP, all data is shared by default. In this case, we are able to parallelize the loop simply by inserting a directive that tells the compiler to parallelize it, and identifying `sum` as a reduction variable. The details of assigning loop iterations to threads, having the different threads build partial sums and their accumulation into a global sum are left to the compiler. Since (apart from the usual variable declarations and initializations) nothing else needs to be specified by the programmer, this code fragment illustrates the simplicity that is possible with OpenMP.

1.9   A Final Word

Given the trend toward bigger SMPs and multithreading computers, it is vital that strategies and techniques for creating shared-memory parallel programs become widely known. Explaining how to use OpenMP in conjunction with the major programming languages Fortran, C, and C++ to write such parallel programs is the purpose of this book. Under OpenMP, one can easily introduce threading in such a way that the same program may run sequentially as well as in parallel. The application developer can rely on the compiler to work out the details of the parallel code or may decide to explicitly assign work to threads. In short, OpenMP is a very flexible medium for creating parallel code.

The discussion of language features in this book is based on the OpenMP 2.5 specification, which merges the previously separate specifications for Fortran and C/C++. At the time of writing, the ARB is working on the OpenMP 3.0 specification, which will expand the model to provide additional convenience and expressivity for the range of architectures that it supports. Further information on this, as well as up-to-date news, can be found at the ARB website `http://www.openmp.org` and at the website of its user community, `http://www.compunity.org`. The complete OpenMP specification can also be downloaded from the ARB website.

2 Overview of OpenMP

In this chapter we give an overview of the OpenMP programming interface and compare it with other approaches to parallel programming for SMPs.

2.1 Introduction

The OpenMP Application Programming Interface (API) was developed to enable portable shared memory parallel programming. It aims to support the parallelization of applications from many disciplines. Moreover, its creators intended to provide an approach that was relatively easy to learn as well as apply. The API is designed to permit an incremental approach to parallelizing an existing code, in which portions of a program are parallelized, possibly in successive steps. This is a marked contrast to the all-or-nothing conversion of an entire program in a single step that is typically required by other parallel programming paradigms. It was also considered highly desirable to enable programmers to work with a single source code: if a single set of source files contains the code for both the sequential and the parallel versions of a program, then program maintenance is much simplified. These goals have done much to give the OpenMP API its current shape, and they continue to guide the OpenMP Architecture Review Board (ARB) as it works to provide new features.

2.2 The Idea of OpenMP

A thread is a runtime entity that is able to independently execute a stream of instructions. OpenMP builds on a large body of work that supports the specification of programs for execution by a collection of cooperating threads [15]. The operating system creates a process to execute a program: it will allocate some resources to that process, including pages of memory and registers for holding values of objects. If multiple threads collaborate to execute a program, they will share the resources, including the address space, of the corresponding process. The individual threads need just a few resources of their own: a program counter and an area in memory to save variables that are specific to it (including registers and a stack). Multiple threads may be executed on a single processor or core via context switches; they may be interleaved via simultaneous multithreading. Threads running simultaneously on multiple processors or cores may work concurrently to execute a parallel program.

Multithreaded programs can be written in various ways, some of which permit complex interactions between threads. OpenMP attempts to provide ease of programming and to help the user avoid a number of potential programming errors,

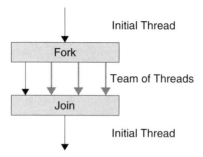

Figure 2.1: **The fork-join programming model supported by OpenMP** –
The program starts as a single thread of execution, the initial thread. A team of threads
is forked at the beginning of a parallel region and joined at the end.

by offering a structured approach to multithreaded programming. It supports the
so-called fork-join programming model [48], which is illustrated in Figure 2.1. Under this approach, the program starts as a single thread of execution, just like a
sequential program. The thread that executes this code is referred to as the *initial thread*. Whenever an OpenMP parallel construct is encountered by a thread
while it is executing the program, it creates a team of threads (this is the *fork*),
becomes the master of the team, and collaborates with the other members of the
team to execute the code dynamically enclosed by the construct. At the end of
the construct, only the original thread, or master of the team, continues; all others
terminate (this is the *join*). Each portion of code enclosed by a parallel construct
is called a parallel region.

OpenMP expects the application developer to give a high-level specification of the
parallelism in the program and the method for exploiting that parallelism. Thus it
provides notation for indicating the regions of an OpenMP program that should be
executed in parallel; it also enables the provision of additional information on how
this is to be accomplished. The job of the OpenMP implementation is to sort out
the low-level details of actually creating independent threads to execute the code
and to assign work to them according to the strategy specified by the programmer.

2.3   The Feature Set

The OpenMP API comprises a set of compiler directives, runtime library routines, and environment variables to specify shared-memory parallelism in Fortran and C/C++ programs. An OpenMP directive is a specially formatted comment or pragma that generally applies to the executable code immediately following it in the program. A directive or OpenMP routine generally affects only those threads that encounter it. Many of the directives are applied to a *structured block* of code, a sequence of executable statements with a single entry at the top and a single exit at the bottom in Fortran programs, and an executable statement in C/C++ (which may be a compound statement with a single entry and single exit). In other words, the program may not branch into or out of blocks of code associated with directives. In Fortran programs, the start and end of the applicable block of code are explicitly marked by OpenMP directives. Since the end of the block is explicit in C/C++, only the start needs to be marked.

OpenMP provides means for the user to

- create teams of threads for parallel execution,

- specify how to share work among the members of a team,

- declare both shared and private variables, and

- synchronize threads and enable them to perform certain operations exclusively (i.e., without interference by other threads).

In the following sections, we give an overview of the features of the API. In subsequent chapters we describe these features and show how they can be used to create parallel programs.

2.3.1   Creating Teams of Threads

A team of threads is created to execute the code in a parallel region of an OpenMP program. To accomplish this, the programmer simply specifies the parallel region by inserting a `parallel` directive immediately before the code that is to be executed in parallel to mark its start; in Fortran programs, the end is also marked by an `end parallel` directive. Additional information can be supplied along with the `parallel` directive. This is mostly used to enable threads to have private copies of some data for the duration of the parallel region and to initialize that data. At the end of a parallel region is an implicit barrier synchronization: this means that no thread can progress until all other threads in the team have reached that point in the program. Afterwards, program execution continues with the thread or threads that previously existed. If a team of threads executing a parallel region encounters another `parallel` directive, each thread in the current team creates a new team of threads and becomes its master. Nesting enables the realization of multilevel parallel programs.

OpenMP is commonly used to incrementally parallelize an existing sequential code, and this task is most easily accomplished by creating parallel regions one at a time.

2.3.2   Sharing Work among Threads

If the programmer does not specify how the work in a parallel region is to be shared among the executing threads, they will each redundantly execute all of the code. This approach does not speed up the program. The OpenMP work-sharing directives are provided for the programmer to state how the computation in a structured block of code is to be distributed among the threads. Unless explicitly overridden by the programmer, an implicit barrier synchronization also exists at the end of a work-sharing construct. The choice of work-sharing method may have a considerable bearing on the performance of the program.

Work Sharing and Loops   Probably the most common work-sharing approach is to distribute the work in a `DO` (Fortran) or `for` (C/C++) loop among the threads in a team. To accomplish this, the programmer inserts the appropriate directive immediately before each loop within a parallel region that is to be shared among threads. Work-sharing directives cannot be applied to all kinds of loops that occur in C/C++ code. Many programs, especially scientific applications, spend a large fraction of their time in loops performing calculations on array elements and so this strategy is widely applicable and often very effective.

All OpenMP strategies for sharing the work in loops assign one or more disjoint sets of iterations to each thread. The programmer may specify the method used to partition the iteration set. The most straightforward strategy assigns one contiguous *chunk of iterations* to each thread. More complicated strategies include dynamically computing the next chunk of iterations for a thread. If the programmer does not provide a strategy, then an implementation-defined default will be used.

When Can the Work Be Shared?   Not every loop can be parallelized in this fashion. It must be possible to determine the number of iterations in the loop upon entry, and this number may not change while the loop is executing. Loops implemented via a `while` construct, for example, may not satisfy this condition. Furthermore, a loop is suitable for sharing among threads only if its iterations are independent. By this, we mean that the order in which the iterations are performed has no bearing on the outcome. The job of the OpenMP programmer is to determine whether this is the case, and sometimes a loop needs to be modified somewhat to accomplish this.

Consider the nested loop in Fortran below which is typical for applications from the field of computational fluid dynamics.

```fortran
!$OMP PARALLEL
!$OMP DO
   do 10 j = 1, jmax
      i = 1
      vv (i,j) = v (i,j,m)
      do 60 i = 2, imax-1
         vv (i,j) = vv (i-1,j) + b(i,j)
 60   continue
      i = imax
      vv (i,j) = vv(i-1,j)
      do 100 i = imax-1, 1, -1
         vv (i,j) = vv (i+1,j) + a (i,j)
100  continue
 10  continue
!$OMP END DO
!$OMP END PARALLEL
```

Loops 60 and 100 are not suitable for parallelization via work sharing. In loop 60, the `i`th iteration writes array element `vv(i,j)` and in the `i+1`th iteration this value is used. Thus iteration `i+1` depends on the outcome of iteration `i`, and the order in which they are executed must be maintained. A similar situation occurs with regard to loop 100 where, for example, the second iteration writes `vv(imax-2,j)`. But this calculation uses the value of `vv(imax-1,j)` that was computed in the previous iteration. All is not lost, however. With some thought one can see that the outermost `j` loop is independent. Thus we can share the iterations of this loop among the executing threads. The two comment lines at the start and end of the example are all that is needed to achieve this in OpenMP.

The data reuse patterns illustrated in the inner loops are examples of *data dependence* [25]. Data dependences prevent us from parallelizing a loop when a value that is written in one loop iteration is either written or read in another iteration. The more complex the loop, the harder it can be to decide whether such dependences exist. Keep in mind that the correct placement of the OpenMP directives is the user's responsibility and that on occasion some insight into the application is needed to decide whether there really is a dependence.

Other Work-Sharing Strategies   Other approaches may be used to assign work to threads within a parallel region. One approach consists of giving distinct pieces of work to the individual threads. This approach is suitable when independent computations are to be performed and the order in which they are carried out is irrelevant. It is straightforward to specify this by using the corresponding OpenMP directive. Just as before, the programmer must ensure that the computations can truly be executed in parallel. It is also possible to specify that just one thread should execute a block of code in a parallel region.

Moreover, the OpenMP API contains a directive for sharing the work in Fortran 90 array statements among threads. It also works for the Fortran 95 `forall` construct. Such operations on an entire array contain considerable exploitable parallelism. The method of distributing the work to threads will be determined by the compiler in this case.

2.3.3   The OpenMP Memory Model

OpenMP is based on the shared-memory model; hence, by default, data is shared among the threads and is visible to all of them. Sometimes, however, one needs variables that have thread-specific values. When each thread has its own copy of a variable, so that it may potentially have a different value for each of them, we say that the variable is *private*. For example, when a team of threads executes a parallel loop, each thread needs its own value of the iteration variable. This case is so important that the compiler enforces it; in other cases the programmer must determine which variables are shared and which are private. Data can be declared to be shared or private with respect to a parallel region or work-sharing construct.[1]

The use of private variables can be beneficial in several ways. They can reduce the frequency of updates to shared memory. Thus, they may help avoid hot spots, or competition for access to certain memory locations, which can be expensive if large numbers of threads are involved. They can also reduce the likelihood of remote data accesses on cc-NUMA platforms and may remove the need for some

---

[1]OpenMP also allows private data objects to persist between parallel regions.

synchronizations. The downside is that they will increase the program's memory footprint.

Threads need a place to store their private data at run time. For this, each thread has its own special region in memory known as the thread stack. The application developer may safely ignore this detail, with one exception: most compilers give the thread stack a default size. But sometimes the amount of data that needs to be saved there can grow to be quite large, as the compiler will use it to store other information, too. Then the default size may not be large enough. Fortunately, the application developer is usually provided with a means to increase the size of the thread stack (for details, the manual should be consulted). Dynamically declared data and persistent data objects require their own storage area. For those who would like to know a little more about this, we describe how data is stored and retrieved at run time in Chapter 8.

In Section 1.2.1 of Chapter 1, we explained that each processor of an SMP has a small amount of private memory called cache. In Section 1.2.2 we showed that this could potentially lead to trouble where shared data is concerned, as the new value of a shared object might be in a cache somewhere on the system instead of main memory, where other threads can access it. Fortunately, the OpenMP programmer does not need to know how a specific system deals with this problem, since OpenMP has its own rules about when shared data is visible to (or accessible by) all threads. These rules state that the values of shared objects must be made available to all threads at synchronization points. (We explain what these are in the next section.) Between the synchronization points, threads may temporarily keep their updated values in local cache. As a result, threads may *temporarily* have different values for some shared objects. If one thread needs a value that was created by another thread, then a synchronization point must be inserted into the code.

OpenMP also has a feature called `flush`, discussed in detail in Section 4.9.2, to synchronize memory. A `flush` operation makes sure that the thread calling it has the same values for shared data objects as does main memory. Hence, new values of any shared objects updated by that thread are written back to shared memory, and the thread gets any new values produced by other threads for the shared data it reads. In some programming languages, a `flush` is known as a *memory fence*, since reads and writes of shared data may not be moved relative to it.

2.3.4   Thread Synchronization

Synchronizing, or coordinating the actions of, threads is sometimes necessary in order to ensure the proper ordering of their accesses to shared data and to prevent

data corruption. Many mechanisms have been proposed to support the synchronization needs of a variety of applications [51, 50, 81]. OpenMP has a rather small
set of fairly well understood synchronization features.

Ensuring the required thread coordination is one of the toughest challenges of
shared-memory programming. OpenMP attempts to reduce the likelihood of synchronization errors, and to make life easier for the programmer, provides for implicit
synchronization. By default, OpenMP gets threads to wait at the end of a work-
sharing construct or parallel region until all threads in the team executing it have
finished their portion of the work. Only then can they proceed. This is known as
a barrier. Synchronizing the actions of a subset of threads is harder to accomplish
in OpenMP and requires care in programming because there is no explicit support
for this.

Sometimes a programmer may need to ensure that only one thread at a time
works on a piece of code. OpenMP has several mechanisms that support this kind
of synchronization. For example, if a thread attempts to execute code that is
protected by a such a feature, and it is already being executed by another thread,
then the former will have to wait for its turn. Alternatively, it may be possible
for it to carry out other work while waiting. If it suffices to protect updates to an
individual variable (more precisely, a memory location), it may be more efficient to
employ the atomic update feature provided by OpenMP.

Synchronization points are those places in the code where synchronization has
been specified, either explicitly or implicitly. They have an additional function in
OpenMP code, as we have just learned: at these places in the code, the system
ensures that threads have consistent values of shared data objects. OpenMP's
synchronization points include explicit and implicit barriers, the start and end of
critical regions, points where locks are acquired or released, and anywhere the
programmer has inserted a *flush* directive.

2.3.5   Other Features to Note

Procedures   Subroutines and functions can complicate the use of parallel programming APIs. In order to accommodate them, major changes to a program
may sometimes be needed. One of the innovative features of OpenMP is the fact
that directives may be inserted into the procedures that are invoked from within
a parallel region. These have come to be known as *orphan directives*, a term that
indicates that they are not in the routine in which the parallel region is specified.
(For compiler buffs, this means that they are not within the lexical extent of the
parallel construct.)

Number of Threads and Thread Numbers For some applications, it can be important to control the number of threads that execute a parallel region. OpenMP lets the programmer specify this number prior to program execution via an environment variable, after the computation has begun via a library routine, or at the start of a parallel region. If this is not done, then the implementation must choose the number of threads that will be used. Some programs need to use the number of threads in a team to set the values of certain variables. Other programs may want to assign computation to a specific thread. OpenMP assigns consecutive numbers, starting from 0, to each thread in a team in order to identify them. There are library routines for retrieving the number of threads as well as for enabling a thread to access its own thread number.

OpenMP has a couple of features that may affect the number of threads in a team. First, it is possible to permit the execution environment to dynamically vary the number of threads, in which case a team may have fewer than the specified number of threads, possibly as a result of other demands made on the system's resources. The default behavior in this regard is implementation defined. Once the number of threads in a given team has been created, however, that number will not change. Second, an implementation is permitted to disallow nested parallelism, or it may be disabled by the programmer.

2.4 OpenMP Programming Styles

OpenMP encourages structured parallel programming and relies heavily on distributing the work in loops among threads. But sometimes the amount of loop-level parallelism in an application is limited. Sometimes parallelization using OpenMP directives leads to unacceptable overheads. Particularly when the application or the number of threads to be used is relatively large, an alternative method of using OpenMP may be beneficial. One can also write OpenMP programs that do not rely on work-sharing directives but rather *assign work explicitly to different threads* using their thread numbers. This approach can lead to highly efficient code. However, the programmer must then insert synchronization manually to ensure that accesses to shared data are correctly controlled. In this mode, programming errors such as deadlock (when all threads wait for each other in perpetuity) may occur and must be avoided via careful code design.

This approach can help solve a broad variety of programming problems. For instance, it may be used to give threads slightly different amounts of work if one knows that the operating system will take up some cycles on a processor. A particularly popular style of programming that can achieve high efficiency based on this approach is suitable for parallelizing programs working on a computational domain that can be subdivided. With it, the user explicitly creates the subdomains (a strategy sometimes called domain decomposition) and assigns them to the threads. Each thread then works on its portion of the data. This strategy is often referred to as SPMD (single program muliple data) programming.

Those approaches that require manual assignment of work to threads and that need explicit synchronization are often called "low-level programming." This style of programming can be very effective and it is broadly applicable, but it requires much more development effort and implies more care on the part of the developer to ensure program correctness. OpenMP provides sufficient features to permit such a low-level approach to parallel program creation.

2.5   Correctness Considerations

One of the major difficulties of shared-memory parallel programming is the effort required to ensure that a program is correct. In addition to all the sources of errors that may arise in a sequential program, shared-memory programs may contain new, and sometimes devious, bugs. Fortunately, the use of directives and a structured programming style is sufficient to prevent many problems; when the programmer adopts a low-level style of programming, however, more care is needed.

One kind of error in particular, a *data race condition*,[2] can be extremely difficult to detect and manifests itself in a shared-memory parallel code through silent data corruption. Unfortunately, the runtime behavior of a program with a data race condition is not reproducible: erroneous data may be produced by one program run, but the problem may not show up the next time it is executed. The problem arises when two or more threads access the same shared variable without any synchronization to order the accesses, and at least one of the accesses is a write. Since it is relatively easy, for example, to create a parallel version of a loop nest without noticing that multiple iterations reference the same array element, the programmer must be aware of the impact that this may have. In general, the more complex the code, the harder it is to guarantee that no such errors have been introduced.

The order of operations actually observed in a code with a data race condition depends on the load on a system and the relative timing of the threads involved. Since threads may execute their instructions at slightly different speeds, and the work of the operating system sometimes affects the performance of one or more threads, the order in which they reach certain code is observed to vary from one

---

[2]This is sometimes also referred to as "data race" or "race condition."

run to another. In some instances, the problem occurs only for a specific number of threads. As a result, a data race bug may escape detection during testing and even for some time when a program is in production use. Thus, the importance of avoiding this problem by paying careful attention during program development can not be overemphasized. Tools may help by pointing out potential problems.

One can identify other potential causes of errors in OpenMP programs. For instance, if the programmer has relied on program execution by a certain number of threads and if a different number is used to execute the code, perhaps because insufficient resources are available, then results may be unexpected. OpenMP generally expects the programmer to check that the execution environment is just what was required, and provides runtime routines for such queries.

Incorrect use of synchronization constructs leads to problems that may not be readily apparent. To avoid them, one must carefully think through the logic of explicit synchronization in a program and must exercise special care with the use of low-level synchronization constructs, such as locks.

2.6   Performance Considerations

How much reduction of the execution time can be expected from OpenMP parallelization and, indeed, by shared-memory parallelization? If we denote by T_1 the execution time of an application on 1 processor, then in an ideal situation, the execution time on P processors should be T_1/P. If T_P denotes the execution time on P processors, then the ratio

$$S = T_1/T_P \qquad (2.1)$$

is referred to as the parallel speedup and is a measure for the success of the parallelization. However, a number of obstacles usually have to be overcome before perfect speedup, or something close to it, is achievable. Virtually all programs contain some regions that are suitable for parallelization and other regions that are not. By using an increasing number of processors, the time spent in the parallelized parts of the program is reduced, but the sequential section remains the same. Eventually the execution time is completely dominated by the time taken to compute the sequential portion, which puts an upper limit on the expected speedup. This effect, known as *Amdahl's law*, can be formulated as

$$S = \frac{1}{(f_{par}/P + (1 - f_{par}))}, \qquad (2.2)$$

where f_{par} is the parallel fraction of the code and P is the number of processors. In the ideal case when all of the code runs in parallel, $f_{par} = 1$, the expected speedup is equal to the number of processors. If only 80 percent of the code runs in parallel ($f_{par} = 0.8$), the maximal speedup one can expect on 16 processors is 4 and on 32 processors is 4.4. Frustrating, isn't it? It is thus important to parallelize as much of the code as possible, particularly if large numbers of processors are to be exploited.

Other obstacles along the way to perfect linear speedup are the overheads introduced by forking and joining threads, thread synchronization, and memory accesses. On the other hand, the ability to fit more of the program's data into cache may offset some of the overheads. A measure of a program's ability to decrease the execution time of the code with an increasing number of processors is referred to as *parallel scalability*.

Note that if the application developer has a specific goal in terms of required performance improvement, it may be possible to select several regions for parallelization, and to ignore the rest, which remains sequential. Note, too, that parallel speedup is often defined as the improvement in performance relative to the "best" sequential algorithm for the problem at hand. This measure indicates whether parallelization provides benefits that could not be obtained by choosing a different approach to solving the problem.

2.7   Wrap-Up

In this chapter, we have given a brief overview of the features that are available in the OpenMP API. In the following chapters, we discuss each of these features in detail, giving their purpose, syntax, examples of their use, and, where necessary, further rules on how they may be applied.

3 Writing a First OpenMP Program

In this chapter, we give a first impression of what it means to use OpenMP to parallelize an application. We familiarize the reader with the OpenMP syntax and give a few basic rules. We also explain how OpenMP can be used to parallelize an existing application in a manner that preserves the original sequential version.

3.1 Introduction

Using OpenMP to parallelize an application is not hard. The impact of OpenMP parallelization is frequently localized, in the sense that modifications to the original source program are often needed in just a few places. Moreover, one usually does not need to rewrite significant portions of the code in order to achieve good parallel performance. In general, the effort of parallelizing a program with OpenMP goes mainly into identifying the parallelism, and not in reprogramming the code to implement that parallelism.

Another benefit of this API is that one can organize the program source in such a way that the original sequential version is preserved. This is a major advantage if one or more validation runs of the parallel code should produce a wrong answer. As a temporary workaround, one can easily have the compiler generate a sequential version of the suspect parts of the application, while debugging the OpenMP code. One can also restructure the sequential code for parallelization first, test this version (without running it in parallel) and then implement the parallelism through the control structures provided by OpenMP. This two-phase approach enables a smoother migration from a sequential to a parallel program than is possible with an "all or nothing" paradigm such as MPI.

For C and C++ programs, pragmas are provided by the OpenMP API to control parallelism. In OpenMP these are called *directives*. They always start with `#pragma omp`, followed by a specific keyword that identifies the directive, with possibly one one or more so-called clauses, each separated by a comma. These clauses are used to further specify the behavior or to further control parallel execution. The directive must not be on the same line as the code surrounding it. The general form of a directive is given in Figure 3.1. The standard continuation symbol (backslash, \) for pragmas can be used in directives. This helps to improve readability by breaking up long pragma sequences into smaller blocks, something we highly recommend for readability and maintenance. White space (spaces and tab characters) can be inserted before and after the `#` and should be used between the words. Note that OpenMP directives in C/C++ are *case-sensitive*.

> **#pragma omp** *directive-name   [clause[[,] clause]. . .] new-line*

Figure 3.1: General form of an OpenMP directive for C/C++ programs –
The directive-name is a specific keyword, for example `parallel`, that defines and controls
the action(s) taken. The clauses can be used to further specify the behavior.

In Fortran all OpenMP directives are special comments that must begin with
a directive *sentinel.* The format of the sentinel differs between fixed- and free-
form source files. In fixed-source format Fortran there are three choices, but the
sentinel *must* start in column one and appear as a single word with no intervening
characters. Fortran fixed-source form line length, white space, continuation, and
column rules apply to the directive line. The sentinels for fixed-source format are
listed in Figure 3.2.

In free-source format only one sentinel is supported. It can appear in any column
as long as it is preceded only by white space. It must also appear as a single word
with no intervening character. Fortran free-format line length, white space, and
continuation rules apply. Figure 3.3 gives the syntax for free-format source.

> **!$omp** *directive-name   [clause[[,] clause]. . .] new-line*
> **c$omp** *directive-name   [clause[[,] clause]. . .] new-line*
> ***$omp** *directive-name   [clause[[,] clause]. . .] new-line*

Figure 3.2: OpenMP directive syntax for fixed-source format in Fortran –
The directive-name is a specific keyword, for example `parallel`, that defines and controls
the action(s) taken. The clauses can be used to further specify the behavior. With
fixed-format syntax the sentinel *must* start in column one.

> **!$omp** *directive-name   [clause[[,] clause]. . .] new-line*

Figure 3.3: OpenMP directive syntax for free-source format in Fortran –
The directive-name is a specific keyword, for example `parallel`, that defines and controls
the action(s) taken. The clauses can be used to further specify the behavior. With
free-format syntax the sentinel can appear in any column.

With Fortran, initial directive lines must have a space after the sentinel. Continued directive lines must have an ampersand (&) as the last nonblank character on
the line, prior to any comment placed inside the directive. Note that the sentinel
has to be repeated, as shown in the example in Figure 3.4.

The need in Fortran to repeat the sentinel on continuation lines distinguishes
Fortran from C/C++. A classical beginner's mistake in Fortran is to forget to

```
!$OMP   PARALLEL PRIVATE(...)   &
!$OMP   SHARED(...)
```

Figure 3.4: **Example of continuation syntax in free-format Fortran** – Note that the sentinel is repeated on the second line.

start the continued line with the required sentinel, resulting in a syntax error at compile time. Another difference from C/C++ syntax is that OpenMP Fortran directives are *case-insensitive*.

We mostly use the `!$omp` sentinel throughout this book.[1] This has the advantage that it is supported with both types of Fortran source text formatting.

A word of caution is needed regarding directives. If a syntax error occurs in their specification (e.g., if a keyword is misspelled in C/C++ or the directive does not start in the first column in a fixed-format Fortran program), an OpenMP compiler ignores the directive and may not issue a warning either. This situation can give rise to some surprising effects at run time. Unfortunately, all we can do here is advise the programmer to double check the syntax of all directives and to read the compiler documentation to see whether there is an option for sending warnings on potential parallelization problems.

3.2   Matrix Times Vector Operation

We now show the use of OpenMP to parallelize a simple operation that realizes a basic, but important, problem: multiplying an m x n matrix B with a vector c of length n, storing the result into a vector a of length m: $a_{mx1} = B_{mxn} * c_{nx1}$. This example was chosen because it is straightforward and is likely to be familiar to most readers, but at the same time it allows us to demonstrate key features of OpenMP. Moreover, it has been used in OpenMP versions of some important application codes [139].

Our example codes also illustrate one of the comments made above: one can take any of the parallelized source codes shown in this chapter, or in the rest of this book for that matter, compile it with an OpenMP compiler, and link the new object instead of the sequential one. At that point one has a parallel program. Typically the same compiler can be used for the sequential and parallel program versions, but with the appropriate option selected to get the compiler to recognize OpenMP features.

---

[1]We may deviate from this rule when source fragments are taken directly from applications.

3.2.1   C and Fortran Implementations of the Problem

The most straightforward serial implementation of the matrix-vector multiply is to calculate the result vector a by computing the dot product of the rows of the matrix B and vector c as shown in Formula (3.1).

$$a_i = \sum_{j=1}^{n} B_{i,j} * c_j \qquad i = 1, \ldots, m \tag{3.1}$$

In the remainder of this chapter we refer to the algorithm based on Formula (3.1) as the "row variant."

3.2.2   A Sequential Implementation of the Matrix Times Vector Operation

In Figures 3.5 and 3.6 on pages 39 and 40, respectively, we present the complete Fortran and C source code for a program that calls a matrix times vector routine with the name mxv. For ease of reference, source line numbers are shown in the program listings.

The main program code is similar for both languages. In the setup part, the user is prompted for the matrix dimensions m and n. Next, memory is allocated that will store the matrix B plus vectors a and c, and the data is initialized. Then, the mxv routine is invoked. After the computations have finished, the memory is released, and the program terminates. The source code for the C version is shown in Figure 3.7; the corresponding Fortran version is shown in Figure 3.8. Note that in Figure 3.7 the *restrict* keyword is used in lines 1–2 to notify the C compiler that pointers a, b, and c are restricted and hence occupy disjoint regions in memory.[2] This gives a compiler more possibilities to optimize the code. Another point worth mentioning is that, for performance reasons in the C version, array b is declared and used as a linear array, rather than a two-dimensional matrix. We explain this action in Section 5.2 of Chapter 5.

The source code for the Fortran implementation also closely follows the mathematical description of this operation. In this case, however, one does not need to specify that a, b, and c are restricted because Fortran does not permit a to overlap in memory with b or c unless this is specifically declared to be the case.

---

[2]This is a feature of the C99 standard. If it is not supported by a compiler, the keyword can be omitted, but performance may not be optimal. If the compiler provides a flag to indicate the pointers are restricted, it should then be used.

```
 1  #include <stdio.h>
 2  #include <stdlib.h>
 3
 4  void mxv(int m, int n, double * restrict a,
 5             double * restrict b, double * restrict c);
 6
 7  int main(int argc, char *argv[])
 8  {
 9     double *a,*b,*c;
10     int i, j, m, n;
11
12     printf("Please give m and n: ");
13     scanf("%d %d",&m,&n);
14
15     if ( (a=(double *)malloc(m*sizeof(double))) == NULL )
16        perror("memory allocation for a");
17     if ( (b=(double *)malloc(m*n*sizeof(double))) == NULL )
18        perror("memory allocation for b");
19     if ( (c=(double *)malloc(n*sizeof(double))) == NULL )
20        perror("memory allocation for c");
21
22     printf("Initializing matrix B and vector c\n");
23     for (j=0; j<n; j++)
24        c[j] = 2.0;
25     for (i=0; i<m; i++)
26        for (j=0; j<n; j++)
27           b[i*n+j] = i;
28
29     printf("Executing mxv function for m = %d n = %d\n",m,n);
30     (void) mxv(m, n, a, b, c);
31
32     free(a);free(b);free(c);
33     return(0);
34  }
```

Figure 3.5: **Main program in C** – Driver program for the mxv routine. The user is prompted for the matrix dimensions m and n. Memory is allocated and initialized prior to the call to mxv. It is released again after the call.

```
1   program main
2   interface
3     subroutine mxv(m, n, a, b, c)
4        integer(kind=4), intent(in)    :: m, n
5        real    (kind=8), intent(in)    :: b(1:m,1:n), c(1:n)
6        real    (kind=8), intent(inout):: a(1:m)
7     end subroutine mxv
8   end interface
9   real(kind=8), allocatable:: a(:), b(:,:), c(:)
10  integer(kind=4)                :: m ,n, i, memstat
11
12  print *, 'Please give m and n:'; read(*,*) m, n
13
14  allocate ( a(1:m), stat=memstat )
15  if ( memstat /= 0 ) stop 'Error in memory allocation for a'
16  allocate ( b(1:m,1:n), stat=memstat )
17  if ( memstat /= 0 ) stop 'Error in memory allocation for b'
18  allocate ( c(1:n), stat=memstat )
19  if ( memstat /= 0 ) stop 'Error in memory allocation for c'
20
21  print *, 'Initializing matrix B and vector c'
22  c(1:n) = 1.0
23  do i = 1, m
24     b(i,1:n) = i
25  end do
26
27  print *, 'Executing mxv routine for m = ',m,' n = ',n
28  call mxv(m, n, a, b, c)
29
30  if ( allocated(a) )   deallocate(a,stat=memstat)
31  if ( allocated(b) )   deallocate(b,stat=memstat)
32  if ( allocated(c) )   deallocate(c,stat=memstat)
33  stop
34  end program main
```

Figure 3.6: **Main program in Fortran** – Driver program for the mxv routine. The user is prompted for the matrix dimensions m and n. Memory is allocated and initialized prior to the call to mxv. It is released after the call.

```
1   void mxv(int m, int n, double * restrict a,
2             double * restrict b, double * restrict c)
3   {
4       int i, j;
5
6       for (i=0; i<m; i++)
7       {
8          a[i] = 0.0;
9          for (j=0; j<n; j++)
10             a[i] += b[i*n+j]*c[j];
11      }
12  }
```

Figure 3.7: **Sequential implementation of the matrix times vector product in C** – This source implements the row variant of the problem. The loop at lines 9–10 computes the dotproduct of row i of matrix b with vector c. The result is stored in element i of vector a. The dotproduct is computed for all rows of the matrix, implemented through the for-loop starting at line 6 and ending at line 11.

3.3   Using OpenMP to Parallelize the Matrix Times Vector Product

We now develop the first OpenMP implementation of our problem, using major OpenMP control structures to do so. Here, we describe them briefly. Details of these and other OpenMP constructs are given in Chapter 4.

The row variant of our problem has a high level of parallelism. The dotproduct implemented in Formula (3.1) on page 38 computes a value a_i for each element of vector a by multiplying the corresponding elements of row i of matrix B with vector c. This computation is illustrated in Figure 3.9. Since no two dotproducts compute the same element of the result vector and since the order in which the values for the elements a_i for $i = 1, \ldots, m$ are calculated does not affect correctness of the answer, these computations can be carried out independently. In other words, this problem can be parallelized over the index value i.

In terms of our implementation this means that we are able to parallelize the outer loop with iteration variable i in both the C and Fortran versions. We give the corresponding listings of the OpenMP source code for mxv in Figure 3.10 on page 44 for the C version and in Figure 3.11 on page 45 for the Fortran implementation.

In both program versions, we have inserted a **parallel** directive at lines 9–10 to define a *parallel* region. Three so-called clauses, **default**, **shared**, and **private**,

```
1          subroutine mxv(m, n, a, b, c)
2
3          implicit none
4          integer(kind=4):: m , n
5          real    (kind=8):: a(1:m), b(1:m,1:n), c(1:n)
6
7          integer(kind=4):: i, j
8
9          do i = 1, m
10            a(i) = 0.0
11            do j = 1, n
12               a(i) = a(i) + b(i,j)*c(j)
13            end do
14         end do
15
16         return
17         end subroutine mxv
```

Figure 3.8: **Sequential implementation of the matrix times vector product in Fortran** – This source implements the row variant of the problem. The loop at lines 11–13 computes the dotproduct of row i of matrix b with vector c. The result is stored in element i of vector a. The dotproduct is computed for all rows of the matrix, implemented by the do loop starting at line 9 and ending at line 14.

have been added. The meaning of these will be explained shortly. To improve readability, we use the continuation feature to break the directive into two pieces.

In the C version, the start of the parallel region is marked by the `#pragma omp parallel for` directive at line 9 and comprises the block of statements that ends at line 16. We have added a comment string to indicate the end of the parallel region, to help avoid the programming error that would arise if the curly braces that define the extent of the parallel region were incorrectly nested. In this particular case no ambiguity exists, but in general we have found this strategy to be helpful.

In the Fortran source code, the parallel region also starts at line 9, where the `!$omp parallel do` directive has been inserted, and ends at line 17 with the `!$omp end parallel do` directive. Fortran programs require an explicit `!$omp end parallel do` directive, since the language does not provide the equivalent of C's curly braces to define a block of statements. Although this directive is not actually required in this specific situation, we use it here to clearly mark the end of the parallel region.

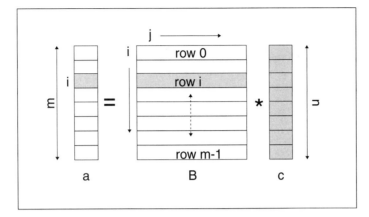

Figure 3.9: **Graphical representation of the row variant of the matrix times vector operation** – Element a_i is obtained by computing the dot product of row i of matrix B with vector c.

The directive is somewhat special. Since just one loop needs to be parallelized, we may use a single directive (the `#pragma omp parallel for` in C and the `!$omp parallel do` construct in Fortran) both to create a parallel region and to specify that the iterations of the loop should be distributed among the executing threads. This is an example of a *combined* parallel work-sharing construct (see Section 4.4.5 in the next chapter).

Data in an OpenMP program either is shared by the threads in a team, in which case all member threads will be able to access the same shared variable, or is private. In the latter case, each thread has its own copy of the data object, and hence the variable may have different values for different threads. The additional information given in the clauses for the directive in our example code specifies what data is shared between threads in the parallel region and which variables are private. Thus, each thread will access the same variable m, but each will have its own distinct variable i.

OpenMP provides built-in data-sharing attribute rules that could be relied on, but we prefer to use the `default(none)` clause instead. This informs the OpenMP compiler that we take it upon ourselves to specify the data-sharing attributes. This approach forces us to explicitly specify, for each variable, whether it is shared by multiple threads, and therefore implies more work on the part of the programmer. The reward, however, is twofold. First, we must now carefully think about the usage of variables, and this action helps us to avoid mistakes. Unless one understands the default data-sharing attribute rules very well, it is safer to be explicit

```
1   #include <stdio.h>
2   #include <stdlib.h>
3
4   void mxv(int m, int n, double * restrict a,
5              double * restrict b, double * restrict c)
6   {
7      int i, j;
8
9   #pragma omp parallel for default(none) \
10          shared(m,n,a,b,c) private(i,j)
11     for (i=0; i<m; i++)
12     {
13        a[i] = 0.0;
14        for (j=0; j<n; j++)
15           a[i] += b[i*n+j]*c[j];
16     } /*-- End of omp parallel for --*/
17  }
```

Figure 3.10: **OpenMP implementation of the matrix times vector product in C** – A single pragma (directive) is sufficient to parallelize the outer loop. We have also opted here to specify explicitly, for each variable, whether it is shared by all threads (`shared`) or whether each thread has a private copy. A comment string is used to clearly mark the end of the parallel region.

about them. Novice OpenMP programmers in particular may easily fall into the trap of making incorrect assumptions about the default rules. The second advantage of explicitly specifying the data-sharing attributes is more subtle. For good performance, one really would like to use private variables as much as possible. By carefully considering which variables have to be shared and which ones could be made private, we are sometimes able to create a faster parallel performance. This topic is discussed in Chapter 5.

Because we have used the `default(none)` clause, we have to decide on the nature of the use of variables in our parallel region. This task may seem harder than it actually is. First, all threads have to be able to access `m,n,a,b`, and `c`. Therefore, they need to be declared as `shared`. If the reason is not immediately clear, consider the alternative. If these variables were to be declared `private`, they would be uninitialized (by one of the rules of OpenMP). But then we would not know how many iterations of the loop to perform. Similarly, array `b` and vector `c` would also not be defined, and the computations could not produce meaningful results.

```
 1          subroutine mxv(m, n, a, b, c)
 2
 3          implicit none
 4
 5          integer(kind=4):: m , n
 6          real    (kind=8):: a(1:m), b(1:m,1:n), c(1:n)
 7          integer         :: i, j
 8
 9  !$OMP PARALLEL DO DEFAULT(NONE)         &
10  !$OMP SHARED(m,n,a,b,c) PRIVATE(i,j)
11          do i = 1, m
12             a(i) = 0.0
13             do j = 1, n
14                a(i) = a(i) + b(i,j)*c(j)
15             end do
16          end do
17  !$OMP END PARALLEL DO
18          return
19          end subroutine mxv
```

Figure 3.11: **OpenMP implementation of the matrix times vector product in Fortran** – One OpenMP directive is sufficient to parallelize the outer loop. We have opted here to specify explicitly, for each variable, whether it is shared by all threads (**shared**) or whether each thread has a private copy. We have used the !$OMP END PARALLEL DO directive to mark the end of the parallel region.

Moreover, if made private, the output vector a would not be accessible outside of the parallel region (another OpenMP rule).[3] Therefore, this vector has to be shared as well. Loop counter variables i and j need to be declared **private**, however. Each thread has to have access to a local, unique copy of these variables. Otherwise, a thread would be able to modify the loop counter of another thread, thereby giving rise to incorrect and unpredictable runtime behavior.

We can now focus on how our code will be executed. Code outside a parallel region will be executed sequentially by a single thread. Only the code that is within a parallel region will be executed in parallel, by a *team of threads*. Typically, threads other than the initial thread are created the first time a parallel region is encountered. They may be reused for subsequent execution of the same parallel region or a different parallel region. More details can be found in Chapter 8.

---

[3]See also Sections 4.5.3 and 4.5.4 on how to initialize and save private variables.

The programmer assigns a portion of the work in the parallel region to each thread in the team by using one or more worksharing directives. In our case, we have specified that the loop immediately following the `#pragma omp parallel for` or `!$omp parallel do` construct (with loop variable i) should be distributed among threads. This means that different threads will execute different iterations of this loop, and each loop iteration will be performed exactly once. For example, thread 0 might work on iteration `i=5`, and iteration `i=10` could be assigned to thread 1. If there are more iterations than threads available, multiple iterations are assigned to the threads in the team. Distributing loop iterations among threads is one of the main *work-sharing* constructs OpenMP offers. By not specifying details of how the work should be distributed, here we have left it up to the implementation to decide exactly which thread should carry out which loop iterations. However, OpenMP also provides a `schedule` clause to allow the user to prescribe the way in which the loop iterations should be distributed. Section 4.5.7 goes into more detail on this.

As each thread in a team completes its portion of the work in a parallel region, it encounters a *barrier*. Here, the threads wait until the last one arrives, indicating that the work inside the parallel region has been completed. Subsequently, only the master thread (the thread that worked on the code prior to the parallel region) proceeds with the execution of statements outside the parallel region. More details on barriers can be found in Section 4.6.1. What happens with the other threads at the end of the parallel region is implementation dependent. All the OpenMP standard says is that the threads are forked at the start of the parallel region and joined at the end. For example, the threads that are no longer needed might be destroyed and threads recreated when another parallel region is encountered. Alternatively, they could be parked for later use or kept around in a busy-wait loop to be available when the program executes the same or another parallel region. It is worthwhile to check the documentation to find out how this situation is handled by an implementation and to discover how to change the behavior (if one is allowed to do so).

The C and Fortran sources listed above also demonstrate the "localized" impact an OpenMP parallelization often has. All it takes to get a parallel version is to compile the source with the appropriate OpenMP compiler option and use this object file to pass on to the linker instead of the original sequential object file.

3.4   Keeping Sequential and Parallel Programs as a Single Source Code

The parallelized version of mxv in Section 3.3 is fully functional. By compiling with the appropriate option, the OpenMP directives are translated into the appropriate multithreaded code, resulting in parallel execution at run time.

One of the powerful features of OpenMP is that one can write a parallel program, while preserving the (original) sequential source. In a way, the sequential version is "built-in." If one does not compile using the OpenMP option (flag), or uses a compiler that does not support OpenMP, the directives are simply ignored, and a sequential executable is generated. However, OpenMP also provides runtime functions that return information from the execution environment. In order to ensure that the program will still compile and execute correctly in sequential mode in their presence, special care needs to be taken when using them. For example, let's say one wishes to use the omp_get_thread_num() function that returns the thread number. If the application is compiled without OpenMP translation, the result will be an unresolved reference at link time. A workaround would be to write one's own dummy function, but a better solution exists.

Specifically, the OpenMP runtime functions in both C/C++ and Fortran can be placed under control of an #ifdef _OPENMP, so that they will be translated only if OpenMP compilation has been invoked. The standard requires that this macro be set to *yyyymm*, with *yyyy* being the year and *mm* the month when the specific standard for the OpenMP version was released. For example. for OpenMP 2.5, _OPENMP is set to 200505.

An example of the use of this macro in a C/C++ program is given in Figure 3.12. Here, the file omp.h will be included only if _OPENMP is defined. This header file is guaranteed to be available if an OpenMP-compliant compiler is used. It includes the interfaces of the OpenMP runtime functions. To be able to use function omp_get_thread_num(), we set its value to zero in sequential mode. This is also the thread number of the initial thread in an OpenMP code.

Figure 3.13 shows an example of similar functionality in Fortran. Just as in the C version, we check whether the _OPENMP macro is defined. If so, we use the omp_lib module, which serves the same purpose as the include file omp.h in C/C++. Unfortunately, the OpenMP standard does not require this module to be present. One must therefore check the compiler documentation to find out whether this module, or a Fortran include file named omp_lib.h, or both are provided. Our Fortran code also sets the thread number (stored in variable TID) to zero if _OPENMP

```
#ifdef _OPENMP
    #include <omp.h>
#else
    #define omp_get_thread_num() 0
#endif
          ......
int TID = omp_get_thread_num();
```

Figure 3.12: **Example of conditional compilation in C** – This mechanism allows us to maintain a single source for sequential and parallel code even if we use OpenMP runtime functions.

has not been defined. Otherwise the value returned by the `omp_get_thread_num()` function call is assigned to `TID`.

```
#ifdef _OPENMP
    use omp_lib
#endif
          ......
integer::  TID
          ......
#ifdef _OPENMP
    TID = omp_get_thread_num()
#else
    TID = 0
#endif
```

Figure 3.13: **Example of conditional compilation in Fortran** – This mechanism allows us to maintain a single source for sequential and parallel code even if we use OpenMP runtime functions. There is an alternative solution in Fortran.

Figure 3.14: **Conditional compilation sentinels in fixed-format Fortran** – At compile time an OpenMP compiler replaces the sentinel by two spaces.

An alternative solution in Fortran uses the *conditional compilation sentinel*. This special sentinel is recognized by the OpenMP compiler and at compile time is replaced by two spaces; when compiled without OpenMP translation, it is simply a comment line and will be discarded. The conditional compilation sentinels recognized in fixed-format source files are listed in Figure 3.14. A line with a conditional compilation sentinel in fixed-format Fortran source will be left unchanged unless it satisfies the following criteria:

- The sentinel *must* start in column 1 and appear as a single word with no intervening space.

- After the sentinel is replaced with two spaces, initial lines must have a space or zero in column 6 and white space and numbers in columns 1 through 5.

- After the sentinel is replaced with two spaces, continuation lines must have a character other than a space or zero in column 6 and only white space in columns 1 through 5.

```
!$
```

Figure 3.15: Conditional compilation sentinel in free-format Fortran – At compile time an OpenMP compiler replaces the sentinel by two spaces.

Free-format source has only one conditional compilation sentinel. The syntax is shown in Figure 3.15. The sentinel will be replaced by two spaces, and thus enable conditional compilation, only if the following four criteria are met:

- The sentinel can appear in any column but must be preceded by white space only.

- The sentinel must appear as a single word with no intervening white space.

- Initial lines must have a space after the sentinel.

- Continued lines must have an ampersand (&) as the last nonblank character on the line, prior to any comment appearing on the conditionally compiled line; continued lines can have an ampersand after the sentinel, with optional white space before and after the ampersand

The conditional compilation mechanism is quite useful. However, one has to be careful not to make a mistake with the syntax because, otherwise, the sentinel will be treated as a comment. Unfortunately, a program might have genuine comments that begin with these characters. If one uses the same style for general documentation of the program (for example `!$ This is my comment`), many syntax errors are going to be generated by an OpenMP compiler.

```
        integer::  TID
              ......
        TID = 0
!$      TID = omp_get_thread_num()
```

Figure 3.16: **Example of the use of the conditional compilation sentinel** –
At compile time an OpenMP compiler will replace the !$ sentinel by two spaces, changing
the comment line into an executable statement.

The most straightforward (and common) use of the conditional compilation sentinel in Fortran is shown in Figure 3.16. In this example, the program variable TID contains the thread number. It is initialized to zero, to be consistent with the thread number of the master thread. If, however, the source has been compiled with OpenMP enabled, the !$ sentinel will be replaced by two spaces. The effect is that the "comment" line becomes the executable statement TID = omp_get_-thread_num(), assigning the runtime thread number to variable TID.

The combination of directive-based syntax and conditional compilation enables one to write an OpenMP program that preserves the sequential version of the application and that can be translated into either sequential or parallel code.

3.5   Wrap-Up

In this chapter, we have introduced the basic idea of OpenMP via a simple example program that has enabled us to demonstrate the use of several of the most common features of the API. We have explained how OpenMP directives are written.

It is often easy to write an OpenMP program where the sequential version of the application is "built-in." A sequential compiler simply ignores the OpenMP directives, because it does not recognize them. By checking whether the _OPENMP symbol has been defined or by using Fortran conditional compilation, one can make a compile-time substitution for the runtime functions to avoid unresolved references at link time. This feature can also be useful in case of a regression. If the numerical results are incorrect, for example, one can simply not compile the suspect source parts under OpenMP. The sequential versions of these sources will then be used as a (temporary) workaround.

4 OpenMP Language Features

In this chapter we introduce the constructs and user-level functions of OpenMP, giving syntax and information on their usage.

4.1 Introduction

OpenMP provides directives, library functions, and environment variables to create and control the execution of parallel programs. In Chapter 3 we informally introduced a few of its most important constructs. In this chapter, we give a fairly extensive overview of the language features, including examples that demonstrate their syntax, usage, and, where relevant, behavior. We show how these OpenMP constructs and clauses are used to tackle some programming problems.

A large number of applications can be parallelized by using relatively few constructs and one or two of the functions. Those readers familiar with MPI will be aware that, despite the relatively large number of features provided by that parallel programming API, just half a dozen of them are really indispensable [69]. OpenMP is a much smaller API than MPI, so it is not all that difficult to learn the entire set of features; but it is similarly possible to identify a short list of constructs that a programmer really should be familiar with. We begin our overview by presenting and discussing a limited set that suffices to write many different programs in Sections 4.3, 4.4, and 4.5. This set comprises the following constructs, some of the clauses that make them powerful, and (informally) a few of the OpenMP library routines:

- Parallel Construct

- Work-Sharing Constructs

    1. Loop Construct

    2. Sections Construct

    3. Single Construct

    4. Workshare Construct (Fortran only)

- Data-Sharing, No Wait, and Schedule Clauses

Next, we introduce the following features, which enable the programmer to orchestrate the actions of different threads, in Section 4.6:

- Barrier Construct

- Critical Construct

- Atomic Construct

- Locks

- Master Construct

The OpenMP API also includes library functions and environment variables that may be used to control the manner in which a program is executed; these are presented in Section 4.7. The remaining clauses for parallel and work-sharing constructs are reviewed in Section 4.8. In Section 4.9, we complete our presentation of the API with a discussion of a few more specialized features.

Where relevant, we comment on practical matters related to the constructs and clauses, but not all details are covered. It is not our objective to duplicate the OpenMP specification, which can be downloaded from [2]. At times, the wording in this chapter is less formal than that typically found in the official document. Our intent is to stay closer to the terminology used by application developers.

4.2   Terminology

Several terms are used fairly often in the OpenMP standard, and we will need them here also. The definitions of *directive* and *construct* from Section 1.2.2 of the OpenMP 2.5 document are cited verbatim for convenience:

- *OpenMP Directive* - In C/C++, a `#pragma` and in Fortran, a comment, that specifies OpenMP program behavior.

- *Executable directive* - An OpenMP directive that is not declarative; that is, it may be placed in an executable context.[1]

- *Construct* - An OpenMP executable directive (and, for Fortran, the paired **end** directive, if any) and the associated statement, loop, or structured block, if any, not including the code in any called routines, that is, the lexical extent of an executable directive.

OpenMP requires well-structured programs, and, as can be seen from the above, constructs are associated with statements, loops, or structured blocks. In C/C++ a "structured block" is defined to be an executable statement, possibly a compound

---

[1] All directives except the `threadprivate` directive are executable directives.

statement, with a single entry at the top and a single exit at the bottom. In Fortran, it is defined as a block of executable statements with a single entry at the top and a single exit at the bottom. For both languages, the point of entry cannot be a labeled statement, and the point of exit cannot be a branch of any type.

In C/C++ the following additional rules apply to a structured block:

- The point of entry cannot be a call to `setjmp()`.

- `longjmp()` and `throw()` (C++ only) must not violate the entry/exit criteria.

- Calls to `exit()` are allowed in a structured block.

- An expression statement, iteration statement, selection statement, or try block is considered to be a structured block if the corresponding compound statement obtained by enclosing it in { and } would be a structured block.

In Fortran the following applies:

- `STOP` statements are allowed in a structured block.

Another important concept in OpenMP is that of a *region* of code. This is defined as follows by the standard: "An OpenMP region consists of all code encountered during a specific instance of the execution of a given OpenMP construct or library routine. A region includes any code in called routines, as well as any implicit code introduced by the OpenMP implementation." In other words, a region encompasses all the code that is in the *dynamic* extent of a construct.

Most OpenMP directives are clearly associated with a region of code, usually the dynamic extent of the structured block or loop nest immediately following it. A few (`barrier` and `flush`) do not apply to any code. Some features affect the behavior or use of threads. For these, the notion of a *binding thread set* is introduced. In particular, some of the runtime library routines have an effect on the thread that invokes them (or return information pertinent to that thread only), whereas others are relevant to a team of threads or to all threads that execute the program. We will discuss binding issues only in those few places where it is important or not immediately clear what the binding of a feature is.

4.3 Parallel Construct

Before embarking on our description of the other basic features of OpenMP we introduce the most important one of all. The *parallel construct* plays a crucial role

#pragma omp parallel *[clause[[,] clause]. . .]*
 structured block

Figure 4.1: Syntax of the parallel construct in C/C++ – The parallel region implicitly ends at the end of the structured block. This is a closing curly brace (}) in most cases.

!$omp parallel *[clause[[,] clause]. . .]*
 structured block
!$omp end parallel

Figure 4.2: Syntax of the parallel construct in Fortran – The terminating `!$omp end parallel` directive is mandatory for the parallel region in Fortran.

in OpenMP: a program without a parallel construct will be executed sequentially. Its C/C++ syntax is given in Figure 4.1; the Fortran syntax is given in Figure 4.2.

This construct is used to specify the computations that should be executed in parallel. Parts of the program that are not enclosed by a parallel construct will be executed serially. When a thread encounters this construct, a team of threads is created to execute the associated parallel region, which is the code dynamically contained within the parallel construct. But although this construct ensures that computations are performed in parallel, it does not distribute the work of the region among the threads in a team. In fact, if the programmer does not use the appropriate syntax to specify this action, the work will be replicated. At the end of a parallel region, there is an implied *barrier* that forces all threads to wait until the work inside the region has been completed. Only the initial thread continues execution after the end of the parallel region. For more information on barriers, we refer to Section 4.6.1 on page 84.

The thread that encounters the parallel construct becomes the *master* of the new team. Each thread in the team is assigned a unique thread number (also referred to as the "thread id") to identify it. They range from zero (for the master thread) up to one less than the number of threads within the team, and they can be accessed by the programmer. Although the parallel region is executed by all threads in the team, each thread is allowed to follow a different path of execution. One way to achieve this is to exploit the thread numbers. We give a simple example in Figure 4.3.

Here, the OpenMP library function `omp_get_thread_num()` is used to obtain the number of each thread executing the parallel region.[2] Each thread will execute

---

[2]We discuss the library functions in Section 4.7; this routine appears in several examples.

```
#pragma omp parallel
   {
      printf("The parallel region is executed by thread %d\n",
         omp_get_thread_num());

      if ( omp_get_thread_num() == 2 ) {
         printf("  Thread %d does things differently\n",
                omp_get_thread_num());
      }
   } /*-- End of parallel region --*/
```

Figure 4.3: **Example of a parallel region** – All threads execute the first `printf` statement, but only the thread with thread number 2 executes the second one.

all code in the parallel region, so that we should expect each to perform the first print statement. However, only one thread will actually execute the second print statement (assuming there are at least three threads in the team), since we used the thread number to control its execution. The output in Figure 4.4 is based on execution of this code by a team with four threads.[3] Note that one cannot make any assumptions about the order in which the threads will execute the first `printf` statement. When the code is run again, the order of execution could be different.

```
The parallel region is executed by thread 0
The parallel region is executed by thread 3
The parallel region is executed by thread 2
  Thread 2 does things differently
The parallel region is executed by thread 1
```

Figure 4.4: **Output of the code shown in Figure 4.3** – Four threads are used in this example.

We list in Figure 4.5 the clauses that may be used along with the parallel construct. They are discussed in Sections 4.5 and 4.8.

There are several restrictions on the parallel construct and its clauses:

---

[3]This is an incomplete OpenMP code fragment and requires a wrapper program before it can be executed. The same holds for all other examples throughout this chapter.

if *(scalar-expression)*	(C/C++)
if *(scalar-logical-expression)*	(Fortran)
num_threads *(integer-expression)*	(C/C++)
num_threads *(scalar-integer-expression)*	(Fortran)
private *(list)*	
firstprivate *(list)*	
shared *(list)*	
default(none | shared)	(C/C++)
default(none | shared | private)	(Fortran)
copyin *(list)*	
reduction *(operator:list)*	(C/C++)
reduction *({ operator | intrinsic_procedure_name} :list)*	(Fortran)

Figure 4.5: **Clauses supported by the parallel construct** – Note that the default(private) clause is not supported on C/C++.

- A program that branches into or out of a parallel region is nonconforming. In other words, if a program does so, then it is *illegal*, and the behavior is undefined.

- A program must not depend on any ordering of the evaluations of the clauses of the parallel directive or on any side effects of the evaluations of the clauses.

- At most one `if` clause can appear on the directive.

- At most one `num_threads` clause can appear on the directive. The expression for the clause must evaluate to a positive integer value.

In C++ there is an additional constraint. A `throw` inside a parallel region must cause execution to resume within the same parallel region, *and* it must be caught by the same thread that threw the exception. In Fortran, unsynchronized use of I/O statements by multiple threads on the *same* unit has unspecified behavior.

Section 4.7 explains how the programmer may specify how many threads should be in the team that executes a parallel region. This number cannot be modified once the team has been created. Note that under exceptional circumstances, for example, a lack of hardware resources, an implementation is permitted to provide fewer than the requested number of threads. Thus, the application may need to check on the number actually assigned for its execution.

The OpenMP standard distinguishes between an *active* parallel region and an *inactive* parallel region. A parallel region is active if it is executed by a team of threads consisting of more than one thread. If it is executed by one thread only, it has been serialized and is considered to be inactive. For example, one can specify that a parallel region be conditionally executed, in order to be sure that it contains enough work for this to be worthwhile (see Section 4.8.1 on page 100). If the condition does not hold at run time, then the parallel region will be inactive. A parallel region may also be inactive if it is nested within another parallel region and this feature is either disabled or not provided by the implementation (see Section 4.7 and Section 4.9.1 for details).

4.4   Sharing the Work among Threads in an OpenMP Program

OpenMP's work-sharing constructs are the next most important feature of OpenMP because they are used to distribute computation among the threads in a team. C/C++ has three work-sharing constructs. Fortran has one more. A work-sharing construct, along with its terminating construct where appropriate, specifies a region of code whose work is to be distributed among the executing threads; it also specifies the manner in which the work in the region is to be parceled out. A work-sharing region must bind to an active **parallel** region in order to have an effect. If a work-sharing directive is encountered in an inactive **parallel** region or in the sequential part of the program, it is simply ignored. Since work-sharing directives may occur in procedures that are invoked both from within a parallel region as well as outside of any parallel regions, they may be exploited during some calls and ignored during others.

The work-sharing constructs are listed in Figure 4.6. For the sake of readability, the clauses have been omitted. These are discussed in Section 4.5 and Section 4.8.

Functionality	Syntax in C/C++	Syntax in Fortran
Distribute iterations over the threads	**#pragma omp for**	**!$omp do**
Distribute independent work units	**#pragma omp sections**	**!$omp sections**
Only one thread executes the code block	**#pragma omp single**	**!$omp single**
Parallelize array-syntax		**!$omp workshare**

Figure 4.6: **OpenMP work-sharing constructs** – These constructs are simple, yet powerful. Many applications can be parallelized by using just a parallel region and one or more of these constructs, possibly with clauses. The **workshare** construct is available in Fortran only. It is used to parallelize Fortran array statements.

The two main rules regarding work-sharing constructs are as follows:

- Each work-sharing region must be encountered by all threads in a team or by none at all.

- The sequence of work-sharing regions and barrier regions encountered must be the same for every thread in a team.

A work-sharing construct does not launch new threads and does not have a barrier on entry. By default, threads wait at a barrier at the end of a work-sharing region until the last thread has completed its share of the work. However, the programmer can suppress this by using the `nowait` clause (see Section 4.5 for more details).

4.4.1 Loop Construct

The *loop construct* causes the iterations of the loop immediately following it to be executed in parallel. At run time, the loop iterations are distributed across the threads. This is probably the most widely used of the work-sharing features. Its syntax is shown in Figure 4.7 for C/C++ and in Figure 4.8 for Fortran.

```
#pragma omp for [clause[[,] clause]...]
        for-loop
```

Figure 4.7: **Syntax of the loop construct in C/C++** – Note the lack of curly braces. These are implied with the construct.

```
!$omp do [clause[[,] clause]...]
        do-loop
[!$omp end do [nowait]]
```

Figure 4.8: **Syntax of the loop construct in Fortran** – The terminating `!$omp end do` directive is optional, but we recommend using it to clearly mark the end of the construct.

In C and C++ programs, the use of this construct is limited to those kinds of loops where the number of iterations can be counted; that is, the loop must have an integer counter variable whose value is incremented (or decremented) by a fixed amount at each iteration until some specified upper (or lower) bound is reached. In particular, this restriction excludes loops that process the items in a list.

The loop header must have the general form shown in Figure 4.9, where *init-expr* stands for the initialization of the loop counter `var` via an integer expression, `b` is

$$\boxed{\textbf{for } (\textit{ init-expr } ; \textit{ var relop b } ; \textit{ incr-expr })}$$

Figure 4.9: **Format of C/C++ loop** – The OpenMP loop construct may be applied only to this kind of loop nest in C/C++ programs.

also an integer expression, and *relop* is one of the following: `<`, `<=`, `>`, `>=`. The *incr-expr* is a statement that increments or decrements `var` by an integer amount using a standard operator (`++`, $-$, `+=`, `-=`). Alternatively, it may take a form such as *var* = *var* + *incr*. Many examples of this kind of loop are presented here and in the following chapters.

We illustrate this construct in Figure 4.10, where we use a parallel directive to define a parallel region and then share its work among threads via the `for` work-sharing directive: the `#pragma omp for` directive states that iterations of the loop following it will be distributed. Within the loop, we again use the OpenMP function `omp_get_thread_num()`, this time to obtain and print the number of the executing thread in each iteration. Note that we have added clauses to the parallel construct that state which data in the region is shared and which is private. Although not strictly needed since this is enforced by the compiler, loop variable `i` is explicitly declared to be a private variable, which means that each thread will have its own copy of `i`. Unless the programmer takes special action (see `lastprivate` in Section 4.5.3), its value is also undefined after the loop has finished. Variable `n` is made shared. We discuss shared and private data in Sections 4.5.1 and 4.5.2.

```
#pragma omp parallel shared(n) private(i)
{
   #pragma omp for
   for (i=0; i<n; i++)
      printf("Thread %d executes loop iteration %d\n",
             omp_get_thread_num(),i);
} /*-- End of parallel region --*/
```

Figure 4.10: **Example of a work-sharing loop** – Each thread executes a subset of the total iteration space $i = 0, \ldots, n - 1$.

In Figure 4.11, we also give output produced when we executed the code of Figure 4.10 using four threads. Given that this is a parallel program, we should not expect the results to be printed in a deterministic order. Indeed, one can easily see that the order in which the `printf` statements are executed is not sorted with respect to the thread number. Note that threads 1, 2, and 3 execute two loop

```
Thread 0 executes loop iteration 0
Thread 0 executes loop iteration 1
Thread 0 executes loop iteration 2
Thread 3 executes loop iteration 7
Thread 3 executes loop iteration 8
Thread 2 executes loop iteration 5
Thread 2 executes loop iteration 6
Thread 1 executes loop iteration 3
Thread 1 executes loop iteration 4
```

Figure 4.11: **Output from the example shown in Figure 4.10** – The example is executed for $n = 9$ and uses four threads.

iterations each. Since the total number of iterations is 9 and since four threads are used, one thread has to execute the additional iteration. In this case it turns out to be thread 0, the so-called master thread, which has done so.

The implementer must decide how to select a thread to execute the remaining iteration(s), and the choice may even change between various releases of the same compiler. In fact, if the programmer does not say how to map the iterations to threads, the compiler must decide what strategy should be used for this. Potentially, it could even choose a different mapping strategy for different loops in the same application. Another of the clauses, the `schedule` clause (see Section 4.5.7 on page 79), is the means by which the programmer is able to influence this mapping. Our second example in Figure 4.12 contains two work-shared loops, or parallel loops. The second loop uses values of `a` that are defined in the first loop. As mentioned above, the compiler does not necessarily map iterations of the second loop in the same way as it does for the first loop. But since there is an implied barrier at the end of a parallel loop, we can be certain that all of the values of `a` have been created by the time we begin to use them.

The clauses supported by the loop construct are listed in Figure 4.13.

4.4.2   The Sections Construct

The *sections construct* is the easiest way to get different threads to carry out different kinds of work, since it permits us to specify several different code regions, each of which will be executed by one of the threads. It consists of two directives: first, `#pragma omp sections` in C/C++ (and `!$omp sections` in Fortran) to indicate the start of the construct (along with a termination directive in Fortran), and second, the `#pragma omp section` directive in C/C++ and `!$omp section` in For-

```
#pragma omp parallel shared(n,a,b) private(i)
{
    #pragma omp for
    for (i=0; i<n; i++)
        a[i] = i;

    #pragma omp for
    for (i=0; i<n; i++)
        b[i] = 2 * a[i];
} /*-- End of parallel region --*/
```

Figure 4.12: **Two work-sharing loops in one parallel region** – One can not assume that the distribution of iterations to threads is identical for both loops but the implied barrier ensures that results are available when needed.

> **private** *(list)*
> **firstprivate** *(list)*
> **lastprivate** *(list)*
> **reduction** *(operator:list)*   (C/C++)
> **reduction** *({ operator | intrinsic_procedure_name} :list)*   (Fortran)
> **ordered**
> **schedule** *(kind[,chunk_size)]*
> **nowait**

Figure 4.13: **Clauses supported by the loop construct** – They are described in Section 4.5 and Section 4.8.

tran, respectively, to mark each distinct section. Each section must be a structured block of code that is independent of the other sections. At run time, the specified code blocks are executed by the threads in the team. Each thread executes one code block at a time, and each code block will be executed exactly once. If there are fewer threads than code blocks, some or all of the threads execute multiple code blocks. If there are fewer code blocks than threads, the remaining threads will be idle. Note that the assignment of code blocks to threads is implementation-dependent.

The syntax of this construct in C/C++ is given in Figure 4.14. The syntax for Fortran is shown in Figure 4.15.

Although the `sections` construct is a general mechanism that can be used to get threads to perform different tasks independently, its most common use is probably to execute function or subroutine calls in parallel. We give an example of this kind of usage in Figure 4.16. This code fragment contains one `sections` construct,

```
#pragma omp sections [clause[[,] clause]...]
    {
    [#pragma omp section ]
        structured block
    [#pragma omp section
        structured block ]
    ...
    }
```

Figure 4.14: **Syntax of the sections construct in C/C++** – The number of sections controls, and limits, the amount of parallelism. If there are "n" of these code blocks, at most "n" threads can execute in parallel.

```
!$omp sections [clause[[,] clause]...]
    [!$omp section ]
        structured block
    [!$omp section
        structured block ]
    ...
!$omp end sections [nowait]
```

Figure 4.15: **Syntax of the sections construct in Fortran** – The number of sections controls, and limits, the amount of parallelism. If there are "n" of these code blocks, at most "n" threads can execute in parallel.

```
#pragma omp parallel
{
   #pragma omp sections
   {
      #pragma omp section
        (void) funcA();

      #pragma omp section
        (void) funcB();
   } /*-- End of sections block --*/

} /*-- End of parallel region --*/
```

Figure 4.16: **Example of parallel sections** – If two or more threads are available, one thread invokes funcA() and another thread calls funcB(). Any other threads are idle.

comprising two sections. The immediate observation is that this limits the parallelism to two threads. If two or more threads are available, function calls `funcA` and `funcB` are executed in parallel. If only one thread is available, both calls to `funcA` and `funcB` are executed, but in sequential order. Note that one cannot make any assumption on the specific order in which section blocks are executed. Even if these calls are executed sequentially, for example, because the directive is not in an active parallel region, `funcB` may be called before `funcA`.

The functions are very simple. They merely print the thread number of the calling thread. Figure 4.17 lists `funcA`. The source of `funcB` is similar. The output of this program when executed by two threads is given in Figure 4.18.

```
void funcA()
{
    printf("In funcA: this section is executed by thread %d\n",
        omp_get_thread_num());
}
```

Figure 4.17: **Source of funcA** – This function prints the thread number of the thread executing the function call.

```
In funcA: this section is executed by thread 0
In funcB: this section is executed by thread 1
```

Figure 4.18: **Output from the example given in Figure 4.16** – The code is executed by using two threads.

Depending on the type of work performed in the various code blocks and the number of threads used, this construct might lead to a *load-balancing* problem. This occurs when threads have different amounts of work to do and thus take different amounts of time to complete. A result of load imbalance is that some threads may wait a long time at the next barrier in the program, which means that the hardware resources are not being efficiently exploited. It may sometimes be possible to eliminate the barrier at the end of this construct (see Section 4.5.6), but that does not overcome the fundamental problem of a load imbalance *within* the sections construct. If, for example, there are five equal-sized code blocks and only four threads are available, one thread has to do more work.[4] If a lot of computation

---

[4]Which thread does so depends on the mapping strategy. The most common way to distribute

is involved, other strategies may need to be considered (see, e.g., Section 4.9.1 and Chapter 6).

The clauses supported by the `sections` construct are listed in Figure 4.19.

private*(list)*
firstprivate*(list)*
lastprivate*(list)*
reduction*(operator:list)*   (C/C++)
reduction*({ operator | intrinsic_procedure_name}:list)*   (Fortran)
nowait

Figure 4.19: **Clauses supported by the sections construct** – These clauses are described in Section 4.5 and Section 4.8.

4.4.3   The Single Construct

The *single construct* is associated with the structured block of code immediately following it and specifies that this block should be executed by one thread only. It does not state which thread should execute the code block; indeed, the thread chosen could vary from one run to another. It can also differ for different `single` constructs within one application. This is not a limitation, however, as this construct should really be used when we do not care which thread executes this part of the application, as long as the work gets done by exactly one thread. The other threads wait at a barrier until the thread executing the single code block has completed.

The syntax of this construct in C/C++ is given in Figure 4.20. The syntax for Fortran is shown in Figure 4.21.

#pragma omp single *[clause[[,] clause]. . .]*   *structured block*

Figure 4.20: **Syntax of the single construct in C/C++** – Only one thread executes the structured block.

The code fragment in Figure 4.22 demonstrates the use of the single construct to initialize a shared variable.[5]

---

code blocks among threads is a round-robin scheme, where the work is distributed nearly evenly in the order of thread number.

[5]The curly braces are not really needed here, as there is one executable statement only; it has been put in to indicate that the code block can be much more complex and contain any number of statements.

!$omp single *[clause[[,] clause]...]*
            structured block
!$omp end single [nowait,[copyprivate]]

Figure 4.21: **Syntax of the single construct in Fortran** – Only one thread executes the structured block.

```
#pragma omp parallel shared(a,b) private(i)
{
   #pragma omp single
   {
      a = 10;
      printf("Single construct executed by thread %d\n",
             omp_get_thread_num());
   }
   /* A barrier is automatically inserted here */

   #pragma omp for
   for (i=0; i<n; i++)
       b[i] = a;

} /*-- End of parallel region --*/

   printf("After the parallel region:\n");
   for (i=0; i<n; i++)
       printf("b[%d] = %d\n",i,b[i]);
```

Figure 4.22: **Example of the single construct** – Only one thread initializes the shared variable a.

The intention is clear. One thread initializes the shared variable a. This variable is then used to initialize vector b in the parallelized **for**-loop. Several points are worth noting here. On theoretical grounds one might think the single construct can be omitted in this case. After all, every thread would write the same value of 10 to the same variable a. However, this approach raises a hardware issue. Depending on the data type, the processor details, and the compiler behavior, the write to memory might be translated into a sequence of store instructions, each store writing a subset of the variable. For example, a variable 8 bytes long might be written to memory through 2 store instructions of 4 bytes each. Since a write operation is not guaranteed to be atomic,[6] multiple threads could do this at the same time, potentially resulting in an arbitrary combination of bytes in memory. This issue is also related to the memory consistency model covered in Section 7.3.1.

Moreover, multiple stores to the same memory address are bad for performance. This and related performance matters are discussed in Chapter 5.

The other point worth noting is that, in this case, a barrier is essential before the `#pragma omp for` loop. Without such a barrier, some threads would begin to assign values to elements of b before a has been assigned a value, a particularly nasty kind of bug.[7] Luckily there is an implicit barrier at the end of the `single` construct. The output of this program is given in Figure 4.23. It shows that in this particular run, thread 3 initialized variable a. This is nondeterministic, however, and may change from run to run.

```
Single construct executed by thread 3
After the parallel region:
b[0] = 10
b[1] = 10
b[2] = 10
b[3] = 10
b[4] = 10
b[5] = 10
b[6] = 10
b[7] = 10
b[8] = 10
```

Figure 4.23: **Output from the example in Figure 4.22** – The value of variable n is set to 9, and four threads are used.

The clauses supported by the single construct are listed in Figure 4.24.

A similar construct, `master` (see Section 4.6.6), guarantees that a code block is executed by the master thread. It does not have an implied barrier.

4.4.4 Workshare Construct

The *workshare construct* is supported in Fortran only, where it serves to enable the parallel execution of code written using Fortran 90 array syntax. The statements

---

[6]Loosely said, if an operation is atomic no other thread can perform the same operation while the current thread executes it.

[7]Chapter 7 covers these kinds of problems in depth.

> **private***(list)*
> **firstprivate***(list)*
> **copyprivate***(list)*
> **nowait**

Figure 4.24: **Clauses supported by the single construct** – These clauses are described in Section 4.5 and Section 4.8 on page 100. Note that in Fortran the `copyprivate` clause (as well as the `nowait` clause) is specified on the `!$omp end single` part of the construct.

in this construct are divided into units of work. These units are then executed in parallel in a manner that respects the semantics of Fortran array operations. The definition of "unit of work" depends on the construct. For example, if the `workshare` directive is applied to an array assignment statement, the assignment of each element is a unit of work. We refer the interested reader to the OpenMP standard for additional definitions of this term.

The syntax is shown in Figure 4.25.

> **!$omp workshare**
> *structured block*
> **!$omp end workshare** [`nowait`]

Figure 4.25: **Syntax of the workshare construct in Fortran** – This construct is used to parallelize (blocks of) statements using array-syntax.

The structured block enclosed by this construct must consist of one or more of the following.

- Fortran array assignments and scalar assignments

- Fortran `FORALL` statements and constructs

- Fortran `WHERE` statements and constructs

- OpenMP `atomic`, `critical`, and `parallel` constructs

The code fragment in Figure 4.26 demonstrates how one can use the `workshare` construct to parallelize array assignment statements. Here, we get multiple threads to update three arrays a, b, and c. In this case, the OpenMP specification states that each assignment to an array element is a unit of work.

Two important rules govern this construct. We quote from the standard (Section 2.5.4):

```
!$OMP PARALLEL SHARED(n,a,b,c)
!$OMP WORKSHARE
        b(1:n) = b(1:n) + 1
        c(1:n) = c(1:n) + 2
        a(1:n) = b(1:n) + c(1:n)
!$OMP END WORKSHARE
!$OMP END PARALLEL
```

Figure 4.26: **Example of the workshare construct** – These array operations are parallelized. There is no control over the assignment of array updates to the threads.

- It is unspecified how the units of work are assigned to the threads executing a `workshare` region.

- An implementation of the `workshare` construct must insert any synchronization that is required to maintain standard Fortran semantics.

In our example the latter rule implies that the OpenMP compiler must generate code such that the updates of `b` and `c` have completed before `a` is computed. In Chapter 8, we give an idea of how the compiler translates `workshare` directives.

Other than `nowait` there are no clauses for this construct.

4.4.5   Combined Parallel Work-Sharing Constructs

Combined parallel work-sharing constructs are shortcuts that can be used when a parallel region comprises precisely one work-sharing construct, that is, the work-sharing region includes all the code in the parallel region. The semantics of the shortcut directives are identical to explicitly specifying the `parallel` construct immediately followed by the work-sharing construct.

For example, the sequence in Figure 4.27 is is equivalent to the shortcut in Figure 4.28.

In Figure 4.29 we give an overview of the combined constructs available in C/C++. The overview for Fortran is shown in Figure 4.30. Note that for readability the clauses have been omitted.

The combined parallel work-sharing constructs allow certain clauses that are supported by both the `parallel` construct and the `workshare` construct. If the behavior of the code depends on where the clause is specified, it is an illegal OpenMP program, and therefore the behavior is undefined.

```
#pragma omp parallel
{
  #pragma omp for
  for (.....)
}
```

Figure 4.27: **A single work-sharing loop in a parallel region** – For cases like this OpenMP provides a shortcut.

```
#pragma omp parallel for
  for (.....)
```

Figure 4.28: **The combined work-sharing loop construct** – This variant is easier to read and may be slightly more efficient.

Full version	Combined construct

#pragma omp parallel
{
   #pragma omp for
    for-loop
}
	#pragma omp parallel for
	   for-loop

#pragma omp parallel
{
#pragma omp sections
{
   [**#pragma omp section**]
    structured block
   [**#pragma omp section**
    structured block]
   ...
}
}
	#pragma omp parallel sections
	{
	   [**#pragma omp section**]
	
	    structured block
	   [**#pragma omp section**
	    structured block]
	   ...
	}

Figure 4.29: **Syntax of the combined constructs in C/C++** – The combined constructs may have a performance advantage over the more general `parallel` region with just one work-sharing construct embedded.

The main advantage of using these combined constructs is readability, but there can also be a performance advantage. When the combined construct is used, a compiler knows what to expect and may be able to generate slightly more efficient

Full version	Combined construct

!$omp parallel
!$omp do
   do-loop
[!$omp end do]
!$omp end parallel
	!$omp parallel do
	   do-loop
	!$omp end parallel do

!$omp parallel
!$omp sections
   [!$omp section]
    structured block
   [!$omp section
    structured block]
   ...
!$omp end sections
!$omp end parallel
	!$omp parallel sections
	   [!$omp section]
	    structured block
	   [!$omp section
	    structured block]
	   ...
	!$omp end parallel sections

!$omp parallel
!$omp workshare
   structured block
!$omp end workshare
!$omp end parallel
	!$omp parallel workshare
	   structured block
	!$omp end parallel workshare

Figure 4.30: **Syntax of the combined constructs in Fortran** – The combined constructs may have a performance advantage over the more general `parallel` region with just one work-sharing construct embedded.

code. For example, it will not insert more than one barrier at the end of the region.

4.5 Clauses to Control Parallel and Work-Sharing Constructs

The OpenMP directives introduced above support a number of *clauses*, optional additions that provide a simple and powerful way to control the behavior of the construct they apply to. Indeed, some of these clauses are all but indispensable in practice. They include syntax needed to specify which variables are shared and which are private in the code associated with a construct, according to the OpenMP memory model introduced in Section 2.3.3 in Chapter 2. We have already indicated which clauses can be used with these constructs and have informally introduced a few of them. Let us now zoom in on them. We focus on practical aspects: what type of functionality is provided, and what are common ways to use them? For other details, including rules and restrictions associated with specific clauses, we refer the reader to the OpenMP standard.

In this section, we introduce the most widely used clauses. In Section 4.8 we introduce the remaining ones. Since the clauses are processed before entering the construct they are associated with, they are evaluated in this "external" context, and any variables that appear in them must be defined there. Several clauses can be used with a given directive. The order in which they are given has no bearing on their evaluation: in fact, since the evaluation order is considered to be arbitrary, the programmer should be careful not to make any assumptions about it.

4.5.1 Shared Clause

The `shared` clause is used to specify which data will be shared among the threads executing the region it is associated with. Simply stated, there is one unique instance of these variables, and each thread can freely read or modify the values. The syntax for this clause is `shared(list)`. All items in the list are data objects that will be shared among the threads in the team.

```
#pragma omp parallel for shared(a)
  for (i=0; i<n; i++)
    {
        a[i] += i;
    } /*-- End of parallel for --*/
```

Figure 4.31: **Example of the shared clause** – All threads can read from and write to vector a.

The code fragment in Figure 4.31 illustrates the use of this clause. In this simple example, vector a is declared to be shared. This implies that all threads are able to read and write elements of a. Within the parallel loop, each thread will access the pre-existing values of those elements a[i] of a that it is responsible for updating and will compute their new values. After the parallel region is finished, all the new values for elements of a will be in main memory, where the master thread can access them.

An important implication of the shared attribute is that multiple threads might attempt to simultaneously update the same memory location or that one thread might try to read from a location that another thread is updating. Special care has to be taken to ensure that neither of these situations occurs and that accesses to shared data are ordered as required by the algorithm. OpenMP places the responsibility for doing so on the user and provides several constructs that may help. They are discussed in Section 4.6.1 and Section 4.6.3. Another construct ensures that new values of shared data are available to all threads immediately, which might not otherwise be the case; it is described in Section 4.9.2.

4.5.2   Private Clause

What about the loop iteration variable i in the example in the previous section? Will it be shared? As we pointed out in Section 4.4.1 on page 58, the answer to that is a firm "no." Since the loop iterations are distributed over the threads in the team, each thread must be given a unique and local copy of the loop variable i so that it can safely modify the value. Otherwise, a change made to i by one thread would affect the value of i in another thread's memory, thereby making it impossible for the thread to keep track of its own set of iterations.

There may well be other data objects in a parallel region or work-sharing construct for which threads should be given their own copies. The private clause comes to our rescue here. The syntax is private(*list*). Each variable in the list is replicated so that each thread in the team of threads has exclusive access to a local copy of this variable. Changes made to the data by one thread are not visible to other threads. This is exactly what is needed for i in the previous example.

By default, OpenMP gives the iteration variable of a parallel loop the private data-sharing attribute. In general, however, we recommend that the programmer not rely on the OpenMP default rules for data-sharing attributes. We will specify data-sharing attributes explicitly.[8]

```
#pragma omp parallel for private(i,a)
  for (i=0; i<n; i++)
    {
        a = i+1;
        printf("Thread %d has a value of a = %d for i = %d\n",
                omp_get_thread_num(),a,i);
    } /*-- End of parallel for --*/
```

Figure 4.32: **Example of the private clause** – Each thread has a local copy of variables i and a.

---

[8]We do make some exceptions: variables declared locally within a structured block or a routine that is invoked from within a parallel region are private by default.

A simple example of the use of the `private` clause is shown in Figure 4.32. Both the loop iteration variable i and the variable a are declared to be private variables here. If variable a had been specified in a shared clause, multiple threads would attempt to update the *same* variable with different values in an uncontrolled manner. The final value would thus depend on which thread happened to last update a. (This bug is a data race condition.) Therefore, the usage of a requires us to specify it to be a private variable, ensuring that each thread has its own copy.

```
Thread 0 has a value of a = 1 for i = 0
Thread 0 has a value of a = 2 for i = 1
Thread 2 has a value of a = 5 for i = 4
Thread 1 has a value of a = 3 for i = 2
Thread 1 has a value of a = 4 for i = 3
```

Figure 4.33: **Output from the example shown in Figure 4.32** – The results are for $n = 5$, using three threads to execute the code.

Figure 4.33 shows the output of this program. As can be seen, threads 0 and 1 each execute two iterations of the loop, producing a different value for a each time. Thread 2 computes one value for a. Since each thread has its own local copy, there is no interference between them, and the results are what we should expect.

We note that the values of private data are *undefined* upon entry to and exit from the specific construct. The value of any variable with the same name as the private variable in the enclosing region is also undefined after the construct has terminated, even if the corresponding variable was defined prior to the region. Since this point may be unintuitive, care must be taken to check that the code respects this.

4.5.3   Lastprivate Clause

The example given in Section 4.5.2 works fine, but what if the value of a is needed after the loop? We have just stated that the values of data specified in the `private` clause can no longer be accessed after the corresponding region terminates. OpenMP offers a workaround if such a value is needed. The `lastprivate` clause addresses this situation; it is supported on the work-sharing loop and `sections` constructs.

The syntax is `lastprivate(list)`. It ensures that the last value of a data object listed is accessible after the corresponding construct has completed execution. In a parallel program, however, we must explain what "last" means. In the case of its use with a work-shared loop, the object will have the value from the iteration of

the loop that would be last in a sequential execution. If the `lastprivate` clause is
used on a `sections` construct, the object gets assigned the value that it has at the
end of the lexically last sections construct.

```
#pragma omp parallel for private(i) lastprivate(a)
  for (i=0; i<n; i++)
    {
       a = i+1;
       printf("Thread %d has a value of a = %d for i = %d\n",
             omp_get_thread_num(),a,i);
    } /*-- End of parallel for --*/

  printf("Value of a after parallel for: a = %d\n",a);
```

Figure 4.34: **Example of the lastprivate clause** – This clause makes the sequentially last value of variable a accessible outside the parallel loop.

In Figure 4.34 we give a slightly modified version of the example code from the
previous section. Variable a now has the `lastprivate` data-sharing attribute, and
there is a print statement after the parallel region so that we can check on the value
a has at that point. The output is given in Figure 4.35. According to our definition
of "last," the value of variable a after the parallel region should correspond to that
computed when i = n-1. That is exactly what we get.

```
Thread 0 has a value of a = 1 for i = 0
Thread 0 has a value of a = 2 for i = 1
Thread 2 has a value of a = 5 for i = 4
Thread 1 has a value of a = 3 for i = 2
Thread 1 has a value of a = 4 for i = 3
Value of a after parallel for: a = 5
```

Figure 4.35: **Output from the example shown in Figure 4.34** – Variable n is
set to 5, and three threads are used. The last value of variable a corresponds to the value
for $i = 4$, as expected.

In fact, all this clause really does is provide some extra convenience, since the
same functionality can be implemented by using an additional shared variable and
some simple logic. We do not particularly recommend doing so, but we demonstrate
how this can be accomplished in the code fragment in Figure 4.36. The additional
variable a_shared has been made shared, allowing us to access it outside the parallel

loop. All that needs to be done is to keep track of the last iteration and then copy the value of a into a_shared.

```
#pragma omp parallel for private(i) private(a) shared(a_shared)
  for (i=0; i<n; i++)
  {
      a = i+1;
      printf("Thread %d has a value of a = %d for i = %d\n",
             omp_get_thread_num(),a,i);
      if ( i == n-1 ) a_shared = a;
  } /*-- End of parallel for --*/
```

Figure 4.36: **Alternative code for the example in Figure 4.34** – This code shows another way to get the behavior of the lastprivate clause. However, we recommend use of the clause, not something like this.

A performance penalty is likely to be associated with the use of lastprivate, because the OpenMP library needs to keep track of which thread executes the last iteration. For a static workload distribution scheme this is relatively easy to do, but for a dynamic scheme this is more costly. More on the performance aspects of this clause can be found in Chapter 5.

4.5.4   Firstprivate Clause

Recall that private data is also undefined on entry to the construct where it is specified. This could be a problem if we need to to pre-initialize private variables with values that are available prior to the region in which they will be used. OpenMP provides the firstprivate construct to help out in such cases. Variables that are declared to be "firstprivate" are private variables, but they are pre-initialized with the value of the variable with the same name before the construct. The initialization is carried out by the initial thread prior to the execution of the construct. The firstprivate clause is supported on the parallel construct, plus the work-sharing loop, sections, and single constructs. The syntax is firstprivate(*list*).

Now assume that each thread in a parallel region needs access to a thread-specific section of a vector but access starts at a certain (nonzero) offset. Figure 4.37 shows one way to implement this idea. The initial value of indx is initialized to the required offset from the first element of a. The length of each thread's section of the array is given by n. In the parallel region, the OpenMP function omp_get_thread_num() is used to store the thread number in variable TID. The

```
for(i=0; i<vlen; i++) a[i] = -i-1;

indx = 4;
#pragma omp parallel default(none) firstprivate(indx) \
                      private(i,TID) shared(n,a)
  {
     TID = omp_get_thread_num();

     indx += n*TID;
     for(i=indx; i<indx+n; i++)
         a[i] = TID + 1;
  } /*-- End of parallel region --*/

printf("After the parallel region:\n");
for (i=0; i<vlen; i++)
    printf("a[%d] = %d\n",i,a[i]);
```

Figure 4.37: **Example using the firstprivate clause** – Each thread has a pre-initialized copy of variable indx. This variable is still private, so threads can update it individually.

start index into the thread-specific section is then given by indx += n*TID which uses the initial value of indx to account for the offset. For demonstration purposes, vector a is initialized with negative values. A part of this vector will be filled with positive values when the parallel region is executed, to make it easy to see which values have been modified.

We have executed this program for indx = 4 using three threads and with n = 2. The output is given in Figure 4.38. It can be seen that the first four elements of a are not modified in the parallel region (as should be the case). Each thread has initialized two elements with a thread-specific value.

This example can actually be implemented more easily by using a shared variable, offset say, that contains the initial offset into vector a. We can then make indx a private variable. This is shown in the code fragment in Figure 4.39.

In general, *read-only* variables can be passed in as shared variables instead of firstprivate. This approach also saves the time incurred by runtime initialization. Note that on *cc-NUMA* systems, however, firstprivate might be the preferable option for dealing with read-only variables. OpenMP typically offers multiple ways to solve a given problem. This is a mixed blessing, however, as the performance implications of the different solutions may not be clearly visible.

```
After the parallel region:
a[0] = -1
a[1] = -2
a[2] = -3
a[3] = -4
a[4] = 1
a[5] = 1
a[6] = 2
a[7] = 2
a[8] = 3
a[9] = 3
```

Figure 4.38: **Output from the program shown in Figure 4.37** – The initial offset into the vector is set to $indx = 4$. Variable $n = 2$ and three threads are used. Therefore the total length of the vector is given by $vlen = 4 * 2 * 3 = 10$. The first $indx = 4$ values of vector a are not initialized.

```
#pragma omp parallel default(none) private(i,TID,indx) \
                shared(n,offset,a)
    {
        TID = omp_get_thread_num();

        indx = offset + n*TID;
        for(i=indx; i<indx+n; i++)
            a[i] = TID + 1;
    } /*-- End of parallel region --*/
```

Figure 4.39: **Alternative to the source shown in Figure 4.37** – If variable indx is not updated any further, this simpler and more elegant solution is preferred.

4.5.5 Default Clause

The default clause is used to give variables a default data-sharing attribute. Its usage is straightforward. For example, default(shared) assigns the shared attribute to all variables referenced in the construct. The default(private) clause, which is not supported in C/C++, makes all variables private by default. It is applicable to the parallel construct only. The syntax in C/C++ is given by default (none | shared). In Fortran, the syntax is default (none | shared | private).

This clause is most often used to define the data-sharing attribute of the majority of the variables in a parallel region. Only the exceptions need to be explicitly listed:

`#pragma omp for default(shared) private(a,b,c)`, for example, declares all variables to be shared, with the exception of a, b, and c.

If `default(none)` is specified instead, the programmer is forced to specify a data-sharing attribute for each variable in the construct. Although variables with a predetermined data-sharing attribute need not be listed in one of the clauses, we strongly recommend that the attribute be explicitly specified for *all* variables in the construct. In the remainder of this chapter, `default(none)` is used in the examples.

4.5.6 Nowait Clause

The `nowait` clause allows the programmer to fine-tune a program's performance. When we introduced the work-sharing constructs, we mentioned that there is an implicit barrier at the end of them. This clause overrides that feature of OpenMP; in other words, if it is added to a construct, the barrier at the end of the associated construct will be suppressed. When threads reach the end of the construct, they will immediately proceed to perform other work. Note, however, that the barrier at the end of a parallel region cannot be suppressed.

Usage is straightforward. Once a parallel program runs correctly, one can try to identify places where a barrier is not needed and insert the `nowait` clause. The code fragment shown in Figure 4.40 demonstrates its use in C code. When a thread is finished with the work associated with the parallelized `for` loop, it continues and no longer waits for the other threads to finish as well.

```
#pragma omp for nowait
  for (i=0; i<n; i++)
   {
      ...........
   }
```

Figure 4.40: **Example of the nowait clause in C/C++** – The clause ensures that there is no barrier at the end of the loop.

In Fortran the clause needs to be added to the **end** part of the construct, as demonstrated in Figure 4.41.

Some care is required when inserting this clause because its incorrect usage can introduce bugs. For example, in Figure 4.12 we showed a parallel region with two parallel loops, where one loop produced values that were used in the subsequent one. If we were to apply a nowait to the first loop in this code, threads might attempt

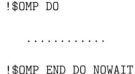

```
!$OMP DO

    . . . . . . . . . . .

!$OMP END DO NOWAIT
```

Figure 4.41: **Example of usage of the nowait clause in Fortran** – In contrast with the syntax for C/C++, this clause is placed on the construct at the end of the loop.

to use values that have not been created. In this particular case, the application programmer might reason that the thread that creates a given value `a[i]` will also be the one that uses it. Then, the barrier could be omitted. There is, however, no guarantee that this is the case. Since we have not told the compiler how to distribute iterations to threads, we cannot be sure that the thread executing loop iteration `i` in the first loop will also execute loop iteration `i` in the second parallel loop. If the code depends on a specific distribution scheme, it is best to specify it explicitly.[9] In the next section, we show how to do so.

4.5.7   Schedule Clause

The `schedule` clause is supported on the loop construct only. It is used to control the manner in which loop iterations are distributed over the threads, which can have a major impact on the performance of a program. The syntax is `schedule(kind [,chunk_size])`.

The schedule clause specifies how the iterations of the loop are assigned to the threads in the team. The granularity of this workload distribution is a *chunk*, a contiguous, nonempty subset of the iteration space. Note that the `chunk_size` parameter need not be a constant; any loop invariant integer expression with a positive value is allowed.

In Figure 4.42 on page 80 the four different schedule kinds defined in the standard are listed, together with a short description of their behavior. The most straightforward schedule is `static`. It also has the least overhead and is the default on many OpenMP compilers, to be used in the absence of an explicit `schedule` clause. As mentioned in Section 4.4.1, one can *not* assume this, however. Both the `dynamic` and `guided` schedules are useful for handling poorly balanced and unpredictable workloads. The difference between them is that with the `guided` schedule, the size

---

[9]This is expected to change in OpenMP 3.0. Under certain conditions the assignment of iteration numbers to threads is preserved across work-sharing loops.

Schedule kind	Description
static	Iterations are divided into chunks of size *chunk_size*. The chunks are assigned to the threads statically in a round-robin manner, in the order of the thread number. The last chunk to be assigned may have a smaller number of iterations. When no *chunk_size* is specified, the iteration space is divided into chunks that are approximately equal in size. Each thread is assigned at most one chunk.
dynamic	The iterations are assigned to threads as the threads request them. The thread executes the chunk of iterations (controlled through the *chunk_size* parameter), then requests another chunk until there are no more chunks to work on. The last chunk may have fewer iterations than *chunk_size*. When no *chunk_size* is specified, it defaults to 1.
guided	The iterations are assigned to threads as the threads request them. The thread executes the chunk of iterations (controlled through the *chunk_size* parameter), then requests another chunk until there are no more chunks to work on. For a *chunk_size* of 1, the size of each chunk is proportional to the number of unassigned iterations, divided by the number of threads, decreasing to 1. For a *chunk_size* of "k" ($k > 1$), the size of each chunk is determined in the same way, with the restriction that the chunks do not contain fewer than k iterations (with a possible exception for the last chunk to be assigned, which may have fewer than k iterations). When no *chunk_size* is specified, it defaults to 1.
runtime	If this schedule is selected, the decision regarding scheduling kind is made at run time. The schedule and (optional) chunk size are set through the `OMP_SCHEDULE` environment variable.

Figure 4.42: **Schedule kinds supported on the schedule clause** – The `static` schedule works best for regular workloads. For a more dynamic work allocation scheme the `dynamic` or `guided` schedules may be more suitable.

of the chunk (of iterations) decreases over time. The rationale behind this scheme is that initially larger chunks are desirable because they reduce the overhead. Load balancing is often more of an issue toward the end of computation. The system then uses relatively small chunks to fill in the gaps in the schedule.

All three workload distribution algorithms support an optional *chunk_size* parameter. As shown in Figure 4.42, the interpretation of this parameter depends on the schedule chosen. For example, a *chunk_size* bigger than 1 on the `static` schedule may give rise to a round-robin allocation scheme in which each thread executes the iterations in a sequence of chunks whose size is given by *chunk_size*. It is not always easy to select the appropriate schedule and value for *chunk_size* up front. The choice may depend (among other things) not only on the code in the loop but also on the specific problem size and the number of threads used. Therefore, the `runtime` clause is convenient. Instead of making a compile time decision, the OpenMP `OMP_SCHEDULE` environment variable can be used to choose the schedule and (optional) *chunk_size* at run time (see Section 4.7).

Figure 4.43 shows an example of the use of the `schedule` clause. The outer loop has been parallelized with the loop construct. The workload in the inner loop depends on the value of the outer loop iteration variable i. Therefore, the workload is not balanced, and the static schedule is probably not the best choice.

```
#pragma omp parallel for default(none) schedule(runtime) \
                    private(i,j) shared(n)
  for (i=0; i<n; i++)
    {
      printf("Iteration %d executed by thread %d\n",
          i, omp_get_thread_num());
      for (j=0; j<i; j++)
          system("sleep 1");
    } /*-- End of parallel for --*/
```

Figure 4.43: **Example of the schedule clause** – The runtime variant of this clause is used. The `OMP_SCHEDULE` environment variable is used to specify the schedule that should be used when executing this loop.

In order to illustrate the various workload policies, the program listed in Figure 4.43 was executed on four threads, using a value of 9 for n. The results are listed in Table 4.1. The first column contains the value of the outer loop iteration variable i. The remaining columns contain the thread number (labeled "TID") for the various workload schedules and chunk sizes selected.

One sees, for example, that iteration i = 0 was always executed by thread 0, regardless of the schedule. Iteration i = 2, however, was executed by thread 0

Table 4.1: **Example of various workload distribution policies** – The behavior for the `dynamic` and `guided` scheduling policies is nondeterministic. A subsequent run with the same program may give different results.

Iteration	TID static	TID static,2	TID dynamic	TID dynamic,2	TID guided	TID guided,2
0	0	0	0	0	0	0
1	0	0	0	0	0	0
2	0	1	3	3	3	3
3	1	1	2	3	2	3
4	1	2	1	2	1	2
5	2	2	0	2	0	2
6	2	3	3	1	3	1
7	3	3	2	1	2	1
8	3	0	1	0	1	0

with the default chunk size on the `static` schedule; but thread 1 executed this iteration with a chunk size of 2. Apparently, this iteration has been executed by thread 3 for both the `dynamic` and the `guided` schedule, regardless of the chunk size.

To illustrate this further, we executed the above loop for `n = 200` using four threads. The results are shown in Figure 4.44. Three scheduling algorithms—`static`, `dynamic,7`, and `guided,7`—have been combined into a single chart. The horizontal axis represents the value of the loop iteration variable `i` in the range `0,...,199`. The vertical axis gives the thread number of the thread that executed the particular iteration.

The first set of four horizontal lines shows the results for the `static` scheme. As expected, thread 0 executes the first 50 iterations, thread 1 works on the next 50 iterations, and so forth. The second set of four horizontal lines gives the results for the `dynamic,7` workload schedule. There are striking differences between this and the `static` case. Threads process chunks of 7 iterations at the time, since a chunk size of 7 was specified. Another difference is that threads no longer work on contiguous sets of iterations. For example, the first set of iterations executed by thread 0 is `i = 0,...,6`, whereas thread 1 processes `i = 21,...,27`, thread 2 handles `i = 7,...,13` and thread 3 executes `i = 14,...,20`. Thread 0 then continues with `i = 28,...,34` and so on.

The results for the `guided,7` schedule clearly demonstrate that the initial chunk sizes are larger than those toward the end. Although there is no notion of time

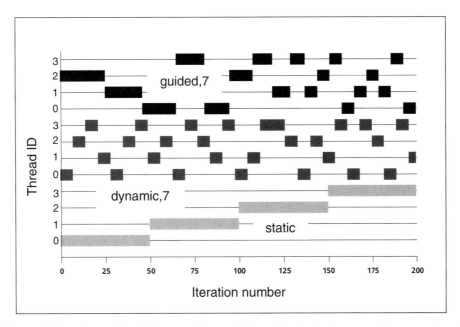

Figure 4.44: **Graphical illustration of the schedule clause** – The mapping of iterations onto four threads for three different scheduling algorithms for a loop of length $n = 200$ is shown. Clearly, both the `dynamic` and the `guided` policy give rise to a much more dynamic workload allocation scheme.

in Figure 4.44, thread 2 was probably the first one to start. With a total of 25 iterations, it gets the largest chunk of iterations. Thread 1 has the next 21 iterations to work on. Thread 0 gets 19 iterations, whereas thread 1 works on the next 16 iterations.

We emphasize that, other than for the `static` schedule, the allocation is nondeterministic and depends on a number of factors including the load of the system. We note, too, that programs that depend on which thread executes a particular iteration are nonconforming. The `static` schedule is most efficient from a performance point of view, since `dynamic` and `guided` have higher overheads. The size of the penalty for using them depends on the OpenMP implementation.

4.6   OpenMP Synchronization Constructs

In this section, we introduce OpenMP constructs that help to organize accesses to shared data by multiple threads. An algorithm may require us to orchestrate the actions of multiple threads to ensure that updates to a shared variable occur in a certain order, or it may simply need to ensure that two threads do not simultaneously attempt to write a shared object. The features discussed here can be used when the implicit barrier provided with work-sharing constructs does not suffice to specify the required interactions or would be inefficient. Together with the work-sharing constructs, they constitute a powerful set of features that suffice to parallelize a large number of applications.

4.6.1   Barrier Construct

A barrier is a point in the execution of a program where threads wait for each other: no thread in the team of threads it applies to may proceed beyond a barrier until all threads in the team have reached that point. We have already seen that many OpenMP constructs imply a barrier. That is, the compiler automatically inserts a barrier at the end of the construct, so that all threads wait there until all of the work associated with the construct has been completed. Thus, it is often unnecessary for the programmer to explicitly add a barrier to a code. If one is needed, however, OpenMP provides a construct that makes this possible. The syntax in C/C++ is given in Figure 4.45. The Fortran syntax is shown in Figure 4.46.

```
#pragma omp barrier
```

Figure 4.45: **Syntax of the barrier construct in C/C++** – This construct binds to the innermost enclosing parallel region.

```
!$omp barrier
```

Figure 4.46: **Syntax of the barrier construct in Fortran** – This construct binds to the innermost enclosing parallel region.

Two important restrictions apply to the `barrier` construct:

- Each barrier *must* be encountered by all threads in a team, or by none at all.

- The sequence of work-sharing regions and barrier regions encountered must be the same for every thread in the team.

Without these restrictions, one could write programs where some threads wait forever (or until somebody kills the process) for other threads to reach a barrier. C/C++ imposes an additional restriction regarding the placement of a barrier construct within the application: The `barrier` construct may only be placed in the program at a position where ignoring or deleting it would result in a program with correct syntax.

The code fragment in Figure 4.47 illustrates the behavior of the barrier construct. To ensure that some threads in the team executing the parallel region take longer than others to reach the barrier, we get half the threads to execute the `sleep 3` command, causing them to idle for three seconds. We then get each thread to print out its the thread number (stored in variable TID), a comment string, and the time of day in the format `hh:mm:ss`. The barrier is then reached. After the barrier, each thread will resume execution and again print out this information. (We do not show the source code of the function called `print_time` that was used to realize the output.)

```
#pragma omp parallel private(TID)
  {
    TID = omp_get_thread_num();
    if (TID < omp_get_num_threads()/2 ) system("sleep 3");
    (void) print_time(TID,"before");

    #pragma omp barrier

    (void) print_time(TID,"after ");
  } /*-- End of parallel region --*/
```

Figure 4.47: **Example usage of the barrier construct** – A thread waits at the barrier until the last thread in the team arrives. To demonstrate this behavior, we have made sure that some threads take longer than others to reach this point.

In Figure 4.48, the output of this program is shown for a run using four threads. Threads 2 and 3 arrive at the barrier 3 seconds before threads 0 and 1, because the latter two were delayed by the system call. The subsequent time stamps show that all threads continue execution once the last two have reached the barrier.

The most common use for a barrier is to avoid a data race condition. Inserting a barrier between the writes to and reads from a shared variable guarantees that the accesses are appropriately ordered, for example, that a write is completed before another thread might want to read the data.

```
Thread 2 before barrier at 01:12:05
Thread 3 before barrier at 01:12:05
Thread 1 before barrier at 01:12:08
Thread 0 before barrier at 01:12:08
Thread 1 after  barrier at 01:12:08
Thread 3 after  barrier at 01:12:08
Thread 2 after  barrier at 01:12:08
Thread 0 after  barrier at 01:12:08
```

Figure 4.48: **Output from the example in Figure 4.47** – Four threads are used. Note that threads 2 and 3 wait for three seconds in the barrier.

4.6.2   Ordered Construct

Another synchronization construct, the ordered construct, allows one to execute a structured block within a parallel loop in sequential order. This is sometimes used, for instance, to enforce an ordering on the printing of data computed by different threads. It may also be used to help determine whether there are any data races in the associated code. The syntax of the ordered construct in C/C++ is shown in Figure 4.49. The Fortran syntax is given in Figure 4.50.

> **#pragma omp ordered**
> *structured block*

Figure 4.49: **Syntax of the ordered construct in C/C++** – This construct is placed within a parallel loop. The structured block is executed in the sequential order of the loop iterations.

> **!$omp ordered**
> *structured block*
> **!$omp end ordered**

Figure 4.50: **Syntax of the ordered construct in Fortran** – This construct is placed within a parallel loop. The structured block is executed in the sequential order of the loop iterations.

An ordered construct ensures that the code within the associated structured block is executed in sequential order. The code outside this block runs in parallel. When the thread executing the first iteration of the loop encounters the construct, it enters the region without waiting. When a thread executing any subsequent iteration encounters the construct, it waits until each of the previous iterations in the sequence has completed execution of the region.

An `ordered` *clause* has to be added to the parallel region in which this construct appears; it informs the compiler that the construct occurs. We defer an example of the usage of this feature to our discussion of the clause in Section 4.8.3. The `ordered` construct itself does not support any clauses.

4.6.3   Critical Construct

The `critical` construct provides a means to ensure that multiple threads do not attempt to update the same shared data simultaneously. The associated code is referred to as a critical region, or a *critical section*.

An optional *name* can be given to a critical construct. In contrast to the rules governing other language features, this name is *global* and therefore should be unique. Otherwise the behavior of the application is undefined.

When a thread encounters a critical construct, it waits until no other thread is executing a critical region with the same name. In other words, there is never a risk that multiple threads will execute the code contained in the same critical region at the same time.

The syntax of the critical construct in C/C++ is given in Figure 4.51. The Fortran syntax is shown in Figure 4.52.

```
#pragma omp critical [(name)]
          structured block
```

Figure 4.51:   **Syntax of the critical construct in C/C++** – The structured block is executed by all threads, but only one at a time executes the block. Optionally, the construct can have a name.

```
!$omp critical [(name)]
       structured block
!$omp end critical [(name)]
```

Figure 4.52:   **Syntax of the critical construct in Fortran** – The structured block is executed by all threads, but only one at a time executes the block. Optionally, the construct can have a name.

To illustrate this construct, consider the code fragment in Figure 4.53. The `for`-loop sums up the elements of vector `a`. This operation can be readily parallelized. One approach is to let each thread independently add up a subset of the elements of the vector. The result is stored in a private variable. When all threads are done, they add up their private contributions to get the total `sum`.

```
sum = 0;
for (i=0; i<n; i++)
    sum += a[i];
```

Figure 4.53: **Loop implementing a summation** – This operation can be parallelized with some help from the compiler.

Figure 4.54 gives pseudo-code showing how two threads might collaborate to form the sum if n is even. Variable `sumLocal` has to be made private to the thread. Otherwise the statement `sumLocal += a[i]` would cause a data race condition, since both threads will try to update the same variable at the same time.

```
/*-- Executed by thread 0 --*/     /*-- Executed by thread 1 --*/

sumLocal = 0;                          sumLocal = 0;
for (i=0; i<n/2; i++)              for (i=n/2-1; i<n; i++)
    sumLocal += a[i];                     sumLocal += a[i];

sum += sumLocal;
                                       sum += sumLocal;
```

Figure 4.54: **Pseudo parallel code for the summation** – This indicates how the operations might be split up among two threads. There is no control over accesses to `sum`, however, so that there is a data race condition.

However, we still have to deal with the updates to `sum`. Without special measures, this also causes a data race condition. We do not need to enforce a certain ordering of accesses here, but we must ensure that only one update may take place at a time. This is precisely what the critical construct guarantees.

The corresponding OpenMP code fragment is shown in Figure 4.55. We have inserted a named critical region ("update_sum") and put a print statement into the critical region. It prints the thread number (stored in variable `TID`), the value of the partial sum that the thread has calculated (stored in variable `sumLocal`), and the value of `sum` so far.

We point out that this example is shown only to illustrate the workings of the critical construct. The explicit reduction algorithm given here is very naive and should not be applied as written. For extensive coverage of explicit reduction algorithms we refer to [123]. OpenMP also provides the `reduction` clause to have the compiler handle these kind of cases.

```
sum = 0;
#pragma omp parallel shared(n,a,sum) private(TID,sumLocal)
  {
     TID = omp_get_thread_num();
     sumLocal = 0;
     #pragma omp for
       for (i=0; i<n; i++)
          sumLocal += a[i];
     #pragma omp critical (update_sum)
      {
        sum += sumLocal;
        printf("TID=%d: sumLocal=%d sum = %d\n",TID,sumLocal,sum);
      }
  } /*-- End of parallel region --*/
printf("Value of sum after parallel region: %d\n",sum);
```

Figure 4.55: **Explicit implementation of a reduction operation** – The critical region is needed to avoid a data race condition when updating variable `sum`. Note that the code is shown only for illustration purposes. OpenMP provides a `reduction` clause to make it even easier to implement a reduction operation. This should be preferred.

Within the parallel region, each thread initializes `sumLocal`. The iterations of the `#pragma omp for` loop are distributed over the threads. This process results in each thread computing a partial sum, stored in `sumLocal`. When the threads are finished with their part of the `for`-loop, they enter the critical region. By definition, only one thread at a time updates `sum`.

The output of this program is given in Figure 4.56. One can clearly see that each thread computes its partial sum and then adds this value to `sum`. Apparently, thread 0 has entered the critical region first, and thread 1 is the last one to enter.

This functionality is required in many situations. One simple example is the need to avoid garbled output when multiple threads print messages, as shown in the code snippet in Figure 4.57.

Another common situation where this construct is useful is when minima and maxima are formed. The code fragment in Figure 4.58 is similar to code in the WUPWISE program used in lattice gauge theory (quantum chromodynamics) and contained in the SPEC OpenMP benchmark suite [16]. It uses a critical region to

```
TID=0: sumLocal=36 sum = 36
TID=2: sumLocal=164 sum = 200
TID=1: sumLocal=100 sum = 300
Value of sum after parallel region: 300
```

Figure 4.56: **Output from the program shown in Figure 4.55** – Three threads
are used and variable $n = 25$.

```
#pragma omp parallel shared(n) private(TID)
    {
        TID = omp_get_thread_num();
        #pragma omp critical (print_tid)
        {
          printf("I am thread %d\n",TID);
        }
    } /*-- End of parallel region --*/
```

Figure 4.57: **Avoiding garbled output** – A critical region helps to avoid intermingled output when multiple threads print from within a parallel region.

ensure that when one thread performs a comparison of the shared `Scale` with its local `LScale` to find out which value is smaller, no other thread can interfere with this sequence of operations. Note that the order in which threads carry out this work is not important here, so that a critical construct is just what is needed.

4.6.4   Atomic Construct

The `atomic` construct, which also enables multiple threads to update shared data without interference, can be an efficient alternative to the critical region. In contrast to other constructs, it is applied only to the (single) assignment statement that immediately follows it; this statement must have a certain form in order for the construct to be valid, and thus its range of applicability is strictly limited. The syntax is shown in Figures 4.59 and 4.60.

The `atomic` construct enables efficient updating of shared variables by multiple threads on hardware platforms which support *atomic* operations. The reason it is applied to just one assignment statement is that it protects updates to an individual memory location, the one on the left-hand side of the assignment. If the hardware supports instructions that read from a memory location, modify the value, and write back to the location all in one action, then `atomic` instructs the compiler to

```
#pragma omp parallel private(ix, LScale, lssq, Temp) \
                      shared(Scale, ssq, x)
  {
  #pragma omp for
      for(ix = 1, ix<N, ix++)
        {
        LScale = ....;
      }
  #pragma omp critical
      {
        if(Scale < LScale){
           ssq = (Scale/LScale) *ssq + lssq;
           Scale = LScale;
        }else
           ssq = ssq + (LScale / Scale) * Lssq
      } /* End of critical region --*/
  } /*-- End of parallel region --*/
```

Figure 4.58: **Critical region usage to determine minimum value** – The critical region is needed to avoid a data race condition when comparing the value of the private variable LSCALE with the shared variable Scale and when updating it and ssq. The execution order does not matter in the case.

> **#pragma omp atomic**
> *statement*

Figure 4.59: **Syntax of the atomic construct in C/C++** – The statement is executed by all threads, but only one thread at a time executes the statement.

> **!$omp atomic**
> *statement*

Figure 4.60: **Syntax of the atomic construct in Fortran** – The statement is executed by all threads, but only one thread at a time executes the statement.

use such an operation. If a thread is atomically updating a value, then no other thread may do so simultaneously. This restriction applies to all threads that execute a program, not just the threads in the same team. To ensure this, however, the programmer must mark *all* potentially simultaneous updates to a memory location by this directive. A simple example is shown is Figure 4.61, where multiple threads update a counter.

```
int ic, i, n;
ic = 0;
#pragma omp parallel shared(n,ic) private(i)
   for (i=0; i++, i<n)
     {
        #pragma omp atomic
           ic = ic + 1;
     }
printf("counter = %d\n", ic);
```

Figure 4.61: **Example for the use of** `atomic` – The `atomic` construct ensures that no updates are lost when multiple threads are updating a counter value.

The `atomic` construct may only be used together with an expression statement in C/C++, which essentially means that it applies a simple, binary operation such as an increment or decrement to the value on the left-hand side. The supported operations are: `+`, `*`, `-`, `/`, `&`, `^`, `|`, `<<`, `>>`. In Fortran, the statement must also take the form of an update to the value on the left-hand side, which may not be an array, via an expression or an intrinsic procedure. The operator may be one of `+`, `*`, `-`, `/`, `.AND.`, `.OR.`, `.EQV.`, `.NEQV.`, and the intrinsic procedure may be one of `MAX`, `MIN`, `IAND`, `IOR`, `IEOR`. There are a number of restrictions on the form that the expression may take; for example, it must not involve the variable on the left-hand side of the assignment statement. We refer the reader to the OpenMP standard for full details.

```
int ic, i, n;
ic = 0;
#pragma omp parallel shared(n,ic) private(i)
   for (i=0; i++, i<n)
     {
        #pragma omp atomic
           ic = ic + bigfunc();
     }
printf("counter = %d\n", ic);
```

Figure 4.62: **Another use of** `atomic` – The `atomic` construct does not prevent multiple threads from executing the function `bigfunc` at the same time.

In our slightly revised example shown in Figure 4.62, the `atomic` construct does not protect the execution of function `bigfunc`. It is only the update to the memory location of the variable `ic` that will occur atomically. If the application developer does not intend to permit the threads to execute `bigfunc` at the same time, then the `critical` construct must be used instead.

4.6.5 Locks

In addition to the synchronization features introduced above, the OpenMP API provides a set of low-level, general-purpose locking runtime library routines, similar in function to the use of semaphores. These routines provide greater flexibility for synchronization than does the use of `critical` sections or `atomic` constructs. The general syntax of the locking library routines is shown in Figures 4.63 and 4.64.

```
void omp_func_lock (omp_lock_t *lck)
```

Figure 4.63: General syntax of locking routines in C/C++ – For a specific routine, *func* expresses its functionality; *func* may assume the values `init`, `destroy`, `set`, `unset`, `test`. The values for nested locks are `init_nest`, `destroy_nest`, `set_nest`, `unset_nest`, `test_nest`.

```
subroutine omp_func_lock (svar)
integer (kind=omp_lock_kind) svar
```

Figure 4.64: General syntax of locking routines in Fortran – For a specific routine, *func* expresses its functionality; *func* may assume the values `init`, `destroy`, `set`, `unset`, `test`. The values for nested locks are `init_nest`, `destroy_nest`, `set_nest`, `unset_nest`, `test_nest`.

The routines operate on special-purpose *lock variables*, which should be accessed via the locking routines only. There are two types of locks: *simple locks*, which may not be locked if already in a locked state, and *nestable locks*, which may be locked multiple times by the same thread. Simple lock variables are declared with the special type `omp_lock_t` in C/C++ and are integer variables of `kind = omp_lock_kind` in Fortran. Nestable lock variables are declared with the special type `omp_nest_lock_t` in C/C++ and are integer variables of `kind = omp_nest_lock_kind` in Fortran. In C, lock routines need an argument that is a pointer to a lock variable of the appropriate type. The general procedure to use locks is as follows:

1. Define the (simple or nested) lock variables.

2. Initialize the lock via a call to `omp_init_lock`.

3. Set the lock using `omp_set_lock` or `omp_test_lock`. The latter checks whether the lock is actually available before attempting to set it. It is useful to achieve asynchronous thread execution.

4. Unset a lock after the work is done via a call to `omp_unset_lock`.

5. Remove the lock association via a call to `omp_destroy_lock`.

A simple example is shown in Figure 4.65.

```
      ...
      CALL OMP_INIT_LOCK (LCK)
      ...
C$OMP PARALLEL SHARED(LCK) PRIVATE(ID)
      ...
  100 CONTINUE
      IF (.NOT. OMP_TEST_LOCK(LCK)) THEN
        CALL WORK2 ()
        GO TO 100
      ENDIF
      CALL WORK(ID)
      CALL OMP_UNSET_LOCK(LCK)
C$OMP END PARALLEL
      CALL OMP_DESTROY_LOCK(LCK)
```

Figure 4.65: **Example of lock usage** – The example demonstrates how asynchronous thread execution can be achieved by using explicit locking

Note that special care is needed when the programmer synchronizes the actions of threads using these routines. If these routines are used improperly, a number of programming errors are possible. In particular, a code may deadlock. We discuss parallel programming pitfalls and problems separately in Chapter 7.

4.6.6   Master Construct

The `master` construct defines a block of code that is guaranteed to be executed by the master thread only. It is thus similar to the `single` construct (covered in Section 4.4.3). The `master` construct is technically not a work-sharing construct, however, and it does not have an implied barrier on entry or exit. The syntax in C/C++ is given in Figure 4.66, and the syntax in Fortran is given in Figure 4.67.

The lack of a barrier may lead to problems. If the `master` construct is used to initialize data, for example, care needs to be taken that this initialization is completed *before* the other threads in the team use the data. The typical solution is either to rely on an implied barrier further down the execution stream or to use an explicit *barrier* construct (see Section 4.6.1).

```
#pragma omp master
      structured block
```

Figure 4.66: Syntax of the master construct in C/C++ – Note that there is *no* implied barrier on entry to, or exit from, this construct.

```
!$omp master
      structured block
!$omp end master
```

Figure 4.67: Syntax of the master construct in Fortran – Note that there is *no* implied barrier on entry to, or exit from, this construct.

Figure 4.68 shows a code fragment that uses the `master` construct. It is similar to the example in Section 4.4.3. The two differences are that the initialization of variable a is now guaranteed to be performed by the master thread *and* the `#pragma omp barrier` needs to be inserted for correctness.

In this simple case, there is no particular reason to choose this rather than the `single` construct. In a more realistic piece of code, there may be additional computation after the `master` construct and before the first use of the data initialized by the master thread. In such a situation, or whenever the barrier is not required, this construct may be preferable.

The output of this program shows that thread 0, the master thread, has performed the initialization of variable a. In contrast to the `single` construct, where it is not known which thread will execute the code, this behavior is deterministic.

4.7   Interaction with the Execution Environment

The OpenMP standard provides several means with which the programmer can interact with the execution environment, either to obtain information from it or to influence the execution of a program. If a program relies on some property of the environment, for example, expects that a certain minimum number of threads will

```
#pragma omp parallel shared(a,b) private(i)
 {
    #pragma omp master
     {
       a = 10;
       printf("Master construct is executed by thread %d\n",
              omp_get_thread_num());
     }

    #pragma omp barrier

    #pragma omp for
     for (i=0; i<n; i++)
         b[i] = a;

 } /*-- End of parallel region --*/

printf("After the parallel region:\n");
for (i=0; i<n; i++)
    printf("b[%d] = %d\n",i,b[i]);
```

Figure 4.68: **Example of the master construct** – This is similar to the example shown in Figure 4.22. The difference is that the master thread is guaranteed to initialize variable a. Note the use of a barrier to ensure availability of data.

```
Master construct is executed by thread 0
After the parallel region:
b[0] = 10
b[1] = 10
b[2] = 10
b[3] = 10
b[4] = 10
b[5] = 10
b[6] = 10
b[7] = 10
b[8] = 10
```

Figure 4.69: **Output from the example in Figure 4.68** – This clearly demonstrates that the master thread has performed the initialization.

execute a parallel region, then the programmer must test for its satisfaction explicitly. Before we discuss these features, we need to explain just how the environment can be manipulated.

The OpenMP standard defines *internal control variables*. These are variables controlled by the OpenMP implementation that govern the behavior of a program at run time in important ways. They cannot be accessed or modified directly at the application level; however, they can be queried and modified through OpenMP functions and environment variables. The following internal control variables are defined.

- *nthreads-var* – stores the number of threads requested for the execution of future parallel regions.

- *dyn-var* – controls whether dynamic adjustment of the number of threads to be used for future parallel regions is enabled

- *nest-var* – controls whether nested parallelism is enabled for future parallel regions

- *run-sched-var* – stores scheduling information to be used for loop regions using the **runtime** schedule clause

- *def-sched-var* – stores implementation-defined default scheduling information for loop regions

Here, we introduce the library functions and environment variables that can be used to access or modify the values of these variables and hence influence the program's execution. The four environment variables defined by the standard may be set prior to program execution. The library routines can also be used to give values to control variables; they override values set via environment variables. In order to be able to use them, a C/C++ program should include the `omp.h` header file. A Fortran program should either include the `omp_lib.h` header file or `omp_lib` module, depending on which of them is provided by the implementation.

Once a team of threads is formed to execute a parallel region, the number of threads in it will not be changed. However, the number of threads to be used to execute future parallel regions can be specified in several ways:

- At the command line, the `OMP_NUM_THREADS` environment variable may be set. The value specified will be used to initialize the *nthreads-var* control variable. Its syntax is `OMP_NUM_THREADS(integer)`, where the integer must be positive.

- During program execution, the number of threads to be used to execute a parallel region may be set or modified via the `omp_set_num_threads` library routine. Its syntax is `omp_set_num_threads(scalar-integer-expression)`, where the evaluation of the expression must result in a positive integer.

- Finally, it is possible to use the `num_threads` clause together with a **parallel** construct to specify how many threads should be in the team executing that specific parallel region. If this is given, it *temporarily* overrides both of the previous constructs. It is discussed and illustrated in Section 4.8.2.

If the parallel region is conditionally executed and the condition does not hold, or if it is a nested region and nesting is not available, then none of these will have an effect: the region will be sequentially executed. During program execution, the number of threads available for executing future parallel regions can be retrieved via the `omp_get_max_threads()` routine, which returns the largest number of threads available for the next parallel region.

One can control the value of *dyn-var* to permit (or disallow) the system to dynamically adjust the number of threads that will be used to execute future parallel regions. This is typically used to optimize the use of system resources for throughput. There are two ways to do so:

- The environment variable `OMP_DYNAMIC` can be specified prior to execution to initialize this value to either *true*, in which case this feature is enabled, or to *false*, in which case the implementation may not adjust the number of threads to use for executing parallel regions. Its syntax is `OMP_DYNAMIC(flag)`, where *flag* has the value *true* or *false*.

- The routine `omp_set_dynamic` adjusts the value of *dyn-var* at run time. It will influence the behavior of parallel regions for which the thread that executes it is the master thread. `omp_set_dynamic(scalar-integer-expression)` is the C/C++ syntax; `omp_set_dynamic(logical-expression)` is the Fortran syntax. In both cases, if the argument of this procedure evaluates to *true*, then dynamic adjustment is enabled. Otherwise, it is disabled.

Routine `omp_get_dynamic` can be used to retrieve the current setting at run time. It returns *true* if the dynamic adjustment of the number of threads is enabled; otherwise *false* is returned. The result is an integer value in C/C++ and a logical value in Fortran.

If the implementation provides nested parallelism, then its availability to execute a given code can be controlled by assigning a value to the *nest-var* variable. If the implementation does not provide this feature, modifications to the *nest-var* variable have no effect.

- This variable can be set to either *true* or *false* prior to execution by giving the OMP_NESTED environment variable the corresponding value. Note that the standard specifies that it is initialized to *false* by default.

- As with the previous cases, a runtime library routine enables the programmer to adjust the setting of *nest-var* at run time, possibly overriding the value of the environment variable. It is omp_set_nested, and it applies to the thread that executes it; in other words, if this thread encounters a parallel construct, then that region will become active so long as the implementation can support such nesting.   The syntax in C/C++ is as follows:

  omp_set_nested(*scalar-integer-expression*).

  The corresponding Fortran is omp_set_nested(*logical-expression*). In both cases, if the argument of this procedure evaluates to *true*, then nesting of parallel regions is enabled; otherwise, it is disabled.

The omp_get_nested routine, whose result is an integer value in C/C++ and a logical value in Fortran, returns the current setting of the *nest-var* variable for the thread that calls it: *true* if nesting is enabled for that thread and otherwise *false*.

The OMP_SCHEDULE environment variable enables the programmer to set *def-sched-var* and thereby customize the default schedule to be applied to parallel loops in a program. Its value, which is otherwise implementation-defined, will be used to determine the assignment of loop iterations to threads for all parallel loops whose schedule type is specified to be runtime. The value of this variable takes the form *type [,chunk]*, where *type* is one of static, dynamic or guided. The optional parameter *chunk* is a positive integer that specifies the *chunk_size*.

The OpenMP standard includes several other user-level library routines, some of which we have already seen:

- The omp_get_num_threads library routine enables the programmer to retrieve the number of threads in the current team. The value it returns has integer data type. This value may be used in the programmer's code, for example, to choose an algorithm from several variants.

- omp_get_thread_num returns the number of the calling thread as an integer value. We have seen its use in many examples throughout this chapter, primarily to assign different tasks to different threads explicitly.

- `omp_get_num_procs` returns, as an integer, the total number of processors available to the program at the instant in which it is called. The number will not depend on which thread calls the routine, since it is a global value.

- `omp_in_parallel` returns *true* if it is called from within an active parallel region (see Section 4.3). Otherwise, it returns *false*. The result value is of type integer in C/C++ and logical in Fortran.

The runtime library also includes routines for implementing locks and portable timers in an OpenMP program. The lock routines are described in Section 4.6.5.

4.8   More OpenMP Clauses

We introduced the most commonly used clauses in Section 4.5. In this section, we introduce the remaining ones. We remind the reader that no assumptions may be made about the order in which the clauses are evaluated. Except for the *if*, *num_threads* and *default* clauses, they may occur multiple times on a given construct, with distinct arguments. We give important rules for the use of clauses here. We refer the reader to the OpenMP standard for other rules and restrictions associated with specific clauses. The syntax for clauses is similar in Fortran and C/C++. The two exceptions are the `copyprivate` (see Section 4.8.6) and `nowait` (Section 4.5.6) clauses.

4.8.1   If Clause

The `if` clause is supported on the `parallel` construct only, where it is used to specify conditional execution. Since some overheads are inevitably incurred with the creation and termination of a parallel region, it is sometimes necessary to test whether there is enough work in the region to warrant its parallelization. The main purpose of this clause is to enable such a test to be specified. The syntax of the clause is `if(scalar-logical-expression)`. If the logical expression evaluates to *true*, which means it is of type integer and has a non-zero value in C/C++, the parallel region will be executed by a team of threads. If it evaluates to *false*, the region is executed by a single thread only.

An example is shown in Figure 4.70. It uses the `if` clause to check whether the value of variable n exceeds 5. If so, the parallel region is executed by the number of threads available. Otherwise, one thread executes the region: in other words, it is then an *inactive* parallel region. Two OpenMP runtime functions are used. The function `omp_get_num_threads()` returns the number of threads

```
#pragma omp parallel if (n > 5) default(none) \
            private(TID) shared(n)
  {
    TID = omp_get_thread_num();
    #pragma omp single
    {
      printf("Value of n = %d\n",n);
      printf("Number of threads in parallel region: %d\n",
        omp_get_num_threads());
    }
    printf("Print statement executed by thread %d\n",TID);
  } /*-- End of parallel region --*/
```

Figure 4.70: **Example of the if clause** – The parallel region is executed by more than one thread only if $n > 5$.

in the current team. As seen before, the thread number is returned by function omp_get_thread_num(). The value is stored in variable TID. A #pragma omp single pragma is used (see also Section 4.4.3) as we want to avoid executing the first two print statements multiple times. Example output for n = 5 and n = 10 is given in Figure 4.71.

```
Value of n = 5
Number of threads in parallel region: 1
Print statement executed by thread 0
Value of n = 10
Number of threads in parallel region: 4
Print statement executed by thread 0
Print statement executed by thread 3
Print statement executed by thread 2
Print statement executed by thread 1
```

Figure 4.71: **Output from the program listed in Figure 4.70** – Four threads are used, but when $n = 5$, only one thread executes the parallel region. For $n = 10$ all four threads are active, because the condition under the if clause now evaluates to true.

4.8.2   Num_threads Clause

The num_threads clause is supported on the parallel construct only and can be used to specify how many threads should be in the team executing the parallel region (cf. Section 4.7). The syntax is num_threads(*scalar-integer-expression*). Any expression that evaluates to an integer value can be used.

Figure 4.72 shows a simple example demonstrating the use of the num_threads and if clauses. To demonstrate the priority rules listed in Section 4.7, we insert a call to the OpenMP runtime function omp_set_num_threads, setting the number of threads to four. We will override it via the clauses.

```
(void) omp_set_num_threads(4);
#pragma omp parallel if (n > 5) num_threads(n) default(none)\
            private(TID) shared(n)
  {
    TID = omp_get_thread_num();
    #pragma omp single
     {
       printf("Value of n = %d\n",n);
       printf("Number of threads in parallel region: %d\n",
          omp_get_num_threads());
     }
    printf("Print statement executed by thread %d\n",TID);
  } /*-- End of parallel region --*/
```

Figure 4.72: **Example of the num_threads clause** – This clause is used on the parallel region to control the number of threads used.

This program has been executed for n = 5 and n = 10. The output is shown in Figure 4.72. For n = 5, the if clause evaluates to false. As a result, the parallel region is executed by one thread only. If n is set to 10, however, the if clause is true and consequently the number of threads is set to 10 by the num_threads(n) clause. In neither of these two cases were four threads used, because of the higher priority of the if and num_threads clauses on the #pragma omp parallel construct.

4.8.3   Ordered Clause

The ordered clause is rather special: it does not take any arguments and is supported on the loop construct only. It has to be given if the ordered construct (see

```
Value of n = 5
Number of threads in parallel region: 1
Print statement executed by thread 0
Value of n = 10
Number of threads in parallel region: 10
Print statement executed by thread 0
Print statement executed by thread 4
Print statement executed by thread 3
Print statement executed by thread 5
Print statement executed by thread 6
Print statement executed by thread 7
Print statement executed by thread 8
Print statement executed by thread 9
Print statement executed by thread 2
Print statement executed by thread 1
```

Figure 4.73: **Output of the program given in Figure 4.72** – For $n = 5$ the if clause evaluates to false and only one thread executes the parallel region. If $n = 10$, however, the if clause is true, and then the num_threads clause causes 10 threads to be used.

Section 4.6.2 on page 86) is used in a parallel region, since its purpose is to inform the compiler of the presence of this construct.

An example of the usage of this clause and the associated construct is shown in the code fragment in Figure 4.74. Note that the schedule(runtime) clause is used (see also Section 4.5.7) to control the workload distribution at run time. The ordered *clause* informs the compiler of the ordered *construct* in the #pragma omp parallel for loop, which is used here on a print statement to ensure that the elements a[i] will be printed in the order i = 0, 1, 2, ..., n-1. The updates of the elements a[i] of array a can and might be processed in any order.

In Figure 4.75 the output obtained using four threads and $n = 9$ is shown. Environment variable OMP_SCHEDULE is set to guided to contrast the dynamic workload distribution for the #pragma omp for loop with the ordered section within the loop. One clearly sees that the second printf statement (the one within the ordered construct) is printed in sequential order, in contrast to the first printf statement.

We note that the ordered clause and construct come with a performance penalty (see also Section 5.4.2). The OpenMP implementation needs to perform additional book-keeping tasks to keep track of the order in which threads should execute the

```
#pragma omp parallel for default(none) ordered schedule(runtime) \
                private(i,TID) shared(n,a,b)
   for (i=0; i<n; i++)
    {
       TID = omp_get_thread_num();

       printf("Thread %d updates a[%d]\n",TID,i);

       a[i] += i;

      #pragma omp ordered
      {printf("Thread %d prints value of a[%d] = %d\n",TID,i,a[i]);}

   }  /*-- End of parallel for --*/
```

Figure 4.74: **Example of the ordered clause** – Regardless of which thread executes which loop iteration, the output from the second `printf` statement is always printed in sequential order.

```
Thread 0 updates a[3]
Thread 2 updates a[0]
Thread 2 prints value of a[0] = 0
Thread 3 updates a[2]
Thread 2 updates a[4]
Thread 1 updates a[1]
Thread 1 prints value of a[1] = 2
Thread 3 prints value of a[2] = 4
Thread 0 prints value of a[3] = 6
Thread 2 prints value of a[4] = 8
Thread 2 updates a[8]
Thread 0 updates a[7]
Thread 3 updates a[6]
Thread 1 updates a[5]
Thread 1 prints value of a[5] = 10
Thread 3 prints value of a[6] = 12
Thread 0 prints value of a[7] = 14
Thread 2 prints value of a[8] = 16
```

Figure 4.75: **Output from the program listed in Figure 4.74** – Note that the lines with "prints value of" come out in the original sequential loop order.

corresponding region. Moreover, if threads finish out of order, there may be an additional performance penalty because some threads might have to wait.

4.8.4 Reduction Clause

```
sum = 0;
for (i=0; i<n; i++)
    sum += a[i];
```

Figure 4.76: **Summation of vector elements** – This operation can be parallelized with the `reduction` clause.

In Section 4.6.3 on page 87, we used a critical construct to parallelize the summation operation shown in Figure 4.76. There is a much easier way to implement this, however. OpenMP provides the `reduction` clause for specifying some forms of recurrence calculations (involving mathematically associative and commutative operators) so that they can be performed in parallel without code modification. The programmer must identify the operations and the variables that will hold the result values: the rest of the work can then be left to the compiler. The results will be shared and it is not necessary to specify the corresponding variables explicitly as "shared." In general, we recommend using this clause rather than implementing a reduction operation manually. The syntax of the reduction clause in C/C++ is given by `reduction(operator:list)`. In Fortran, certain intrinsic functions are also supported. The syntax is as follows:
`reduction({operator | intrinsic_procedure_name}:list)`.
The type of the result variable must be valid for the reduction operator (or intrinsic in Fortran).

We now show how easily the example given in Section 4.6.3 on page 87 can be implemented using the `reduction` clause. In Figure 4.77, this clause has been used to specify that `sum` will hold the result of a reduction, identified via the + operator. Based on this, an OpenMP compiler will generate code that is roughly equivalent to our example in Section 4.6.3, but it may be able to do so more efficiently. For example, the final summation could be computed through a binary tree, which scales better than a naive summation. Output of this program from a run using three threads is given in Figure 4.78.

Reductions are common in scientific and engineering programs, where they may be used to test for convergence or to compute statistical data, among other things. Figure 4.79 shows an excerpt from a molecular dynamics simulation. The code

```
#pragma omp parallel for default(none) shared(n,a) \
               reduction(+:sum)
      for (i=0; i<n; i++)
         sum += a[i];
  /*-- End of parallel reduction --*/
printf("Value of sum after parallel region: %d\n",sum);
```

Figure 4.77: **Example of the reduction clause** – This clause gets the OpenMP compiler to generate code that performs the summation in parallel. This is generally to be preferred over a manual implementation.

```
Value of sum after parallel region: 300
```

Figure 4.78: **Output of the example shown in Figure 4.77** – Three threads are used. The other values and settings are also the same as for the example output given in Figure 4.56 on page 90.

collects the forces acting on each of the particles as a result of the proximity of other particles and their motion and uses it to modify their position and velocity. The fragment we show includes two reduction operations to gather the potential and kinetic energy.

We note that, depending on the operator or intrinsic used, the initial value of the shared reduction variable (like sum in our example) may be *updated*, not overwritten. In the example above, if the initial value of sum is, for example, 10 prior to the reduction operation, the final value is given by $sum = 10 + \sum_{i=0}^{n-1} a[i]$. In other words, for this operator the original value is updated with the new contribution, not overwritten.

The order in which thread-specific values are combined is *unspecified*. Therefore, where floating-point data are concerned, there may be numerical differences between the results of a sequential and parallel run, or even of two parallel runs using the same number of threads. This is a result of the limitation in precision with which computers represent floating-point numbers: results may vary slightly, depending on the order in which operations are performed. It is not a cause for concern if the values are all of roughly the same magnitude. The OpenMP standard is explicit about this point: "There is no guarantee that bit-identical results will be obtained or that side effects (such as floating-point exceptions) will be identical" (see Section 2.8.3.6 of the 2.5 standard). It is good to keep this in mind when using the reduction clause.

```
! The force computation for each particle is performed in parallel
!$omp   parallel do
!$omp&  default(shared)
!$omp&  private(i,j,k,rij,d)
!$omp&  reduction(+ : pot, kin)
      do i=1,nparticles
        ! compute potential energy and forces
        f(1:nd,i) = 0.0
        do j=1,nparticles
            if (i .ne. j) then
               call distance(nd,box,pos(1,i),pos(1,j),rij,d)
               ! result is saved in variable d
               pot = pot + 0.5*v(d)
               do k=1,nd
                  f(k,i) = f(k,i) - rij(k)*dv(d)/d
               enddo
            endif
        enddo
        ! compute kinetic energy
        kin = kin + dotprod(nd,vel(1,i),vel(1,i))
      enddo
!$omp   end parallel do
      kin = kin*0.5*mass

      return
      end
```

Figure 4.79: **Piece of a molecular dynamics simulation** – Each thread computes displacement and velocity information for a subset of the particles. As it is doing so, it contributes to the summation of potential and kinetic energy.

The operators supported (plus the intrinsic functions available in Fortran for this clause) are given in the first column of Figures 4.80 (C/C++) and 4.81 (Fortran). Each operator has a specific initial value associated with it, listed in the second column. This is the initial value of each *local* copy of the reduction variable.

OpenMP defines which type of statements are applicable to the reduction clause. In Figure 4.82 all the reduction statements supported in C/C++ are listed. The statements and intrinsic functions available in Fortran are given in Figure 4.83. In Fortran, the *array reduction* is also supported, which permits the reduction

Operator	Initialization value
+	0
*	1
–	0
&	~0
|	0
^	0
&&	1
||	0

Figure 4.80: **Operators and initial values supported on the reduction clause in C/C++** – The initialization value is the value of the local copy of the reduction variable. This value is operator, data type, and language dependent.

Operator	Initialization value
+	0
*	1
–	0
.and.	.true.
.or.	.false.
.eqv.	.true.
.neqv.	.false.
.neqv.	.false.

Intrinsic	Initialization value
max	Smallest negative machine representable number in the reduction variable type
min	Largest negative machine representable number in the reduction variable type
iand	All bits on
ior	0
ieor	0

Figure 4.81: **Operators, intrinsic functions, and initial values supported on the reduction clause in Fortran** – The initialization value is the value of the local copy of the reduction variable. This value is operator, data type, and language dependent.

"variable" to be an entire array; see the example in Figure 4.84, where array `a` is updated in parallel in a manner that is similar to the scalar case. Each thread computes a *partial* update by calculating `a(1:n) = a(1:n) + b(1:n,j)*c(j)` for specific values of j, storing the result in a private array. This partial solution is then added to the global solution, the (shared) result array a. The details of the implementation depend on the specific OpenMP compiler.

```
x = x op expr
x binop = expr
x = expr op x (except for subtraction)
x++
++x
x--
--x
```

Figure 4.82: **Typical reduction statements in C/C++** – Here, expr has scalar type and does not reference x, *op* is not an overloaded operator, but one of +, *, -, &, ¬ |, &&, or | |, and *binop* is not an overloaded operator, but one of +, *, -, &, ^, or |.

```
x = x op expr
x = expr op x (except for subtraction)
x = intrinsic(x, expr_list)
x = intrinsic(expr_list, x)
```

Figure 4.83: **Typical reduction and intrinsic statements in Fortran** – Here, *op* is one of the operators from the list +, *, -, .and., .or., .eqv., or .neqv.. The expression does not involve x, the reduction *op* is the last operation performed on the right-hand side, and *expr_list* is a comma-separated list of expressions not involving x. The *intrinsic* function is one from the list given in Figure 4.81.

```
!$OMP PARALLEL DO DEFAULT(NONE) PRIVATE(j) SHARED(n,b,c) &
!$OMP             REDUCTION(+:a)
      do j = 1, n
         a(1:n) = a(1:n) + b(1:n,j)*c(j)
      end do
!$OMP END PARALLEL DO
```

Figure 4.84: **Example of an array reduction** – This type of reduction operation is supported in Fortran only.

We note that there are some further restrictions on both the variables and the operators that may be used. In C/C++ the following restrictions apply:

- Aggregate types (including arrays), pointer types, and reference types are not supported.

- A reduction variable must not be `const`-qualified.

- The operator specified on the clause can not be overloaded with respect to the variables that appear in the clause.

In Fortran there are some restrictions as well:

- A variable that appears in the clause must be definable.

- A list item must be a named variable of intrinsic type.

- Fortran pointers, Cray pointers, assumed-size array and allocatable arrays are not supported.

4.8.5   Copyin Clause

The `copyin` clause provides a means to copy the value of the master thread's threadprivate variable(s) to the corresponding threadprivate variables of the other threads. As explained in Section 4.9.3, these are global variables that are made private to each thread: each thread has its own set of these variables. Just as with regular private data, the initial values are undefined. The `copyin` clause can be used to change this situation. The copy is carried out after the team of threads is formed and prior to the start of execution of the `parallel` region, so that it enables a straightforward initialization of this kind of data object.

The clause is supported on the `parallel` directive and the combined parallel work-sharing directives. The syntax is `copyin(list)`. Several restrictions apply. We refer to the standard for the details.

4.8.6   Copyprivate Clause

The `copyprivate` clause is supported on the `single` directive only. It provides a mechanism for broadcasting the value of a private variable from one thread to the other threads in the team. The typical use for this clause is to have one thread read or initialize private data that is subsequently used by the other threads as well.

After the single construct has ended, but before the threads have left the associated barrier, the values of variables specified in the associated list are copied to the other threads. Since the barrier is essential in this case, the standard prohibits use of this clause in combination with the *nowait* clause.

The syntax is of this clause is: `copyprivate (list)`. In Fortran this clause is added to the `end` part of the construct. With C/C++, `copyprivate` is a regular clause, specified on the `single` construct.

4.9   Advanced OpenMP Constructs

We have covered the most common features of the API. These are sufficient to parallelize the majority of applications. Here, we complete our overview of the OpenMP API by covering a few remaining, specialized constructs. These are considered special-purpose because the need to use them strongly depends on the application. For example, certain recursive algorithms can take advantage of nested parallelism in a natural way, but many applications do not need this feature.

4.9.1   Nested Parallelism

If a thread in a team executing a parallel region encounters another parallel construct, it creates a new team and becomes the master of that new team. This is generally referred to in OpenMP as "nested parallelism."

In contrast to the other features of the API, an implementation is free to not provide nested parallelism. In this case, parallel constructs that are nested within other parallel constructs will be ignored and the corresponding parallel region serialized (executed by a single thread only): it is thus inactive. Increasingly, OpenMP implementations support this feature. We note that frequent starting and stopping of parallel regions may introduce a non-trivial performance penalty.

Some care is needed when using nested parallelism. For example, if the function `omp_get_thread_num()` is called from within a nested parallel region, it still returns a number in the range of zero up to one less than the number of threads of the *current* team. In other words, the thread number may no longer be unique. This situation is demonstrated in the code fragment in Figure 4.85, where `omp_get_nested()` is used to test whether nested parallelism is available. The `num_threads` clause is used (see Section 4.8.2 on page 102) to specify that the second level parallel region should be executed by two threads.

The output obtained when using three threads to execute the first, "outer," parallel region is given in Figure 4.86. We have used indentation to see that a message comes from the inner parallel region, but it is no longer possible to distinguish messages from the individual threads that execute this region.

The code fragment from Figure 4.87 shows one way to address the problem for this specific case. Here, variable `TID` is used to store the number of the thread at

```
printf("Nested parallelism is %s\n",
        omp_get_nested() ? "supported" : "not supported");
#pragma omp parallel
    {
      printf("Thread %d executes the outer parallel region\n",
              omp_get_thread_num());

      #pragma omp parallel num_threads(2)
      {
        printf("  Thread %d executes inner parallel region\n",
                omp_get_thread_num());
      } /*-- End of inner parallel region --*/
    } /*-- End of outer parallel region --*/
```

Figure 4.85: **Example of nested parallelism** – Two parallel regions are nested. The second parallel region is executed by two threads.

```
Nested parallelism is supported
Thread 0 executes the outer parallel region
  Thread 0 executes the inner parallel region
  Thread 1 executes the inner parallel region
Thread 2 executes the outer parallel region
  Thread 0 executes the inner parallel region
Thread 1 executes the outer parallel region
  Thread 0 executes the inner parallel region
  Thread 1 executes the inner parallel region
  Thread 1 executes the inner parallel region
```

Figure 4.86: **Output from the source listed in Figure 4.85** – Three threads are used. The values returned by the OpenMP function omp_get_thread_num() do not reflect the nesting level. It is not possible to use the thread number to uniquely identify a thread.

the outer level. This variable is then passed on to the inner level parallel region by means of the firstprivate clause. Thus, each thread has a local copy of variable TID that is *initialized* with the value it had prior to entering the inner parallel region. This is exactly what is needed.

The output from the code fragment in Figure 4.87 is shown in Figure 4.88. As before, three threads execute the outer parallel region. One can now determine which inner level thread has executed the printf statement within the inner parallel

```
printf("Nested parallelism is %s\n",
        omp_get_nested() ? "supported" : "not supported");
#pragma omp parallel private(TID)
  {
    TID = omp_get_thread_num();

    printf("Thread %d executes the outer parallel region\n",TID);

    #pragma omp parallel num_threads(2) firstprivate(TID)
    {
      printf("TID %d: Thread %d executes inner parallel region\n",
             TID,omp_get_thread_num());
    }  /*-- End of inner parallel region --*/
  }  /*-- End of outer parallel region --*/
```

Figure 4.87: **Modified version of nested parallelism example** – A thread at the first parallel level stores the thread number and passes it on to the second level.

```
Nested parallelism is supported
Thread 0 executes the outer parallel region
TID 0: Thread 0 executes inner parallel region
Thread 1 executes the outer parallel region
TID 1: Thread 0 executes inner parallel region
Thread 2 executes the outer parallel region
TID 2: Thread 0 executes inner parallel region
TID 2: Thread 1 executes inner parallel region
TID 0: Thread 1 executes inner parallel region
TID 1: Thread 1 executes inner parallel region
```

Figure 4.88: **Output from the source listed in Figure 4.87** – At least one can now distinguish at what nesting level the message is printed.

region.

Where nested parallelism is concerned, it is not always obvious what region a specific construct relates to. For the details of *binding* rules we refer to the standard.

4.9.2   Flush Directive

We have seen that the OpenMP memory model distinguishes between shared data, which is accessible and visible to all threads, and private data, which is local to an individual thread. We also explained in Chapter 2 that, where the sharing of values is concerned, things are more complex than they appear to be on the surface. This is because, on most modern computers, processors have their own "local," very high speed memory, the registers and cache (see Fig. 1.1). If a thread updates shared data, the new values will first be saved in a register and then stored back to the local cache. The updates are thus not necessarily immediately visible to other threads, since threads executing on other processors do not have access to either of these memories. On a cache-coherent machine, the modification to cache is broadcast to other processors to make them aware of changes, but the details of how and when this is performed depends on the platform.

OpenMP protects its users from needing to know how a given computer handles this data *consistency* problem. The OpenMP standard specifies that all modifications are written back to main memory and are thus available to all threads, at *synchronization points* in the program. Between these synchronization points, threads are permitted to have new values for shared variables stored in their local memory rather than in the global shared memory. As a result, each thread executing an OpenMP code potentially has its own *temporary view* of the values of shared data. This approach, called a *relaxed consistency model,* makes it easier for the system to offer good program performance.

But sometimes this is not enough. Sometimes updated values of shared values must become visible to other threads in-between synchronization points. The OpenMP API provides the `flush` directive to make this possible.

The purpose of the `flush` directive is to make a thread's temporary view of shared data consistent with the values in memory. The syntax of the directive in C/C++ is given in Figure 4.89.

$$\boxed{\textbf{\#pragma omp flush } [\textit{(list)}]}$$

Figure 4.89:   **Syntax of the flush directive in C/C++** – This enforces shared data to be consistent. Its usage is not always straightforward.

The syntax in Fortran is shown in Figure 4.90.

The `flush` operation applies to all variables specified in the list. If no list is provided, it applies to all thread-visible shared data. If the `flush` operation is invoked by a thread that has updated the variables, their new values will be flushed

```
!$omp flush [(list)]
```

Figure 4.90: **Syntax of the flush directive in Fortran** – This enforces shared data to be consistent. Its usage is not always straightforward.

to memory and therefore be accessible to all other threads. If the construct is invoked by a thread that has not updated a value, it will ensure that any local copies of the data are replaced by the latest value from main memory. Some care is required with its use. First, this does *not* synchronize the actions of different threads: rather, it forces the executing thread to make its shared data values consistent with shared memory. Second, since the compiler reorders operations to enhance program performance, one cannot assume that the flush operation will remain exactly in the position, relative to other operations, in which it was placed by the programmer. What can be guaranteed is that it will not change its position relative to any operations involving the flushed variables. Implicit flush operations with no list occur at the following locations.

- All explicit and implicit barriers (e.g., at the end of a parallel region or work-sharing construct)

- Entry to and exit from `critical` regions

- Entry to and exit from lock routines

This design is to help avoid errors that would probably otherwise occur frequently. For example, if flush was not implied on entry to and exit from locks, the code in Figure 4.91 would not ensure that the updated value of `count` is available to threads other than the one that has performed the operation. Indeed, versions of the OpenMP standard prior to 2.5 required an explicit `flush(count)` before and after the update. The implied flushing of all shared variables was introduced to ensure correctness of the code; it may, however carry performance penalties.

The following example demonstrates how to employ `flush` to set up pipelined thread execution. We consider the NAS Parallel Benchmark LU from the NPB version 3.2.1. This is a simulated computational fluid dynamics application that uses a symmetric successive overrelaxation method to solve a seven-band block-diagonal system resulting from finite-difference discretization of the 3D compressible Navier-Stokes equations. The OpenMP parallelization of the code is described in [90] and is summarized below. All of the loops involved carry dependences that prevent straightforward parallelization. A code snippet is shown in Figure 4.92.

```
!$omp parallel shared (lck, count)
      ...
      call omp_set_lock (lck)
      count = count + 1
      call omp_unset_lock (lck)
      ...
!$omp end parallel
```

Figure 4.91: **A lock implies a** `flush` – The example uses locks to increment a shared counter. Since a call to a lock routine implies flushing of all shared variables, it ensures that all threads have a consistent view of the value of variable `count`.

```
do k=2,nz
   do j = 2, ny
      do i = 2, nx
         v(i,j,k) = v(i,j,k) + v(i-1,j,k)
                  + v(i,j-1,k) + v(i,j,k-1)
         ...
      end do
   end do
end do
```

Figure 4.92: **Code snippet from a time consuming loop in the LU code from the NAS Parallel Benchmarks** – Dependences in all three dimensions prevent straightforward parallelization of the loop.

A certain amount of parallelism can be exploited by setting up pipelined thread execution. The basic idea is to enclose the outer loop in a parallel region but share the work on the next inner level. For our example, an `!$omp parallel do` directive is placed on the k-loop, and the `!$omp do` work-sharing directive is placed on the j-loop. On entry to the parallel region, the team of threads is created and starts executing. Since the work in the k-loop is not parceled out, all threads will execute all iterations of it.

For a given iteration of the k-loop, each thread will work on its chunk of iterations of the j-loop. But because of data dependences, the threads cannot all work on the same iteration of the k-loop at the same time. Each thread needs data that will be updated by another thread, with the exception of the thread that receives the first chunk of iterations. If we explicitly schedule this code so that thread 0 receives the first chunk, thread 1 the second, and so forth, then thread 0 can start to work

```
!$OMP PARALLEL PRIVATE(k, iam)

   iam = OMP_GET_THREAD_NUM()
   isync(iam) = 0 ! Initialize synchronization array

! Wait for neighbor thread to finish

!$OMP BARRIER
   do k = 2, nz
      if (iam .gt. 0) then
         do while(isync(iam-1) .eq. 0)
!$OMP FLUSH(isync)
         end do
         isync(iam 1) = 0
!$OMP FLUSH(isync,v)
      end if

!$OMP DO SCHEDULE(STATIC, nchunk)
      do j = 2, ny; do i = 2, nx
            v(i,j,k) = v(i,j,k) + v(i-1,j,k) + ....
      end do; end do
!$OMP END DO NOWAIT

! Signal the availability of data to neighbor thread

      if (iam .lt. nt) then
!$OMP FLUSH(isync,v)
         do while (isync(iam) .eq. 1)
!$OMP FLUSH(isync)
         end do
         isync (iam) = 1
!$OMP FLUSH(isync)
      end if
   end do

!$OMP END PARALLEL
```

Figure 4.93: **One-dimensional pipelined thread execution in the NAS Parallel Benchmark LU** – The flush directive is used several times here. Note that ny is assumed to be a multiple of the number of threads nt.

immediately on its first chunk of data in the j direction. Once thread 0 finishes, thread 1 can start on its chunk of the j-loop for iteration k=2 and, in the meantime, thread 0 moves on to work on iteration k=3. Eventually, all threads will be working on their chunk of data in the j dimension, but on different iterations of the k-loop. Implementing this kind of pipelined thread execution is a more challenging problem for the programmer because it requires synchronization of individual threads, rather than global barrier synchronization. A thread has to wait for the availability of the data it needs before it can start on a new chunk, and it must signal the availability of updated data to the thread that is waiting for that data. The `flush` directive can be used for this purpose, as shown in Figure 4.93.

The code invokes OpenMP runtime library routines `omp_get_thread_num`, to obtain the current thread identifier, and `omp_get_num_threads` for the total number of threads. The shared array `isync` is used to indicate the availability of data from neighboring threads. Static scheduling has to be specified for this technique. In addition, loop lengths are assumed to be a multiple of the number of threads, thereby eliminating unpredictable behavior introduced by compiler-specific treatment of end cases. Thread 0 can start processing right away. All other threads have to wait until the values they need are available. To accomplish this, we place the `flush` directive inside two subsequent `while`-loops. The first `flush` ensures that the array `isync` is read from memory, rather than using a value stored locally in a register or cache. The second `flush` ensures that the updated value of `isync` is visible to other threads and that array `v` is read from memory after the `while`-loop has exited.

After processing its chunk of the j-loop, a thread needs to signal the availability of the data to its successor thread. To this end we use two `flush` directives, one of which is placed in a `while`-loop. The first `flush` ensures that the updated values of array `v` are made visible to the successor thread before the synchronization takes place. The second `flush` ensures that the synchronization array `isync` is made visible after it has been updated.

4.9.3   Threadprivate Directive

We have seen clauses for declaring data in parallel and work-sharing regions to be shared or private. However, we have not discussed how to deal with global data (e.g., static in C and common blocks in Fortran). By default, global data is shared, which is often appropriate. But in some situations we may need, or would prefer to have, private data that persists throughout the computation. This is where the `threadprivate` directive comes in handy.[10] The effect of the `threadprivate` directive is that the named global-lifetime objects are replicated, so that each thread has its own copy. Put simply, each thread gets a private or "local" copy of the specified global variables (and common blocks in case of Fortran). There is also a convenient mechanism for initializing this data if required. See the description of the `copyin` clause in Section 4.8.5 for details.

The syntax of the `threadprivate` directive in C/C++ is shown in Figure 4.94. The Fortran syntax is given in Figure 4.95.

#pragma omp threadprivate *(list)*

Figure 4.94: **Syntax of the threadprivate directive in C/C++** – The *list* consists of a comma separated list of file-scope, namespace-scope, or static block scope variables that have incomplete types. The `copyin` clause can be used to initialize the data in the threadprivate copies of the list item(s).

!$omp threadprivate *(list)*

Figure 4.95: **Syntax of the threadprivate directive in Fortran** – The *list* consists of a comma-separated list of named variables and named common blocks. Common block names must appear between slashes, for example, `!$omp threadprivate (/mycommonblock/)`. The `copyin` clause can be used to initialize the data in the threadprivate copies of the list item(s).

Among the various types of variables that may be specified in the `threadprivate` directive are pointer variables in C/C++ and Fortran and allocatables in Fortran. By default, the threadprivate copies are not allocated or defined. The programmer must take care of this task in the parallel region. The example in Figure 4.96 demonstrates this point.

In order to exploit this directive, a program must adhere to a number of rules and restrictions. For it to make sense for global data to persist, and thus for data created within one parallel region to be available in the *next* parallel region, the regions need to be executed by the "same" threads. In the context of OpenMP, this means that the parallel regions must be executed by the same number of threads. Then, each of the threads will continue to work on one of the sets of data previously produced. If all of the conditions below hold, and if a threadprivate object is referenced in two consecutive (at run time) parallel regions, then threads with the same thread

---

[10]Technically this is a directive, not a construct.

number in their respective regions reference the same copy of that variable.[11] We refer to the OpenMP standard (Section 2.8.2) for more details on this directive.

- Neither parallel region is nested inside another parallel region.

- The number of threads used to execute both parallel regions is the same.

- The value of the *dyn-var* internal control variable is false at entry to the first parallel region and remains false until entry to the second parallel region.

- The value of the *nthreads-var* internal control variable is the same at entry to both parallel regions and has not been modified between these points.

```
1 int *pglobal;
2
3 int main()
4 {
5            . . . . . . . . . . .
6
7  for (i=0; i<n; i++)
8  {
9   if ((pglobal=(int *) malloc(length[i]*sizeof(int))) != NULL) {
10
11      for (j=sum=0; j<length[i]; j++) pglobal[j] = j+1;
12      sum = calculate_sum(length[i]);
13      printf("Value of sum for i = %d is %d\n",i,sum);
14      free(pglobal);
15
16  } else {
17      printf("Fatal error in malloc - length[%d] = %d\n",
18             i,length[i]);
19  }
20  }
21
22          . . . . . . . . . . .
```

Figure 4.96: **Program fragment** – This program uses a global pointer pglobal to allocate, initialize, and release memory.

---

[11]Section 4.7 on page 95 defines and explains these control variables.

The need for and usage of the `threadprivate` directive is illustrated by a somewhat elaborate example in Figure 4.96, where the fragment of a sequential program is listed. At line 1 a global pointer `pglobal` to an `int` is defined. The main for-loop spans lines 7 through 20. In this loop, storage is allocated at line 9. Pointer `pglobal` is used to point to this block of memory, which is initialized in the for-loop (line 11). At line 12 function `calculate_sum` is called; it sums up the elements of `pglobal`. At line 13 the checksum called `sum` is printed. At line 14 the memory block is released again through the call to the `free` function. If the memory allocation should fail, the code block under the `else` branch is executed. Function `calculate_sum` is given in Figure 4.97. It simply adds up all the elements pointed to by `global`, using parameter `length` as an argument to the function.

```
1   extern int *pglobal;
2
3   int calculate_sum(int length)
4   {
5      int sum = 0;
6
7      for (int j=0; j<length; j++)
8         sum += pglobal[j];
9
10     return(sum);
11  }
```

Figure 4.97: **Source of function calculate_sum** – This function sums up the elements of a vector pointed to by the global pointer `pglobal`.

The main loop over `i` at line 7 in Figure 4.96 can be easily parallelized with a `#pragma omp parallel for` combined work-sharing construct. However, this requires care when using pointer `pglobal` in particular. By default, `pglobal` is a shared variable. This creates various (related) problems. In the parallelized loop over `i`, multiple threads update `pglobal` simultaneously, creating a data race condition. If we do not find a way to overcome this, we already have a fatal error of course. But on top of that, the size of the memory block depends on `i` and is therefore thread-dependent. As a result, some threads access memory outside of the area that has been allocated, another fatal error. The third problem encountered is that one thread may release memory (through the call to `free`) while another thread or multiple threads still need to access this portion of memory. This results in undetermined runtime behavior, leading to a wrong answer (because of the data race condition) or a segmentation violation caused by the out-of-bounds access or premature release of memory. Luckily, the `threadprivate` directive helps out. The OpenMP version of the code fragment using this is shown in Figure 4.98.

```
 1 int *pglobal;
 2
 3 #pragma omp threadprivate(pglobal)
 4
 5 int main()
 6 {
 7             . . . . . . . . . . .
 8
 9  #pragma omp parallel for shared(n,length,check) \
10          private(TID,i,j,sum)
11  for (i=0; i<n; i++)
12  {
13    TID = omp_get_thread_num();
14
15    if ((pglobal=(int *) malloc(length[i]*sizeof(int))) != NULL) {
16
17        for (j=sum=0; j<length[i]; j++) pglobal[j] = j+1;
18        sum = calculate_sum(length[i]);
19        printf("TID %d: value of sum for i = %d is %d\n",
20               TID,i,sum);
21        free(pglobal);
22
23    } else {
24        printf("TID %d: fatal error in malloc - length[%d] = %d\n",
25               TID,i,length[i]);
26    }
27  } /*-- End of parallel for --*/
28
29             . . . . . . . . . . .
```

Figure 4.98: **OpenMP version of the program fragment** – The `threadprivate` directive is used to give each thread a private copy of the global pointer `pglobal`. This is needed for the parallel loop to be correct.

The source code changes needed to parallelize this loop are minimal. A `#pragma omp threadprivate` directive is used at line 3 to give each thread a local copy of our pointer `pglobal`. At line 9 the `#pragma omp parallel for` directive is inserted to parallelize the main loop over i. For diagnostic purposes the thread number is stored in variable TID at line 13. This identifier is used in the print statements. The output is given in Figure 4.99.

```
TID 0: value of sum for i = 0 is 55
TID 0: value of sum for i = 1 is 210
TID 2: value of sum for i = 4 is 1275
TID 1: value of sum for i = 2 is 465
TID 1: value of sum for i = 3 is 820
```

Figure 4.99: **Output of the program listed in Figure 4.98** – Variable n is set to 5, and three threads are used.

Sometimes a private variable, such as a pointer with the private data-sharing attribute, can be used to achieve the same result. In the example here, this is not possible without modifying the source of function calculate_sum and all the places in the source program where it is called. Since this requires more work, and most likely additional testing, the threadprivate directive is more convenient to use.

4.10   Wrap-Up

In the early sections of this chapter, we introduced some terminology and then presented and discussed a basic set of OpenMP constructs, directives, and clauses. This set is more than sufficient to parallelize many different applications. We next introduced synchronization constructs and explained how to influence and exchange information with the execution environment. We then showed some slightly less common clauses and, finally, some advanced features.

OpenMP is straightforward to use. The programmer's time is often spent thinking about where the parallelism is in the application. Once this has been identified, implementing it using the features provided by OpenMP is often straightforward. Challenges may arise if an algorithm implies tricky synchronization or if additional performance is needed.

What helps when parallelizing an application is to have a clean sequential version to start with. In particular, the control and data flow through the program should be straightforward. Use of global data that is modified should be minimized to reduce the chance of introducing a data race condition. Something else that helps when parallelizing loops is to avoid a bulky loop body, which makes the specification of data-sharing attributes tedious and error prone. If the loop body performs a substantial amount of work, one should push it into a function. All variables local to the function are private by default, often dramatically reducing the data-sharing list. This is not only more pleasing to the eye but also easier to maintain. The use of block scoping in C can also help in this respect.

5 How to Get Good Performance by Using OpenMP

In this chapter, we give an overview of major performance considerations with respect to OpenMP programming and explain how to measure performance. We give tips on how to avoid common performance problems. Much of this chapter is taken up with a case study that illustrates a number of the points made, as well as providing insight into the process of exploring and overcoming performance problems.

5.1 Introduction

The relative ease of parallel programming with OpenMP can be a mixed blessing. It may be possible to quickly write a correctly functioning OpenMP program, but not so easy to create a program that provides the desired level of performance. When performance is poor, it is often because some basic programming rules have not been adhered to.

Programmers have developed some rules of thumb on how to write efficient sequential code. If these rules are followed, a certain base level of performance is usually achieved. This can often be gradually improved by successive fine tuning aspects of this program. The same is true for OpenMP programs. As we explain below, following some basic guidelines can help avoid first-level performance problems. For good performance, especially with a larger numbers of threads, more work may be required.

Our goal in this chapter is to give the programmer enough information to get things right from the start and to have the insight needed to improve a code's performance.

Chapter 6 expands on this goal. Several case studies are discussed in detail there. The aim is to show not only how to apply the basic performance rules to real-world applications but also how to use more advanced strategies to obtain good performance, scalable to a high number of threads.

5.2 Performance Considerations for Sequential Programs

One may be surprised to find a discussion of sequential performance in a book on OpenMP. We have good reason for covering this topic, however. Scalar performance is still a major concern when creating a parallel program.

These days, poor single-processor ("sequential") performance is often caused by suboptimal usage of the cache memory subsystem found in contemporary computers. In particular, a so-called cache miss at the highest level in the cache hierarchy is expensive because it implies the data must be fetched from main memory before it can be used. That is typically at least 5–10 times more expensive than fetching data from one of the caches. If this situation happens frequently on a single-processor system, it can severely reduce program performance.

On a shared-memory multiprocessor system, the adverse impact is even stronger: the more threads involved, the bigger the potential performance problem. The reason is as follows. A miss at the highest cache level causes additional traffic on the system interconnect. No matter how fast this interconnect is, parallel performance degrades because none of the systems on the market today have an interconnect with sufficient bandwidth to sustain frequent cache misses simultaneously by all processors (or cores) in the system.

We briefly discuss the memory hierarchy and its impact, since this is so important for OpenMP programs. The programmer can adopt many strategies, in addition to those discussed here, to improve sequential performance. The extent to which the user is willing and able to tune the sequential program before inserting OpenMP constructs will vary, as will the performance gains that can be achieved by doing so. We highly recommended, however, that the programmer consider sequential performance when creating OpenMP code, especially if the goal is a scalable OpenMP application.

5.2.1   Memory Access Patterns and Performance

A modern memory system is organized as a hierarchy, where the largest, and also slowest, part of memory is known as main memory. Main memory is organized into pages, a subset of which will be available to a given application. The memory levels closer to the processor are successively smaller and faster and are collectively known as cache. When a program is compiled, the compiler will arrange for its data objects to be stored in main memory; they will be transferred to cache when needed. If a value required for a computation is not already in a cache (we call this a cache "miss"), it must be retrieved from higher levels of the memory hierarchy, a process that can be quite expensive. Program data is brought into cache in chunks called blocks, each of which will occupy a line of cache. Data that is already in cache may need to be removed, or "evicted", to make space for a new block of data. Different systems have different strategies for deciding what must go.

The memory hierarchy is (with rare exceptions) not explicitly programmable by either the user or the compiler. Rather, data are fetched into cache and evicted from it dynamically as the need arises. Given the penalty paid whenever values must be retrieved from other levels of memory, various strategies have been devised that can help the compiler and the programmer to (indirectly) reduce the frequency with which this situation occurs. A major goal is to organize data accesses so that values are used as often as possible while they are still in cache. The most common strategies for doing so are based on the fact that programming languages (including both Fortran and C) typically specify that the elements of arrays be stored contiguously in memory. Thus, if an array element is fetched into cache, "nearby" elements of the array will be in the same cache block and will be fetched as part of the same transaction. If a computation that uses any of these values can be performed while they are still in cache, it will be beneficial for performance.

In C, a two-dimensional array is stored in rows. For instance, element [0][2] follows element [0][1], which in turn follows element [0][0] in memory. Element [1][1] is followed by [1][2], and so forth. This is often referred to as "rowwise storage." Thus, when an array element is transferred to cache, neighbors in the same row are typically also transferred as part of the same cache line. For good performance, therefore, a matrix-based computation should access the elements of the array row by row, not column by column. Figures 5.1 and 5.2 illustrate both types of memory access.

```
for (int i=0; i<n; i++)
   for (int j=0; j<n; j++)
      sum += a[i][j];
```

Figure 5.1: **Example of good memory access** – Array a is accessed along the rows. This approach ensures good performance from the memory system.

The loop in Figure 5.1 exhibits good memory access. When data has been brought into the cache(s), all the elements of the line are used before the next line is referenced. This type of access pattern is often referred to as "unit stride."

```
for (int j=0; j<n; j++)
   for (int i=0; i<n; i++)
      sum += a[i][j];
```

Figure 5.2: **Example of bad memory access** – Array a is accessed columnwise. This approach results in poor utilization of the memory system. The larger the array, the worse its performance will be.

In contrast, the loop in Figure 5.2 is not cache friendly. Each reference to a[i][j] may bring a new block of data into the cache. The next element in the line it occupies is not referenced until the next iteration of the outer loop is begun, by which time it might have been replaced in cache by other data needed during the execution of the inner loop. Hence, the execution time of this loop may be dominated by the time taken to repeatedly copy data into cache. This situation is especially likely if variable n is fairly large (relative to the cache size).

The storage order is different in Fortran: entire arrays are stored contiguously by column. This means that for an m x n array a, element a(1,1) is followed by element a(2,1). The last element a(m,1) of the first column in followed by a(1,2), etc. This is called "columnwise storage." Just as in C, it is critical for performance that a Fortran array be accessed in the order in which the elements are stored in memory.

5.2.2   Translation-Lookaside Buffer

We have skipped one important detail about the memory system. On a system that supports virtual memory, the memory addresses for different applications are "virtualized": they are given logical addresses, arranged into virtual pages. The size of a page is determined by the size(s) the system supports, plus the choice(s) offered by the operating system. A typical page size is 4 or 8 KByte, but much larger ones exist. In fact, the physical pages that are available to a program may be spread out in memory, and so the virtual pages must be mapped to the physical ones. The operating system sets up a special data structure, called a page table, that records this mapping. It is used to locate the physical page corresponding to a virtual page when it is referenced during execution. The page table resides in main memory, however, and this procedure is time-consuming. In order to alleviate the expense of looking up page addresses, a special cache was developed that stores recently accessed entries in the page table. It is known as the *translation-lookaside buffer*, or TLB, and may considerably improve the performance of the system and of individual applications.[1]

The TLB is on the critical path for performance. Whenever data is needed for a calculation and the information needed to determine its physical location is not in the TLB, the processor waits until the requested information is available. Only then is it able to transfer the values and resume execution. Therefore, just as with data cache, it is important to make good use of the TLB entries. We would like a page to be heavily referenced while its location is stored in the TLB. Whenever a program does not access data in storage order (as shown in Figure 5.2, for example), frequent cache reloads plus a large number of TLB misses may result.

---

[1]There can be a hierarchy of TLBs similar to that of data (and instruction) caches.

5.2.3 Loop Optimizations

Both the programmer and the compiler can improve the use of memory. To show how, we first note that the difference between the two code fragments in Figures 5.1 and 5.2 is minor. If we were to encounter the latter loop in a piece of code, we could simply exchange the order of the loop headers and most likely experience a significant performance benefit. This is one way in which loops can be restructured, or transformed, to improve performance. This particular strategy is called *loop interchange* (or *loop exchange*).

Since many programs spend much of their time executing loops and since most array accesses are to be found there, a suitable reorganization of the computation in loop nests to exploit cache can significantly improve a program's performance. A number of loop transformations can help achieve this. They can be applied if the changes to the code do not affect correct execution of the program. The test for this is as follows:

If any memory location is referenced more than once in the loop nest and if at least one of those references modifies its value, then their relative ordering must not be changed by the transformation.

Although this is often intuitive, the loop's code must be carefully examined to be sure this is the case for all data accesses. A compiler is not always able to determine whether this property holds, which is why the application developer can sometimes do a better job of optimizing loops. This is most likely to be the case if pointers are used or array subscripts refer to variables or other arrays.

A programmer should consider transforming a loop if accesses to arrays in the loop nest do not occur in the order in which they are stored in memory, or if a loop has a large body and the references to an array element or its neighbors are far apart. A simple reordering of the statements inside the body of the loop nest may make a difference. Note that loop transformations have other purposes, too. They may help the compiler to better utilize the instruction pipeline or may increase the amount of exploitable parallelism. They can also be applied to increase the size of parallel regions. Here we describe some of the most important transformations. We refer to [181, 178] for a deeper discussion. Some of these transformations are used in the case study in Section 5.6.

Loop unrolling is a powerful technique to effectively reduce the overheads of loop execution (caused by the increment of the loop variable, test for completion and branch to the start of the loop's code). It has other benefits, too. Loop unrolling can help to improve cache line utilization by improving data reuse. It can also help to increase the instruction-level parallelism, or ILP (see also Section 1.1). In order to accomplish all of this, the transformation packs the work of several loop iterations into a single pass through the loop by replicating and appropriately modifying the statements in the loop.

```
for (int i=1; i<n; i++) {
     a[i] = b[i] + 1;
     c[i] = a[i] + a[i-1] + b[i-1];
}
```

Figure 5.3: **A short loop nest** – Loop overheads are relatively high when each iteration has a small number of operations.

The loop in Figure 5.3 loads four array elements, performs three floating-point additions, and stores two values per iteration. Its overhead includes incrementing the loop variable, testing its value and branching to the start of the loop. In contrast, the unrolled loop shown in Figure 5.4 loads five values, carries out six floating-point additions, and stores four values, with the same overheads. The overall overhead of executing the loop nest has been roughly halved. The data reuse has improved, too. When one is updating `c[i+1]`, the value of `a[i]` just computed can be used immediately. There is no risk that the reference to `a[i]` might force new data to be brought into cache. The newly computed value is still in a register and hence available for use.

```
for (int i=1; i<n; i+=2) {
     a[i] = b[i] + 1;
     c[i] = a[i] + a[i-1] + b[i-1];
     a[i+1] = b[i+1] + 1;
     c[i+1] = a[i+1] + a[i] + b[i];
}
```

Figure 5.4: **An unrolled loop** – The loop of Figure 5.3 has been unrolled by a factor of 2 to reduce the loop overheads. We assume the number of iterations is divisible by 2.

In this example, the loop body executes 2 iterations in one pass. This number is called the "unroll factor." The appropriate choice depends on various constraints. A higher value tends to give better performance but also increases the number of registers needed, for example.

Nowadays, a programmer seldom needs to apply this transformation manually, since compilers are very good at doing this. They are also very good at determining the optimal unroll factor.

A downside of loop unrolling is that the performance of the resulting code may vary somewhat as a function of the iteration count. If the unroll factor does not divide the iteration count, the remaining iterations must be performed outside this loop nest. This is implemented through a second loop, the "cleanup" loop. By definition it is a short loop and somewhat reduces potential performance gains.

Loop unrolling usually is not a good idea if the loop already contains a lot of computation or if it contains procedure calls. The former situation is likely to mean that this will make cache use less efficient, and the latter introduces new overheads that are likely to outweigh the savings. If there are branches in the loop, the benefits may also be low.

Unroll and jam is an extension of loop unrolling that is appropriate for some loop nests with multiple loops. We consider only the case here with two loops that are tightly nested, as illustrated in Figure 5.5.

```
for (int j=0; j<n; j++)
   for (int i=0; i<n; i++)
       a[i][j] = b[i][j] + 1;
```

Figure 5.5: **A loop that does not benefit from inner loop unrolling** – In this case, unrolling the loop over i results in poor cache utilization. It is assumed the iteration count is divisible by 2.

This loop nest is a prime candidate for unrolling because there is not much computation per iteration. Unfortunately, unrolling the inner loop over i results in strided access to elements of arrays a and b. If, however, we unroll the outer loop, as in Figure 5.6, then we have the desired rowwise array access.

```
for (int j=0; j<n; j+=2){
   for (int i=0; i<n; i++)
       a[i][j] = b[i][j] + 1;
   for (int i=0; i<n; i++)
       a[i][j+1] = b[i][j+1] + 1;
}
```

Figure 5.6: **Outer loop unrolling** – The outer loop of the code in Figure 5.5 has been unrolled by a factor of 2.

We can do better than this, however, since we can reduce the loop overhead by "jamming" the replicated inner loops to recreate a single inner loop, as shown in Figure 5.7 for our example loop nest. Since the resulting loop includes work from several iterations of the outer loop, it has more computation and reduces the overall overhead.

```
for (int j=0; j<n; j+=2)
   for (int i=0; i<n; i++) {
      a[i][j]   = b[i][j] + 1;
      a[i][j+1] = b[i][j+1] + 1;
}
```

Figure 5.7: **Unroll and jam** – The bodies of the two inner loops have been "jammed" into a single inner loop that performs the work of two iterations of the outer loop, reducing the overall overhead.

Loop interchange exchanges the order of loops in a nest. The example in Section 5.2.1 showed how this transformation can be applied to improve memory access. It can also be profitably used to increase the amount of work inside a loop that will be parallelized, by moving loops inside the parallel loop.

Code between the loop headers, a function call, a data dependence, or branches within the loop are some of the possible reasons a compiler may not be able to apply this optimization. An example of such an inhibitor is shown in Figure 5.8.

```
for (int j=0; j<n; j++)
  for (int i=0; i<m; i++)
    a[i][j+1] = a[i+1][j] + b;
```

Figure 5.8: **Loop with complex array access pattern** – Array a is updated in column order here. This is not good for performance, but the compiler cannot improve this by exchanging the loop headers.

Since it involves strided access to elements of a, swapping the loop headers might lead to a substantial speedup. To see why we cannot do so here, consider how this change affects the value of just one array element. In the original loop, a[2][2] is computed in iteration j=1,i=2. It is subsequently used to assign a new value to a[1][3] in iteration j=2,i=1.

In the loop given in Figure 5.9, where the loop headers are swapped, these iterations are executed in the opposite order. As a result, when the value of a[1][3] is computed, the *old* value of a[2][2] will be taken instead and a different result produced.

The problem here is that we have swapped the order in which a value is computed and then used, thereby violating our test for a legal loop transformation. Careful reasoning is needed by the compiler or programmer to determine whether this can happen: fortunately it is not all that common.

```
for (int i=0; i<n; i++)
  for (int j=0; j<m; j++)
    a[i][j+1] = a[i+1][j] + b ;
```

Figure 5.9: **Illegal loop interchange** – This loop has improved memory access, but the values it computes for array a are *not* the same as those produced by the loop of Figure 5.8.

Loop fusion merges two or more loops to create a bigger loop. This might enable data in cache to be reused more frequently or might increase the amount of computation per iteration in order to improve the instruction-level parallelism (see Section 1.1), as well as lowering loop overheads because more work gets done per loop iteration. Sometimes a reordering of loops beforehand, or of statements inside one or more loops, may enhance the results.

For example, consider the pair of loops in Figure 5.10. Especially if n is large, values of a accessed in the first loop will no longer be in cache when they are needed in the second loop. Loop fusion enables us to rewrite this computation as a single loop, given in Figure 5.11. Some care may be needed to ensure that the result does not violate the test for a legal transformation.

```
for (int i=0; i<n; i++)
    a[i] = b[i] * 2;
for (int i=0; i<n; i++)
  {
    x[i] = 2 * x[i];
    c[i] = a[i] + 2;
  }
```

Figure 5.10: **A pair of loops that both access array** a – The second loop reuses element a[i], but by the time it is executed, the cache line this element is part of may no longer be in the cache.

```
for (int i=0; i<n; i++)
{
     a[i] = b[i] * 2;
     c[i] = a[i] + 2;
     x[i] = 2 * x[i];
}
```

Figure 5.11: **An example of loop fusion** – The pair of loops of Figure 5.10 have been combined and the statements reordered. This permits the values of array a to be immediately reused.

Loop fission is a transformation that breaks up a loop into several loops. Sometimes, we may be able to improve use of cache this way or isolate a part that inhibits full optimization of the loop. This technique is likely to be most useful if a loop nest is large and its data does not fit into cache or if we can optimize parts of the loop in different ways.

Figure 5.12 shows a loop nest which first assigns a value to an element of array c and then updates a column of array a. The accesses to arrays a and b in the inner loop imply poor cache locality and bad memory access, but the assignment to array c prevents us from simply applying loop interchange. Loop fission solves this problem. It results in two different loops: we can swap the loop headers in the second of them to get the desired effect. Moreover, the first loop is amenable to further optimization, like replacement by a vectorized version of the exp intrinsic function, if available. We show the result of the loop fission in Figure 5.13.

```
for (int i=0; i<n; i++)
 {
   c[i] = exp(i/n) ;
   for (int j=0; j<m; j++)
      a[j][i] = b[j][i] + d[j] * e[i];
 }
```

Figure 5.12: **A loop with poor cache utilization and bad memory access** – If we can split off the updates to array c from the rest of the work, loop interchange can be applied to fix this problem.

Loop tiling or *blocking* is the last loop transformation presented and discussed here. It is a powerful transformation designed to tailor the number of memory references inside a loop iteration so that they fit into cache. If data sizes are large

```
for (int i=0; i<n; i++)
  c[i] = exp(i/n) ;

for (int j=0; j<m; j++)
  for (int i=0; i<n; i++)
      a[j][i] = b[j][i] + d[j] * e[i];
```

Figure 5.13: **Loop fission** – The loop nest of Figure 5.12 has been split into a pair of loops, followed by loop interchange applied to the second loop to improve cache usage.

and memory access is bad, or if there is data reuse in the loop, chopping a loop into chunks (tiles) may make this possible.

Loop tiling replaces the original loop by a pair of loops. This may be done for as many different loops in a loop nest as appropriate. It may be necessary to experiment with the size of the tiles. Note that if we spread the work of a loop nest among threads via an OpenMP work-sharing directive, then each thread receives a portion of the overall computation. That will have an impact on the number of memory references in that loop and has to be taken into account when tiling.

We now show the use of this transformation for a related, but slightly different, purpose. We cannot ensure that the values of both arrays a and b will be in cache in the code of Figure 5.14, which transposes a. If the values of b are used in cache order, we end up with strided access to the elements of a (as shown) and vice versa.

```
for (int i=0; i<n; i++)
  for (int j=0; j<m; j++)
      b[i][j] = a[j][i];
```

Figure 5.14: **A nested loop implementing an array transpose operation** – Loop interchange does not improve its use of cache or TLB. A fresh approach is needed.

The penalty incurred for the strided accesses to a can be reduced by improving locality in terms of memory pages used. This should lower the number of TLB misses. The modified code is shown in Figure 5.15, where the inner loop is replaced by a pair of loops with loop variables j1 and j2. Here, we update rows of array b in segments of length nbj, which is called the "blocking size." If we choose this size carefully, we can keep data from b in cache and reuse a set of pages of data from a before moving on to the next set of elements of b.

```
for (int j1=0; j1<n; j1+=nbj)
  for (int i=0; i<n; i++)
    for (int j2=0; j2 < MIN(n-j1,nbj); j2++)
        b[i][j1+j2] = a[j1+j2][i];
```

Figure 5.15: **Loop tiling applied to matrix transpose** – Here we have used loop tiling to split the inner loop into a pair of loops. This reduces TLB and cache misses.

We illustrate the change in the way that a and b are accessed in Figure 5.16.

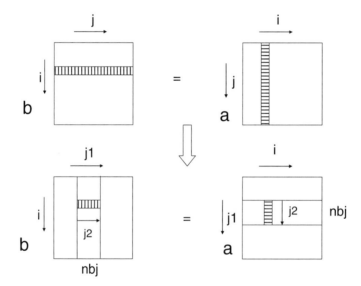

Figure 5.16: **Array access pattern** – Here we see how arrays a and b are accessed before and after *loop tiling*. The revised version accesses fewer pages per outer loop iteration.

5.2.4   Use of Pointers and Contiguous Memory in C

Pointers are commonly used in C applications, but they pose a serious challenge for performance tuning. The memory model in C is such that, without additional information, one must assume that all pointers may reference any memory address. This is generally referred to as the *pointer aliasing problem*. It prevents a compiler from performing many program optimizations, since it cannot determine that they are safe. As a result, performance will suffer. But if pointers are guaranteed to point to portions of nonoverlapping memory, for example because each pointer targets memory allocated through a distinct call to the "malloc" function, more aggressive optimization techniques can be applied. In general, only the programmer knows what memory locations a pointer may refer to. The `restrict` keyword used in the example of Section 3.2.2 is provided in C99 to inform the compiler that the memory referenced by one pointer does not overlap with a memory section pointed to by another pointer. Some compilers also provide options to specify this information. Note that even though the Fortran standard does not permit such "aliasing" except in a restricted context, some programs violate the standard, and compilers may take this into account. It can be worth checking the compiler's documentation for information and options related to aliasing in Fortran programs also.

The example in Section 3.2.2 also declares a linear array to represent array b in the implementation, rather than a two-dimensional array. This is a technique specific to C. If b is declared and used as an array of pointers, not all rows of the matrix need to be equal in length. As a result, the compiler has to make a more conservative assumption regarding the memory layout. This has a negative impact on the compiler's ability to optimize code. The linearization of the matrix ensures that a contiguous block of memory is used, and this helps the compiler to analyze and optimize loop nests to improve memory usage. It is also likely to result in fewer memory accesses and might enhance software-controlled data prefetch, if supported.

5.2.5   Using Compilers

Modern compilers implement most, if not all, of the loop optimizations presented in Section 5.2.3. They perform a variety of analyses to determine whether they may be applied (the main one is known as data dependence analysis). They also apply a variety of techniques to reduce the number of operations performed and reorder code to better exploit the hardware. The amount of work they carry out can be influenced by the application developer. Once correctness of the numerical results is assured, it is worthwhile to experiment with compiler options to squeeze the maximum performance out of the application. These options (or *flags*) differ a good deal from one compiler to another, so they must be explored afresh for each compiler. Recall that the compiler's ability to transform code is limited by its ability to analyze the program and to determine that one can safely modify it. We have just seen that this may be hindered by the presence of pointers, for example (Section 5.2.4). A different kind of problem arises when the compiler is not able to improve memory usage because that involves changing the structure of nonlocal data. Here the programmer has to take action: some rewriting of the source code may lead to better results.

5.3   Measuring OpenMP Performance

Before considering how to achieve good OpenMP performance, we need to discuss how it can be measured and identify what factors determine overall program performance. With a serial program, timing how long the program takes is straightforward. Common practice is to use a standard operating system command. For instance, an application might be executed under control of the `/bin/time` command available on Unix systems (for example `/bin/time ./a.out`). The "real," "user," and "system" times are then printed after the program has finished execution. An example is shown in Figure 5.17.

```
$ /bin/time ./program.exe

real    5.4
user    3.2
sys     1.0
```

Figure 5.17: **Example output from the /bin/time command** – These three numbers can be used to get a first impression on the performance. For a deeper analysis a more sophisticated performance tool is needed.

This output contains some useful information. The first number tells us that the program took 5.4 seconds from beginning to end. Next we see that it spent 3.2 seconds in user mode; this is the time the program spent executing outside any operating system services. The last number is the time spent on operating system services, such as input/output routines. Generally, the sum of the user and system time is referred to as the *CPU time*. The "real" time is also referred to as *wall-clock time,* or *elapsed time*.[2] We observe a difference between the elapsed time of 5.4 seconds and the CPU time. There can be several reasons for this, but a common cause is that the application did not get a full processor to itself, because of a high load on the system.

The same timing mechanism can be used to measure the performance of (shared memory) parallel programs. If sufficient processors are available, the elapsed time

---

[2]The `omp_get_wtime()` function provided by OpenMP is convenient for measuring the elapsed time of blocks of source code.

should be less than the CPU time. But, we didn't get the parallelism for free. An OpenMP program has additional overheads. After all, something has to happen to make the sequential program run in parallel. These overheads are collectively called the *parallel overhead* It includes the time to create, start, and stop threads, the extra work needed to figure out what each task is to perform, the time spent waiting in barriers and at critical sections and locks, and the time spent computing some operations redundantly. Hence, the *total* CPU time is likely to exceed the CPU time of the serial version.

In Section 2.6 on page 33, Amdahl's law was discussed. This is used as a basis for the simple performance model given in Formulas (5.1) and (5.2) below. The difference here is that the effect of parallel overhead is accounted for.

$$T_{CPU}(P) = (1 + O_p \cdot P) \cdot T_{serial} \tag{5.1}$$

$$T_{Elapsed}(P) = (\frac{f}{P} + 1 - f + O_p \cdot P) \cdot T_{serial} \tag{5.2}$$

In this model, T_{serial} is the CPU time of the original serial version of the application. The number of processors is given by P. The parallel overhead is denoted by $O_p \cdot P$, with O_p assumed to be a constant percentage (this is a simplification, as the overheads may well increase as the number of processors grows).

The fraction of execution time that has been parallelized is specified by $f \in [0, 1]$. Both $f = 0$ and $f = 1$ are extreme cases. A value of zero for f implies that application is serial. A perfectly parallel application corresponds to $f = 1$.

In Table 5.1 we see what happens if the original program takes $T_{serial} = 10.20$ seconds to run and code corresponding to 95% of the execution time has been parallelized. In this case, $f = 0.95$. It is also assumed that each additional processor adds a 2% overhead to the total CPU time ($O_p = 0.02$).

The *parallel speedup*, or just "speedup" for short, is calculated by taking the ratio of the elapsed time on P processors and the elapsed time of the serial version.[3] The *parallel efficiency*, or simply "efficiency", is obtained by dividing the speedup by the number of processors. The combination of the increased parallel overhead and the fact that 5% of the execution time is serial quickly limits scalability. The performance on four processors is already far from optimal. There are clearly diminishing returns on adding even more processors, given that the speedup on 8 processors is just a little over three.

---

[3]It is implicitly assumed that all processors requested are available to the application throughout the execution of the program.

Table 5.1: **Parallel performance and speedup for f=0.95 and 2% overhead**
– The elapsed time goes down, whereas the total CPU time goes up. Parallel speedup is
calculated from the elapsed time, using the serial version as the reference.

Version	Number of Processors	CPU time (seconds)	Elapsed time (seconds)	Speedup	Efficiency (%)
Serial	1	10.20	10.20	1.00	100
Parallel	1	10.40	10.40	0.98	98
	2	10.61	5.76	1.77	88
	4	11.02	3.75	2.72	68
	8	11.83	3.35	3.04	38

The performance information obtained from an external timer is useful for a
first diagnosis. For a deeper analysis of the inhibitor(s) to scalable performance,
sophisticated tools are needed. In the remainder of this section, we give an overview
of the factors that influence the performance of OpenMP code and offer tips on how
to gather performance information. In Section 6.6 on page 228 we dig deeper into
the topic of performance tuning, including performance analysis tools and their use.

5.3.1   Understanding the Performance of an OpenMP Program

We have seen in earlier sections that memory behavior is critical for the performance of sequential applications, and we noted that this also holds for an OpenMP
code. The relevance of Amdahl's law for the performance improvement that can
be obtained by creating a parallel program has also been discussed. In this section,
an overview of the kinds of overheads that may be incurred is given.

The observable performance of OpenMP programs is influenced by at least the
following factors, in addition to those that play a role in sequential performance:

- The manner in which memory is accessed by the individual threads. This
  has a major influence on performance, as seen later. If each thread accesses
  a distinct portion of data consistently throughout the program, it probably
  makes excellent use of the memory hierarchy, including the thread-local cache.
  In such cases, the performance improvement obtained by the larger fraction
  of data references that can be served by cache might more than offset the
  total overheads.

- The fraction of the work that is sequential, or replicated. By the latter,
  we mean the computations that occur once in the sequential program, but

are performed by each thread in the parallel version. Some amount of such *sequential overheads* are inevitable in almost all parallel programs.

- The amount of time spent handling OpenMP constructs. Each of the directives and routines in OpenMP comes with some overheads. For example, when a parallel region is created, threads might have to be created, or woken up and some data structures have to be set up to carry information needed by the runtime system. When a work-sharing directive is implemented, the work to be performed by each thread is usually determined at run time. Since this work is not needed in the sequential code, it is an additional performance penalty introduced by the OpenMP translation. We collectively call these the *(OpenMP) parallelization overheads*. Different constructs inherently incur different overheads. They can be measured (see Section 5.3.2).

- The load imbalance between synchronization points. If threads perform different amounts of work in a work-shared region, the faster threads have to wait at the barrier for the slower ones to reach that point. Similarly, threads might have to wait for a member of their team to carry out the work of a `single` construct. When threads are inactive at a barrier, they are not contributing to the work of the program. During this time, the other threads are idle. If they are actually busy on some other work for part of that time, there is no performance hit. We might call the corresponding penalty the *load imbalance overheads*. (Note that if the operating system uses one of the threads to carry out an operation, this can lead to idle time at the next barrier that is not caused by a load imbalance in the application itself.)

- Other synchronization costs. Threads typically waste time waiting for access to a critical region or a variable involved in an atomic update, or to acquire a lock. If they are unable to perform useful work during that time, they remain idle. These are collectively the *synchronization overheads*.

With a parallel program, there can also be a positive effect, offsetting some of the performance loss caused by sequential code and the various overheads. This is because a parallel program has more aggregate cache capacity at its disposal, since each thread will have some amount of local cache. This might result in a *superlinear* speedup: the speedup exceeds the number of processors used. In this chapter several examples of this are shown (see also Sections 5.6.3, 5.6.4, and 5.7).

A programmer can exploit knowledge of these basic performance considerations in many ways. In the remainder of this chapter, we explore some of them. We show, in particular, how memory usage influences performance.

5.3.2   Overheads of the OpenMP Translation

A cost is associated with the creation of OpenMP parallel regions, with the sharing of work among threads, and with all kinds of synchronization. The actual overheads experienced by an application depend on the OpenMP translation strategy used by the compiler, characteristics of the runtime library routines and the way they are used, the target platform, and the way the compiler otherwise optimizes code. The sources of overheads include the cost of starting up threads and creating their execution environment, the potential additional expense incurred by the encapsulation of a parallel region in a separate function, the cost of computing the schedule, the time taken to block and unblock threads, and the time for them to fetch work and signal that they are ready. Minor overheads also are incurred by using `firstprivate` and `lastprivate`. In most cases, however, these are relatively modest compared to the cost of barriers and other forms of thread synchronization, as well as the loss in speedup whenever one or more threads are idle. Dynamic forms of scheduling can lead to much more thread interaction than do static schedules, and therefore inevitably incur higher overheads: on the other hand, they may reduce thread idle time in the presence of load imbalance. A good OpenMP implementation takes care to use the most efficient means possible to create, deploy, and synchronize threads.

The EPCC microbenchmarks were created to help programmers estimate the relative cost of using different OpenMP constructs [30]. They are easy to use and provide an estimate of the overheads each feature causes. SPHINX [47] is another set of microbenchmarks, which also considers the cost of using OpenMP constructs in conjunction with MPI. Sphinx provides a powerful environment that helps the user obtain more accurate measurements, but it requires a little more effort [150].

Figure 5.18 shows overheads for major OpenMP constructs as measured by the EPCC microbenchmarks for the first version of the OpenUH compiler [112]. A few results are striking here. First, the overheads for the `for` directive and for the `barrier` are almost identical. Indeed, the overheads for the parallel loop consist of calling the static loop schedule and the barrier. So this is not such a surprising result. Overheads for the `parallel for` are just slightly higher than those for `parallel`, a result that can be accounted for by the overheads of sharing the work, which is negligible for the default static scheduling policy. The `single` directive has higher overheads than a `barrier`. This is also not surprising, as the overheads consist of a call to a runtime library routine that ensures that one thread executes the region, and then a barrier at the end. In this implementation, the `reduction` clause is costly because it is implemented via a critical region. This was a simple,

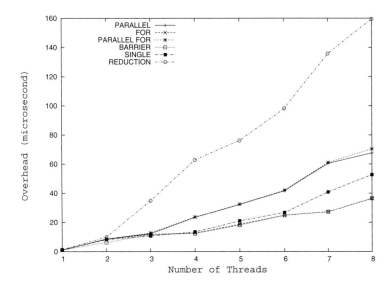

Figure 5.18: **Overheads of some OpenMP directives** – The overhead of several common directives and constructs is given in microseconds.

portable way to achieve the required functionality, but it is not an efficient way to realize this construct. Most implementations will be more efficient.

Overheads for the different kinds of loop schedules are given in Figure 5.19. They clearly show the performance benefits of a static schedule, and the penalties incurred by a dynamic schedule, where loops must grab chunks of work—especially small chunks—at run time. The guided schedule, where chunk sizes are gradually reduced, may be a good alternative in this region. Note that the scale to the left is logarithmic.

5.3.3   Interaction with the Execution Environment

When one is measuring and analyzing performance, it is important to be able to control the execution environment. To start with, one has to make sure that, when running the parallel application, the load on the system does not exceed the number of processors. If it does, the system is said to be oversubscribed. This not only degrades performance but also makes it hard to analyze the program's behavior. On an SMP system we strongly recommend that a program use fewer than the total number of processors, even if the system is dedicated to a single application. The reason is that the operating system daemons and services need

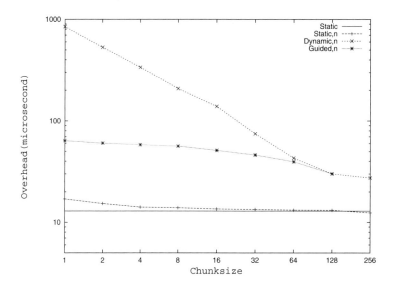

Figure 5.19: **Overhead of OpenMP scheduling** – The overheads for the different kinds of loop schedules are shown. Note that the scale to the left is logarithmic.

to run on a processor, too. If all processors are in use by the application, even a relatively lightweight daemon disrupts the execution of the user program, because one thread has to give way to this process. This might delay all other threads at the next synchronization point. Even for a scalable code, the speedup curve may then flatten out for the run that used all processors in the system.

In an ideal scenario, the system is dedicated to the application. This strategy avoids possible negative interference from the other program(s) running on the system. If this is not the case, process context switches may reduce performance. After such a switch, the cache contents of the previously running thread may be invalidated by the other program that is scheduled to run. Even if the previous thread is rescheduled onto the same processor, the data will most likely have to be reloaded into the cache(s). Things are worse if the thread is rescheduled onto a different processor after a context switch.

Even on modest-sized SMPs, the performance of an application could be influenced by the way its data has been stored in physical memory. The reason is that some real-world systems have cc-NUMA memory. As a result, timings of a program with the same data set may vary considerably. OpenMP does not provide any features to bind threads to processors or to specify the placement of data in a cc-NUMA memory. If available, such a feature is part of the interface with the operating system. For example, some systems provide command line controls to specify the placement of threads across a system, as well as a means to request that data be placed in the vicinity of a given thread. This kind of feature and its use is discussed in Chapter 6.

5.4   Best Practices

The flexibility and convenience of OpenMP as a programming model come with a risk. One may often be able to come up with several different parallelization strategies, all of which deliver a correct OpenMP program. But the performance of these versions can be vastly different. The most intuitive implementation is often not the best one when it comes to performance, but the parallel inefficiency is not directly visible simply by inspecting the source. In part, this is an unfortunate side-effect of a programming model that does not require the user to specify all details of parallel execution. It sometimes occurs because the programmer did not follow the basic rules for obtaining OpenMP performance. On other occasions, additional problems must be overcome. In this section, we provide some general recommendations on how to write an efficient OpenMP program.

5.4.1   Optimize Barrier Use

No matter how efficiently barriers are implemented, they are expensive operations. It is always worthwhile to reduce their usage to the minimum required by the code. Fortunately, the `nowait` clause (see also Section 4.5.6 on page 78) makes it easy to eliminate the barrier that is implied on several constructs.

One of the simplest cases is shown in Figure 5.20. The `#pragma omp for` loop construct has an implied barrier. Since the second parallel loop is back to back with the end of the parallel region, we can safely omit the implied barrier for the second loop. (A compiler might do this anyway.)

A recommended strategy is to first ensure that the OpenMP program works correctly and then use the `nowait` clause where possible, carefully inserting explicit barriers (see also Section 4.6.1 on page 84) at specific points in the program as needed. When doing this, one needs to take particular care to identify and order computations that write and read the same portion of memory.

This is demonstrated in Figure 5.21. Here vectors `a` and `c` are independently updated. There is no reason why a thread that has finished its work in the first loop should not enter the second loop. This is enabled by adding the `nowait` clause

```
#pragma omp parallel
{
         .........
   #pragma omp for
     for (i=0; i<n; i++)
         .........
   #pragma omp for nowait
     for (i=0; i<n; i++)

} /*-- End of parallel region - barrier is implied --*/
```

Figure 5.20: **A construct with one barrier less** – The nowait clause is used to omit the implied barrier at the end of the second loop.

```
#pragma omp parallel default(none) \
        shared(n,a,b,c,d,sum) private(i)
{
   #pragma omp for nowait
   for (i=0; i<n; i++)
      a[i] += b[i];

   #pragma omp for nowait
   for (i=0; i<n; i++)
      c[i] += d[i];

   #pragma omp barrier

   #pragma omp for nowait reduction(+:sum)
   for (i=0; i<n; i++)
      sum += a[i] + c[i];
} /*-- End of parallel region --*/
```

Figure 5.21: **A reduced number of barriers** – Before reading the values of vectors a and b all updates on these vectors have to be completed. The barrier ensures this.

to the first loop. Since the new values of a and c are subsequently used to calculate sum, we can either retain the implied barrier on the second #pragma omp for loop or remove it and insert an explicit #pragma omp barrier as shown. The version presented reflects the dependences clearly; however, the choice is largely a matter of taste and style. Either way, a barrier *must* be present before the last loop. The third `nowait` clause is applied to the loop with the `reduction` clause. As before, this is safe because the parallel region ends with a barrier anyhow and the value of `sum` is not used before the end of the region.

5.4.2 Avoid the Ordered Construct

As explained in Section 4.6.2 on page 86, the `ordered` construct ensures that the corresponding block of code within a parallel loop is executed in the order of the loop iterations. It is expensive to implement. The runtime system has to keep track which iterations have finished and possibly keep threads in a wait state until their results are needed. This inevitably slows program execution.

The ordered construct can often (perhaps always) be avoided. It might be better, for example, to wait and perform I/O outside of a parallelized loop. We do not claim that other solutions are always trivial to implement, but they are certain to be rewarding from a performance point of view.

5.4.3 Avoid Large Critical Regions

A critical region is used to ensure that no two threads execute a piece of code simultaneously. It can be used when the actual order in which threads perform the computation is not important. The more code contained in the critical region, however, the greater the likelihood that threads have to wait to enter it, and the longer the potential wait times. Therefore the programmer should minimize the amount of code enclosed within a critical region. If a critical region is very large, program performance might be poor.

For example, in the code in Figure 5.22, each thread updates the shared variable `a`. However, the second statement assigns a new value to a private variable, and hence there is no chance of a data race. This second statement unnecessarily increases the amount of work in the region and potentially extends the amount of time threads must wait for each other. It should thus be removed from the critical region. A more likely scenario occurs when the critical region contains a loop with some computation that requires exclusive access by a single thread at a time and some computation that does not. Since the latter could considerably degrade performance, it is usually worthwhile rewriting the portion of code to minimize the amount of work contained in the critical region.

We recall that whereas a critical region forces threads to perform all of the code enclosed within it one at a time, an atomic update enforces exclusive access to just one memory location. If the work to be performed only occasionally leads threads

```
#pragma omp parallel shared(a,b) private(c,d)
{
    ......
#pragma omp critical
    {
      a += 2 * c;
      c = d * d;
    }
} /*-- End of parallel region --*/
```

Figure 5.22: **A critical region** – Without the critical region, the first statement here leads to a data race. The second statement however involves private data only and unnecessarily increases the time taken to execute this construct. To improve performance it should be removed from the critical region.

to access the same data, a critical region might be an expensive choice. If at all possible, an atomic update is to be preferred. An alternative is to rewrite the piece of code and separate, as far as possible, those computations that cannot lead to data races from those operations that do need to be protected.

5.4.4 Maximize Parallel Regions

Indiscriminate use of parallel regions may give rise to suboptimal performance. Overheads are associated with starting and terminating a parallel region. Large parallel regions offer more opportunities for using data in cache and provide a bigger context for other compiler optimizations. Therefore it is worthwhile to minimize the number of parallel regions.

For example, if we have multiple parallel loops, we must choose whether to encapsulate each loop in an individual parallel region, as sketched in Figure 5.23, or to create one parallel region encompassing all of them.

The alternative is outlined in Figure 5.24. It has fewer implied barriers, and there might be potential for cache data reuse between loops. The downside of this approach is that one can no longer adjust the number of threads on a per loop basis, but this is often not a real limitation.

5.4.5 Avoid Parallel Regions in Inner Loops

Another common technique to improve performance is to move parallel regions out of innermost loops. Otherwise, we repeatedly experience the overheads of the

```
#pragma omp parallel for
for (.....)
{
    /*-- Work-sharing loop 1 --*/
}

#pragma omp parallel for
for (.....)
{
    /*-- Work-sharing loop 2 --*/
}
        .........

#pragma omp parallel for
for (.....)
{
    /*-- Work-sharing loop N --*/
}
```

Figure 5.23: **Multiple combined parallel work-sharing loops** – Each parallelized loop adds to the parallel overhead and has an implied barrier that cannot be omitted.

```
#pragma omp parallel
{
    #pragma omp for  /*-- Work-sharing loop 1 --*/
    { ...... }

    #pragma omp for  /*-- Work-sharing loop 2 --*/
    { ...... }

        .........

    #pragma omp for  /*-- Work-sharing loop N --*/
    { ...... }
}
```

Figure 5.24: **Single parallel region enclosing all work-sharing for loops** – The cost of the parallel region is amortized over the various work-sharing loops.

parallel construct. For example, in the loop nest shown in Figure 5.25, the overheads of the #pragma omp parallel for construct are incurred n^2 times.

```
for (i=0; i<n; i++)
    for (j=0; j<n; j++)
        #pragma omp parallel for
        for (k=0; k<n; k++)
            { .........}
```

Figure 5.25: **Parallel region embedded in a loop nest** – The overheads of the parallel region are incurred n^2 times.

A more efficient solution is indicated in Figure 5.26. The #pragma omp parallel for construct is split into its constituent directives and the #pragma omp parallel has been moved to enclose the entire loop nest. The #pragma omp for remains at the inner loop level. Depending on the amount of work performed in the innermost loop, one should see a noticeable performance gain.

```
#pragma omp parallel
    for (i=0; i<n; i++)
        for (j=0; j<n; j++)
            #pragma omp for
            for (k=0; k<n; k++)
                { .........}
```

Figure 5.26: **Parallel region moved outside of the loop nest** – The parallel construct overheads are minimized.

5.4.6 Address Poor Load Balance

In some parallel algorithms, threads have different amounts of work to do. Transposing a triangular matrix is a standard example. It is natural to assign each thread the work associated with a consecutive block of rows or columns. But since these are not equal in length, the workload is different for each thread, resulting in a load imbalance. When this occurs, the threads wait at the next synchronization point until the slowest one completes. One way to overcome this problem is to use the schedule clause covered in Section 4.5.7 on page 79 with a nonstatic schedule. The caveat here is that the **dynamic** and **guided** workload distribution schedules have higher overheads than does the `static` scheme. If the load imbalance is severe enough, however, this cost is offset by the more flexible allocation of work to threads. It might be a good idea to experiment with these schemes, as well as with various values for the chunk size parameter. Here the `runtime` clause comes in handy, as it allows easy experimentation without the need to recompile the program.

For example, the code in Figure 5.27 reads, writes, and processes data in chunks. A substantial amount of performance is lost if the parallel version does not overlap reading the data, processing it, and writing the results. The idea here is to read in a new data set, while at the same time processing the previous set and writing out results from the one before that.

```
for (i=0; i<N; i++) {
    ReadFromFile(i,...);
    for (j=0; j<ProcessingNum; j++ )
        ProcessData(); /* lots of work here */
    WriteResultsToFile(i);
 }
```

Figure 5.27: **Pipelined processing** – This code reads data in chunks, processes each chunk and writes the results to disk before dealing with the next chunk.

The resulting code is shown in Figure 5.28. To minimize the overheads of setting up parallel regions, the entire computation is enclosed in a single parallel region.

The code first reads in the chunk of data needed for the first iteration of the `i` loop. Since execution cannot proceed until this data is available, the implicit barrier is not removed. Next, one of the threads starts to read the next chunk of data. Because of the `nowait` clause, the other threads immediately begin to execute the processing loop.

If a static schedule was used here, the thread performing the read operation would have had the same amount of work to do as the other threads. All other threads then effectively wait for about as long as the read operation takes. The dynamic schedule overcomes this problem and leads to a significant speedup: the thread performing I/O joins the others once it has finished reading data, and shares in any computations that remain at that time. But it will not cause them to wait unless they have, in fact, performed all of the work by the time the I/O is done. After this, one thread writes out the results. Since there is a `nowait` clause, the other threads move on to the next iteration. Again, another thread starts reading while the others can immediately move on to the computation.

```
#pragma omp parallel
{
   /* preload data to be used in first iteration of the i-loop */
   #pragma omp single
      {ReadFromFile(0,...);}

   for (i=0; i<N; i++) {

      /* preload data for next iteration of the i-loop */
      #pragma omp single nowait
         {ReadFromFile(i+1...);}

      #pragma omp for schedule(dynamic)
         for (j=0; j<ProcessingNum; j++)
            ProcessChunkOfData();  /* here is the work */
      /* there is a barrier at the end of this loop */

      #pragma omp single nowait
         {WriteResultsToFile(i);}

   }  /* threads immediately move on to next iteration of i-loop */
} /* one parallel region encloses all the work */
```

Figure 5.28: **Parallelized pipelined processing** – This code uses a dynamic work-sharing schedule to overlap I/O and computation.

The dynamic schedule used here not only provides the overlap of computation and I/O that is required in many codes; it also provides the necessary, but minimum, amount of synchronization needed by the computation. The barrier at the end of the j loop ensures that data for the next loop iteration is available and that the results of the previous iteration have been written out before work proceeds. Assuming that the j loop contains sufficient work, all but the first read and the final write of data are fully overlapped in this code.

5.5 Additional Performance Considerations

Unfortunately, situations also arise where it is harder to give rules of thumb how to get the best performance out of an OpenMP application. The best approach might depend not only on the application but also on the system and OpenMP implementation. We discuss some of these situations next.

5.5.1 The Single Construct Versus the Master Construct

The functionality of the `single` and `master` constructs is similar. The difference is that a `single` region can be executed by any thread, typically the first to encounter it, whereas this is not the case for the `master` region. The former also has an implied barrier, although it can be omitted through a `nowait` clause.

Which construct is more efficient? The answer unfortunately depends on the details. In general, one should expect the `master` construct to be more efficient, as the `single` construct requires more work in the OpenMP library. The `single` construct might be more efficient if the master thread is not likely to be the first one to reach it and the threads need to synchronize at the end of the block. However, the relative performance difference is implementation and application dependent.

On a cc-NUMA architecture it might even get more complicated. See also Section 6.2.3 on page 199 for a discussion on this.

5.5.2 Avoid False Sharing

One of the factors limiting scalable performance is *false sharing*. It is a side effect of the cache-line granularity of cache coherence implemented in shared-memory systems (see also Section 1.2 on page 3). The cache coherence mechanism keeps track of the status of cache lines by appending "state bits" to the line that indicate whether the data on the cache line is still valid or is "stale", that is, has been invalidated. Any time a cache line is modified, cache coherence starts to do its work. It notifies other caches holding a copy of the same line that the line has been modified elsewhere.[4] At such a point, the copy of the line on other processors is invalidated. If the data in the line is still needed, a new, up-to-date copy of it must be fetched. Depending on the implementation, the data might be fetched from main memory or from the cache of another processor. One of the problems with this mechanism is that the state bits do not keep track of the cache line state on a byte basis, but at the line level instead. As a result, a processor is not able to detect that individual bytes in a line have not been modified and can still be safely read. Instead, an entire new line has to be fetched. Consequently, when two

---

[4] A write-back cache design is assumed here, as is common for at least certain levels of the cache hierarchy.

threads update different data elements in the same cache line, they interfere with each other. This effect is known as *false sharing*.

We note that a modest amount of false sharing does not have a significant impact on performance. If, however, some or all of the threads update the same cache line frequently, performance degrades. The coherence transactions take time, and the cache line hops from one cache to the other. An extreme case of false sharing is illustrated by the example shown in Figure 5.29. To simplify our explanation of what happens at run time, we assume that a cache line contains eight elements of vector a. Furthermore, we assume that element a[0] is the first item in the cache line, all threads have a copy of a in their cache prior to the update, and Nthreads is eight. In the loop, thread P updates a[P]. If sufficient processors are available, the threads are likely to execute this update simultaneously. In this case, false sharing substantially degrades performance.

```
#pragma omp parallel for shared(Nthreads,a) schedule(static,1)
    for (int i=0; i<Nthreads; i++)
        a[i] += i;
```

Figure 5.29: **Example of false sharing** – Nthreads equals the number of threads executing the for-loop. The chunk size of 1 causes each thread to update one element of a, resulting in false sharing.

The explanation is as follows. Assume thread 0 first updates a[0]. This update invalidates the other copies of the cache line containing a[0]. Since a[1] through a[7] are in the same line, this single invalidation also impacts threads 1 through 7. All of them find out that the element to be updated is part of a line that has just been invalidated, forcing them to get a new copy even though their respective elements have not been modified yet. This effect is then repeated each time one of the other threads updates its element. For instance, when thread 1 modifies element a[1], it invalidates the copies of the cache line containing a[0] and a[2], ..., a[7] in the caches of the processors the other threads are running on.

In this case, *array padding* can be used to eliminate the problem. Under the assumptions made, extending, or "padding," the array by dimensioning it as a[n][8] and changing the indexing from a[i] to a[i][0] eliminates the false sharing. Accesses to different elements a[i][0] are now separated by a cache line. As a result, the update of an element no longer affects the state bits of the lines other elements are part of.

Although array padding works well, it is a low-level optimization. Given that the size of a cache line needs to be taken into account, it is also potentially non-portable: the performance benefit on a different system may be reduced, or even be nonexistent.

False sharing is likely to significantly impact performance under the following conditions:

1. Shared data is *modified* by multiple threads.

2. The access pattern is such that multiple threads modify the same cache line(s).

3. These modifications occur in rapid succession.

All of these conditions need to be met for the degradation to be noticeable. There is no false sharing with read-only data, because the cache lines are not invalidated.

In general, using private data instead of shared data significantly reduces the risk of false sharing. In contrast with padding, this is also a portable optimization.

The exception is a situation where different private copies are held in the same cache line or where the end of one copy shares a cache line with the start of another copy. Although this might occasionally occur, the performance impact is not likely to be significant. The compiler may have a minor effect on false sharing, depending on how it allocates data and where the object code stores data in registers back in cache. If it has reduced the number of times a variable is written, it can (slightly) reduce the occurrence of false sharing.

```
#pragma omp parallel shared(a,b)
{
    a = b + 1;
    ......
}
```

Figure 5.30: **An initialization that causes false sharing** – This statement meets the first two criteria for false sharing. If multiple threads execute it at the same time, performance is degraded. Note that there could even be another runtime error in this example. Depending on the data type and hardware details, the write operation to memory might be broken into several smaller stores, corrupting the result. For more details we refer to page 65.

In our example of Figure 5.30, the executing threads all evaluate b+1 and assign the result to variable a. Since b is not modified, this does not cause false sharing.

However, variable `a` does. If there are a number of such initializations, they could reduce program performance. In a more efficient implementation, variable `a` is declared and used as a private variable instead. Assuming the various copies of `a` are part of different cache lines, false sharing no longer occurs.

5.5.3 Private Versus Shared Data

The programmer may often choose whether data should be shared or private. Either choice might lead to a correct application, but the performance impact can be substantial if the "wrong" choice is made.

For example, if threads need unique read/write access to a one dimensional array, one could declare a two-dimensional shared array with one row (in C/C++) or column (in Fortran) per thread. Alternatively, each thread might allocate a one-dimensional private array within the parallel region. In general, the latter approach is to be preferred over the former. When modifying shared data, a data element might be in the same cache line as data that is to be modified by another thread. If this is the case and if modifications are frequent, performance degrades because of false sharing (see also Section 5.5.2). With private data there is much less risk of such interference.

Accessing shared data also requires dereferencing a pointer, which incurs a performance overhead.

If data is read but not written in a parallel region, it could be shared, ensuring that each thread has (read) access to it. But it could also be privatized so that each thread has a local copy of the data, using the `firstprivate` clause (see Section 4.5.4) to initialize it to the values prior to the parallel region. Both approaches work, but the performance could be different. Sharing the data seems the most reasonable choice here. There is no risk of false sharing because the data is not modified, memory usage does not increase, and there is no runtime overhead to copy the data. This may not be the case on a cc-NUMA architecture though. See also Section 6.2.3 on this topic.

5.6   Case Study: The Matrix Times Vector Product

In this section, we revisit the parallel version of the matrix times vector product. We first consider the performance of a slightly modified version of the code introduced in Section 3.3. We then show how OpenMP features can be used to improve the performance. At that point a distinction needs to be made between the C and Fortran implementations of this problem. We show that the behavior of this code is significantly affected by the way in which it uses memory. We also show that a compiler could be able to overcome some performance problems. Moreover, we give some insight into the process of studying the behavior of a parallel program.

5.6.1 Testing Circumstances and Performance Metrics

In general, performance results are significantly influenced by the following factors.

- The coding style used by the application developer

- The compiler, the choice of compiler options used, and its runtime libraries

- Relevant features of the operating system, including its support for memory allocation and thread scheduling

- Characteristics of the hardware, including its memory hierarchy, cache coherence mechanisms, support for atomic operations, and more

All results given here were obtained on a Sun Fire^{TM} E6900 SMP system with the dual-core UltraSPARC® IV [132] processor. The system had 24 processors (48 cores) and was running the Solaris^{TM} 9 operating system in multiuser mode. No special precautions were taken to tune the system for these tests.

We emphasize that the results presented are system-dependent and that this is no more than a case study. The behavior of the code shown here might be different on another platform and under another compiler, or even with a different release of the same compiler and libraries. Our purpose here is to shed some light on the process of studying the performance of a multithreaded program.

In all the graphs, the performance is shown over a range of square matrix sizes. The amount of memory required for a given matrix size is referred to as "the memory footprint." The smallest matrix size tested is 5 x 5. This corresponds to a memory footprint of just $(m + m \text{ x } n + n) * 8 = (5 + 5 \text{ x } 5 + 5) * 8 = 280$ bytes. The largest matrix is 2000 x 2000. The memory footprint for this problem is a little over 3 GByte. The parallel performance is given in million floating-point operations per second (Mflop/s). In some cases, we also report on the parallel efficiency. Formula (2.1) in Section 2.6 is used to calculate the parallel speedup. For T_1, the elapsed time for the OpenMP code on one thread is used. The efficiency is obtained by dividing the speedup by the number of threads. OpenMP code has unavoidable overheads that do not exist in a sequential program. Nevertheless, although the overheads depend largely on the compiler, libraries, and hardware, a well-parallelized OpenMP application can be nearly as efficient on a single thread as its sequential counterpart. It is good practice to compare the performance for both versions, and we do so. In practice, sequential results are often obtained by compiling without the OpenMP option, effectively deactivating the parallelism.

To measure the effectiveness of the parallel version executed on one thread, we compute the *single thread overhead* by subtracting 1 from the ratio of the performance of the sequential version and the OpenMP version executed on a single thread. This metric is given in Formula (5.3). Note that the value is computed as a percentage.

$$Overhead_{single\ thread} = 100 * (\frac{ElapsedTime(OpenMP_{single\ thread})}{ElapsedTime(Sequential)} - 1)\ \%\ (5.3)$$

In the ideal case, the elapsed time of the OpenMP version is equal to the sequential version. This corresponds to an overhead value of 0. If the sequential version is faster, the overhead is strictly positive. There is always a chance that the OpenMP version on a single thread might be faster because of a difference in compiler optimizations. If so, the overhead is strictly negative.

5.6.2   A Modified OpenMP Implementation

We have adapted the OpenMP implementations of the matrix times vector problem given in Figures 3.10 and 3.11 in Chapter 3. The sources are listed in Figures 5.31 and 5.32. In this version, the `#pragma omp parallel for` directive in C/C++, and the `!$omp parallel do` directive in Fortran are used to replace the parallel region with only one work-sharing `#pragma omp for` or `!$omp do` construct, respectively. The initialization of the result vector a has also been optimized for sequential execution. A common approach is to set the elements to zero first. But why initialize the value of a_i to zero, only to immediately add $B_{i,j} * c_j$ to it for $j = 0$ in C and $j = 1$ in Fortran? These redundant instructions can be eliminated by pre-initializing element a_i to the result of the first computation. Consequently, the inner loop starts with a value of 1 instead of 0 for j in the C version and with $j = 2$ in the Fortran implementation. There is a second reason not to initialize elements of vector a to zero. When values are assigned to variables that are needed later on, they are written back to cache, where they might displace other data. Although the impact may not be measurable here, it is always a good idea to reduce the number of stores as well as the total number of instructions.

Admittedly, the compiler does not have to store a_i until all computations on this element have completed, and the effect is probably very minor in this case anyhow,

```
 1  void mxv(int m, int n, double * restrict a,
 2              double * restrict b, double * restrict c)
 3  {
 4     int i, j;
 5
 6  #pragma omp parallel for default(none) \
 7          shared(m,n,a,b,c) private(i,j)
 8     for (i=0; i<m; i++)
 9     {
10       a[i] = b[i*n]*c[0];
11       for (j=1; j<n; j++)
12         a[i] += b[i*n+j]*c[j];
13     } /*-- End of parallel for --*/
14  }
```

Figure 5.31: **OpenMP version of the matrix times vector product in C –**
The result vector is initialized to the first computed result here.

but it is a simple example of a sequential optimization (see also Section 5.2) that
improves the cache utilization and reduces the number of instructions executed.

5.6.3   Performance Results for the C Version

In Figure 5.33, the single thread overheads are given as a function of the memory
footprint for the C version of the matrix times vector product. The smallest matrices (starting with a 5 x 5 matrix) have a significant overhead. Although not easy
to derive from the graph, the overhead for a 200 x 200 matrix (corresponding to a
memory footprint of 0.3 MByte) is 2%. It is less for larger matrices. Although the
actual numbers are specific to the application, implementation, compiler, and system, we recall that an OpenMP application executed using one thread inherently
has overheads that do not exist in a pure sequential version.

In Figure 5.34, the performance in Mflop/s for 1, 2, 4, and 8 threads is plotted
as a function of the memory footprint. The curves reveal several interesting facts:

- If the memory footprint is less than 0.05 MByte, the performance on 2, 4,
  and 8 threads is below single-thread performance. This threshold value corresponds to $m = n = 80$.

- For a certain range of problem sizes, superlinear speedup is observed. The
  range depends on the number of threads.

```
 1          subroutine mxv(m, n, a, b, c)
 2
 3          implicit none
 4          integer(kind=4)  :: m , n
 5          real    (kind=8)  :: a(1:m), b(1:m,1:n), c(1:n)
 6
 7          integer          :: i, j
 8
 9   !$OMP PARALLEL DO DEFAULT(NONE) &
10   !$OMP SHARED(m,n,a,b,c) PRIVATE(i,j)
11          do i = 1, m
12             a(i) = b(i,1)*c(1)
13             do j = 2, n
14                a(i) = a(i) + b(i,j)*c(j)
15             end do
16          end do
17   !$OMP END PARALLEL DO
18
19          return
20          end subroutine mxv
```

Figure 5.32: **The OpenMP version of the matrix times vector product in Fortran** – The result vector is initialized to the first computed result here.

- For the largest problem sizes tested, the performance for 2 threads scales quite well. For higher thread counts this gets progressively worse.

The *superlinear* speedup is a pleasant performance bonus. With a superlinear speedup, the performance on P threads is more than P times higher than the single-thread performance. This can be attributed mainly to the fact that more aggregate cache space is available when using more than one processor.

This effect is more clearly seen in the parallel efficiency chart given in Figure 5.35. In this chart, perfect (100%) efficiency is used as a reference. This line corresponds to linear scaling. A value below this line indicates the scaling is less than linear. If the value exceeds the line, superlinear speedup is realized.

For a given number of threads, the efficiency improves as the matrix gets larger, but only up to a given point. After that, the efficiency decreases. The extent of the decrease depends on the number of threads used. Typically, the higher the number

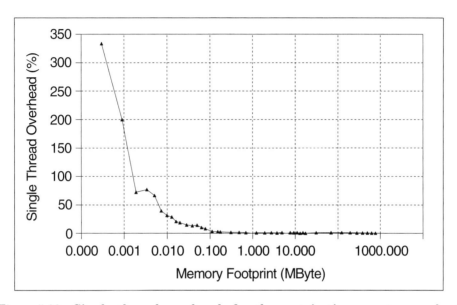

Figure 5.33: **Single-thread overheads for the matrix times vector product in C** – Formula (5.3) has been used to compute the overhead for a wide range of matrix sizes. For a matrix of size 200 **x** 200 the overhead is 2%. It is less for larger matrices.

of threads, the more substantial the degradation is. This behavior is consistent with Amdahl's law.

For a memory footprint on the order of 1 MByte, the efficiency for 2 threads is 95%. For 8 threads this threshold is at around 4 MByte. At 8 MByte something interesting happens: the implementation exhibits a superlinear speedup of up to 450%. The higher the number of threads, the longer this behavior lasts. For example, if the memory footprint is 30 MByte, the efficiency using 2 threads drops back to 98%, but it is over 400% for 4 and 8 threads. For a 70 MByte memory footprint, the efficiency for 8 threads is over 200% but drops to around 95% for 4 threads. These numbers should not really come as a surprise. The processor used in our experiments has a level-2 cache of 8 Mbyte per core. If, for example, 8 threads are used, a problem size corresponding to a memory footprint of 64 MByte fits into the aggregated level-2 caches. If, however, 4 threads are used for the same problem size, only half of the data is cache-resident on average.[5] As a result, many more

---

[5]Because of cache mapping effects and cache line invalidations, lines may be evicted prematurely. This is why "half" is approximate only.

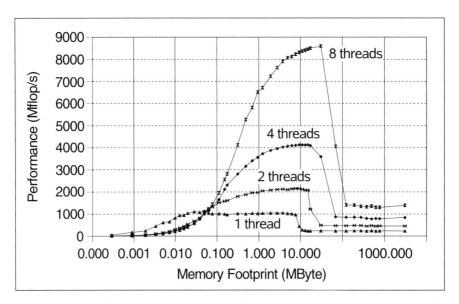

Figure 5.34: **OpenMP performance of the matrix times vector product in C** – If the memory footprint is less than 0.05 MByte, the single thread performance is higher than the performance for multiple threads. For a certain range of problem sizes, a superlinear speedup is realized. For problem sizes exceeding this range, the performance curves follow Amdahl's law.

of the array references come out of the slower main memory, not from the faster cache memory.

The reduced efficiency for a larger memory footprint can be explained by Amdahl's law. There is still some benefit from the aggregated cache space available; but as the problem size increases, the relative benefit decreases. This is illustrated in Table 5.2. If we measure one efficiency value, Amdahl's law can be used to estimate the other values. For our data point, we determine that the parallel efficiency for 2 threads on the largest matrix (20, 000 by 20, 000) used is 96.3%. The table shows that our estimates for 4 and 8 threads using Amdahl's law are quite accurate. It also demonstrates how ruthless this law is. A fairly respectable 96.3% efficiency on 2 threads is not sufficient to scale to a large number of threads. Based on these numbers, the efficiency for 16 threads drops to 63%. Using 32 threads, the efficiency drops further to 45%. In other words, more than half of the threads are effectively not used in this case.

The performance degradation for small matrices can be avoided by using an `if`-clause (see also Section 4.8.1) on the parallel region, as shown in Figure 5.36. In

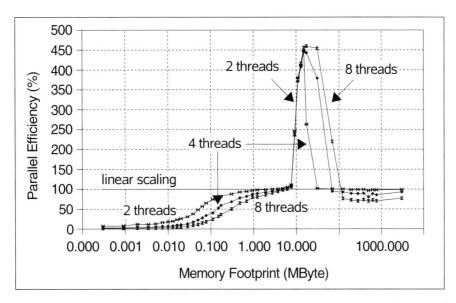

Figure 5.35: **Parallel efficiency of the matrix times vector product in C** –
Several interesting effects are observed. Up to a specific memory footprint, the efficiency
increases as the matrix gets larger. A superlinear speedup is even observed. The higher
the number of threads, the longer this lasts. At a certain point, however, the efficiency
drops, basically following Amdahl's law.

Table 5.2: **Estimated parallel efficiency for the OpenMP version in C**
– The measured efficiency of 96.3% for the largest, 20, 000 by 20, 000, matrix using 2
threads serves as the basis to estimate the efficiencies for 4 and 8 threads. The measured
values are in good agreement with these estimates.

Threads	Amdahl's Law (%)	Measured (%)
2	96.3	96.3
4	89.7	89.4
8	78.8	75.6

order to avoid changing the interface of the matrix times vector routine, a global
integer variable with the name `threshold_omp` is used to control the parallel execution. It is included in file `globals.h`.

The program has been rerun with a value of 100 for `threshold_omp`. This is a
higher value than strictly needed, but it means we can safely use more than eight

```
1   #include "globals.h"
2
3   void mxv(int m, int n, double * restrict a,
4             double * restrict b, double * restrict c)
5   {
6     int i, j;
7
8   #pragma omp parallel for if (m > threshold_omp) \
9           default(none) \
10          shared(m,n,a,b,c) private(i,j)
11    for (i=0; i<m; i++)
12    {
13      a[i] = b[i*n]*c[0];
14      for (j=1; j<n; j++)
15        a[i] += b[i*n+j]*c[j];
16    } /*-- End of parallel for --*/
17  }
```

Figure 5.36: **Second OpenMP version of the matrix times vector product in C** – Compared to the source listed in Figure 5.31, the if-clause has been included. The threshold_omp variable can be used to avoid a performance degradation for small matrices. If the clause evaluates to false, only one thread executes the code.

threads. Some of the overhead, especially for the barrier, may increase as a function of the number of threads.[6] The results given in Figure 5.37 show that the threshold value enables us to avoid performance degradation. The parallel performance is now either equal to or higher than the single-thread performance.

5.6.4   Performance Results for the Fortran Version

The Fortran version of the matrix times vector product is discussed next. Just as for the C version, the single thread overhead is shown first, followed by the parallel performance results. The single-thread overhead is given as a function of the memory footprint in Figure 5.38 for the implementation listed in Figure 5.32. Similar to the C version, the single-thread overhead is 2% for a 200 by 200 matrix and less for larger matrices. A comparison of the graphs in Figures 5.33 and 5.38 shows that the single-thread overhead is approximately the same for both the C and Fortran versions.

---

[6]A more elegant solution is to make the threshold a function of the number of threads.

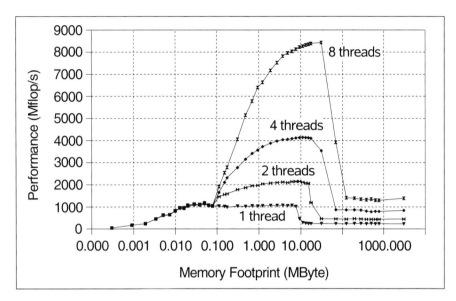

Figure 5.37: **OpenMP performance of the matrix times vector product in C** – The performance is now either equal to or higher than single-thread performance.

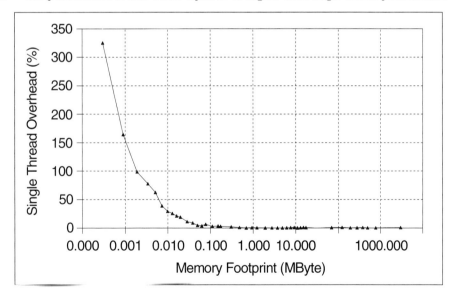

Figure 5.38: **Single-thread overhead for the row implementation in Fortran** – Formula 5.3 has been used to compute the overhead for a wide range of matrix sizes. For a matrix of size 200 x 200 the overhead is 2% and less for larger matrices.

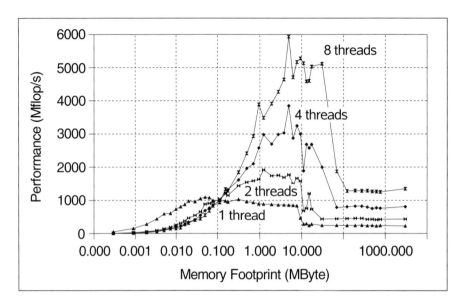

Figure 5.39: **OpenMP performance of the matrix times vector product in Fortran** – If the memory footprint is less than 0.1 MByte, the single-thread performance is higher than the performance for multiple threads. For a certain range of problem sizes, a superlinear speedup is realized. For problem sizes exceeding this range, the performance curves follow Amdahl's law.

In Figure 5.39 the performance in Mflop/s is plotted as a function of the memory footprint using 1, 2, 4, and 8 threads. The shapes of the performance curves are similar to those shown in Figure 5.34:

- For problem sizes exceeding 0.10 MByte, the multithreaded performance exceeds the single-thread performance. This corresponds to a matrix of size 120 by 120. This threshold is only slightly higher than for the C version.

- For a memory footprint in the 10–70 MByte range, a superlinear speedup is observed. The extent also depends on the number of threads used.

- For large problem sizes, the performance follows Amdahl's law. On the largest matrix size tested, the efficiency for 2 threads is 96.1%, very close to the 96.3% measured for the C version. The performance using 4 and 8 threads can be explained by this efficiency.

As with the C version, the `if`-clause is used to avoid performance degradation when the matrix is too small. The source of this version is listed in Figure 5.40.

```
 1        subroutine mxv(m, n, a, b, c)
 2
 3        use globals
 4
 5        implicit none
 6        integer(kind=4)  :: m, n
 7        real    (kind=8)  :: a(1:m), b(1:m,1:n), c(1:n)
 8
 9        integer          :: i, j
10
11  !$OMP PARALLEL DO DEFAULT(NONE) IF (m > threshold_omp) &
12  !$OMP SHARED(m,n,a,b,c) PRIVATE(i,j)
13        do i = 1, m
14           a(i) = b(i,1)*c(1)
15           do j = 2, n
16              a(i) = a(i) + b(i,j)*c(j)
17           end do
18        end do
19  !$OMP END PARALLEL DO
20
21        return
22        end subroutine mxv
```

Figure 5.40: **Second OpenMP version of the matrix times vector product in Fortran** – Compared to source listed in Figure 5.32, the if-clause has been included. The threshold_omp variable can be used to avoid a performance degradation if the matrix is too small. In cases when the clause evaluates to true, only one thread executes the code.

We avoid having to change the interface of the routine by using a Fortran module called globals to pass in the threshold_omp. In Figure 5.41 the performance is given for a threshold value of 100, meaning that it will be executed by a single thread if $m \leq 100$. The threshold has the desired effect on performance.

5.7   Fortran Performance Explored Further

The results given in the previous section warrant some deeper analysis. In particular, the following is observed:

- If more than one thread is used, the *absolute* performance for the Fortran version is lower than for the C version in certain ranges of the memory footprint.

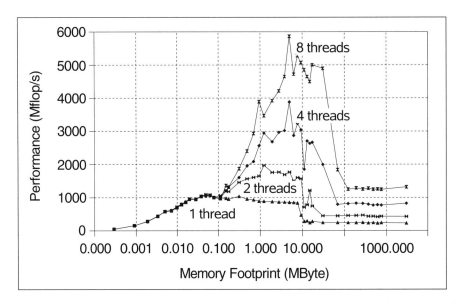

Figure 5.41: **OpenMP performance of the second version of the matrix times vector product in Fortran** – The performance of the implementation is now either equal to or higher than the single-thread performance.

- Compared to the results for the C version, the curves for 2, 4, and 8 threads are more "spiky" for a specific part of the memory footprint. The size of this region is approximately in the 1–18 MByte range.

To make these differences clear, Figure 5.42 plots the performance for both C and Fortran versions, using 1 and 2 threads. The single-threaded performance of the C version is up to 20% higher than the Fortran version for a memory footprint that does not exceed 8 MByte. The biggest differences are in the 70 KByte to 8 MByte range. This corresponds to matrix sizes that no longer fit in the level-1 data cache (64 KByte) but do fit into the level-2 unified cache (8 MByte). There is no difference for a footprint exceeding 8 MByte. On 2 threads, the performance is the same for very small matrices, but as soon as the memory footprint is about 5 KByte or more, the C version is faster. For a footprint of around 30 MByte, the performance is equal again.

In fact, the Fortran performance is quite remarkable. The implementation of the C version was straightforward. The matrix times vector product has a natural level of parallelism at the outer loop level, *and* the data is accessed in the most suitable way for performance. But in the Fortran version, access to elements of the

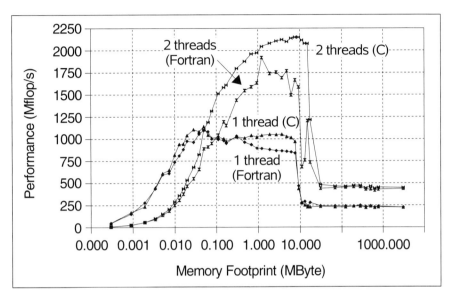

Figure 5.42: **Performance comparison using 1 and 2 threads in C and Fortran** – The performance of the C version is either equal to or better than the Fortran version. Given that the latter suffers from a bad memory access pattern, this is rather remarkable.

two-dimensional array b is by row. This is very bad for performance, especially for larger matrices, as Fortran stores arrays by column. Why does the Fortran version perform quite well, then? One should not expect the single-thread performance to be so close, especially for large matrices, where excessive data and TLB cache misses dominate the performance.

This gives rise to an interesting dilemma. The natural level of parallelism for this algorithm is at the row level, but this is bad from a memory access point of view in Fortran. Apparently, something is done to give us the best of both worlds.

Although it is compiler specific, let us examine this case a little further. Essentially, the compiler breaks the i loop into chunks and assigns one chunk to each thread as indicated below, where the values of i_start and i_end depend on the thread number:

```
do i = i_start, i_end
   a(i) = b(i,1)*c(1)
   do j = 2, n
      a(i) = a(i) + b(i,j)*c(j)
```

```
      end do
   end do
```

This is, however, only a first step. Next the compiler begins to optimize. Among other actions, it splits the loop over i into two loops. The pair of loops surrounding the second assignment statement are then interchanged, resulting in code like the following:

```
do i = i_start, i_end
   a(i) = b(i,1)*c(1)
end do
do j = 2, n
   do i = i_start, i_end
      a(i) = a(i) + b(i,j)*c(j)
   end do
end do
```

The resulting program structure obtained by manually applying similar transformations to the source code is represented in Figure 5.43. Not shown here is the unroll-and-jam optimization applied by the compiler to all three loops. As shown in Section 5.2.3, unrolling the j loop creates multiple copies of the innermost loop over i. Next these loops are then fused (or "jammed") back into a single loop over i. This new innermost loop is further unrolled.

At source lines 10 and 11 the number of threads and thread number are stored in variables nthreads and tid, respectively. These are used to calculate how many iterations each thread has to execute. Hence the computation of the values for i_start and i_end in lines 12 to 23. The loop at lines 25–27 initializes a portion of the result vector a. The crucial part of the optimized code is shown at lines 28–32. The loops over i and j have been interchanged to eliminate the bad memory access. As a result, array b is accessed by column.

This idea can be implemented in other ways. If the number of threads is known in advance, for example, the call to omp_get_num_threads() is not needed. Note, however, that the use of the if-clause may complicate the situation. We could have gotten one thread to retrieve the number of threads and pass this on to the other threads as a shared variable. But this requires an explicit barrier before line 12, which we have avoided here. The solution chosen has the advantage of forming an independent block of OpenMP code. It can be used "as is" instead of the source given in Figure 5.40.

```
1          subroutine mxv(m, n, a, b, c)
2          use globals
3          use omp_lib
4              <declarations omitted>
5   !$OMP PARALLEL DEFAULT(NONE) IF (m > threshold_omp)   &
6   !$OMP SHARED(m,n,a,b,c)                               &
7   !$OMP PRIVATE(i,j,i_start,i_end,nthreads,mrem,mchunk) &
8   !$OMP PRIVATE(mrem,tid,incr,offset)
9
10         nthreads = OMP_GET_NUM_THREADS()
11         tid      = OMP_GET_THREAD_NUM()
12         mrem     = mod(m,nthreads)
13         mchunk   = (m-mrem)/nthreads
14
15         if ( tid < mrem ) then
16             incr   = mchunk + 1
17             offset = 1
18         else
19             incr   = mchunk
20             offset = mrem + 1
21         end if
22         i_start = tid*incr + offset
23         i_end   = i_start + incr - 1
24
25         do i = i_start, i_end
26             a(i) = b(i,1)*c(1)
27         end do
28         do j = 2, n
29             do i = i_start, i_end
30                 a(i) = a(i) + b(i,j)*c(j)
31             end do
32         end do
33
34   !$OMP END PARALLEL
35
36         return
37         end subroutine mxv
```

Figure 5.43: **Explicitly optimized version of the Fortran implementation**
– This code has one parallel region only. It mimics the optimizations applied by the compiler to the code of Figure 5.40.

Just to demonstrate how close the manually parallelized version given in Figure 5.43 is to what the compiler generates, the performance curves for this version are shown in Figure 5.44.

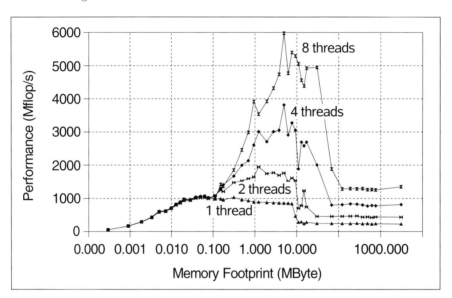

Figure 5.44: **Performance for the source given in Figure 5.43** – The performance is virtually identical to the results shown in Figure 5.41.

The loop interchange at lines 28–29 eliminates an important performance bottleneck, but it still has its drawbacks:

1. The optimized Fortran version has three memory references: For each value of the loop variable i, elements b(i,j) and a(i) are loaded, and the result value a(i) has to be stored. In the C implementation there are two loads only. The fewer loads and stores there are, the less risk there is of premature cache evictions. Fortunately, the references have unit stride, so the impact is limited here. In this particular case, the unroll-and-jam transformation reduces the number of loads and stores of a(i).

2. In the C version, the length of the innermost loop is the same, regardless of the number of threads used. This is not the case for the Fortran version, where the chunk size is a decreasing function of the number of threads. A short innermost loop is in general not good for performance. The loop over-

head dominates, and the processor pipeline might stall as results may not be available soon enough.

3. The Fortran version is more sensitive to false sharing. Although in both the C and Fortran implementations, multiple threads update a portion of the same vector a, the update in the Fortran version is performed $O(n)$ times: for every iteration of the j-loop, the same section of a is read and written. In the C version, false sharing is at the outer loop level only. The impact of false sharing is reduced by the unroll and jam transformation performed by the compiler, because this reduces the number of loads and stores of a(i). Still, this implementation inherently suffers more from false sharing than the C version.

Figure 5.42 shows that for sufficiently large matrix sizes, the performance of the C and Fortran versions are equal. For small matrix sizes the last two factors in particular degrade the performance of the Fortran version. One might be tempted to use the if-clause to prevent this from occurring. Figure 5.42 shows that, although the performance on 2, 4, and 8 threads is lower than for the C version, it is still higher than single-threaded code. In other words, although not as fast as the C version, it still pays to execute the code in parallel if $m > 100$.

This section concludes with a detailed investigation of the performance spikes observed for the Fortran version. In particular for a certain range of the memory footprint, the performance changes noticeably from one matrix size to another. The C version does not exhibit this kind of pronounced fluctuation.

Figure 5.45 zooms in on the performance for values of variable m between 300 and 500. Square matrices have been used throughout ($m = n$). These detailed results reveal interesting behavior. For a certain relatively small subset of the values for m, the performance drops, or peaks. The location of peaks depends on the number of threads used. We now examine two of these outliers, a dip and a peak, in detail. In both cases, a "good" and a "bad" value for m have been selected. By comparing their performance characteristics, we hope to obtain more insight into the behavior.

Figure 5.3 lists the performance for m=381 and m=385. Speedup is based on the single-thread performance. The way to interpret the results is that a dip in the performance occurs on a single thread. This dip does scale with the number of threads though. The speedup values even suggest the performance catches up for an increasing number of threads.

In order to explore how this performance dip arises, the Sun Performance Analyzer [128] was used to obtain timing information at the level of the hardware

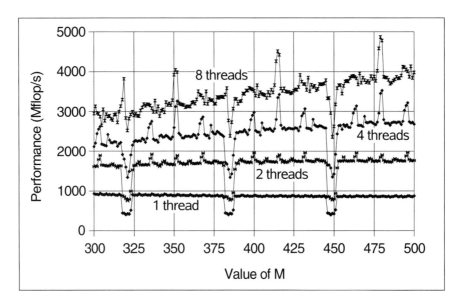

Figure 5.45: **Detailed performance results for the source given in Figure 5.43** – The performance for all values of m in the range [300, 500] is plotted. For very specific values of m, the performance exhibits a dip or peak. The peaks are also a function of the number of threads used.

Table 5.3: **Performance and speedup for** $m = 381$ **and** $m = 385$ – The performance difference for these nearby values of m is remarkable. Although still much lower in absolute performance, on 4 and 8 threads a higher speedup is realized for $m = 385$. This suggests the performance catches up for an increasing number of threads.

Threads	M = 381 (Mflop/s)	Speedup	M = 385 (Mflop/s)	Speedup
1	834.4	1.00	440.6	1.00
2	1638.7	1.96	767.1	1.74
4	2369.4	2.84	1341.2	3.04
8	3353.8	4.02	2384.7	5.41

counters in the processor. Such counters are system specific and are typically documented in the reference manual for the processor.[7] We report the counter data for m=381 and m=385 in Figures 5.46 and 5.47.

---

[7]Performance counter details for the UltraSPARC IV processor can be found in [131, 132].

Excl. CPU Cycles		Excl. D$ and E$ Stall Cycles		Excl. E$ Stall Cycles		Name
sec.	%	sec.	%	sec.	%	
17.583	100.00	6.404	100.00	0.	0.	\<Total\>
17.417	99.05	6.379	99.62	0.	0.	mxv_ -- OMP parallel region from line 12 [_$p1A12.mxv_]
0.133	0.76	0.016	0.25	0.	0.	\<OMP-overhead\>
0.033	0.19	0.004	0.07	0.	0.	mxv_
0.	0.	0.002	0.03	0.	0.	\<OMP-implicit_barrier\>

Figure 5.46: **Single-thread profile for** $m = 381$ – The CPU cycles, as well as the stall times for the L1 data cache ("D\$") and L2 unified cache ("E\$"), are shown. The timings are given in seconds and as a percentage of the total.

Excl. CPU Cycles		Excl. D$ and E$ Stall Cycles		Excl. E$ Stall Cycles		Name
sec.	%	sec.	%	sec.	%	
33.892	100.00	24.166	100.00	0.	0.	\<Total\>
33.550	98.99	24.089	99.68	0.	0.	mxv_ -- OMP parallel region from line 12 [_$p1A12.mxv_]
0.250	0.74	0.060	0.25	0.	0.	\<OMP-overhead\>
0.025	0.07	0.006	0.02	0.	0.	\<OMP-implicit_barrier\>
0.017	0.05	0.003	0.01	0.	0.	mxv_

Figure 5.47: **Single-thread profile for** $m = 385$ – The CPU cycles, as well as the stall times for the L1 data cache ("D\$") and L2 unified cache ("E\$"), are shown. The timings are given in seconds and as a percentage of the total.

In both figures, the name of the function or subroutine to which the data applies is given on the right. The timings and percentages for the entire application are summarized under "\<Total\> ." Subsequent lines give the numbers for the various user and system functions. The leftmost pair of columns ("Excl. CPU Cycles") shows the number of CPU cycles for the program unit, converted to seconds. This figure is also given as a percentage of the total CPU time. Under the heading "Excl. D\$ and E\$ Stall Cycles" the number of seconds the processor waits ("stalls") for data to arrive out of the cache subsystem is shown. "D\$" stands for the L1 data cache. The unified L2 cache is called "E\$." The percentage of the total stall time this corresponds to is also given. The numbers are for the D$ and E$ cache stalls combined. The third pair of columns lists the stall times for the L2 E$ cache only.

As expected, 99% of the time is spent in the parallel region shown in Figure 5.43. There are two OpenMP-related entries in the profiles ("<OMP-overhead>" and "<OMP-implicit-barrier>"). These are present because even on a single thread, the underlying OpenMP infrastructure is executed. Their contributions are negligible though.

There are no E$ Stall Cycles, indicating the program did not spend any time waiting for data to be copied from main memory into the L2 cache. For both values of m, the memory footprint is on the order of 1.1 MByte. Since the L2 cache on this processor is 8 MByte per core, the matrix and vectors easily fit in. In general this does not automatically imply there are no cache misses in the L2 cache. Because of cache mapping conflicts, cache lines could be evicted prematurely. Apparently that is not the case here.

What is striking is the difference in the combined cache stall time. Indeed, if we subtract this time from the total, we see that the CPU time spent other than waiting is about $17.4 - 6.4 = 11.0$ seconds for m=381 and $33.6 - 24.1 = 9.5$ seconds for m=385. In other words, the main cause for the performance difference lies in the time spent waiting for data to arrive in the L1 data cache. For m=381 this is 36.7% of the total time, whereas it doubles to 71.7% for m=385. Now we must find out why this has increased so dramatically.

As mentioned earlier, this implementation has three memory references in the innermost loop, including a store. The compiler applies the unroll-and-jam optimization to the nested loop, unrolling the outer loop to a depth of 8. The corresponding pseudocode is listed in Figure 5.48. This optimization has a definite, positive impact on the overall performance. The downside is that more elements of b and c are read, increasing the chances of cache conflicts.

The performance dip seems to be caused by the combination of the unroll factor chosen for this particular loop and the L1 data cache characteristics. This causes premature cache line evictions for *specific* value(s) of variable m. Theoretically, the other dips in performance could be caused by something quite different. But this is not very likely.

Next, we investigate the program's behavior for m=479, where there is a peak in performance, when using 2, 4, and 8 threads. Here, we compare data for two different values of m. Table 5.4 gives the performance for m=476 and m=479. The relative speedup is based on single-thread performance. Given that the number of threads doubles each time, perfect scaling corresponds to an entry of 2.00. In

```
do j = 2, n-mod(n-1,8), 8
   do i = i_start, i_end
      a(i) = a(i) + b(i,j  )*c(j  ) + b(i,j+1)*c(j+1) &
                  + b(i,j+2)*c(j+2) + b(i,j+3)*c(j+3) &
                  + b(i,j+4)*c(j+4) + b(i,j+5)*c(j+5) &
                  + b(i,j+6)*c(j+6) + b(i,j+7)*c(j+7)
   end do
end do
do j = mod(n-1,8)+1, m
   do i = i_start, i_end
      a(i) = a(i) + b(i,j)*c(j)
   end do
end do
```

Figure 5.48: **Pseudocode fragment after the unroll-and-jam optimization** – The outer level loop unrolling reduces the number of loads and stores for element a(i).

the last column the relative difference between the results for m=479 and m=471 is shown.

Table 5.4: **Performance and speedup for $m = 476$ and $m = 479$** – As the number of threads increases, the performance gap between the two increases to 29%. Going from one to two threads, the performance scales superlinearly for m=479.

Threads	M = 476 (Mflop/s)	Relative Speedup	M = 479 (Mflop/s)	Relative Speedup	Relative Difference
1	874.8	1.00	859.5	1.00	-1.7%
2	1736.5	1.99	1847.6	2.15	6.4%
4	2665.4	1.53	3448.3	1.87	29.4%
8	3768.7	1.41	4866.4	1.41	29.1%

In contrast with the results for m=381 and m=385, the single-thread performance is nearly identical. The performance for m=479 is even slightly less than for m=476. When two or more threads are used however, the results for m=479 quickly exceed those for m=476; the relative speedup is higher. On two threads, a small superlinear speedup is even realized. This actually turns out to provide the answer to our question.

In Table 5.5 we give the hardware performance counter data obtained for the two different values of m on 1 and 2 threads using the Sun Performance Analyzer [128].

Table 5.5: **Hardware performance counter data for** $m = 476$ **and** $m = 479$ – All values are in seconds and per thread, except for the last one, which shows the "Total" values aggregated over the 2 threads.

Threads/	CPU sec.		D$+E$ stalls		E$ stalls	
Number	m=476	m=479	m=476	m=479	m=476	m=479
1/0	207.4	214.0	76.9	76.3	0.00	0.00
2/0	102.8	95.5	36.2	28.5	6.27	0.00
2/1	103.5	96.7	41.2	28.3	5.83	0.15
Total	206.3	192.2	77.4	56.8	12.10	0.15

All values are in seconds and are given on a per thread basis. The first column contains two numbers, separated by a slash. The first is the number of threads used, the second one is the OpenMP thread number. The second column gives the CPU time in seconds for each value of m. The next one contains the number of seconds the CPU stalls while waiting for data from the cache subsystem. The last column gives the stall data for the E$ cache only. The line labeled "Total" shows the values aggregated over the 2 threads for the parallel run. The total number of CPU cycles for 2 threads is about 10% less than for the single thread for m=479. This is not what one would expect because usually the number of CPU cycles goes up if the number of threads increases. The key data is found in the remaining columns. When only one thread is used, the time spent servicing cache misses is about 76 seconds for both values of m. Given that there are no stalls at the E$ L2 unified cache level for both values of m, it is clear that all misses come from the D$ L1 data cache. On two threads the situation is different. First, the total stall time is reduced by $76.3 - 56.8 = 19.5$ seconds for m=479, whereas it goes up a little (77.4 versus 76.9) for m=476. Second, for m=476 the E$ stall time is no longer zero. Each of the two threads waits for about 6 seconds, whereas the number is negligible for m=479. There are several possible explanations. Cache mapping effects might play a role. Another factor could be false sharing. Depending on the value of m and the number of threads used, the same cache line(s) might be modified simultaneously by multiple threads. If this situation happens, there are more premature cache line evictions.

We also see that for m=479 the D$ cache waiting time is lower than for m=476. Therefore, the peak in performance for m=479 is mostly explained by a decrease in the number of cache misses at both the D$ L1 and E$ L2 cache level. This difference in cache behavior gives rise to the modest (15%) superlinear speedup observed on

2 threads. This behavior is continued when 4 and 8 threads are utilized, resulting in the peak observed.

Although the details differ, both the dip and peak can be largely explained by cache effects. We emphasize that these special values for m are the exceptions. Similar behavior is likely to be observed on other cache-based systems and for other compilers, although the specific values of m for which these dips and peaks occur are likely to be different.

```
for (i=0; i<m; i++)
  a[i] = b[i*n]*c[0];
for (i=0; i<m-m%8; i++)
{
  for (j=1; j<n; j++)
  {
    a[i  ] += b[(i  )*n+j]*c[j];
    a[i+1] += b[(i+j)*n+j]*c[j];
    a[i+2] += b[(i+2)*n+j]*c[j];
    a[i+3] += b[(i+3)*n+j]*c[j];
    a[i+4] += b[(i+4)*n+j]*c[j];
    a[i+5] += b[(i+5)*n+j]*c[j];
    a[i+6] += b[(i+6)*n+j]*c[j];
    a[i+7] += b[(i+7)*n+j]*c[j];
  }
}
for (i=m-m%8; i<m; i++)
  for (j=1; j<n; j++)
    a[i] += b[i*n+j]*c[j];
```

Figure 5.49: **Pseudocode fragment of the compiler optimized C version** – The compiler applies loop splitting and unroll and jam to enhance the performance of the original code.

To show why the performance curves for the C version are much smoother, we observe that the memory access pattern is different. The pseudocode for the compiler-optimized C version is listed in Figure 5.49. Similar to the Fortran case, the C compiler performs loop fission, followed by an unroll and jam to a depth of 8. Not shown here is the subsequent unrolling performed on the three innermost loops. Other than for very small values of m, most of the execution time is spent in the second, nested loop. The loads and stores of elements of a in the j loop are loop invariant. The absence of stores is good, especially as this avoids false sharing.

Thanks to the unroll and jam, element `c[j]` is reused seven more times, but it also results in eight different references to the elements of `b`. However, all these nine elements are accessed with unit stride. From a memory access point of view, this is optimal. Cache conflicts might arise only if there are collisions between `c[j]` and one or more of the elements of `b`, or between the various elements of `b` themselves. Whether the former occurs depends on the difference between the starting addresses of `b` and `c`, as well as the values of `m` and `n`. Although one cannot exclude this possibility, cache collisions between `b` and `c` are expected to be rare. Conflicts between individual elements of `b` are more likely. Depending on the cache characteristics, the compiler optimizations, and the value of `n`, dips in the performance may occur as a result. In particular, if `n` is a power of 2, or close to such a number, the performance should be expected to drop significantly.[8]

5.8   An Alternative Fortran Implementation

The performance of the row-oriented strategy has been discussed extensively. Fortran developers familiar with the basic concepts of memory access patterns probably would have used a column-based version from the outset. In this section, several OpenMP variants of such an implementation are discussed. Where relevant, a comparison with the results obtained in Section 5.6 is made.

From a performance point of view, the implementation indicated by Formula (5.4) is more suitable for Fortran. Here, a refers to the entire vector; c_j denotes the jth element of vector c and B_j is used to refer to column j of matrix B. The solution is reached by accumulating the partial products $B_j * c_j$ into vector a. As the memory access on matrix B is over the columns, we will refer to this as the "column variant."

$$a = a + B_j * c_j \qquad j = 1, \dots, n \qquad (5.4)$$

We again optimize the initialization of the result vector a (see also Figure 5.32 on page 160). Lines 9–11 implement the incremental update. Mainly for demonstration purposes, array syntax is used to update all elements of `a`.

As written, the column implementation cannot be parallelized over the `j` loop in Figure 5.50 because then multiple threads simultaneously update the *same* vector `a`, resulting in a data race. If the update at line 10 were to be put into a critical region, the computation is effectively serialized, defeating the whole purpose of parallelization. An alternative is to parallelize the work of line 10, so that each

---

[8]Additional experiments not reported upon here confirm this to be the case.

```
1       subroutine mxv(m, n, a, b, c)
2
3       implicit none
4       integer(kind=4)  :: m, n, i, j
5       real    (kind=8)  :: a(1:m), b(1:m,1:n), c(1:n)
6
7       a(1:m) = b(1:m,1)*c(1)
8
9       do j = 2, n
10          a(1:m) = a(1:m) + b(1:m,j)*c(j)
11      end do
12
13      return
14      end subroutine mxv
```

Figure 5.50: **Column-oriented sequential implementation of the matrix times vector product in Fortran** – The result vector a is built up step by step. For each value of the loop variable j a new contribution is added.

thread updates a unique subset of the elements of a. As array syntax is used, a `!$omp workshare` directive is required to do so. The initialization at line 7 can be similarly parallelized. The OpenMP code is given in Figure 5.51. In order to use as few parallel regions as possible, two `workshare` directives within one enclosing `parallel` directive are applied. The `!$omp workshare` directive embedded in the j loop requires some explanation. The entire do-loop at line 16 is executed by all threads. For the same value of j, each thread then updates a subset of the elements of a, after which execution proceeds to the next value of j. This is correct, but inefficient. In particular, the OpenMP overheads associated with the second `!$omp workshare` directive are incurred $n - 1$ times, each time the j-loop is executed. Moreover, for a fixed value of m, increasing the number of threads also increases the occurrences of false sharing in the parallel loop.

The poor performance for this version is demonstrated in Figure 5.52. The first point to note is the much higher threshold needed to amortize the parallel overhead. There are benefits in using multiple threads only for a memory footprint exceeding 8 MByte (corresponding to $m = n = 1,000$). Although the performance scales reasonably beyond this point, in absolute terms it is very poor compared to the row version. Another difference is that the performance using 4 and 8 threads does not stabilize. This problem has been investigated further. It turns out that the

```
 1          subroutine mxv(m, n, a, b, c, threshold_omp)
 2
 3          implicit none
 4          integer(kind=4)  :: m, n, threshold_omp
 5          real    (kind=8)  :: a(1:m), b(1:m,1:n), c(1:n)
 6
 7          integer :: j
 8
 9  !$OMP PARALLEL DEFAULT(NONE) &
10  !$OMP SHARED(m,n,a,b,c) PRIVATE(j)
11
12  !$OMP WORKSHARE
13          a(1:m) = b(1:m,1)*c(1)
14  !$OMP END WORKSHARE
15
16          do j = 2, n
17  !$OMP WORKSHARE
18              a(1:m) = a(1:m) + b(1:m,j)*c(j)
19  !$OMP END WORKSHARE
20          end do
21
22  !$OMP END PARALLEL
23
24          return
25          end subroutine mxv
```

Figure 5.51: **Column-oriented OpenMP implementation of the matrix times vector product in Fortran** – A single parallel region is used to enclose both work-sharing directives. Although technically correct, this is a very inefficient parallel implementation of the problem.

performance continues to increase as a function of the memory footprint. Only for a footprint in the order of 10 GByte and above is the performance more or less constant. This situation is clearly not practical.

But this is not the end of the story. In fact, the column version of this problem actually performs an *array reduction* (see also Section 4.8.4 on page 105). Source code that makes this explicit is shown in Figure 5.53. The array reduction is implemented in lines 17–23. The array operations are rewritten to use the `reduction` clause on the work-sharing DO-loop. At run time, the threads compute a partial

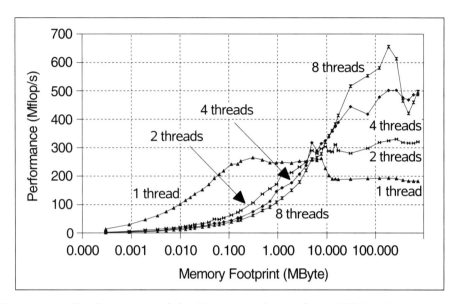

Figure 5.52: **Performance of the Fortran column OpenMP implementation**
– These results clearly demonstrate this is *not* an efficient implementation. Overheads
are high. The performance does not stabilize using 4 and 8 threads. Although it scales
reasonably well beyond the threshold point, the absolute performance is disappointing.

reduction in the iterations of the j-loop assigned to them. The values are stored
in a local copy of vector a. The partial contributions are then merged to form the
final result. The performance results and parallel efficiency of this variant are given
in Figures 5.54 and 5.55 respectively. For values up to the threshold ($m = 600$ in
this case), the parallel efficiency on P threads is $100/P$ %.

In general, we recommend use of the (array) reduction clause, both for convenience and for readability of the code.

We note the following substantial performance improvements over the results
reported in Figure 5.52:

- The threshold value is reduced from $m = 1,000$ to $m = 600$. The latter
  corresponds to a memory footprint of 2.8 MByte.

- Absolute performances for the smallest, 5 x 5, and the largest matrices tested
  are slightly lower for the new version. Otherwise, it is considerably faster.

- The parallel efficiency is much higher.

```
 1          subroutine mxv(m, n, a, b, c)
 2          use globals
 3
 4          implicit none
 5          integer(kind=4)  :: m, n, threshold_omp
 6          real   (kind=8)  :: a(1:m), b(1:m,1:n), c(1:n)
 7
 8          integer :: i, j
 9
10   !$OMP PARALLEL DEFAULT(NONE) IF (n > threshold_omp) &
11   !$OMP SHARED(m,n,a,b,c) PRIVATE(i,j)
12
13   !$OMP WORKSHARE
14          a(1:m) = b(1:m,1)*c(1)
15   !$OMP END WORKSHARE
16
17   !$OMP DO REDUCTION(+:a)
18          do j = 2, n
19             do i = 1, m
20                a(i) = a(i) + b(i,j)*c(j)
21             end do
22          end do
23   !$OMP END DO
24
25   !$OMP END PARALLEL
26
27          return
28          end subroutine mxv
```

Figure 5.53: **Array reduction implementation of the matrix times vector product in Fortran** – The reduction clause is used to compute the result vector a. This type of reduction is supported in Fortran only. The if-clause is used to avoid a performance degradation if m is too small.

- For a certain range of the memory footprint, a superlinear speedup is realized.

- Although the curves are not entirely smooth, the performance appears to stabilize somewhat for the largest matrix sizes tested.

Although the performance has improved substantially, this version is still not as fast as the code in Figure 5.43 that the Sun compiler generated from the original

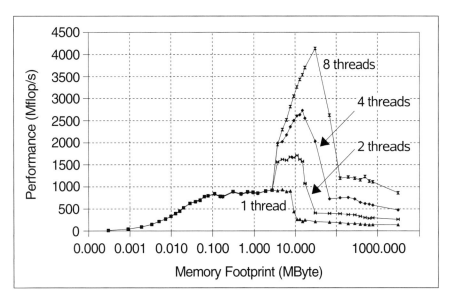

Figure 5.54: **Performance of the array reduction version** – Results here are much better than those in Figure 5.52, for a wide range of matrix sizes. Only for the smallest and largest matrices is the array reduction marginally slower.

code shown in Figure 5.32.

The third version of the problem is partially given in Figure 5.56. As before, the initialization of vector `a` has been parallelized through a `!$omp workshare` directive (lines 5–7). We make use of an allocatable array `col_sum`. This is private to a thread and used to store the partial results. If the memory allocation on line 9 succeeds, `col_sum` is initialized to zero. In case of a failure, the shared counter `ier`, initialized to zero prior to the parallel region, is incremented by one. In order to ensure the correct count is obtained, this update is guarded through the critical region at lines 27–31. As `ier` is a shared variable, it is accessible and can be tested outside the parallel region: if it is nonzero, an error has occurred, and appropriate action can be taken. Note that simply setting this variable to one in case of an error is often sufficient. The solution given here may serve as a template for other, more sophisticated scenarios. For example, with some additional bookkeeping, and by recording the thread number(s) in case of a failure, one can compute the result for the remaining loop iterations postmortem (either in parallel again or on a single thread) and proceed with the execution of the program.

The main computational part is found at lines 13–17. Each thread is assigned

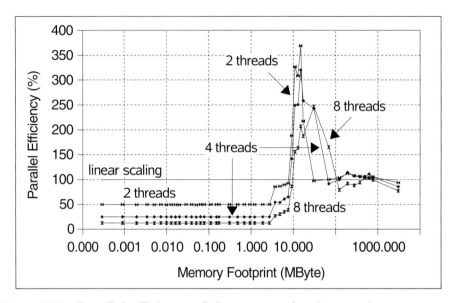

Figure 5.55: **Parallel efficiency of the array reduction version** – For matrix sizes up to the threshold value ($m = 600$ in this case), the efficiency on P threads is $100/P$ %. For a memory footprint in the 10–100 MByte range a superlinear speedup is realized. As observed before, this range depends on the number of threads used. For large matrices the efficiency is good, but not perfect.

a number of iterations of the j loop, effectively computing a partial result. This result is accumulated into the private vector col_sum. In the critical section at lines 21–23 the partial results are merged to form the final result vector a. Finally, at line 25, the temporary storage is released again.

We have inserted nowait clauses at source lines 7 and 17 in order to reduce the number of barriers. As a result, threads do not synchronize until they reach the explicit !$omp barrier directive at line 19. This barrier is needed to ensure that both the initial values of a and the partial results stored in col_sum are available before entering critical section "update_a." The alternative to the barrier is to rely on the implied barrier that is part of the !$omp end do directive by omitting the nowait clause at line 17. Our version makes the synchronization point explicit.

In Figure 5.57 the performance of this version is given. It performs better than the previous one. Although not easily visible from the chart, the threshold value is further reduced from $m = 600$ to $m = 500$. For larger matrix sizes, the performance is higher and constant. For instance, on 8 threads the performance is flat for a memory footprint of 122 MByte and beyond. This crossover point corresponds

```
 1         ier  = 0
 2  !$OMP PARALLEL DEFAULT(NONE) IF ( n > threshold_omp) &
 3  !$OMP SHARED(m,n,a,b,c,ier) PRIVATE(i,j,memstat,col_sum)
 4
 5  !$OMP WORKSHARE
 6         a(1:m) = b(1:m,1)*c(1)
 7  !$OMP END WORKSHARE NOWAIT
 8
 9         allocate ( col_sum(1:m), STAT=memstat )
10         if ( memstat == 0 ) then
11            col_sum(1:m) = 0.0
12
13  !$OMP DO
14         do j = 2, n
15             col_sum(1:m) = col_sum(1:m) + b(1:m,j)*c(j)
16         end do
17  !$OMP END DO NOWAIT
18
19  !$OMP BARRIER
20
21  !$OMP CRITICAL(UPDATE_A)
22         a(1:m) = a(1:m) + col_sum(1:m)
23  !$OMP END CRITICAL(UPDATE_A)
24
25         if (allocated(col_sum)) deallocate(col_sum)
26         else
27  !$OMP CRITICAL(ERROR_FLAG)
28         ier = ier + 1
29  !$OMP END CRITICAL(ERROR_FLAG)
30         end if
31
32  !$OMP END PARALLEL
```

Figure 5.56: **Third implementation of the column oriented version** – After initializing the result vector a, the vector col_sum is allocated. This vector is local to the thread and is used to store a partial result. The update_a critical region is used to merge the partial results into result vector a. This implementation has been optimized to reduce the number of barriers. The program exits gracefully in case of a memory allocation failure.

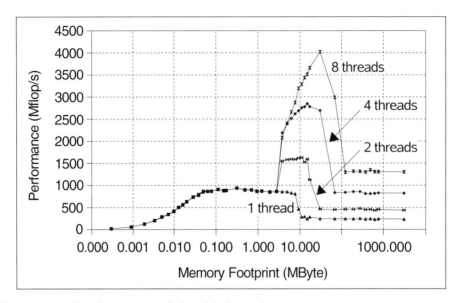

Figure 5.57: **Performance of the third version** – The performance curves are very similar to those for the array reduction version shown in Figure 5.54. The main difference is observed for larger matrices. The performance remains constant, whereas this is not the case for the previous version.

to a matrix of size $m = n = 4,000$. For the array reduction version a similar crossover point is observed, but the performance continues to degrade somewhat as the matrix gets larger. To magnify the differences, the speedup of the version shown in Figure 5.56 over the version given in Figure 5.53 is plotted in Figure 5.58.

Up to their respective threshold value, both implementations execute on a single thread only. Thus the speedup is independent of the number of threads up to this point. On small matrices, the third version performs better than the second, array reduction-based, version, but the benefit decreases as the matrix increases in size. At a certain point the array reduction is up to 10% faster. Eventually, however, the third version outperforms the second version again. The memory footprint for which this occurs also depends on the number of threads used. For the largest matrix size tested, the performance gain is in the 50–70% range.[9]

An intriguing point is that, if we compare Figures 5.41 on page 168 and Figure 5.54, we see that their performance is quite similar. Although not easy to derive

---

[9]A brief analysis of the compiler generated code indicates this cannot be attributed to differences in the optimizations performed at the thread level.

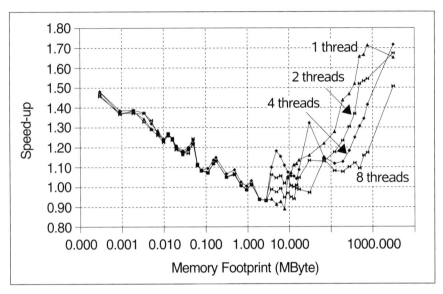

Figure 5.58: **Speedup of the third version over the second column version** – Outside a relatively small region of the memory footprint, the explicitly parallelized version outperforms the version using the array reduction.

from the charts, the row implementation is actually somewhat faster or about equal in performance for all matrix sizes tested.

5.9 Wrap-Up

In the first part of this chapter, we presented simple guidelines on how to write an efficient OpenMP application. Compilers are sometimes able to make up for suboptimal code. They might be capable of performing optimizations such as those described in Section 5.4.5. However, a compiler is always limited by its ability to analyze a program and if for no other reason, it is good practice to write efficient OpenMP code from the start. There is also some debate over the question how much optimization a compiler should be permitted to perform at the OpenMP level, and a pragmatic answer may depend on the context. For example, a redundant, explicitly parallelized initialization loop might be put in by the programmer to ensure first touch data placement on a cc-NUMA architecture (see also Chapter 6). If the compiler eliminates such a redundant operation, performance may suffer.

Performance is always affected by a number of factors that include the compiler, the compiler options selected, libraries, operating system features, the coding style, and the system state at run time. In the second part of this chapter, we have used the simple matrix times vector product to investigate parallel program behavior.

The implementation is fairly straightforward in C. Other than using the `if`-clause, there is not much need to further optimize the implementation. In Fortran the situation is different. The row-oriented implementation was expected to perform poorly, because the memory access pattern is bad. Instead, it performs surprisingly well. Through code transformations the compiler is able to overcome the poor memory access, while preserving the parallelization at the outermost loop level.

It was then observed that for very specific matrix sizes, performance dips or peaks occur. Our exploration showed that these are related to cache effects. As such, they can be expected to show up on other cache-based systems, too, although the matrix size(s) for which these occur and the performance impact are likely to be different.

Fortran developers probably would have started out using the column version of the problem instead. After all, that gives the optimal memory access pattern for single-processor performance. It turns out that a naive OpenMP implementation performs poorly. Once it is realized that an array reduction is performed, the `reduction` clause can be used to get significantly better performance. Next, a handcrafted version of this approach was shown. Although this version gives an improvement, the first row version in Fortran performs just as well and sometimes even better. This somewhat surprising result is of course specific to the algorithm, implementation, system, and software used and would not be possible if the code were not so amenable to compiler analysis.

The lesson to be learned from this study is that, for important program regions, both experimentation and analysis are needed. We hope that the insights given here are sufficient for a programmer to get started on this process.

6 Using OpenMP in the Real World

Up to this point we have discussed the most common usage of OpenMP, namely, to parallelize loops by incrementally inserting compiler directives into the code. This approach offers the benefit of ease of use, but in certain situations it may also have its limitations when it comes to the efficient use of a large number of CPUs. The purpose of this chapter is to show that OpenMP is not limited to loop-level parallelism and to demonstrate how OpenMP supports scalability to a large number of threads. We also discuss performance analysis techniques applicable to large-scale OpenMP programs.

6.1   Scalability Challenges for OpenMP

As the number of processors in a shared-memory system increases, the scalability of an OpenMP program becomes a greater concern. To create a parallel program that scales to a large number of threads, a programmer must carefully consider the nature of the parallelism that can be exploited. Assuming that there is enough parallelism to keep the machine busy, the next step is to express the parallelism identified in a suitable manner.

As we have seen, OpenMP is well suited for expressing loop-level parallelism. One might therefore conclude that OpenMP is limited to fine-grained parallelism, but this is not true. Coarse-grained parallelism, in which very large program regions are parallelized, can also be achieved. Indeed, an entire program can be enclosed in one large parallel region and the work divided up explicitly between the threads. We will discuss this approach to OpenMP parallelism in Section 6.3. We briefly discussed MPI programming for distributed-memory architectures in Section 1.8. Combining MPI and OpenMP is a software trend to support parallelization for clusters of SMP processors. This *hybrid programming model*, which offers the potential to increase the scalability of large-scale applications, will be discussed in Section 6.4. Nested OpenMP, which was discussed in Section 4.9.1, offers a way to exploit multiple levels of parallelism in order to increase the parallel scalability. Examples will be provided in Section 6.5.

The challenge of creating a parallel application begins with a program's data. If this data set can be logically partitioned in such a way that a portion of the data is associated with each thread, this might form the basis of the parallelization. In the corresponding parallel program, each thread will be responsible for performing computations that update the data assigned to it. Each thread essentially carries out the same work, but on its own portion of the data set. Data updated by one thread and used by another must be handled carefully: synchronization must be inserted to ensure that the correct ordering of accesses is enforced. This approach is well suited to applications such as computational fluid dynamics codes that find the discrete solution of partial differential equations. Characteristic is that the same computations are performed on a large number of points of a computational grid. This parallelization strategy, often termed *data parallelism* because the partition of the data is at the heart of the approach, can be realized in several different ways with OpenMP. It has the specific benefit of providing good data locality for many programs, since threads consistently access the same portions of the data set. This potentially enables a high level of data cache reuse, which can be particularly important on cc-NUMA systems, where data is physically distributed across a network. Data at "remote" locations on a network is generally more expensive to access, and frequent remote accesses can lead to network congestion. One can think of this as adding another level of memory to the hierarchy. Since a strategy based on data parallelism also generally leads to a program that is identical for each thread (other than the data used), it is also known as the *single program multiple data*, or SPMD, approach to parallel programming.

Another approach for keeping a machine busy with useful work is to give the threads different kinds of work to do. This may be natural for computations where two or more different kinds of tasks interact with each other. However, it is inherently more difficult to scale programs of this type to a large number of threads, unless there are sufficient tasks to be distributed. This, too, has many natural applications. In quite a few programs, a number of essentially independent, but similar, tasks must be performed. These may be farmed out to the threads. For example, if a large number of input images must be variously analyzed and transformed in a given sequence, it may be easier to have each process or thread do its piece of this work for all images rather than to divide out the images. A drawback of this kind of parallelism is that it tends to lead to a fixed structure, and if the number of available processors varies, it may not be easy to adjust the code to match. Moreover, some computations may dynamically create tasks that can be mapped to the threads. Parallelization strategies that parcel out pieces of work to different threads are generally referred to as *task parallelism*. It, too, can be used as the basis for creating an OpenMP program. Moreover, it may be combined with a data-parallel approach to create scalable code.

Many books on parallel programming describe different ways to parallelize programs for distributed memory [152] and discuss programming patterns that may help determine how best to exploit concurrency in an application [123]. We refer the reader to these for more information on this topic. The point here is that the programmer needs to determine a strategy for creating a parallel program that considers both, the data as well as the work of the entire program.

The OpenMP programming model not only assumes a globally shared address space for all threads but also assumes that the cost of accessing a memory location is uniform across the system. In practice, however, memory access latency is often not uniform. Although non-uniform memory access (NUMA) is most commonly associated with large platforms with hundreds or thousands of CPUs, even small SMPs may be NUMA. Large-scale cc-NUMA (cache-coherent NUMA) shared-memory multiprocessor systems consist of processors and memory connected via a network. Any memory location can be read from or written to, but the access time could differ. Memory that is at the same node within the network as a processor is considered to be local to it; memory that is accessed across a network is remote. It is not unusual that remote memory latency is three to five times the latency to local memory on such platforms. Recent efforts have sought to provide the benefits of cache coherence to networks of workstations and PCs at the cost of even higher differences in remote access latency. Since this enables system-wide global addressing, OpenMP can similarly be deployed on them.

Given the large remote-access latencies of these cc-NUMA architectures, obtaining a program with a high level of data locality is potentially the most important challenge for performance. In addition to making suitable modifications to a code, the programmer may be able to exploit features of the architecture and its operating system, such as the ability to bind threads to particular CPUs, arrange for the placement and dynamic migration of memory pages, and use page replication to substantially increase application performance.

6.2   Achieving Scalability on cc-NUMA Architectures

OpenMP does not provide a direct means of optimizing code for cc-NUMA systems and therefore we can only indirectly influence the performance of a program on such a platform. To make clear the specific challenges posed by these machines, we first give a general discussion of data placement and then discuss some ways to run an OpenMP job on them.

6.2.1   Memory Placement and Thread Binding: Why Do We Care?

Data allocation—or, more accurately, page allocation—is under control of the operating system. On a cc-NUMA architecture, the pages of data belonging to a given program may, for example, be distributed across the nodes of the system. A commonly used allocation policy is called *First Touch*. Under this policy, the thread initializing a data object gets the page associated with that data item in the memory local to the processor it is currently executing on. First Touch is an approximate strategy that works surprisingly well, especially for programs where the updates to a given data element are typically performed by the same thread throughout the computation. Things are harder if the data access pattern is not uniform throughout the code. Several operating systems provide features that give the user a certain level of control over the placement and movement of pages. It is a good investment of time to study the documentation to find out what features are available and how to use them.

The challenge on a cc-NUMA platform is not simply to appropriately map data to the distributed memory; the placement of threads onto the compute nodes requires care. To explain why this is the case, we make our discussion more concrete by using a hypothetical cc-NUMA architecture with 8 processors (P1-P8), 2 processor boards (B1 and B2) and 2 memory modules (M1 and M2), shown in Figure 6.1. We will assume that it is used to execute an OpenMP application with 8 OpenMP threads. In an ideal situation, each OpenMP thread would run on the same processor for the duration of the program: thread T1 on processor P1, T2 on P2, and so on. The data for the threads running on P1, P2, P3, P4 would be placed in M1, and the data for threads running on P5, P6, P7, P8 would be placed on M2. In real life this usually is not the case, partly because of the nature of the application and its use of data, and partly because of the way the runtime library and operating system work in a typical multiuser environment.

Here are some example scenarios that may lead to inefficient thread and memory placement while an OpenMP code is executed:

Unwanted thread migration. Given a system such as the one depicted in Figure 6.1 where 8 OpenMP threads are spread across the 8 processors, and assume that, when the first parallel region is encountered, the data needed by the threads is placed in memory according to the First Touch policy described above. The operating system (OS for short) might decide, particularly when running in multiuser mode, to suspend the program's execution so that the CPUs are available to execute some other task. When the threads are placed back onto the processors, there is no guarantee that they will end up on the same CPU. The data, however, will remain on the same memory module. In such a situation threads that started out running on processor board B1 might end up running on B2, but the data they need to access remains on memory module M1. The remote memory accesses introduced by this effect

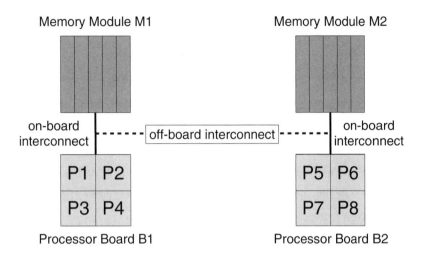

Figure 6.1: **A generic cc-NUMA architecture** – Processor P1, P2, P3, P4 can access memory module M1 with a low latency, while the access time from these processors for data on M2 is high.

can greatly increase the execution time of the program. We discuss possible solutions to this problem below.

The application requires irregular or changing memory access patterns. If the threads access data on different pages in an unpredictable or highly irregular fashion, the First Touch policy may not work well. Here it may be advantageous to select a policy that places the pages of data across the memory modules in a round robin fashion. Although this might lead to a larger number of remote memory accesses, the strategy is probably less susceptible to bottlenecks. As an added benefit, performance problems as the result of relocation of threads are less likely. A similar situation arises if the memory access pattern changes during the programs execution. In this case the First Touch policy may result in long memory access times for later phases of the program. An example for such a scenario is adaptive mesh refinement, which requires dynamic load-balancing when implemented using OpenMP [144]. If the system provides an interface for migrating memory pages between the different program phases, exploiting it might be advantageous. Examples are *migrate-on-next-touch* support via library routines or compiler directives, such as those provided on the HP Compaq Alpha GS-series [26] and Sun Fire^{TM} Servers [127]. Note, however, that a penalty is associated with the migration, so this feature should be used sparingly.

Inefficient thread placement for hybrid codes. Additional problems may arise if a hybrid program consisting of multiple MPI processes, each with several OpenMP threads, is launched. The runtime system might decide to map the MPI processes onto adjacent CPUs, which is a sensible strategy when they are single-threaded but potentially problematic if they employ multiple OpenMP threads. As an example we consider the hypothetical architecture depicted in Figure 6.1. If a hybrid code consists of 2 MPI processes with 4 threads each, the runtime system may decide to place the 2 MPI processes on adjacent CPUs on processor board B1. When the time comes to create the OpenMP threads for both processes, some of them will end up running on processor board B2, thereby introducing remote memory access to the data of their master threads. This might lead to frequent remote memory accesses for some of the threads. In the worst case, data in cache may "ping-pong" (i.e., move frequently) between two different nodes of the machine. This situation could be avoided by placing one of the MPI processes on P1 and the other MPI process on P5, allowing each of them to use 4 adjacent CPUs for their work.

Changing thread team compositions in nested OpenMP codes. The programmer cannot assume that the same resources will be used to execute two different inner parallel regions when nested parallelism is employed. At the beginning of a nested parallel region, a new team of threads is created, and the encountering thread becomes the master of the new team. If this situation happens multiple times in a program, the OpenMP 2.5 standard does not require that the threads be started in the same location each time. Thus, the first time a nested parallel region is encountered, the program might be executed by threads running on processors P1, P2, P3, and P4, but the next time it might be carried out by threads running on P1, P4, P5, and P7. If these teams work on the same chunks of data, many remote memory accesses can result.

6.2.2 Examples of Vendor-Specific cc-NUMA Support

To achieve scalability of OpenMP codes on large-scale cc-NUMA architectures, one may wish to bind threads explicitly to specific processors so that they remain close

to the memory where their data has been stored. Using appropriate methods to
bind threads to specific CPUs, to allocate data pages, and to migrate data according
to access patterns can substantially improve the performance of an application. To
show what kind of support for such features may be provided, we give examples
from two distinct vendor platforms. The purpose of the discussion is to give the
reader an idea of what to look for on a system; other systems also provide similar
features. For more details on the features introduced here, and those on other
platforms, we refer the user to the documentation.

SGI Origin and **SGI Altix**^{TM} [160] systems employ the concept of *CPU sets*.
This allows the user to run an application on a restricted set of processors and
associated memory. The CPU sets are created by the *super user*, invoking the
cpuset command, or automatically by the batch scheduling system. The *dplace*
command allows a user to bind an application to a particular set of processors at
start up time. The default strategy for memory allocation is the First Touch policy
described earlier.

For example, if P1, P2, P3, and P4 in Figure 6.1 form a CPU set, then the
commands

```
setenv OMP_NUM_THREADS 4
dplace -c0-3 a.out
```

can be used to execute `a.out` on processors P1,P2,P3, and P4.

For the Origin systems the MIPSPro^{TM} compiler provided informal extensions
that permitted a higher-level user description of the strategy for distributing data,
as well as for instructing the compiler to assign work to threads based on the data
locality [165]. These directives are now outmoded. There are also OS commands to
place and migrate data that may be invoked while the code is running. The latter
may help if a program has distinct computational phases.

When hybrid MPI/OpenMP programs are run on an SGI Altix^{TM} or Origin
system, special memory placement features are available to ensure that OpenMP
threads run on processors close to the parent MPI process. That is, the MPI processes must be spread out across the processors. To achieve this behavior, the user
must indicate to the runtime system that a hybrid program is being run by setting the environment variable `MPI_OPENMP_INTEROP`. MPI reserves nodes for this
hybrid placement model based on the number of MPI processes and the number
of OpenMP threads per process. For example, if 2 MPI processes with 4 OpenMP
threads per MPI process are used on the platform in Figure 6.1, MPI will request
a placement for 2x4 processes at startup time. The MPI processes will be spread
out such that there is one per node and the corresponding threads share the same

memory. All MPI processes are assumed to start with the same number of OpenMP threads, as specified by the `OMP_NUM_THREADS` environment variable. The SGI Origin supports an additional environment variable, `MPI_DSM_PLACEMENT`. If this is set to `threadroundrobin`, the runtime system attempts to satisfy requests for new memory pages for the MPI process in a round-robin fashion. Additional environment variables `MPI_DSM_CPULIST` and `MPI_DSM_MUSTRUN` are available to place MPI processes onto particular processors and to ensure that they are bound to them.

For example, to run a hybrid MPI/OpenMP code on the architecture in Figure 6.1, the user could specify the following.

```
setenv OMP_NUM_THREADS 4
setenv MPI_OPENMP_INTEROP
setenv MPI_DSM_PLACEMENT threadroundrobin
setenv MPI_DSM_CPULIST 1,5
setenv MPI_DSM_MUSTRUN TRUE
mpirun -np 2 a.out
```

For more detailed documentation of these features, the reader is referred to [162] and [161].

The Sun Microsystems Solaris™ operating system provides the *pbind* command to bind or unbind processes or threads to physical processors. It can also be used to query the binding policy in effect. The command takes the processor id, plus one or more processes IDs, with or without thread IDs.

In the example shown in Figure 6.2, the two threads (or "lightweight processes", lwp, in Solaris terminology) of an OpenMP program with process id 704 are first bound to processor 1. Next we query what processes are specifically bound to this processor and then release the binding of the second thread again. To verify this, we check what processes are bound to processor 1 and 0, respectively. The *processor_bind* system call provides similar functionality at the source level. This type of control may be necessary in the case of hybrid MPI/OpenMP or nested OpenMP codes.

The Sun OpenMP implementation provides the `SUNW_MP_PROCBIND` environment variable to bind the threads to physical processors, or cores in case of a multicore architecture.

Since Version 9, the Solaris operating system has provided a way to optimize memory placement. By default, the operating system attempts to place memory pages according to the First Touch policy described earlier. The policy can be changed by using the `madvise` system call. The `pmadvise` tool provides similar

```
# pbind -b 1 704/1 704/2
lwp id 704/1: was 1, now 1
lwp id 704/2: was not bound, now 1
# pbind -Q 1
lwp id 704/1: 1
lwp id 704/2: 1
# pbind -u 704/2
lwp id 704/2: was 1, now not bound
# pbind -Q 1
lwp id 704/1: 1
# pbind -Q 0
#
```

Figure 6.2: **Examples of binding on the Solaris operating system** – The `pbind` command is used to bind the threads to a specific processor first; the binding is verified and then released again for the second thread. The last two commands verify the binding again.

functionality at the command line level. The `meminfo` system call can be used to obtain more information about the virtual and physical memory behavior, for example, which locality group the page is part of. Commands such as `lgrpinfo`, `plgrp`, and `pmap` are useful to query the topology, policies, and mappings in effect.

This is by no means a comprehensive collection of the available support on all cc-NUMA architectures. For example, the IBM AIX^{TM} operating system provides the `bindprocessor` command and a runtime library routine with the same name to bind threads to processors [86]. Under the Linux operating system, various system calls as well as the `taskset` and `numactl` commands may be used to query and control the placement of data and threads.

We recommend that the programmer check the availability of environment variables, system calls, runtime library routines, or command line tools to control data placement, data movement, and thread binding on a cc-NUMA platform.

6.2.3   Implications of Data and Thread Placement on cc-NUMA Performance

The relative placement of data and threads may significantly influence the performance of certain OpenMP constructs. This was not considered when discussing the behavior of some features in Chapter 5. For example, in Section 5.5.1 the performance differences between the `single` and `master` constructs were discussed. Even on a relatively simple SMP architecture there is no uniform best choice. If data has been carefully mapped to a cc-NUMA system (e.g., via First Touch placement), then it may not be a good idea to permit an arbitrary thread to update the data via the `single` construct. Not only might this result in a general performance loss, but it might also give rise to large performance variations, depending on which thread executes the region. If the data was previously initialized by the master thread, then the `master` construct is likely to work better. Otherwise, it might be beneficial to explicitly map the corresponding work to individual threads based on the location of the data.

The use of private data can be beneficial on such systems. Typically, private data is allocated on the stack (see Chapter 8 for a brief discussion of the stack). In a cc-NUMA aware OpenMP implementation, the stack should be in memory local to the thread. With shared data, this configuration cannot always be ensured, even when First Touch is appropriately used. When shared data is fetched from remote memory, the data cache(s) local to the processor will buffer it, so that subsequent accesses should be fast. However, data may be displaced from the cache in order to make way for another block of data. If so, another relatively expensive transfer from remote memory will occur the next time it is needed. As a result, privatizing data often pays off on a cc-NUMA platform.

6.3   SPMD Programming

While OpenMP is well suited for realizing fine-grained parallelization, one also can use it to accomplish very coarse-grained parallelism. To do so, one creates code that encloses a program's entire computation in one large parallel region. This approach typically involves a higher programming effort but can provide high levels of scalability. It requires the programmer to assign data and work explicitly to threads. The most typical usage is to employ *data parallelism*, where some or all of the data is partitioned so that each thread receives its own portion. The threads will work on their part of the data. Shared data structures are created to hold those values that are shared in the resulting program; in many cases, this is just a small fraction of the total amount of program data. This is the SPMD (single program multiple data) programming style. Note that the availability of shared memory permits variants of this idea to be used. For example, it is possible that a major part of the program is an SPMD code while other parts are not. Likewise, some of the data structures might be distributed among the threads while others remain shared. In reality, SPMD style programs are examples of a low-level thread-specific programming style that has the following characteristics:

- The code contains a small number of large parallel regions.

- Work sharing is controlled by the user, based on the thread identifier (*ID*).

- For true SPMD codes, work sharing is based on distributing major data structures among threads. Usually, most of the data is private.

Figures 6.3 and 6.4 demonstrate a directive-based code fragment and an equivalent SPMD style code.

```
!$OMP PARALLEL DO PRIVATE(i,j), SHARED(a, b, n, m)
 do i = 1, n
     do j = 1, m
        a(i,j) = a(i,j) + 0.25 * (b(i-1, j) + b(i+1, j) &
                              + b(i,j-1)  + b(i,j+1))
     end do
  end do
```

Figure 6.3: **Parallelization of a stencil operation** – The parallelism is implemented by applying the parallel loop directive to the outer loop.

The simple example shows that the SPMD programming style requires more user effort than simply inserting directives into the code. So, what is the advantage? Why would the code shown in Figure 6.4 perform better than that from Figure 6.3? For this code fragment alone, it might not—unless the data size is large [35] or there are more threads available than there are iterations in either of the loops. Assume, for example, that n=m=32 and that 64 threads are available. In the code in Figure 6.3 the work is distributed in one dimension. There will not be any speedup beyond 32, since 32 threads will not have any work to do. The code in Figure 6.4 divides the work in two dimensions. This way, there is work for all of the 64 threads, each one working on a **4x4** chunk of iterations. The true strength of the SPMD style becomes apparent when it is applied to large applications. It permits the user to precisely control details of work assignment and thus to ensure that threads consistently update specific parts of the data, which may substantially reduce the cost of memory accesses even on small SMPs. This increases the potential for scalability.

Case Study 1: A CFD Flow Solver

An example of a successful OpenMP parallelization is `flowCart`, a solver for the inviscid steady-state Euler equations in compressible fluids [24]. The solver is in-

```
!$OMP  PARALLEL PRIVATE(i, j, iam, low_i, low_j, up_i, up_j)  &
!$OMP           SHARED(nt, nti, ntj, a, b)

!$OMP SINGLE
   nt = OMP_GET_NUM_THREADS()
   nti = int(sqrt(real(nt)))
   ntj = int(sqrt(real(nt)))
!$OMP END SINGLE

  iam = OMP_GET_THREAD_NUM()
  low_i = n * iam/nti + 1
  up_i  = n * (iam+1)/nti
  low_j = m * iam/ntj + 1
  up_i  = m * (iam+1)/ntj
!$OMP DO
   do i = low_i, up_i
       do j = low_j, up_j
           a(i,j) = a(i,j) + 0.25 * (b(i-1, j) + b(i+1, j) &
                                     + b(i,j-1)  + b(i,j+1))
       end do
   end do
!$OMP END DO

!$OMP END PARALLEL
```

Figure 6.4: **SPMD style parallelization of a stencil operation** – The example assumes that a square number of threads is available. Loop bounds are explicitly calculated based on the thread ID. This allows the programmer to control the assignment of work precisely.

tegrated into the Cart3D [7] package, a high-fidelity inviscid analysis package for conceptual and preliminary aerodynamic design developed at NASA Ames Research Center. The flowCart solver employs a finite-volume discretization scheme, where the flow quantities are stored at the centroid of each cell. An explicit Runge-Kutta iteration scheme is used to reach a steady state. OpenMP and MPI versions of flowCart are available and use the same command line arguments.

The following design decisions made during the development of the OpenMP version of the flowCart application were critical to achieving high performance and ensuring scalability to hundreds of threads.

Domain Decomposition Approach: Each thread is assigned its own subdomain with a certain number of cells. The thread is responsible for updating its set of cells, an action referred to as the *owner computes* rule. There are a number of cells in surrounding subdomains whose values are needed in order to perform the stencil operations for all cells within the subdomain. These are referred to as *overlap cells*, and their values must be obtained from the thread responsible for them. The code fragment in Figure 6.5 shows the overall structure of the application.

The domain decomposition happens *on the fly*, in that the number of subdomains is determined at run time based on the value of the `OMP_NUM_THREADS` environment variable. The number of cells per thread is calculated by using a workload balancing scheme. The cells are assigned sequentially to the threads, until each thread has reached its quota. The threads responsible for updating each subdomain allocate and then immediately touch every element of their own arrays. This approach is taken to achieve data locality via the First Touch policy. Each thread operates on its own private data. The only shared data structure is a small array of pointers to the subdomain structures. If there are `N` subdomains, this will be an array of `N` pointers to the `N` subdomain structures on the different processors.

Note that the code shown in Figure 6.5 has no explicitly declared private variables. Instead, the variables, such as `pMyGrid`, are declared within the parallel region and are private by default. Only a small array of pointers to the chunks of privately allocated arrays, `pGrid`, is declared outside of the parallel region and is explicitly shared.

The calculations within each subdomain can proceed fairly independently from each other. The threads do not update their overlap cells, but they receive updated values from their neighbors. At this point, information needs to be exchanged among neighboring subdomains, requiring synchronization.

Explicit Data Exchange: After performing each chunk of computation within each subdomain, the updated values of the overlap cells need to be exchanged. Rather than making calls to a communication library as required in a message-passing implementation, here the data exchange is implemented by directly taking advantage of shared memory. For each overlap cell, the location of the updated values is computed once and saved. A pointer into the corresponding subdomain is used to access the values. The code fragment in Figure 6.6 outlines the basic structure of the loop implementing the exchange of values for overlap cells.

Note that most MPI implementations on shared-memory systems leverage the available shared address space for efficiency. Using nonblocking communication may allow overlapping of calculation and communication. Nevertheless, the MPI-based approach requires matching send and receive pairs as well as the packing

```
//
// pGrid is a small shared array of pointers to each
// subdomain structure for a particular thread.
//
  struct subdomain pGrid[MaxNumThreads];
  int N = omp_get_num_threads();
  pGrid = (subdomain *) malloc (N * sizeof(double *));

#pragma omp parallel shared(pGrid, N)
{
//
// pMyGrid is a pointer to a chunk of data that holds the
// subdomain for a particular thread. The memory is allocated
// within a parallel region and therefore private to each thread.
//
  struct subdomain pMyGrid;
//
// perform the domain decomposition
//
#pragma omp parallel
  iam = omp_get_thread_num();
  pMyGrid = (subdomain) malloc(sizeof(subdomain));
  initSubdomain(pMyGrid);
  pGrid[iam] = pMyGrid;
//
// Time step iteration to compute the solution
//
  for (i=0; i<itmax; i++) {
    computeGradient(pMyGrid);
    copyGradient(pNeighborGrid);
    computeResiduals(pMyGrid);
    updateCells(pMyGrid);
    copyOverlapCells(pMyNeigborGrid);
  }
}
```

Figure 6.5: **Structure of the flowCart solver** – Basic code structure outlining the decomposition approach used in the highly scalable flow solver flowCart of Cart3D.

```
#pragma omp barrier
  for (k=0; k<Neighbors; k++){
     for (j = 0; j < overlapCells; j++) {
        set_pointers (pNeighborGrid);
        XchangeIndex = pNeighborGrid->index;
    /*
     actual copying takes place here
    */
        pMyGrid->a[j] = pNeighborGrid->a[XchangeIndex];
     }
  }
#pragma omp barrier
```

Figure 6.6: **OpenMP-based boundary exchange in Cart3D** – The code fragment shows the structure of the OpenMP-based implementation of the exchange of values for overlap cells in the flowCart solver of Cart3D.

and unpacking of message buffers. The corresponding loop implemented in MPI is outlined in Figure 6.7.

Data Replication: In order for the calculations on the cells within each subdomain to proceed independently for some time, a number of overlap cells are replicated on neighboring subdomains. Traditionally, shared-memory implementations would define one large array of cells. Each thread is assigned a range of indices to work on, using the neighboring cells as needed. This approach does not require explicit communication. However, it does not leave the opportunity to control memory locality for each subdomain.

Both the OpenMP and MPI implementations of `flowCart` show excellent scalability on a variety of hardware platforms. On some large-scale shared memory systems, the OpenMP version outperforms the MPI implementation. For example, on an SGI Origin 3600, the speedup for a problem size of 4.7 million cells on 512 CPUs is about 450 for OpenMP versus 350 for MPI. Running the OpenMP-based implementation on a larger problem (25 million cells) employing 496 CPUs of a single node of an SGI Altix^{TM} system showed a speedup of 400 and a performance of 0.63 TFlop/s. Most recent performance results can be obtained from the Cart3D website [7], and considerable information on the scalability of the code is contained in [124]. Figure 6.8 shows an example Cartesian mesh and the corresponding pressure contours of the solution for a Cart3D application.

The lesson learned from this case study is that OpenMP can achieve scalability

```
/* allocate send and receive buffers */
malloc(sbuf);
malloc(rbuf);
/* fill up the send buffers */
for (k=0; k<Neighbors; k++){
    ncount = 0;
    for (j=0; j < overlapCells; j++) {
        set_pointers (pMyGrid, k);
        XchangeIndex = pMyGrid->index
        sbuf[ncount]= pMyGrid->a[XchangeIndex];
        ncount++;
     }
    /* send buffer */
    Size = ncount;
    MPI_Isend(sbuf, Size, Type,
        recvID, Tag, MPI_COMM_WORLD, &(rbuf[k]));
}
for (k=0; k<Neighbors; k++){
 /* receive data from any source that has sent data */
   MPI_Recv(rbuf, Size, Type, MPI_ANY_SOURCE,
                    MPI_COMM_WORLD, &status);
   ncount = 0;
    /*  unpacking data */
    for (j=0; j < overlapCells; j++) {
        pMyGrid->a[j] = rbuf[ncount];
        ncount++;
    }
}
if (Neighbors > 0) {
        MPI_Waitall(Neighbors);
}
```

Figure 6.7: **MPI-based boundary exchange in Cart3D** – The code fragment shows the structure of the MPI-based implementation of the exchange of values for overlap cells in the flowCart solver of Cart3D.

that meets or even exceeds that of message passing, if the user is willing to invest a similar amount of programming effort into parallelizing the application. The resulting code is generally easier to maintain.

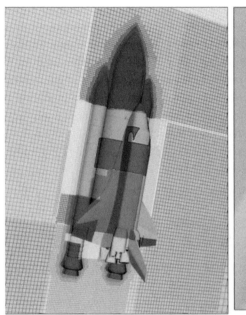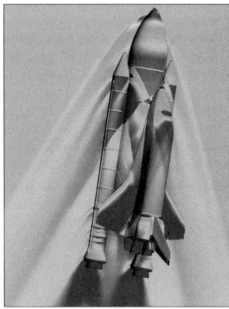

Figure 6.8: **Example application of Cart3D** – The image on the left depicts a Cartesian mesh around a full space shuttle launch vehicle configuration including orbiter, external tank, solid rocket boosters, and fore and aft attach hardware. The image on the right shows the computed pressure contour lines for the same configuration. The OpenMP-based implementation of the application shows excellent performance and scalability on large shared-memory systems. (The figure has been provided courtesy of Michael Aftosmis and Marsha Berger from NASA Ames Research Center.)

6.4   Combining OpenMP and Message Passing

Message-passing-based parallelization has the potential for high performance and good scalability because communication of data and synchronization of processes are completely under user control. The message-passing model supported by MPI provides a portable way to create parallel programs on distributed as well as shared-memory architectures. Some discussion of MPI can be found in Section 1.8. We assume that the reader of this section is familiar with it. We will occasionally describe certain features of MPI that are relevant for OpenMP programming here. For more details, please refer to the MPI-1 and MPI-2 standard [58]. A good introduction to MPI is provided in [69].

Combining MPI and OpenMP offers an approach to exploit hierarchical parallelism inherent in the application or the underlying hardware. The hybrid programming style is most efficient when MPI processes work on a coarse level of parallelism, taking advantage of the user-controlled data distribution and work scheduling. Parallelization based on OpenMP is used within the shared address space of each process for additional fine-grained parallelization. The situation is depicted in Figure 6.9.

Hybrid MPI/OpenMP programming has the potential to increase the scalability of an application, but there are drawbacks. The following is a list of issues that should be considered when using hybrid parallelism.

Reasons to Combine MPI and OpenMP:

1. This software approach matches the hardware trend toward clusters of SMPs by using MPI across nodes and OpenMP within nodes. Hybrid code offers the possibility of reducing MPI communication overhead by using OpenMP within the node and by taking advantage of the shared memory, such as depicted in Figure 6.9. By exploiting shared data, parallelizing parts of the application with OpenMP improves performance, without noticeably increasing the memory requirements of the application.

2. Some applications expose two levels of parallelism: coarse-grained parallelism, implemented by using MPI, where a large amount of computation can be performed independently, with only the occasional exchange of information between different processes; and fine-grained parallelism, which may be available at the loop level. The hybrid programming may be suitable for exploiting such multiple levels of parallelism.

3. Application requirements or system restrictions may limit the number of MPI processes that can be used. In this case using OpenMP in addition to MPI can increase the amount of parallelism.

4. Some applications show an unbalanced work load at the MPI level that might be hard to overcome. In this case, OpenMP provides a convenient way to address the imbalance, by exploiting extra parallelism on a finer granularity and by assigning a different number of threads to different MPI processes, depending on the workload.

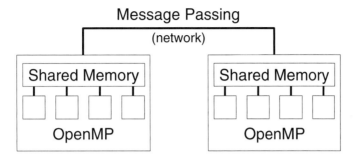

Figure 6.9: **Combining MPI and OpenMP** – Hybrid programming offers a natural match on a software level with respect to the concept and architecture of SMP clusters.

Reasons Not to Combine MPI and OpenMP:

1. Introducing OpenMP into an existing MPI code also means introducing the drawbacks of OpenMP, such as the following.

   - Limitations when it comes to control of work distribution and synchronization

   - Overhead introduced by thread creation and synchronization

   - Dependence on the quality of compiler and runtime support for OpenMP

   - Dependence on the availability of shared memory and related issues such as data placement.

2. The interaction of MPI and OpenMP runtime libraries may have negative side effects on the program's performance, depending on the support (or rather the lack thereof) on a particular system.

3. Some applications naturally expose only one level of parallelism, and there may be no benefit in introducing hierarchical parallelism.

If, after considering all the issues above, one decides that hybrid parallelism is the way to go, here are some rules of thumb how to go about it.

Starting from an existing sequential code, the first step usually consists of decomposing the problem for MPI parallelization, adding the OpenMP directives later on. This way only the master thread will perform communication between MPI tasks. The simplest and least error-prone way is to use MPI only outside of parallel regions. If the program is parallelized in such a way that MPI calls are issued from within parallel regions, then several threads may call the same routines from the MPI library at the same time, and a thread-safe MPI library is needed.

MPI support for OpenMP: There are no special requirements for OpenMP support if calls to the MPI library are always made outside of parallel regions. If this is the case, keep in mind that only the master thread is active during communication and the remaining threads are not used, as in the sequential sections of the code. Calling MPI from within parallel regions may enable overlapping communication and computation, but it requires paying a lot more attention to the interaction of MPI and OpenMP. In this case, the MPI library has to be aware of the fact that it can be called by different threads of the same program. The MPI-1 standard does not provide any support for multithreading. The MPI-2 [58] standard does include several levels of thread support. This needs to be specified in a call to `MPI_Init_-thread`, rather than just using `MPI_Init`, which is equivalent to initializing with no thread support. Many MPI implementations now support the `MPI_Init_thread` call, even if full MPI-2 support is lacking. The syntax in C is as follows.

```
int MPI_Init_thread(int *argc,
    char *((*argv)[]), int required, int *provided)
```

The syntax in Fortran is as follows.

```
MPI_INIT_THREAD(required, provided, ierr)
integer required, provided, ierr
```

The call to `MPI_Init_thread` initializes MPI in the same way that a call to `MPI_init` would. In addition, it initializes the thread support level. The argument `required` is used to specify the desired level of thread support. The argument `provided` is returned as output, indicating the actual level provided by the system. Possible values are listed below in increasing order of thread support.

- `MPI_THREAD_SINGLE`: Only one thread will execute. This is the same as initializing with `MPI_init`.

- `MPI_THREAD_FUNNELED`: Process may be multithreaded, but only the master thread will make MPI calls.

- `MPI_THREAD_SERIALIZED`: Multiple threads may make MPI calls, but only one at a time.

- `MPI_THREAD_MULTIPLE`: Multiple threads may make MPI calls with no restrictions.

Thread support at levels `MPI_THREAD_FUNNELED` or higher allows potential overlap of communication and computation. For example, in an SPMD style of programming, certain threads can perform communication while others are computing. This is outlined in Figure 6.10.

```
!$OMP PARALLEL
    if (thread_id .eq. id1) then
        call mpi_routine1()
    else if (thread_id .eq. id2) then
        call mpi_routine2()
    else
        do_compute()
    end if
!$OMP END PARALLEL
```

Figure 6.10: **Example of overlapping computation and communication** – The code fragment illustrates how this could be implemented in an MPI application.

6.4.1   Case Study 2: The NAS Parallel Benchmark BT

The following example demonstrates how the choice of domain decomposition affects the interaction between MPI and OpenMP. The code is derived from the NAS Parallel Benchmarks. The benchmarks are described in [20] and [21] and can be downloaded from [154]. We discuss the BT benchmark, which is a simulated CFD application using an ADI (alternating directions iteration) method to solve the discretized Navier Stokes Equations in three dimensions. The three spatial dimensions are decoupled, and a tridiagonal system of equations is solved in each dimension. The flow of the program is depicted in Figure 6.11. We consider two different approaches to hybrid parallelization of the application.

Three-dimensional domain decomposition: In this approach, the MPI parallelization is based on a 3D domain decomposition. Each MPI process is assigned a number of 3D blocks. Data dependences in each of the spatial dimensions require an exchange of boundary values after updating a block. Figure 6.12 shows, as an example, the structure of the loop in routine `z_solve`. It is easy to exploit loop level parallelism via the OpenMP `!$omp parallel do` directive. The most suitable loop for parallelization in routine `z_solve` is the j-loop, since data dependences

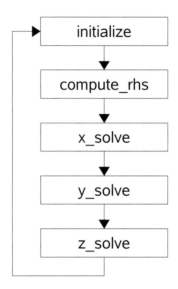

Figure 6.11: **The NAS Parallel Benchmark BT** – The basic computational flow through the various phases is shown.

prevent parallelization of the k-loop. Parallelization of the i-loop would result in unfavorable memory access, giving rise to false sharing of data. The hybrid parallel version of routine `z_solve` is shown in Figure 6.13. No special thread support is required so that it is sufficient to use the regular `MPI_init`.

One-dimensional domain decomposition. OpenMP is applied in the prior approach to a dimension that is distributed for the MPI parallelization. Another strategy is to parallelize using MPI in one spatial dimension and OpenMP in another. In this variant, each MPI process is responsible for one slice of the decomposed domain, rather than a number of 3D cubes. Data dependences require that boundary values have to be exchanged before and after updating the slice. OpenMP is now employed to parallelize one of the nondistributed dimensions. The 1D domain decomposition requires MPI thread support of level `MPI_THREAD_MULTIPLE` because all threads associated with an MPI process issue MPI calls. Figure 6.14 depicts the structure of routine `z-solve` if the data is distributed in the k dimension. The rank `ID` in `MPI_send` and `MPI_receive` identifies the MPI process, not a particular thread. Distinct message tags are used to avoid conflicts in the communication calls issued by different threads within the same process.

```
call MPI_init(...)

do ib = 1, nblock
   call mpi_receive

   do j = j_low, j_high
      do i = i_low, i_high
         do k = k_low, k_high
            rhs(i,j,k,ib) = rhs(i, j, k-1, ib) +  ...
         end do
      end do
   end do
   call mpi_send
end do
```

Figure 6.12: **Structure of the MPI-based solver routine** – MPI implementation of routine z-solve in the NAS Parallel Benchmark BT based on a 3D domain decomposition.

```
call MPI_init(...)

do ib = 1, nblock
   call mpi_receive
!$OMP PARALLEL DO
   do j = j_low, j_high
      do i = i_low, i_high
         do k = k_low, k_high
            rhs(i,j,k,ib) = rhs(i, j, k-1, ib) +  ...
         end do
      end do
   end do
!$OMP END PARALLEL DO
   call mpi_send
```

Figure 6.13: **Structure of the MPI/OpenMP based solver routine** – Hybrid parallelization of routine z-solve in the NAS Parallel Benchmark BT based on a 3D domain decomposition. The OpenMP directive is placed on the outermost loop, in this case the second spatial dimension j. Data dependences prevent OpenMP parallelization of the k-loop and require communication between neighboring MPI processes.

```
call MPI_init_thread(MPI_THREAD_MULTIPLE,...)
...
!$OMP PARALLEL DO
 do j = 1, ny
    call mpi_receive(pid_1, tag_rec_tid, ...)
    do k = k_low, k_high
      do i = 1, nx
          rhs(i, j, k) = rhs(i, j, k-1) + ...
      end do
    end do
    call mpi_send(pid_2, tag_my_tid, ...)
 end do
!$OMP END PARALLEL DO
```

Figure 6.14: **Hybrid parallelization based on 1D domain decomposition** –
OpenMP directives are placed on loops over unpartitioned dimensions. This requires calls
to the MPI library from within the parallel regions.

Which of these strategies is preferable? The 3D domain decomposition employs
OpenMP on the same dimension as MPI, which is in a sense redundant. However,
it requires very little interaction between MPI and OpenMP. Furthermore, if the
MPI code already exists, one can easily develop the hybrid code by simply inserting
OpenMP directives. In some situations, the hybrid implementation can outperform
the pure MPI code, such as when the number of MPI processes is limited because of
system restrictions or when using MPI introduces a high communication overhead.
The 1D domain decomposition approach applies MPI and OpenMP to different
dimensions. It requires tight interaction between MPI and OpenMP and it is a lot
harder to implement, with plenty of opportunity to introduce errors. However, this
approach requires MPI communication with only 2 neighbor processes, as opposed
to 6 neighbors in the 3D domain decomposition approach. This can potentially be
advantageous on slow networks. A detailed case study of the example above with
performance results is given in [93].

6.4.2   Case Study 3: The Multi-Zone NAS Parallel Benchmarks

The application discussed in Section 6.4.1 does not expose multiple levels of parallelism: parallelization occurs along the 3 spatial dimensions, which are all equal, in
the sense that there is no natural hierarchy between them.

Applications that exposes a natural hierarchical parallelism include multi-zone computational fluid dynamics codes [52] and climate models such as the ocean circulation model POP version 2.0.1 [103]. In these applications a geometrically complex domain is covered by sets of partially overlapping discretization grids, called zones. The solution within each zone can be calculated fairly independently, requiring only an occasional update of boundary values. This gives rise to coarse-grained parallelism. The solver routines invoked for the discretization grids within each zone offer the possibility for loop-level parallelization. The Multi-zone NAS Parallel Benchmarks are a set of benchmarks that capture the behavior of multi-zone codes from the area of computational fluid dynamics. They are described in [49] and are publicly available [154]. A hybrid MPI/OpenMP implementation of the benchmarks is part of the distribution package.

The benchmarks `LU-MZ`, `SP-MZ`, and `BT-MZ` are multi-zone versions of the well-known single-zone NAS Parallel Benchmarks [20] `LU`, `SP`, and `BT`. They compute solutions of unsteady, compressible Navier-Stokes equations in three spatial dimensions. The `LU` benchmark uses a lower-upper symmetric Gauss-Seidel algorithm, `SP` employs a scalar pentadiagonal solver, and `BT` a block tridiagonal algorithm. The program flow of the benchmarks is shown in Figure 6.15. The structure of the program is given in Figure 6.16. The fragment of the `z_solve` subroutine, parallelized with OpenMP, is listed in Figure 6.17.

The benchmarks are categorized in classes according to the problem size. In this example we consider the benchmarks for problem size B, which implies a domain of 304 by 208 by 17 grid points, divided into 64 zones. The test cases require about 200 MByte of memory. The major difference between the benchmarks, which is relevant for hybrid programming, is the workload distribution. In the `LU-MZ` benchmark, the number of zones is 16, which limits the number of MPI processes that can be employed to 16. The number of zones for `SP-MZ` and `BT-MZ` is 64. For `SP-MZ` all zones are of equal size. For `BT-MZ` the size of the zones varies widely, with a ratio of about 20 between the largest and the smallest zone. Figures 6.18 and 6.19 show the effects of varying the number of MPI processes on a fixed number of CPUs.

The timings were obtained by using a total of 128 threads on an SGI Origin 3000 and 64 threads on an UltraSPARC IV+ based Sun Fire E25K. The charts compare the timings obtained on **n** MPI processes versus 64 MPI processes, which is the maximum number of MPI processes that can be employed. On both architectures `SP-MZ` fares best when using as many MPI processes as possible to exploit coarse-grained parallelism. Using multiple OpenMP threads per MPI process was advantageous only when more CPUs than zones were available. The situation is different for BT-MZ. Because of the large difference in the number of grid points per

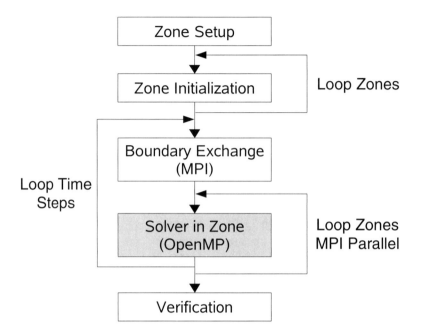

Figure 6.15: **The NAS Parallel Benchmark BT-MZ** – The basic computational flow through the various phases is shown.

zone, good load-balance cannot be achieved for BT-MZ on MPI-level. In this case the load must be balanced at the fine-grained level of parallelism, which means we should use fewer processes with multiple threads each. For LU-MZ, the outer level of parallelism is limited to 16. In this case, one must use multiple threads per MPI process to exploit a higher number of available CPUs. For all benchmarks, proper thread binding and memory placement, such as discussed in Section 6.2, were necessary to achieve good performance. A detailed discussion of the performance characteristics of the benchmarks can be found in [89].

6.5 Nested OpenMP Parallelism

The previous section described how to employ a combination of MPI and OpenMP to exploit multiple levels of parallelism. Another approach is to use nested OpenMP parallelism. Recall that the OpenMP standard allows the nesting of parallel regions, although an implementation need not support this feature (see also Sections 4.9.1

```
      program bt-mz-mpi-openmp

      call mpi_init()
C
C  Apply load-balancing heuristics to determine
C  zones and threads per MPI processes
C
      call get_zones_threads(my_zones, my_nt)
C
C  Each process sets number of threads.
C
      call omp_set_num_threads (my_nt)
C
      do step = 1, niter
C
        call exch_boundary      ! Boundary data exchange
                                ! using MPI
        do zone = 1, my_zones
          ...
          call z_solve(zone) ! Solver within zone
        end do
      end do
      end
```

Figure 6.16: **Structure of the Multi-Zone NAS Parallel Benchmark BT-MZ**
– The code outlines the structure of an implementation employing hybrid parallelism.

and 4.7). When a thread in the outer parallel region encounters the inner !$omp
parallel, it becomes the master thread of a new team of threads. If nested parallelism is supported and enabled, the new team will consist of multiple threads.
There is an implicit barrier synchronization at the end of an inner parallel region.
Only the master thread of the inner team continues execution after the barrier.
There is also an implicit barrier synchronization point at the end of the outer
parallel region. This is illustrated in Figure 6.20.

Work-sharing directives cannot be tightly nested; hence, there cannot be nested
#pragma omp for (in C) or nested !$omp do (in Fortran), without introducing
nested #pragma omp parallel or !$omp parallel constructs. This implies the
introduction of barrier synchronization points at the end of inner parallel regions,
in addition to the barrier synchronization points at the outer parallel regions. Fig-

```
      subroutine z_solve(zone, ... )
C
C Fine grain parallelization
C
!$OMP PARALLEL DO PRIVATE(m, i, j, k)
  do j = 2, nz-1
    do i = 2, ny-1
      do k = 2, ny-1
        do m = 1, 5
            rhs(m,i,j,k) = rhs(m,i,j,k-1) + ...
        end do
      end do
    end do
  end do
!$OMP END PARALLEL DO
  return
  end
```

Figure 6.17: **Solver used by the Multi-Zone NAS Parallel Benchmark BT-MZ** – This routine has been parallelized with OpenMP.

ure 6.21 demonstrates this issue. The barrier synchronization points introduced by !$omp do can be removed by using the NOWAIT clause. The implicit barriers introduced by !$omp parallel cannot be removed. This restriction introduces a high synchronization overhead and may have bad effects on the program flow, as we describe later.

The default data-sharing attributes for nested regions are as follows:

- If a variable is shared in the outer region, it is shared by all threads in the teams of the inner regions.

- If a variable is private in the outer region and accessible by a thread that becomes the master thread of the team executing the inner parallel region, then this variable is by default shared by all threads executing the inner region.

We now describe some situations suitable for employing nested OpenMP parallelism.

Overlapping I/O and computation. For many codes, reading and writing of data can be overlapped with computation. For example, seismic applications

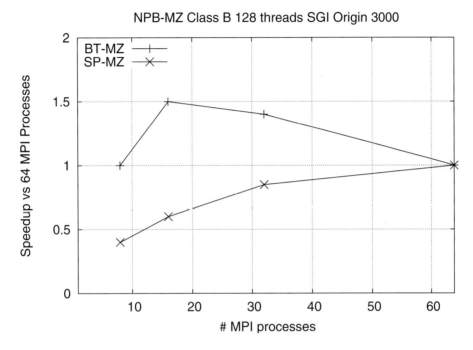

Figure 6.18: **Timing comparisons for BT-MZ and SP-MZ on SGI Origin 3000** – The timings were obtained for runs of Class B on 128 CPUs on an SGI Origin 3000. Displayed is the speedup compared to a run employing 64 MPI processes. The charts show that SP-MZ runs fastest using the maximum number of MPI processes, which is 64 for Class B. BT-MZ fares best using 16 MPI processes, each employing multiple threads.

process large amounts of data, and overlapping may improve performance. If the input data is read in chunks, one chunk may be processed while the next one is read. These chunks are processed by fast Fourier transform computations, and the results are written to an output file. The amount of seismic data typically is rather large, and overlapping I/O and computation is therefore beneficial. This can be accomplished by creating three parallel sections, one to read the input, one to do the computations, and one to write output data. Additional data parallelism can be exploited by parallelizing the computationally intensive loops, as shown in the code example in Figure 6.22. The chunks of data are processed in a pipelined fashion. This requires point-to-point synchronization between the threads executing the outer level of parallelism, which can be accomplished by synchronization mechanisms such as those described in Section 4.9.2. The flow of the program is

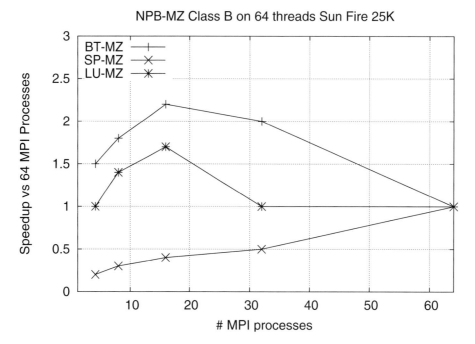

Figure 6.19: **Timing comparisons for BT-MZ, LU-MZ, and SP-MZ on Sun Fire** – The timings are obtained for runs of Class B on 64 CPUs of a 72 UltraSPARC IV+ processor Sun Fire E25K. Displayed is the speedup compared to a run employing 64 MPI processes. The charts show that SP-MZ runs fastest using 64 the number of MPI processes, each running on 1 thread. BT-MZ runs best running on 16 MPI processes, each on multiple threads. For LU-MZ the number of MPI processes is limited to 16. The speedup for a higher number of MPI processes is set to 1 in the chart.

depicted in Figure 6.23. For more details on this technique see [36].

Overlapping functional parallelism. The previous example can be extended to a general overlap of functional parallelism. Examples are multimedia applications such as discussed in [174]. Task parallelism can be exploited by breaking the input stream into chunks and having them processed by different parallel sections in a pipelined fashion: once the audio processing is done for the first chunk, the video work can begin to work on it while the audio work continues to the second chunk, and so on. This requires synchronization between the threads executing the two parallel sections. Synchronization mechanisms such as those described in Section 4.9.2 can be used for this purpose. Further parallelism can be exploited

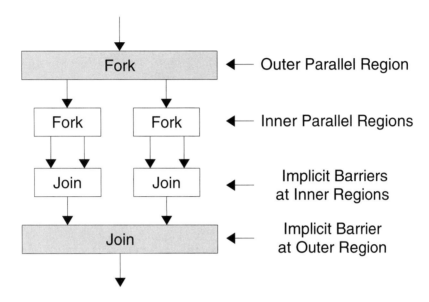

Figure 6.20: **Nested OpenMP parallel regions** – Inner parallel regions introduce implicit synchronization points in addition to the barrier synchronization points at the outer parallel regions.

at the loop level within the parallel sections. If the video processing, for example, is a lot more expensive than the audio processing, more threads can be assigned to work on the video part's computationally intensive loops in order to achieve a balanced workload between the two parallel sections.

6.5.1   Case Study 4: Employing Nested OpenMP for Multi-Zone CFD Benchmarks

Nested OpenMP can be employed to handle multiple levels of data parallelism, as demonstrated in the following case study.

The benchmarks described in Section 6.4.2 can be parallelized by using nested OpenMP rather than MPI/OpenMP hybrid programming. On shared-memory systems with a large number of processors, nested OpenMP is a feasible alternative to the hybrid approach. Rather than using MPI for the coarse-grained part and

```
#pragma omp parallel
{
#pragma omp for private(i, j)
    for (i=0; i <n; i++) {
#prgama omp parallel              <= required
  {
#pragma omp for private(j)
        for (j=0; i<n; j++) {
            do_work(i,j)
        }
    }           <= required implicit barrier
}               <= required implicit barrier
```

Figure 6.21: **Synchronization within a nested parallel region** – When using nested OpenMP directives there are implicit barrier synchronization points at the end of outer as well as the inner parallel regions. Work-sharing directives cannot be tightly nested: An inner !$omp for requires an inner !$omp parallel.

OpenMP on the fine-grained level, OpenMP can be used on both levels. The code fragments in Figures 6.24 and 6.25 outline such an implementation based on nested OpenMP directives.

A comparison of the code to the hybrid implementation in Figure 6.16 shows that the structure of both implementations is very similar. Differences between the nested OpenMP and the hybrid code are as follows:

- **Startup.** The hybrid code contains a call to mpi_init to set up the execution environment, and the number of MPI processes is specified by the user. For example, assume the name of the program is bt-mz-mpi, and *mpirun* is the command used to execute MPI-based programs. The following two commands cause this hybrid program to use 32 CPUs, distributed over 8 MPI processes, each using 4 OpenMP threads each on average:[1]

```
setenv OMP_NUM_THREADS 4
mpirun -np 8 ./bt-mz-mpi
```

The nested OpenMP code needs a mechanism to allow the user to specify the number of outer parallel regions. This can be accomplished in several ways.

---

[1]Note that this application employs load-balancing heuristics to calculate the appropriate number of threads for the inner-level parallel loop.

```
...
#pragma omp parallel sections
#pragma omp section
for (i=0; i < N; i++) {
    read_input(i);
    signal_read(i);
}
#pragma omp section
for (i=0; i < N; i++) {
    wait_read(i);
    process_data(i);
    signal_processed(i);
}
#pragma omp section
for (i=0; i < N; i++) {
    wait_processed (i)
    write_output(i);
}
...

void process_data(i)
{
  ...
#prgama omp parallel for num_threads(4)
 for (j=0; j<M; j++) {
    do_compute(i,j)
 }
}
```

Figure 6.22: **Overlapping computation and I/O with nested OpenMP** –
The code demonstrates how to employ nested parallelism to overlap I/O and computation.
Functional parallelism is exploited by creating different parallel sections for reading input
data, performing the computation, and writing the results. Additional data parallelism
is exploited within the computationally intensive section that processes the data. In the
example a total of 6 threads are being used, with 4 threads involved in producing the
results.

For example, we can introduce the environment variable MY_OUTER_LEVEL to
specify the number of outer-level threads. If we want to use 8 such threads,
plus 4 threads at the second level, the nested OpenMP version of the code
would be executed as follows.

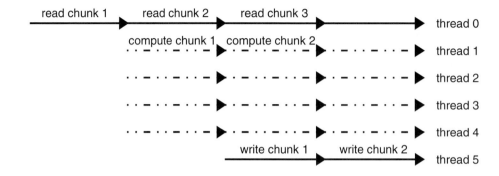

Figure 6.23: **Pipelined flow of the thread execution** – Nested parallelism is employed to overlap computation and I/O.

```
setenv OMP_NUM_THREADS 32; setenv MY_OUTER_LEVEL 8
./bt-mz-nested-omp
```

- **Outer-level parallelism.** In the hybrid version of the code, outer-level parallelism is based on MPI processes updating a subset of the zones. In the nested OpenMP version, outer-level parallelism is achieved by inserting an `!$omp parallel` directive for the loop over the zones. Note that there is no work-sharing directive for the outer parallel region. The work is shared in an SPMD-style fashion, by explicit use of the thread *ID*.

- **Boundary exchange.** Data exchange at the boundaries is done by reading from and writing to the data structures as defined in the sequential version of the code.

- **Inner-level parallelism.** Just as in the hybrid version, inner-level parallelism is achieved by placing an `!$omp parallel do` directive on the loops within the solver routines. A difference in the nested OpenMP code is that the number of threads working on the inner region has to be specified for each team via the `num_threads` clause. This makes it necessary that the mapping of zones onto threads be visible within the solver routines. In our example this is achieved by the use of the common block `thread_info`.

A problem with this sort of nested parallelism is that the OpenMP 2.5 standard does not provide a way for the user to specify that the same team of OpenMP

```
      program bt-mz-nested-omp
      common/thread_info/nt_inner(1:nt_outer)
C
C  The user specifies the number of outer parallel
C  regions. Load-balancing heuristics are applied
C  to assign zones to outer parallel regions and determine
C  the number of inner level threads per outer parallel regions.

      call get_zones_threads (my_zones, nt_outer, nt_inner)
C
      do step = 1, niter
C
C  Copying data between zones as in sequential code
C
        call exch_boundary
C
C  Create parallel regions for coarse grain parallelism.
C
!$OMP  PARALLEL PRIVATE(iam, zone,..)
!$OMP& NUM_THREADS(nt_outer)
C
        iam = omp_get_thread_num ()
C
C SPMD style explicit user controlled work sharing:
C
        do zone = 1, zones
           if (my_zones(zone) .eq. iam) then
              ...
              call z_solve(zone, iam)
           end if
        end do
      end do
    end
```

Figure 6.24: **The Multi-Zone NAS Parallel Benchmark BT-MZ** – The example outlines the structure of the code when coarse-grained parallelism is based on (nested) OpenMP.

```fortran
      subroutine z_solve(zone, iam, ... )
      common/thread_info/nt_inner(1:nt_outer)
C
C Inner parallel region
C
!$OMP  PARALLEL DO DEFAULT(SHARED) PRIVATE(m, i, j, k)
!$OMP& NUM_THREADS(nt_inner(iam))
      do j = 2, nz-1
        do i = 2, ny-1
          do k = 2, ny-1
            do m = 1, 5
              rhs(m, i, j, k) =
                  rhs(m, i, j, k-1) +  ...
            end do
          end do
        end do
      end do
!$OMP END PARALLEL DO
      return
      end
```

Figure 6.25: **Source of subroutine z_solve** – This routine is called from within a parallel region. Nested OpenMP directives are used to exploit fine-grained parallelism.

threads should be working together in subsequent inner parallel regions. A typical OpenMP implementation of nested parallelism requests threads for inner parallel regions from a pool of available threads. This has the effect that the composition of the inner thread teams could change between different instances of the inner parallel region, which makes efficient thread binding and memory placement very hard, if not impossible. Some research compilers, such as the NanosCompiler [66], provide extended support for nested parallelism and allow fixed thread teams to be created. A study [18] has shown that with this extra support, nested OpenMP can be a feasible alternative to employing MPI/OpenMP for the parallelization of multi-zone CFD codes. For the example of the benchmark BT-MZ run on an SGI Origin 3000 and using the NanosCompiler for nested OpenMP parallelization, the chart in Figure 6.26 shows little performance difference between the two different implementations.

Nested OpenMP parallelization can be an alternative to employing hybrid parallelism on large shared-memory architectures, but a number of performance con-

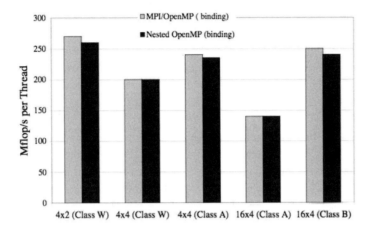

Figure 6.26: **Performance comparison of MPI/OpenMP and nested OpenMP** – The chart compares the performance, measured in Mflop/s per thread and run on an SGI Origin 3000, of the MPI/OpenMP-based multi-zone NAS Parallel Benchmark BT-MZ to its counterpart implemented using nested OpenMP and additional support provided by the NanosCompiler. Thread binding was applied for both versions. There is little performance difference between the different implementations across the various combinations of outer- and inner-level parallelization.

siderations must be taken into account:

1. Increased demand for forking and joining of threads at inner parallel regions requires an extremely efficient thread runtime library and operating system support.

2. Synchronization overhead will increase because of the implicit barrier synchronization at inner parallel regions.

3. Point-to-point synchronization between threads from different inner parallel regions is problematic because of implicit barrier synchronization at the end of inner parallel regions.

4. Thread pool-based implementations of nested parallelism may lead to loss of data locality and increased memory access on cc-NUMA architectures.

6.6   Performance Analysis of OpenMP Programs

Assuming that the performance of an application is satisfactory in single-threaded mode, the most likely performance question is "Why does my application not get the expected speed-up when running on multiple threads?" The performance of large-scale parallel applications depends on many factors, including sequential performance (Section 5.2), load imbalance (Section 5.4.6), and parallelization overheads (Section 5.3).

Section 5.3.1 lists additional factors that influence OpenMP programs. The issue of replicated work is of particular interest for SPMD programs, which contain very large parallel regions. For hybrid codes it is of interest to examine the interaction of the OpenMP runtime library with the MPI communication library. Careful performance analysis is required if an application does not show the expected scalability.

6.6.1   Performance Profiling of OpenMP Programs

Profile data from a representative run of the application will show where the program spends most of its time and what resources are being used. Programmer effort can then concentrate on the particularly time-consuming routines. The basic components of most performance analysis tools consist of a module to record the performance-related information and a module to examine the results. These either can be separate components or can be integrated in one tool. Depending on the profiling technology used, the program may have to be specifically prepared to record the information.

The application has to be executed to collect the performance data. Typically, the recorded information is stored on disk and can be subsequently examined to detect potential performance problems. In those cases where the production run takes a long time to execute and requires a large amount of memory, a test case that makes fewer demands on resources should be selected.

There is a risk with this approach, though. The parameters that define the problem to be solved may have a profound effect on the profile. It is therefore important to choose a reduced test case that has the same computational characteristics as the production workload. When one is in doubt whether the selected problem reflects the targeted job, we recommend making a profile of the production run as well and ensuring that the profiles are similar. If they are, the performance analysis can focus on the smaller test case, but it is still good practice to occasionally verify whether the performance gains apply to the production job as well.

Several approaches can be used to obtain performance data. One of these is called *sampling*, which is based on periodic clock-based OS interrupts or hardware counter traps, such as the overflow hardware counter registers. At these sampling points, the values of performance data, such as the program counter, the time, call stacks, and hardware-counter overflow data are collected and recorded. Examples of sampling-based profiling tools are the Unix^{TM} *gprof* tool, the *Sun Performance Analyzer* [128], and *oprofile* [3].

An alternative approach is to collect data by *code instrumentation* rather than interrupting execution. In this approach, calls to a tracing library are inserted in the code by the programmer, the compiler, or a tool. These library calls will write performance information into a *performance profile* file during program execution. An advantage of this approach is that the user has control over when and where information is collected. Moreover, the trace data represents a true time line of the flow of the program. The disadvantage is that modification of the source code and recompilation are required, which is not always an option. Also, the instrumentation can affect the compiler optimizations and therefore performance behavior, and it can be very costly in terms of additional resources needed, in particular with respect to disk and memory consumption. Some packages support dynamic instrumentation of the executable program, thereby eliminating the need for recompilation. An example is the *ompitrace* module, which is part of the Paraver [56] Performance Analysis System.

Regardless of the recording technology, examples of pertinent performance information are as follows:

- The state of a thread at given times, such as waiting for work, synchronizing, forking, joining, or doing useful work

- Time spent in parallel regions and work-sharing constructs

- Time spent in user and system level routines

- Hardware counter information such as CPU cycles, instructions, and cache misses

- Time spent in communication, message length, and the number of messages

Performance data is usually recorded as a series of events tagged with a thread ID, a process ID (in case of MPI programs), a CPU ID, a timestamp, and—depending on the recording method—a call stack. The event data is used to compute performance metrics which are then mapped onto, for example, source or assembly code, thread IDs, and process IDs. The more flexibility the tracing and analysis packages provide in calculating, mapping, and comparing these metrics, the more insight one will be able to obtain into the nature of the obstacles to perfect scalability.

The performance data collected, whether it is based on statistical sampling or on instrumentation-based tracing, contains a huge amount of information. The challenge in analyzing the performance lies in the meaningful interpretation of collected data. Some useful features to have in a tool are the ability to:

- Map performance metrics onto source code, assembler code, threads, and processes;

- Observe the behavior of metrics over time; and

- Calculate user defined performance metrics.

In the following we discuss a number of performance metrics and give suggestions on how to determine them. We use the OpenMP versions of the NAS Parallel Benchmarks version 3.2 and the Multi-zone NAS Parallel benchmarks version 3.1 as example codes, which are freely available and can be downloaded at [154].

6.6.2   Interpreting Timing Information

When obtaining timing profiles for parallel programs, one has to distinguish between *wall-clock time* and *CPU time*. As explained in Section 5.3, wall-clock time is the actual time that passes between the beginning and the end of a timing interval. It is also referred to as the *elapsed time*. The CPU time is the time the program spends in user mode. For a sequential program, the wall-clock time is typically the sum of CPU time and system time. CPU time is usually reported as the sum of the CPU times over all threads. Because of the overhead introduced by the parallelization, the CPU time will not decrease with an increasing number of threads. At best, it will be stationary, but in many cases an increase will be observed. A profiling tool helps to understand where this additional cost comes from.

Timing information can be used to obtain the following metrics:

- **Parallelization coverage.** In view of Amdahl's law (see also Formula (2.2) in Section 2.6), it is important to know how much of an application actually runs in parallel. The ratio of the total execution time spent outside of parallel regions versus the total execution time provides a rough idea of what to expect of the scalability of the application. As will be explained in Section 8.3.4, most compilers put parallel regions into separate routines, a technique often referred to as *outlining*. The naming convention for these compiler-generated routines will usually be such that it can be associated with the original function from which it was extracted. Depending on the system, it may even be possible to determine the line number and the loop identifier. If the parallel program is run on a single thread, one can determine the percentage of time spent in parallel regions and work-sharing constructs versus the time spent outside of parallel regions. This will provide an upper bound on the scaling that can be expected when increasing the number of threads.

To demonstrate this, we ran the NAS Parallel Benchmark BT of problem size Class A on a Sun Fire E6900 system with 24 UltraSPARC IV processors. The benchmark reports the following information.

```
BT Benchmark Completed.
Class            =                          A
Size             =              64x  64x  64
Iterations       =                        200
Time in seconds  =                     418.82
Total threads    =                          1
Avail threads    =                          1
Mop/s total      =                     401.80
Mop/s/thread     =                     401.80
Operation type   =             floating point
Verification     =                 SUCCESSFUL
Version          =                        3.2
```

The *gprof* output for a run on a single thread looks like the following.

```
      %   cumulative              total
    time    seconds    calls     ms/call  name
    16.4      73.10       201    590.56   _$d1A40.y_solve_
    16.3     145.54       201    587.28   _$d1A40.z_solve_
    15.7     215.59       201    575.39   _$d1A43.x_solve_
    14.6     280.54  146029716     0.00   binvcrhs_
     8.2     316.91  146029716     0.00   matmul_sub_
     7.4     349.71  146029716     0.00   matvec_sub_
     5.8     383.51       202     82.82   _$d1I67.compute_rhs_
     3.7     400.06       202     81.93   _$d1H176.compute_rhs_
```

```
3.1    413.74       202    67.72   _$d1G298.compute_rhs_
1.7    421.36       202    37.72   _$d1E380.compute_rhs_
1.3    427.23       202    29.06   _$d1A23.compute_rhs_
0.9    435.92       202    20.00   _$d1B48.compute_rhs_
0.9    439.78       201    19.20   _$d1A18.add_
0.5    442.17   2317932     0.00   lhsinit_
0.4    444.13       202     9.70   _$d1C423.compute_rhs_
0.1    444.43   2317932     0.00   binvrhs_
...
```

The routines with names starting with a _$ sign are the *outlined routines* generated by the compiler to execute parallel loops and parallel regions. The name indicates the subroutine name as well as the line number of the parallel construct. For example, _$d1A40.y_solve_ refers to a parallel construct in routine y_solve in line 40. Note that this is just an example and that the nomenclature depends on the particular compiler and system that is being used. Routines binvcrhs, matmul_sub, matvec_sub, lhsinit, and binvrhs are called within parallel regions, so we can count them as being executed in parallel. Adding up the percentage contributions of the routines that are executed in parallel shows 98 percent of the total execution time is spent in parallel regions. According to Amdahl's law an upper bound for the speedup when running, for example, on 4 threads is given by

$$S = \frac{1}{(0.98/4 + 0.02)} = 3.8. \tag{6.1}$$

Running the same application on 4 threads yields the following benchmark information.

```
BT Benchmark Completed.
Class            =                    A
Size             =        64x  64x  64
Iterations       =                  200
Time in seconds  =               123.32
Total threads    =                    4
Avail threads    =                    4
Mop/s total      =              1364.60
Mop/s/thread     =               341.15
```

```
Operation type  =           floating point
Verification    =              SUCCESSFUL
Version         =                     3.2
```

The profile information looks like this.

% time	cumulative seconds	calls	total ms/call	name
16.6	87.27	804	164.81	_$d1A40.y_solve_
16.5	174.19	804	164.38	_$d1A40.z_solve_
15.9	257.69	804	160.12	_$d1A43.x_solve_
13.6	329.31	146029716	0.00	binvcrhs_
6.9	365.62	146029716	0.00	matmul_sub_
4.8	390.80	146029716	0.00	matvec_sub_
3.0	428.35	808	19.55	_$d1H176.compute_rhs_
2.9	443.65	808	18.94	_$d1I67.compute_rhs_
2.8	458.26	808	18.08	_$d1G298.compute_rhs_
2.6	471.91			tree_barrier_and_reduction
1.6	489.81	804	10.71	_$d1A18.add_
1.5	497.70	808	9.76	_$d1E380.compute_rhs_
1.1	503.55			mt_nop
1.1	509.37	808	7.20	_$d1B48.compute_rhs_
1.1	515.02	808	6.99	_$d1A23.compute_rhs_
0.4	522.10	2317932	0.00	lhsinit_
0.4	523.99	808	2.34	_$d1C423.compute_rhs_
0.1	524.35	808	0.45	_$d1F356.compute_rhs_
0.1	524.69	2317932	0.00	binvrhs_
0.1	524.99	4195072	0.00	exact_solution_
...				

The overall execution time decreased from 419 seconds to 123 seconds, resulting in a speedup of 3.4. As mentioned in Section 5.3, Amdahl's law ignores the overhead introduced by parallel execution. As in this case, it tends to predict a more optimistic speedup than that observed in reality.

- **Useful parallel time.** Not all time spent in parallel regions will decrease linearly as the number of threads increases. For example, threads may be in a parallel region but spend time waiting for work or at synchronization points. Notice that in the profiling output above, additional time is reported for `tree_barrier_and_reduction` in the profile for 4 threads, an item that is not present in the profile listing for 1 thread. This is a routine from the specific OpenMP library used. It is part of the implementation of the barrier construct and can be considered to be part of the parallel overhead.

Determining how much time is spent in performing useful work and how much time is spent in synchronization may or may not be easy, depending on the system and performance analysis tool. Below is the output of the Sun Performance Analyzer [128] for the example of the NAS parallel benchmark BT for a run using 4 threads. The profile information indicates for each routine how much time is spent in actual work.

Incl. User CPU sec.	Incl. OMP Work sec.	Incl. OMP Wait sec.	Name
577.424	522.906	165.826	\<Total\>
101.811	0.	165.316	\<OMP-implicit_barrier\>
159.341	146.442	41.279	_$d1A40.y_solve_
167.707	151.436	53.668	_$d1A40.z_solve_
147.903	136.616	31.272	_$d1A43.x_solve_
71.440	77.274	0.	binvcrhs_
34.414	35.785	0.	matmul_sub_
26.829	32.002	0.	matvec_sub_
23.286	17.492	12.529	_$d1H176.compute_rhs_
15.671	17.492	0.	_$d1I67.compute_rhs_
20.464	17.732	10.367	_$d1G298.compute_rhs_
14.330	10.517	8.456	_$d1A18.add_
7.996	9.537	0.	_$d1E380.compute_rhs_
8.076	6.204	2.212	_$d1B48.compute_rhs_
5.704	5.844	0.	_$d1A23.compute_rhs_
2.212	2.212	0.	lhsinit_
1.871	1.871	0.	_$d1C423.compute_rhs_
0.390	0.	0.390	\<OMP-idle\>
0.280	0.280	0.	_$d1F356.compute_rhs_
0.260	0.260	0.	exact_solution_

To detect, for example, load imbalance between the threads, one must see the value of the metric not only for each routine but also for each thread. To this end, we use a two-dimensional display such as that provided by the Paraver Performance Analysis system [56]. An example is shown in Figure 6.27, which displays the CPU time in micro-seconds per thread for the four most time consuming parts of the BT benchmarks. The timings were obtained using 4 threads on an SGI Origin 2000.

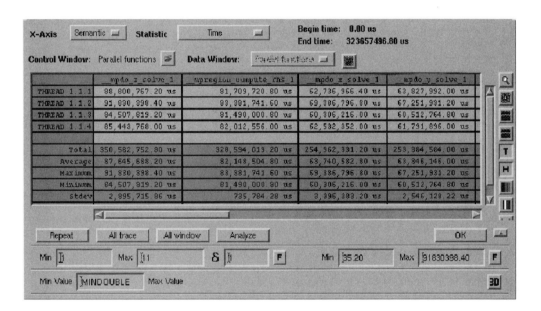

Figure 6.27: **Paraver view of CPU time per thread per parallel region** – A two-dimensional view of CPU time per thread and per parallel region as displayed by the Paraver performance analysis system.

- **Estimating the parallel efficiency.** The parallel efficiency is defined as the speedup divided by the number of threads. To determine the speedup, one must measure the execution time for a single-threaded run, a task that could be prohibitively expensive. The concept of useful parallel time can be used to estimate the parallel efficiency from just one run on multiple threads,

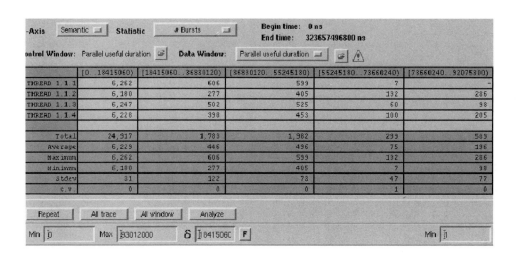

Figure 6.28: **Paraver histogram of the distribution of OpenMP workshare durations** – The histogram shows the distribution of OpenMP workshare durations in routine `compute_rhs` of NAS Parallel Benchmark BT as displayed by the Paraver Performance Analysis System. The timings were obtained on a SGI Origin 2000 employing 4 threads. The OpenMP workshare constructs are sorted by duration in bins of 0.18 seconds. The overview shows that for all threads the majority of the durations are shorter than 0.18 seconds.

without needing to execute on a single thread. The following equation can be used for this purpose:

$$EstParEfficiency = \frac{ElapsedTime}{MasterSeqTime + \sum_{j=1}^{P} ParTime_j}, \qquad (6.2)$$

where

– $ElapsedTime$ is the elapsed execution time,

- *MasterSeqTime* is the time the master thread spends outside of parallel regions,

- *ParTime$_j$* is the useful parallel time of thread j, and

- P is the number of threads.

- **The workshare duration.** This is the time between entry and exit of one chunk of work within a work-sharing construct. Measuring this requires instrumentation-based profiling. The metric can provide insight into various performance metrics. For one, it serves as a measure of the *granularity of the parallelization*. Executing a large number of very small chunks introduces more overhead than the execution of fewer, but larger, chunks of work. The quantification of *large* and *small* depends on the particular system. Therefore, the comparison between different durations is more interesting than the absolute value. A suitable way to display this metric is in the form of histograms. For each thread the execution times of the work-sharing constructs are sorted by duration into bins. This approach not only indicates the distribution of long and short work-sharing constructs, but also differences between the individual threads. An example of this type of information is given in Figure 6.28.

  Comparing histograms of workshare durations for different parallel regions helps to identify areas with inefficient fine grained parallelization. Comparing the workshare duration between threads can help to spot areas where high latencies introduced by the memory subsystem cause increased execution times for some threads. If certain threads take considerably longer to execute their chunks of work and the workload is balanced, nonoptimal memory placement could be the reason on a cc-NUMA architecture.

- **Thread synchronization.** The impact of this on the execution time can be determined by analyzing the following timing information:

  - Time spent within MASTER, SINGLE, and CRITICAL regions

  - Time spent in atomic operations

  - Time spent handling locks, such as setting, testing, and waiting to acquire them

  - Time spent in array reduction operations

- **Load balancing.** Poor scalability could be caused because of the work not being equally spread over the number of threads or because of other asymmetries. Profile information can be used to diagnose the following possible causes for this behavior:

  - Per thread barrier synchronization time at the end of parallel loops
  - Per thread useful time
  - Per thread number of instructions executed by each thread during the useful time in parallel regions
  - Time per chunk of a work sharing construct

- **Work scheduling.** Dynamic scheduling (see Section 4.5.7) provides for a well-balanced workload distribution. It should be used with care, however, since it introduces inefficiencies. First, the overhead of assigning chunks to threads is higher than with static scheduling, where the distribution of work is determined at the beginning of the loop and remains fixed during the whole execution. Second, dynamic scheduling may lead to a loss of data locality because the threads will possibly work on different chunks of data during the execution of the loops. As an example we consider the NAS BT benchmark of class A, executed by using 16 threads on a Sun Fire E6900 system with 24 UltraSPARC IV processors. If static scheduling is applied, the profile for some of the most time-consuming parallel loops looks like the following:

```
Excl.     Incl.     Incl.     Name
User CPU  User CPU  OMP Work  OMP Wait
  sec.      sec.      sec.      sec.
 81.817   143.420   136.616    6.845   _$d1A40.z_solve_
 79.205   122.426   117.312    5.164   _$d1A43.x_solve_
 79.095   125.368   119.794    5.574   _$d1A40.y_solve_
  ...
 15.871    17.132    15.871    1.261   _$d1G298.compute_rhs_
  ...
```

The same code when executed on the same system but using dynamic scheduling yields the following.

```
Excl.      Incl.      Incl.        Name
User CPU   User CPU   OMP Work   OMP Wait
   sec.       sec.       sec.       sec.
 80.186    139.588    132.753      6.865 _$d1A40.z_solve_
 80.146    138.997    133.233      5.764 _$d1A43.x_solve_
 79.786    126.398    121.165      5.324 _$d1A40.y_solve_
 ...
 64.485     70.920     64.485      6.435 _$d1G298.compute_rhs_
 ...
```

While the parallel loops in the routines x_solve, y_solve, and z_solve are not affected by the scheduling policy, the loop in compute_rhs shows a significant performance decrease when dynamic scheduling is used. There is some increase in the time waiting for work and a huge increase in the time actually performing the calculations, most likely due to loss of data locality.

6.6.3   Using Hardware Counters

In addition to execution time-related information, hardware counter data provides important means to understand the performance of the parallel program. What hardware counters are available and how to read them depend on the processor and system used. In this section we discuss a small set of counters that are most commonly available and useful to measure.

- The *number of executed instructions* per thread provides various interesting insights. Comparing this metric between threads can point to a *workload imbalance* within parallel regions. Keep in mind, though, that threads may execute instructions while they are idle or during synchronization[2]. In order to determine workload differences between threads it is therefore important to consider only the instructions executed while performing useful work.

  Consider, for example, the NAS Parallel Benchmark LU. As discussed in Section 4.9.2, this application uses a pipelined thread execution model, implemented via explicit point-to-point synchronization. Counting the instructions during one of the solver routines may indicate that some threads are executing many more instructions than others. This does not necessarily indicate a work

---

[2]Be aware that the OpenMP 2.5 specifications leave it up to the implementation what idle threads should do. It is best to check the documentation to find out what the specific environment used supports, as well as what the default is.

load imbalance, however. Depending on the thread, idle policy instructions could be issued while a thread is waiting for work.

The number of executed instructions can show an excessive amount of *replicated work*. If the number of instructions performed during the useful parallel time increases considerably when increasing the number of threads, it could be an indication of replicated work, a problem that is particularly prone to arise in SPMD programs. Recall that the characteristic for SPMD programming, which was discussed in Section 6.3, is a small number of large parallel regions. This might result in large sections of identical code being executed by all of the threads, thereby limiting the scalability.

- It is often useful to correlate certain metrics, such as time and the value of hardware counters. The number of *instructions per second* during the thread useful time is an indicator of how well the processor pipelines are being used. If the ratio is low for certain routines, one might want to check whether threads spend their time waiting for work, are waiting in a synchronization phase or are waiting for the cache and memory system.

- The *number of data cache and translation-lookaside buffer (TLB) misses* are important metrics to consider. Both provide measures for the efficiency of memory accesses. Details are given in Chapter 5.

  Just as in the case of instructions, the actual value of the hardware counter is hard to interpret. Insight is gained by comparing values between threads, observing the behavior over a period of time or by combining the values with other metrics. For example, an interesting statistic is the ratio of cache or TLB misses per instruction. If this ratio is high for certain routines or threads, it is worth trying to change the memory access pattern, as was discussed by way of an example in Section 5.6.

- The *cost per cache miss* can provide a measure for the impact of remote memory access on a cc-NUMA architecture or DSM system. An estimate for this metric can be obtained by combining the time, the number of instructions, and the number of cache misses, as shown in the following formula:

$$EstCacheMissCost = \frac{ElapsedTime - \frac{NumInsts}{IdealMIPS}}{NumCacheMisses}, \tag{6.3}$$

where

- *ElapsedTime* is the elapsed execution time;

- *NumInsts* is the number of instructions executed during the useful parallel time;

- *IdealMIPS* is the number of millions of instructions per second that could be obtained if the cost for a cache miss were zero (this is a machine-specific constant, for example, the inverse of the clock rate); and

- *NumCacheMisses* is the number of cache misses that occurred during the useful parallel time.

More interesting than the absolute value of this metric is how it compares between threads. If the cost per cache miss for certain routines varies widely between the threads, some data could be stored in such a way that it causes remote memory access for some threads, thereby increasing the overall execution time. The metric was used to detect inefficient memory placement when executing a hybrid MPI/OpenMP application in [94].

- On some systems, the counters can be used to detect *false sharing*, described in Section 5.5.2. Unfortunately, it is very hard to give general recommendations. If cache coherency related counters are available, their values can be monitored as a function of the number of threads used. If false sharing occurs, they tend to increase exponentially. The same is true for cache misses at the outermost level.

6.7 Wrap-Up

Writing an OpenMP application that performs well is often fairly straightforward, but there are exceptions worth considering

On cc-NUMA architectures, the placement of data can critically affect performance. By exploiting the First Touch placement policy, most or all of the data often can be placed close to the threads that need it most. In those cases where this policy is not sufficient, system-specific support may be needed to further enhance performance.

Using OpenMP in an SPMD style requires more programming effort but can achieve performance and scalability comparable to that of message passing code.

On a cluster of SMP, or multicore, nodes, the hybrid MPI/OpenMP model can be an attractive solution to exploit the two levels of parallelism this kind of architecture offers. The downside of this approach is that one needs to master and combine two different parallel programming paradigms. Nested parallelism applied in an SPMD style can be a feasible alternative. In view of the rising importance of multicore technology, one can expect that in the near future shared-memory systems will support a large number of processing nodes, tied together by using a two-level interconnect topology. The SPMD programming style maps nicely onto this.

Performance analysis tools are indispensable for identifying and addressing performance bottlenecks. The two most common techniques are sampling and tracing, each with their pros and cons. A high-quality tool allows the user to derive a wealth of information to guide the tuning process.

7 Troubleshooting

One of the toughest problems facing an OpenMP programmer is to learn how to avoid introducing bugs into a program as part of the parallelization process. The desire to avoid bugs in any program seems obvious, but bugs in shared-memory parallel programs tend to be very subtle and harder to find than in sequential programs. This chapter discusses the most typical kinds of errors that occur in OpenMP programs, as well as some more complicated cases.

7.1 Introduction

Up to now the emphasis has been on the ease with which OpenMP can be used to create parallel programs. Indeed, this was one of the primary goals of the OpenMP designers. It still remains the programmer's responsibility to identify and properly express the parallelism. Unfortunately, errors made while expressing the parallelism can lead to incorrect code. The details of implementing the parallelism are handled implicitly by the compiler and the runtime library and are transparent to the programmer. This situation can make debugging an OpenMP code difficult. In this chapter, we discuss common and fairly straightforward errors as well as some more complicated cases. We also describe good practices to help avoid problems, and we outline some debugging strategies.

7.2 Common Misunderstandings and Frequent Errors

In this section we describe concepts, constructs, and programming techniques that are most likely to introduce (subtle) errors. We also provide recommendations on how these errors can be avoided.

7.2.1 Data Race Conditions

One of the biggest drawbacks of shared-memory parallel programming is that it might lead to the introduction of a certain type of bug that manifests itself through silent data corruption. To make matters worse, the runtime behavior of code with this kind of error is also not reproducible: if one executes the same erroneous program a second time, the problem might not show up.

OpenMP has several safety nets to help avoid this kind of bug. But OpenMP cannot prevent its introduction, since it is typically a result of faulty use of one of the directives. For example it may arise from the incorrect parallelization of a loop or an unprotected update of shared data. In this section we elaborate on this type of error, commonly known as a *data race condition*. This is sometimes also referred to simply as a *data race* or *race condition*.

A data race condition exists when two threads may concurrently access the same shared variable between synchronization points, without holding any common locks and with at least one thread modifying the variable. The order of these accesses is nondeterministic. The thread reading the value might get the old value or the updated one, or some other erroneous value if the update requires more than one store operation. This usually leads to indeterministic behavior, with the program producing different results from run to run.

Consider the following `for`-loop:

```
for (i=0; i<n-1; i++)
   a[i] = a[i] + b[i];
```

The iterations of this loop are independent. The order in which they are executed does not affect the result. If, for example, we were to run the loop backwards, the results would be the same. What about the following loop, then?

```
for (i=0; i<n-1; i++)
   a[i] = a[i+1] + b[i];
```

The only change is that we now use `a[i+i]` to update `a[i]`. This is called a *loop-carried dependence*: the loop iterations are dependent on each other. This minor change in the indexing destroys the parallelism. As written, the above loop can no longer be executed in parallel. The explanation is the following. When we update `a[i]`, we read the *old* value of `a[i+1]`. In the next iteration, `a[i+1]` is then updated. Of course, this is a small change to the loop, but it is not a minor change in the algorithm at all.

If we do go ahead and execute the second loop in parallel, different threads will simultaneously execute the statement `a[i] = a[i+1] + b[i]` for different values of `i`. Thus there arises the distinct possibility that for some value of `i`, the thread responsible for executing iteration `i+1` does so *before* iteration `i` is executed. At this point we have an error in our program. When the statement is executed for iteration `i`, the *new* value of `a[i+1]` is read, leading to an incorrect result. Unfortunately, there is no easy way to detect that this has occurred. This is an example of a data race condition introduced by the inappropriate parallelization of a loop.

Generally speaking, whether a data race condition affects a program's numerical results depends on various factors:

- Load on the system. The relative timing between the threads matters.

- Input data set. This might, for instance, lead to some load imbalance that affects the speed with which individual threads reach the incorrectly parallelized code.

- Number of threads used. In some cases the problem shows up only for a specific number of threads.

Therefore, a bug caused by a data race condition leads to nondeterministic behavior.[1] A bug clearly exists in the parallel application, but one might not notice it during the test phase or even in production mode, for example because the number of threads used has been such that the problem was not exposed. Changing the number of threads or some other aspect of its execution could cause the bug to (re)surface.

To demonstrate the typical behavior of a data race condition, we have executed the second loop above in parallel, and observe the impact of its deliberate bug. We use integer values for vectors a and b. Our measure of correctness is the checksum of the relevant values of a, defined as $checksum \equiv \sum_{i=0}^{n-2} a_i$. The correct result is printed together with the actual value, computed after vector a is updated in the parallel loop. The program has been executed using 1, 2, 4, 32, and 48 threads. These runs are performed four times each to see whether the error surfaces. We have set n to a value of 64. The results are listed in Figure 7.1. The second column gives the number of threads used. Column four contains the value of the checksum that is computed after the parallel loop. The last column has the correct value of the checksum. Note that we used the *same* binary program for all these runs. To change the number of threads, we modified the value for the OMP_NUM_THREADS environment variable only.

As to be expected, the single thread results are correct. Surprisingly, the results on two threads are all correct, too. On four threads, the results are wrong in three out of the four cases. Two of the incorrect results are the same. For 32 and 48 threads none of the results are correct, and they are always different. This unpredictable runtime behavior is typical for a data race condition.

At the OpenMP level, data race conditions could also be introduced as the result of missing `private` clauses, missing `critical` regions, or incorrectly applied `nowait` clauses. Because of the lack of a barrier, the `master` construct can also introduce a data race if not used carefully. Other potential sources of data race conditions are the SAVE and DATA statements in Fortran and static or extern in C. Throughout this chapter, examples of these kinds of error are given.

---

[1] A data race also implies that false sharing occurs, possibly degrading performance. See also Section 5.5.2 on page 153.

```
threads:   1 checksum   1953 correct value   1953
threads:   1 checksum   1953 correct value   1953
threads:   1 checksum   1953 correct value   1953
threads:   1 checksum   1953 correct value   1953

threads:   2 checksum   1953 correct value   1953
threads:   2 checksum   1953 correct value   1953
threads:   2 checksum   1953 correct value   1953
threads:   2 checksum   1953 correct value   1953

threads:   4 checksum   1905 correct value   1953
threads:   4 checksum   1905 correct value   1953
threads:   4 checksum   1953 correct value   1953
threads:   4 checksum   1937 correct value   1953

threads:  32 checksum   1525 correct value   1953
threads:  32 checksum   1473 correct value   1953
threads:  32 checksum   1489 correct value   1953
threads:  32 checksum   1513 correct value   1953

threads:  48 checksum    936 correct value   1953
threads:  48 checksum   1007 correct value   1953
threads:  48 checksum    887 correct value   1953
threads:  48 checksum    822 correct value   1953
```

Figure 7.1: **Output from a loop with a data race condition** - On a single thread the results are always correct, as is to be expected. Even on two threads the results are correct. Using four threads or more, the results are wrong, except in the third run. This demonstrates the non-deterministic behavior of this kind of code.

7.2.2 Default Data-Sharing Attributes

We think it is good practice (although arguably a matter of personal preference and style) to explicitly specify the data-sharing attributes of variables and not rely on the default data-sharing attribute. Doing so reduces the possibility of errors. Moreover, for good performance, it is often best to minimize sharing of variables (see also Sections 5.5.2 and 5.5.3).

Probably the most important rule to watch out for is that, in many cases, variables are shared by default. This is illustrated in Figure 7.2. The variable Xshared is shared by default. If multiple threads execute the parallel region, they all try to simultaneously write a different value into the same variable `Xshared`. This is an example of a data race.

```
#pragma omp parallel
{
  int Xlocal  = omp_get_thread_num();
  Xshared = omp_get_thread_num(); /*-- Data race --*/

  printf("Xlocal = %d Xshared = %d\n",Xlocal,Xshared);

} /*-- End of parallel region --*/
```

Figure 7.2: **Example of implied sharing** – By default, variable `Xshared` is shared. The assignment to `Xshared` causes a data race: if multiple threads are used, they simultaneously store a different value in the same variable.

Errors like this can easily sneak in. The code example in Figure 7.3 shows a data race condition introduced by the fact that variable `x` is shared by default, rather than having been explicitly declared `private`.

```
void compute(int n)
{
  int    i;
  double h, x, sum;

  h = 1.0/(double) n;
  sum = 0.0;
#pragma omp for reduction(+:sum) shared(h)
  for (i=1; i <= n; i++) {
      x = h * ((double)i - 0.5);
      sum += (1.0 / (1.0 + x*x));
  }
  pi = h * sum;
}
```

Figure 7.3: **Data Race Condition due to missing private declaration** – The variables i and x are not explicitly declared as private. Variable i is implicitly declared to be private according to the OpenMP default data-sharing rules. Variable x is shared by default. It is written to by multiple threads, leading to a race condition.

In the example in Figure 7.4, multiple threads update elements of the shared
data structure `material`. In order to ensure deterministic results, the update loop
over `i` in the parallel region should be enclosed by a critical region.

```
    integer ind (1:numt)
    ....
    allocate (material(1:numt), istat)
    do i = 1, numt
       material(i) = 0.
       material(i)%x = val1
    end do
       ...
!$OMP PARALLEL DO DEFAULT(PRIVATE) SHARED(material,plq,ind, numt)
    do n = 1, numt
       mid = ind(i)
       qm = material(mid)%x * plq(n)
       do i = 1, 4
          material(mid)%x = material(mid)%x + qm * px(i)
       end do
    end do
!$OMP END PARALLEL DO
```

Figure 7.4: **Data race condition due to missing** `critical` **region** – The value
of the private variable `mid` could be the same for different threads, causing the shared
variable `material(mid)%x` to be updated by multiple threads at the same time. In order
to guarantee predictable output, the i-loop in the parallel region must be enclosed by a
`critical` region.

A subtle distinction exists between Fortran and C/C++ regarding the default
data-sharing rules. In Fortran, loop index variables are private by default. In C,
the index variables of the parallel `for`-loop are private by default, but this does
not extend to the index variables of loops at a deeper nesting level. An example is
shown in Figure 7.5. Loop variable `j` is shared by default, resulting in undefined
runtime behavior. It is another example of a data race.

The error is easy to avoid through an explicit `private` clause for the loop variables, or by using a local variable instead. For example loop variable `k` is private
by default if used as follows: `for (int k=0; ...)`.

Our recommendation to be specific on the data-sharing attributes is also language
dependent. Fortran has more need of this approach than does C/C++. The main

```
int i, j;
#pragma omp parallel for
for (i=0; i<n; i++)
    for (j=0; j<m; j++) {
        a[i][j] = compute(i,j);
    }
```

Figure 7.5: **Example of a loop variable that is implicitly shared** – Loop variable i is private by default, but this is not the case for j: it is shared by default. This results in undefined runtime behavior.

reason is that in Fortran, variables cannot be declared locally in a code block, such as a loop.

7.2.3 Values of Private Variables

One of the most important decisions to be made when developing a shared memory parallel program is what data should be shared between threads and what should be local to a thread.

Whenever each thread requires its own "local" copy of a variable in a calculation, this variable needs to be listed in a `private` clause.

One can avoid errors that result from not adding variables to the `private` clause. The key is to use the `default(none)` clause, thereby forcing all data sharing attributes to be specified explicitly rather than by relying on defaults. Additionally, one should keep in mind two points:

- The value of the private copy is uninitialized on entry to the parallel region.

- The value of the original variable is undefined on exit from the parallel region.[2]

An example of using an uninitialized private variable is given in Figure 7.6. The programmer uses variable b without realizing that it does not have an initial value within the parallel loop, despite the fact it has a value prior to the loop. As a result, the variable is undefined and can take any value. If the intent is to initialize b with the value it had before the parallel region, then the `firstprivate` clause achieves exactly this. Alternatively, it can be made `shared`, since it is not modified in the parallel loop. There is also a problem with variables a and b, both of which are undefined after the parallel loop. The `lastprivate` clause is a convenient

---

[2]This will probably not be true in OpenMP 3.0.

feature to make the last value of a private list item available after the parallel region terminates, so this problem can easily be avoided as well. As explained in Section 4.5.3 the interpretation of "last" depends on the construct. There is also a (modest) performance penalty when using this construct. A correct version of this code is shown in Figure 7.7.

```
void main ()
{
    . . . . . . . . . . . .
    #pragma omp parallel for private(i,a,b)
    for (i=0; i<n; i++)
    {
          b++;
          a = b+i;
    } /*-- End of parallel for --*/
    c = a + b;
    . . . . . . . . . . . .
}
```

Figure 7.6: **Incorrect use of the private clause** – This code has two problems. First, variable b is used but not initialized within the parallel loop. Second, variables a and b should not be used after the parallel loop. The values after the parallel loop are undefined and therefore implementation dependent.

7.2.4   Problems with the Master Construct

Whenever a piece of work within a parallel region needs to be performed by only one thread, either the **single** or the **master** construct can be used. For many tasks involving reading, writing or general control, the **master** construct is the natural choice. Unfortunately, the **master** construct does not have an implied barrier. Figure 7.8 shows a simple, but erroneous, example of its use. Not only is there no synchronization, but there is also no guaranteed flushing of any modified data upon completion of this construct (see also Section 7.3.1). As a result, a potential problem arises if data is read in, initialized, or updated in this construct and subsequently used by other threads. For correct results, a barrier *must* be inserted before any accesses to the variables modified in the master construct. In many cases, the simplest solution is to use the **single** construct, because it implies a **barrier** at the end of the construct.

```
void main ()
{
    .............
    #pragma omp parallel for private(i), firstprivate(b) \
            lastprivate(a,b)
    for (i=0; i<n; i++)
    {
        b++;
        a = b+i;
    } /*-- End of parallel for --*/
    c = a + b;
    .............
}
```

Figure 7.7: **Corrected version using** firstprivate **and** lastprivate **variables** – This is the correct version of the code in Figure 7.6.

```
#include <stdio.h>
#include <stdlib.h>

void main()
{
    int Xinit, Xlocal;

    #pragma omp parallel shared(Xinit) private(Xlocal)
    {
        #pragma omp master
        {Xinit = 10;}

        Xlocal = Xinit; /*-- Xinit might not be available yet --*/

    } /*-- End of parallel region --*/
}
```

Figure 7.8: **Incorrect use of the** master **construct** – This code fragment implicitly assumes that variable Xinit is available to the threads after initialization. This is incorrect. The master thread might not have executed the assignment when another thread reaches it, or the variable might not have been flushed to memory.

7.2.5 Assumptions about Work Scheduling

Earlier we saw (for example, in Section 5.4.1) that the `nowait` clause can help to
increase performance by removing unnecessary barriers at the end of work-sharing
constructs for example. In such a case, however, care must be taken not to rely
on assumptions about which thread executes which loop iterations. An example
of such an incorrect assumption is shown in Figure 7.9. If the loop bound `n` is
not a multiple of the number of threads, then, according to the OpenMP 2.5 specifications, there are several compliant algorithms for distributing the remaining
iterations. As of OpenMP 2.5 there is no requirement that the same algorithm has
to be used in different loops. A compiler may choose to employ different strategies
for dealing with remainder iterations in order to take advantage of memory align-
ment. Therefore, the second loop in Fig. 7.9 might read values of array `b` that have
not yet been written to in the first loop. This action, however, results in a data
race condition.

```
#pragma omp parallel
{
    #pragma omp for schedule(static) nowait
        for (i=0; i<n; i++)
            b[i] = (a[i] + a[i-1]) / 2.0;
    #pragma omp for schedule(static) nowait
        for (i=0; i<n; i++)
            z[i] = sqrt(b[i]);
}
```

Figure 7.9: **Example of incorrect assumptions about work scheduling in
the OpenMP 2.5 specifications** – The `nowait` clause might potentially introduce a
data race condition, even with static work scheduling, if `n` is not a multiple of the number
of threads.

7.2.6 Invalid Nesting of Directives

In many programs it may seem natural to further subdivide the work that has
been handed out to the threads in a team. For example, if a number of different
`sections` have been defined, one or more of them might contain enough work for
multiple threads. Indeed, the computation can be further distributed in this way.
Before doing so, however, the programmer must take care to create a new team of
threads to carry out this work. The way to do so is to introduce a new parallel

region. A common cause of error is to nest work-sharing directives in a program, without providing a new parallel region. An example of such incorrect use is given in Figure 7.10.[3]

```
#pragma omp parallel shared(n,a,b)
  {
    #pragma omp for
    for (int i=0; i<n; i++)
    {
        a[i] = i + 1;
        #pragma omp for // WRONG - Needs a new parallel region
        for (int j=0; j<n; j++)
            b[i][j] = a[i];
    }
  } /*-- End of parallel region --*/
```

Figure 7.10: **Example of incorrectly nested directives** – Nested parallelism is implemented at the level of parallel regions, not work-sharing constructs, as erroneously attempted in this code fragment.

```
  #pragma omp parallel shared(n,a,b)
  {
    #pragma omp for
    for (int i=0; i<n; i++)
    {
        a[i] = i + 1;
        #pragma omp parallel for // Okay - This is a parallel region
        for (int j=0; j<n; j++)
            b[i][j] = a[i];
    }
  } /*-- End of parallel region --*/
```

Figure 7.11: **Example of correctly nested directives** – This is correct use of nested parallelism. This code fragment has two nested parallel regions.

However, nested work-sharing constructs without nested parallel regions cannot work. The threads in the current team have already been assigned their portion of the work by the existing work-sharing directive, and no idle threads are waiting

---

[3]Compilers will probably flag this kind of incorrect use and issue a warning.

for more work. The new parallel region must supply the new threads. The correct code is shown in Figure 7.11.

This kind of error may also inadvertently occur if orphan directives are used.

There are other ways in which invalid nesting of directives can lead to unexpected program behavior. The following are examples of the erroneous use of directives:

- A `barrier` is in a work-sharing sharing construct, a `critical` section, or a `master` construct.

- A `master` construct is within a work-sharing construct.

- An `ordered` directive is within a `critical` section.

- The `barrier` is not executed by all threads in the team.

Another example of an error in the use of a `barrier` is illustrated in the code fragment in Figure 7.12. According to the OpenMP 2.5 specifications, one of the restrictions on the `barrier` is as follows: "Each barrier region must be encountered by all threads in a team, or none at all" (Section 2.7.3 in [2]). This rule is violated in the code fragment shown here.

```
#pragma omp parallel // Incorrect use of the barrier
{
   if ( omp_get_thread_num() == 0 )
   {
         .....
      #pragma omp barrier
   }
   else
   {
         .....
      #pragma omp barrier
   }
} /*-- End of parallel region --*/
```

Figure 7.12: **Illegal use of the** `barrier` – The `barrier` is not encountered by all threads in the team, and therefore this is an illegal OpenMP program. The runtime behavior is undefined.

The example in Figure 7.12 could have an interesting side effect. The pragma translates to a function call that implements the barrier functionality. An optimizing compiler might potentially detect that in this case the barrier function can be called unconditionally, effectively executing the following code fragment.

```
if ( omp_get_thread_num() == 0 )
{ ..... }
else
{ ..... }
#pragma omp barrier
```

This use of the barrier no longer violates the specifications. The question is, of course, whether a compiler is able to perform this transformation. This would require it to be able to analyze and transform parallel code, an area of active research.

Another illegal use of a barrier in a work-sharing construct is demonstrated in the example in Figure 7.22 in Section 7.3.5 on page 269. This is erroneous because all threads in the team must encounter the barrier.

7.2.7   Subtle Errors in the Use of Directives

Errors in the directives can have subtle undesired effects. Section 3.1 describes the OpenMP directive syntax and cautions that not all errors in the directives are detected at compile time. In the example in Figure 7.13, the continuation line with the private declaration of variables i and cl contains an extra exclamation mark. As a result, the compiler no longer recognizes this as an OpenMP directives, and the private clause is ignored. Following the default data-sharing rules in OpenMP, loop variable i is private. This is exactly what was intended, but by virtue of these rules variable cl is shared, thereby introducing a data race. This error is caught by the compiler if the default(none) clause is used.

In C, curly brackets are used to define a parallel region that spans more than a single statement. If these brackets are not placed correctly or are left out entirely, unexpected runtime behavior may occur, ranging from a reduced speedup to an incorrect result. The code fragment in Figure 7.14 illustrates such a situation. In the first parallel region, both functions work1 and work2 are executed in parallel, but in the second parallel region, only function work1 is.

7.2.8   Hidden Side Effects, or the Need for Thread Safety

Using libraries can potentially introduce side effects if they are not *thread-safe*. The terminology *thread-safe* refers to the situation that, in a multithreaded program, the

```
      subroutine dot(n, a, b, c)
      implicit none

      integer(kind=4):: n
      real   (kind=8):: a(1:n), b(1:n), c, cl
      integer       :: i
!$OMP PARALLEL SHARED(n,a,b,c)
!!$OMP& PRIVATE(i,cl)
!$OMP DO
      do i = 1, n
         cl = cl + b(i)*a(i)
      end do
!$OMP END DO
!$OMP CRITICAL
      c = c + cl
!$OMP END CRITICAL
!$OMP END PARALLEL
      return
      end
```

Figure 7.13: **Example of an error in the OpenMP directive** – The continuation contains an extra exclamation mark. As a result the compiler ignores the private clause. Loop variable i is private by default, as intended, but variable cl is shared. This introduces a data race. If the default(none) clause is used, the compiler catches this kind of error.

```
main()
{
#pragma omp parallel
   {
      work1(); /*-- Executed in parallel --*/
      work2(); /*-- Executed in parallel --*/
   }

#pragma omp parallel
   work1(); /*-- Executed in parallel  --*/
   work2(); /*-- Executed sequentially --*/
}
```

Figure 7.14: **Example of the impact of curly brackets on parallel execution** – It is very likely an error was made in the definition of the second parallel region: function work2 is executed by the master thread only.

same functions and the same resources may be accessed concurrently by multiple flows of control. The use of global data is not thread-safe. For example, library routines for multithreaded programs that make use of global data must be written such that shared data is protected from concurrent writes.

The code in Figure 7.15 shows a global variable being incremented every time a library routine is executed. If the library is called from within a parallel region, multiple threads may try to access variable `icount` concurrently. Because the increment `++` is not an atomic operation, it can be interrupted before completion. This constitutes a data race condition and might yield indeterministic results, as discussed in Section 7.2.1. In order to make the routine thread-safe, access to variable `icount` has to be protected by a lock, an **atomic** construct or a critical section.

```
int icount;

void lib_func()
{
  icount++;
  do_lib_work();
}

main ()
{
   #pragma omp parallel
   {
     lib_func();
   } /*-- End of parallel region -- */
}
```

Figure 7.15: **Example of a function call that is not thread-safe** – The library keeps track of how often its routines are called by incrementing a global counter. If executed by multiple threads within a parallel region, all threads read and modify the shared counter variable, leading to a race condition.

Library routines written in Fortran should be built such that all local data is allocated on the stack for thread-safety. This could be a problem in cases where the SAVE statement is used. Originally introduced for sequential processing, the SAVE statement has an unpleasant side effect in a parallel context.

According to Section 2.8.1.2 in the OpenMP 2.5 specifications [2], a local variable that is used in a SAVE statement changes from private to shared. If multiple threads update such a variable, the risk of a data race arises.

An example of this kind of use can be found in the linear algebra library package LAPACK [13].[4] A number of its auxiliary library routines contain SAVE statements on some or all of the variables. An example is routine dlamch, which is called to determine double precision machine parameters. A number of variables are listed in a SAVE statement, for example to indicate the first usage of the routine to perform certain initializations. A code snippet is provided in Figure 7.16.

```
DOUBLE PRECISION FUNCTION DLAMCH( CMACH )
*       .. Local Scalars ..
LOGICAL   FIRST
*       .. Save statements ..
SAVE                FIRST
*       .. Data statements ..
DATA                FIRST / .TRUE. /
*       ..
...
IF( FIRST ) THEN
   FIRST = .FALSE.
   CALL DLAMC2( BETA, IT, LRND, EPS, IMIN, RMIN, IMAX, RMAX )
   ...
ENDIF
```

Figure 7.16: **Example of a Fortran library call that is not thread-safe** – The library routine performs certain initializations the first time it is called. When it is called from within a **parallel** region, access to variable FIRST has to be protected to avoid data race conditions.

One possibility to make such a routine thread-safe is to serialize access to the shared data. Most vendors provide thread-safe implementations of important libraries, such as LAPACK. It is good practice, however, to check the documentation when in doubt.

Another source of hidden side effects is shared class objects and methods in C++. When class objects with methods defined on them are used as shared variables within OpenMP parallel regions, race conditions can result. An example is shown in Figure 7.17. In order to make the code thread-safe, the invocation of the method

---

[4]The Fortran source code can be downloaded at [14].

should be enclosed in a critical region, or the update of the shared variable within the method should be enclosed by a critical region.

```
class anInt {
    public:
        int x;
        anInt(int i = 0){ x = i; };
        void addInt (int y){ x = x + y; }
    };
    main()
    {
        anInt a(10);
        #pragma omp parallel
        {
            a.addInt(5);
        }
    }
```

Figure 7.17: **Example of unsafe use of a shared C++ object** – When executed on 2 threads, the expected result is 20. However, data race conditions may yield indeterministic results.

7.3 Deeper Trouble: More Subtle Problems

Classifying bugs is risky, but the ones discussed next are probably harder to find than those presented so far. The reason is that their occurrence depends on a combination of factors. The bug manifests itself only if a set of conditions is met.

7.3.1 Memory Consistency Problems

Various memory models have been proposed for shared-memory parallel programming. What they regulate is, from the viewpoint of the programmer, the point at which new values of shared data (are guaranteed to) become available to those threads that did not perform the update. They therefore dictate when the updating thread must write its new values back to memory or otherwise invalidate other copies of data, and enable their update. The reason for the potential difference is clear: data may initially be in the local memory only (registers or cache). They should also regulate the order in which updates should be performed, if there is one. One possible model is called *sequential consistency*. This is based on our intuitive notion of what happens on a uniprocessor system and requires that the values of shared data be available just as they would be in some sequential execution of the code. Lamport [105] has defined this as follows:

"A multiprocessor system is sequentially consistent if the result of any execution is the same as if the operations of all the processsors were executed in some sequential order, and the operations of each individual processor appear in this sequence in the order specified by its program."

A sequentially consistent model of memory requires that values of shared data be uniformly consistent among the executing threads. In other words, if one thread creates a new value and this value is immediately used in a subsequent statement, then the thread that executes this second statement must make use of the new value. This is good news for the programmer, who does not need to worry about coordinating access to data, but it is bad news for the performance of the resulting program. It would require a memory update after each operation that modifies a shared variable and, potentially, before each use of a shared variable. This might well negate the performance benefit offered by shared-memory machines. Because it is hard to write efficient programs in this way, OpenMP does not provide a sequentially consistent memory model.

Many other shared-memory consistency models have been proposed. The choices are collectively known as relaxed consistency models. The good point about such models is that they make it easier for the system to provide high performance; the bad point is that they make programming harder. The programmer has to consider when data will be available and, if this is not sufficient for the purposes of a code, explicitly introduce language features to enforce availability of data, such as synchronizing the actions of two or more threads. The more flexible the memory model, the more freedom given to the compiler to reorder operations, but the more effort potentially required from the programmer.

OpenMP has attempted to balance the ease of programming with the need to provide adequate levels of performance. It defines points in the program at which data in shared memory must be made current and at which each thread must make its modifications available to all other threads. The threads do not need to update data in any specific order. And, as long as there are no data race conditions, there should be no impact on the resulting values. Issues of consistency most commonly arise in OpenMP is when a barrier is executed. It does not matter whether this was explicitly programmed or implied by another construct.

One can explicitly require that memory be made consistent by inserting a flush directive (see also Section 4.9.2 on page 114) into the code. If this style of programming is employed, however, the programmer must determine the points at which memory needs to be made consistent and then insert any necessary operations to enforce such consistency. These points are ordered with respect to one another in the code—with the exception of flush operations that have disjoint sets of variables to be flushed. Many consider the explicit `flush` directive in OpenMP to be too low level, and we recommend either avoiding explicit use of `flush` or exercising great care when using it. Indeed, the goal for OpenMP is to take care of such situations behind the scenes, for example with the implied flush on a barrier.

On very large machines, new values of shared data might be transferred to other threads through messages. Potentially, one message might be transmitted faster than another one (perhaps because it is very small), and the messages may arrive out of order. Even in such cases, the original order of memory updates must be preserved if there is any overlap in the memory locations being modified.

Note that the OpenMP model is distinct from any hardware realization of consistency. Different machines have different ways of enforcing memory consistency: they may write blocks of data back to main memory and require a replacement of that block in any other caches that store it, or they may transfer data between different caches directly. Such differences need not bother the programmer. However, the cost of this operation may well be of interest: the more expensive it is on a given machine, the more one will want to avoid having too many points in the program requiring consistency, and the higher the pay-off for privatizing data. Thus OpenMP provides the portability and the ability to reason about correctness without the need to know how an architecture implements consistency, but it does not necessarily provide full performance portability (although the vendors make every attempt to do so). For those who wish to pursue this topic further, an excellent discussion of memory consistency models for shared-memory machines is given in [6].

So where is the problem? The memory consistency model adopted by OpenMP implies that each thread has its own *temporary view* of the values of shared data between explicit or implicit barrier synchronization points. If shared variables are accessed between these points, care has to be taken to keep the temporary memory view of the threads consistent. Making false assumptions about the behavior of OpenMP programs in this respect is another potential source of error.

A common misconception is that cache coherence is sufficient to avoid data races. The aspect overlooked is the memory consistency model. Cache coherence is a protocol to ensure cache lines are correctly updated, but it does *not* specify when and in what order the results are written back to memory. That is the responsibility of the memory consistency model. If a relaxed model is used, for example, there is no guarantee that the write operation of a thread has finished before another thread performs a read operation on the same address in memory. As a result, the value of the variable stored at that address gets corrupted, leading to a data race.

7.3.2 Erroneous Assumptions about Memory Consistency

We illustrate the kind of problem that may arise if a programmer is not aware of the memory consistency model adopted by OpenMP. In the example the programmer has chosen to use shared variables to implement point-to-point thread synchronization. Such a case is discussed in Section 4.9.2. The source in Figure 7.18 is the naive, and incorrect, version. The correct code fragment is shown in Figure 4.93 on page 117.

Implementing the communication as shown most likely yields unexpected behavior during execution. This program is intended to work as follows: each thread, except the master, requires data from the thread with a thread id (stored in variable iam) that is one less than its own. We call this the "predecessor" thread. Similarly, we use the notion of a "successor" thread to indicate the thread that will use the new data the current thread produces. The issue is that threads need some way to determine whether the data from the predecessor thread is available. They also need to be able to signal their successor thread that updated data is available.

The programmer has arranged for threads to use the values of array isync to allow threads to synchronize with their "neighbors" to accomplish this. Array element isync(iam) contains the status of the thread with identifier iam, isync(iam-1) thus contains the status of its predecessor. The check of the values of isync is carried out in a while-loop.

The problem with this strategy is that the values are most likely read from registers. An optimizing compiler tries hard to optimize the use of registers and minimize the number of load and store instructions. Cache coherence triggers on a store instruction. As a result, if a value is changed in a register but is not stored back, the modification is not propagated up the memory chain.

In this case changes in array isync are not necessarily seen by all threads. Unfortunately, the changes in this array are used to notify the other threads of a change in the situation. Therefore, they keep waiting indefinitely, causing the program to hang.[5]

To ensure that values are written back to shared memory and the updated values are used in a subsequent read, flush directives need to be inserted in the while-loops, as well as after the write to an element of array isync.

---

[5]This is a special case of a deadlock and is referred to as *livelock*.

```
!$OMP PARALLEL PRIVATE(K, IAM, NT)
C
C  Initialize a synchronization array isync
C
   iam = OMP_GET_THREAD_NUM()
   nt = OMP_GET_NUM_THREADS()
   isync(iam) = 0
C
C Wait for predecessor thread to finish
C
!$OMP BARRIER
   do k = 2,nz
      if (iam .gt. 0) then
         do while(isync(iam-1) .eq. 0)
         end do
         isync(iam-1) = 0
      end if
C
!$OMP DO SCHEDULE(STATIC)
      do j = 2, ny
         do i = 2, nx
            v(i,j,k) = v(i,j,k) + v(i-1,j,k)
                     + v(i,j-1,k) + v(i,j,k-1)
            ...
         end do
      end do
!$OMP END DO NOWAIT
C
C Signal the availability of data to the successor thread
C
      if (iam .lt. nt) then
         do while (isync(iam) .eq. 1)
         end do
         isync (iam) = 1
      end if
   end do
```

Figure 7.18: **Point-to-point thread communication implemented using shared variables** – This code contains several memory consistency problems. The correct code fragment is shown in Figure 4.93 on page 117.

Doing so is not sufficient, however. Array v is modified. Values are obtained from a predecessor thread and passed to a successor thread. To guarantee that the correct values (just updated by the predecessor) are read before the next computation starts, and to make newly updated values available to the successor thread, one should flush array v before and after the update.

We note that the LU code of the NAS Parallel Benchmark Version 3.2 (and prior versions) does not contain an explicit flush of array v, but only of array isync. Nevertheless, the code has executed correctly on most hardware platforms for many years. The reason is most likely that the compiler ignores the explicit list in the flush, thereby forcing *all* shared variables to be synchronized in memory. In the example, array v is also synchronized, and the bug in the program is not exposed.

7.3.3   Incorrect Use of Flush

The flush directive is provided to enable the programmer to ensure that values of certain (or all) shared data are available between synchronization points if that is required by the algorithm. Unfortunately, incorrect assumptions about the use of this directive may result in another kind of programming error. Here is why (we discuss this again briefly in Chapter 8). First, the compiler is at liberty to reorder the instructions in a program, as long as this does not lead to an incorrect program. In the case of flush operations, this means the compiler is permitted to move a flush operation relative to code that does not affect the variable(s) being flushed: "Implementations must not reorder the code for a memory operation for a given variable, or the code for a flush operation for the variable, with respect to a flush operation that refers to the same variable." (Section 1.4.2 in [2]).

To see the impact, consider the program fragment in Figure 7.19. The code shown implements the following idea. Thread 0 initializes some data, represented by the assignment to newdata. Variable signal is used to notify the other thread(s) the data has been modified. The change in signal is monitored by the other thread(s). Once this variable has been modified, the thread reads the updated value of newdata and uses it for some local computations, symbolized by the assignment to localdata. This type of communication resembles the example discussed in Section 7.3.2.

Here, however, the programmer has added flush directives to ensure that the changes in variables newdata and signal are made visible to the other thread(s).

The problem is that nothing prevents the compiler from moving the flush operations with respect to each other. In particular, the compiler may move the two

```
      signal = 0
!$omp parallel default(none) shared(signal,newdata) &
!$omp private(TID,localdata)
      TID = omp_get_thread_num()
      if (TID == 0 ) then
         newdata = 10
!$omp flush(newdata)
         signal = 1
!$omp flush(signal)
       else
!$omp flush(signal)
         do while (signal == 0 )
!$omp flush(signal)
         end do
!$omp flush(newdata)
         localdata = newdata
      end if
!$omp end parallel
```

Figure 7.19: **Wrong use of the `flush` directive to synchronize access to shared data** – Wrong assumptions about the reordering the compiler is permitted to perform lead a programmer to incorrectly assume that all threads but 0 do not access variable `newdata` until after it has been updated by thread 0.

statements that update and flush `signal` in thread 0's code so that they are executed *before* the update and flush of `newdata`. If that happens, the other thread may pick up the change in `signal` *before* `newdata` has been modified.

The situation is remedied in Figure 7.20, where `signal` has been added to the list of items in the first `flush` directive for the code executed by thread 0. The addition ensures that this flush operation may not be moved relative to the surrounding code for this thread, thereby preventing the compiler from changing `signal` before `newdata` has been modified. Variable `signal` now indeed acts as a flag that the update has occurred.

Whether the compiler is allowed to move instructions past a flush has been a matter of some debate. Not only did some implementations previously not do so: even the examples in earlier releases of the OpenMP specification assumed that this did not occur. The OpenMP 2.5 specification clarifies this matter. As a result, compilers may move operations that do not affect the flushed variables relative to the flush operations.

```
      signal = 0
!$omp parallel default(none) shared(signal,newdata) &
!$omp private(TID,localdata)
      TID = omp_get_thread_num()
      if (TID == 0 ) then
         newdata = 10
!$omp flush(newdata,signal)
         signal = 1
!$omp flush(signal)
      else
!$omp flush(signal)
         do while (signal == 0 )
!$omp flush(signal)
         end do
!$omp flush(newdata)
         localdata = newdata
      end if
!$omp end parallel
```

Figure 7.20: **Correct use of the flush directive to synchronize access to shared data** – The only change is the addition of variable **signal** to the first **flush** directive, preventing the compiler from interchanging the order of the two assignments in thread 0. Now it is guaranteed that **newdata** is modified before **signal** changes value.

7.3.4   A Well-Masked Data Race

The example discussed next is derived from a real application. The program sporadically crashed. The error turned out to be a data race, but a very subtle one. It is similar to the example given in Figure 7.16, but it turns out to have an additional problem. The code is listed in Figure 7.21.

This program uses a classical Fortran method to minimize the amount of work performed. Apparently, variable a needs to be initialized only once. This is implemented in lines 16–19. An initial value of .true. is given to variable **first**. The first time the if-statement on line 16 is encountered, the condition is true, and statements 17–18 are executed. Variable a is initialized to 10 on line 17. By setting **first** to .false. *and* by preserving this value through the **SAVE** attribute (line 13), the next time this code block is encountered it will be skipped.

This subroutine is executed in parallel (lines 3–5), thereby introducing two bugs. It might happen that the compiler interchanges the assignments to a (line 17) and

```
1          program main
2
3   !$OMP PARALLEL DEFAULT(NONE) PRIVATE(...)
4             call mysubroutine()
5   !$OMP END PARALLEL
6
7          stop
8          end
9          subroutine mysubroutine()
10         implicit none
11         real, save   :: a
12         real         :: a_inv
13         logical, save:: first
14         data first /.true./
15
16         if ( first ) then
17            a = 10.0
18            first = .false.
19         end if
20         a_inv = 1.0/a
21
22         return
23         end
```

Figure 7.21: **A very subtle data race** – If the compiler interchanges the assignments to variables a and first and the thread executing the if-statement first is context switched out before a is initialized, the other thread(s) use an undefined value for a in the division. This example is not far fetched: it is derived from a real application.

first (line 18). If so, the following scenario may occur. The thread that encounters the if-statement first changes first to .false.; but *before* the assignment a = 10.0 is executed, it is context switched out by the operating system. Another thread that encounters the if-statement shortly afterwards skips it because first is already set to .false. by the other thread. As a result, it uses an uninitialized value of a in the division on line 20. If the system pre-initializes variables to zero, a division by zero results, causing the second thread to crash. A second bug is the implied assumption that both variables a and first are immediately visible after a thread has changed their value. As discussed in Section 7.3.2, this is incorrect.

Fortunately, both bugs can be fixed with one change in the source.

```
!$omp single
      if ( first ) then
          a = 10.0
          first = .false.
      end if
!$omp end single
```

By enclosing lines 16–19 in a `single` work-sharing construct, the work is still performed only once, but the implied barrier ensures that no thread uses variable `a`
before it is initialized, and the implied `flush` ensures that both `a` and `first` are
made visible to the other threads executing the subroutine.

7.3.5   Deadlock Situations

The term *deadlock* refers to the runtime situation that occurs when a thread is
waiting for a resource that is never going to be available. Various actions can create
a deadlock situation in an OpenMP program. A typical example is to incorrectly
insert a barrier that is not encountered by all threads of the same team. This is
demonstrated in the code fragment in Figure 7.22.

The explicit barrier in function `work1` is erroneous, causing the program to deadlock if more than one thread is used. In such a case, one thread of the team executes
this barrier. After another thread has executed function `work2`, it waits in the implied barrier at the end of the `parallel sections` construct. The other thread
does not arrive at this point, however, because it waits in the explicit barrier. As
a result, no progress is made.

Not surprisingly, erroneous use of the OpenMP locking routines can also lead to
deadlocks. A common error is to forget to release a lock, as demonstrated in the
source fragment in Figure 7.23.

As long as function `work1` does not return a nonzero value of variable `ierr`, all is
well. If it does so, however, lock variable `lck` is not released. If the thread executing
this code section acquired the lock first, the thread executing the second section
waits forever for the lock to become available. Hence, the program hangs.

Another type of error made relatively frequently is to incorrectly nest locks. The
code fragment in Figure 7.24 shows such an example.

If the thread executing the first section acquires lock variable `lck1` first *and* the
thread executing the second section acquires `lck2` before the other thread does so,
a deadlock situation has occurred.

```
work1()
{
  /*-- Some work performed here --*/

  #pragma omp barrier
}

work2()
{
  /*-- Some work performed here --*/
}

main()
{
 #pragma omp parallel sections
   {
   #pragma omp section
     work1();
   #pragma omp section
     work2();
   }
 }
```

Figure 7.22: **Example of a deadlock situation** – If executed by two threads, this program never finishes. The thread executing work1 waits forever in the explicit barrier. The other thread waits in vain for the other thread to arrive in the implicit barrier at the end of the **parallel sections** construct.

The first thread waits for lck2 to become available, but meanwhile the second thread waits for the first thread to release lck1. As a result, no progress will be made, and the program hangs.

```
      call OMP_INIT_LOCK(lck)
!$OMP PARALLEL SECTIONS
!$OMP SECTION
      call OMP_SET_LOCK(lck)
        call work1(ierr)
        if ( ierr .eq. 0) then
           call OMP_UNSET_LOCK(lck)
        else
           print*,"Error"
        endif
!$OMP SECTION
      call OMP_SET_LOCK(lck)
        call work2()
      call OMP_UNSET_LOCK(lck)
!$OMP END PARALLEL SECTIONS
```

Figure 7.23: **Example of a deadlock situation due to an unreleased lock** –
If `lck` is set in the first section and routine `work1` returns a nonzero value for `ierr`, the
lock is not released. The thread executing the second section may then wait forever.

```
      call OMP_INIT_LOCK(lck1)
      call OMP_INIT_LOCK(lck2)
!$OMP PARALLEL SECTIONS
!$OMP SECTION
      call OMP_SET_LOCK(lck1)
        call OMP_SET_LOCK(lck2)
          call work1(lck1,lck2)
        call OMP_UNSET_LOCK(lck2)
      call OMP_UNSET_LOCK(lck1)
!$OMP SECTION
      call OMP_SET_LOCK(lck2)
        call OMP_SET_LOCK(lck1)
          call work2 (lck1,lck2)
        call OMP_UNSET_LOCK(lck1)
      call OMP_UNSET_LOCK(lck2)
!$OMP END PARALLEL SECTIONS
```

Figure 7.24: **Example of a possible deadlock situation caused by incorrectly nested locks** – A deadlock arises if `lck1` is set by one thread and `lck2` by
another.

7.4 Debugging OpenMP Codes

Even if all the rules on safe programming have been taken into account, an occasional error may still sneak its way into the code. How should one proceed when an OpenMP code crashes, produces wrong results, or exhibits nondeterministic behavior? This section presents techniques for debugging OpenMP programs.

We strongly encourage the use of tools (e.g., a debugger or a tool to detect data races) for debugging. This topic is covered in Section 7.4.3. Before using these tools, however, one may want to spend some time isolating the nature and (possibly) location of the bug. Especially if the bug is expected to be hard to find, tools can help speed troubleshooting. For example, if the error has its roots in a data race, a standard debugger may not be very helpful because the behavior is not reproducible.

7.4.1 Verification of the Sequential Version

Parallel execution of the code may expose problems in the sequential code that have not manifested themselves earlier. Therefore, the first step when debugging a parallel application should always be the verification of the sequential version.

To this end, the programmer should disable the OpenMP directives. To do so requires no source code changes, but it does require a recompilation without the option that enables the recognition of the directives. If care has been taken when inserting OpenMP runtime functions (through the appropriate use of `#ifdef`, for example), this is probably a relatively simple effort.

Next, the programmer should verify the behavior of this version under the following circumstances:

- Run the source code through syntax checking tools such as *lint* or *ftncheck*.

- Enable as many compiler diagnostic options as possible.

- Try different compiler optimizations. The bug might already show up for a specific set of options applied to the sequential version.

- For Fortran, check what happens if all local data is allocated on the stack (in case this is not the default).

- Run the loops parallelized with OpenMP backwards. If the result is wrong, the loop(s) cannot be executed in parallel. The reverse is not true. If the result is okay, it does not automatically mean the loop can be parallelized.

7.4.2   Verification of the Parallel Code

Once the correctness of the sequential version has been established beyond a reasonable doubt, it is time to move on to investigate the specific effects of the OpenMP parallelization.

At this point it can be helpful to consider the nature of the runtime behavior. For example, if the bug is predictable and does not seem to depend on the number of threads used, a data race is less likely.

It is also good practice to find the lowest compiler optimization level for which the bug occurs. As explained in Section 7.3.3 for example, a bug in the use of the `flush` directive may show up only if the compiler reorders the statements.

The program should be compiled such that all local data is allocated on the stack. For most compilers this task is done automatically when enabling the OpenMP directives, but one should check the documentation to be sure.

Several scenarios are now worth exploring:

- Run the OpenMP version of the program on one thread. If the error shows up then, there is most likely a basic error in the code.

- Selectively enable/disable OpenMP directives to zoom in on the part of the program where the error originates.

- If a data race is suspected:

  - Use as many threads as possible. The higher the number of threads, the more likely the data race is to show up.

  - `DATA` and `SAVE` statements in Fortran programs and the use of `static` and external variables in C/C++ might cause data to be shared unintentionally.

- Check that the libraries used are thread-safe in case one or more of their functions are called within a parallel region.

7.4.3   How Can Tools Help?

Some compilers support a static analysis of the OpenMP program. This goes beyond syntax checks, which all compilers report on. At compile time, an attempt is made to detect possible runtime errors, for example, a shared variable being updated simultaneously by multiple threads.

Such an analysis may not be sufficient, though. While the code may have no semantic errors, the program may still fail to deliver the correct results. In this case the use of a *dynamic* tool is the logical next step.

Some compilers and OpenMP libraries also support runtime checking for erroneous usages of OpenMP directives. This feature can be very helpful for detecting errors caused by the incorrect use of an orphan directive, such as a barrier within a work-sharing construct. This might not be detectable by a compiler's static analysis since it requires insight into the program's runtime behavior.

For example, the Sun Studio C and Fortran compilers [129] support an option to statically detect errors in an OpenMP program. The OpenMP runtime library supports the SUNW_MP_WARN environment variable. If set to TRUE, runtime error checking in the library is activated. We strongly recommend checking the documentation of the specific OpenMP compiler one uses for features like this. They can save a significant amount of time and frustration.

But, even this may not be sufficient to find the cause of the error. Two tools to consider next are a debugger and a data race detection tool.

Most people are familiar with a debugger. This is a tool that allows the user to stop a running program more or less at any point in the source and, at that point, examine and also change variables to do a "what if" kind of analysis. Some debuggers also support a "watch" function to monitor the change of a specific memory location.

A number of debuggers also provide support for multithreaded programs. Examples are the Berkeley UNIX^{TM} symbolic debugger dbx, DDT^{TM} by Allinea [166], the public domain GNU gdb [151] debugger, Sun Studio [129] from Sun Microsystems, and TotalView^{TM} by Etnus [54].

The major additional feature of a parallel debugger is that the typical debugging functionality is supported at the thread level. A thread can be stopped, its variables and call stack can be examined, and so forth. In addition, there are commands that perform a specific action (like setting a breakpoint) for all threads. We now give some examples of this type of functionality.

Setting breakpoints and stepping through parallel regions – The majority of OpenMP compilers apply *procedure outlining* when transforming parallel regions. This is discussed in more detail in Section 8.3.4. In a nutshell, the compiler pushes the body of a parallel region into a function.

Outlining offers advantages to the compiler implementation. The downside is that it may not be possible to step into or out of a parallel region. A standard method for dealing with this is to let the user set the breakpoint inside the parallel region. Once the breakpoint is hit, single stepping can proceed, as shown in Figure 7.25. This example is based on the Sun Studio dbx debugger applied to the code shown in Figure 7.6 when run on 4 threads.

```
(dbx) stop at 8
dbx: Line "trouble1.c":8 maps to 2 addresses in "trouble1.o"
dbx: Line "trouble1.c":8 maps to 2 addresses in "trouble1.o"
dbx: Line "trouble1.c":8 maps to 2 addresses in "trouble1.o"
dbx: Line "trouble1.c":8 maps to 2 addresses in "trouble1.o"
(dbx) run
5 100 100
Before parallel loop: a = 5, b = 100
t@1 (l@1) stopped in _$d1A7.main at line 8 in file "trouble1.c"
    8             for (i=0; i<n; i++)
t@2 (l@2) stopped in _$d1A7.main at line 8 in file "trouble1.c"
    8             for (i=0; i<n; i++)
t@3 (l@3) stopped in _$d1A7.main at line 8 in file "trouble1.c"
    8             for (i=0; i<n; i++)
t@4 (l@4) stopped in _$d1A7.main at line 8 in file "trouble1.c"
    8             for (i=0; i<n; i++)
```

Figure 7.25: **Example of setting a breakpoint within a parallel region** – The code from Figure 7.6 is run on 4 threads using the dbx debugger. A breakpoint is set at the entry to the parallel region. All four threads stop execution at this point.

When single stepping through a parallel region in an OpenMP program, the execution sequence may not correspond to the actual source code sequence because the compiler has transformed the code. This is similar to single stepping through sequential code optimized by the compiler.

State examination of individual threads – When execution is stopped in a parallel region, the stack trace usually contains the outlined routine plus several OpenMP runtime library calls[6]. The stack trace may look different for master and worker threads, as shown in Figure 7.26.

Most OpenMP compilers transform private variables to local variables within the outlined routine(s). Shared variables are typically kept in the master thread's original stack frame and their address passed to the outlined routine as parameters. The stack context of the master thread can thus be used to display the variables for the worker threads.

---

[6]The library function names differ across the various OpenMP implementations.

```
(dbx) threads
*  t@1  breakpoint          in  _$d1A7.main()
   t@2  slave_startup_function() running    in  run_my_job()
*  t@3  slave_startup_function() breakpoint in  _$d1A7.main()
*> t@4  slave_startup_function() breakpoint in  _$d1A7.main()
where
current thread: t@4
=>[1] _$d1A7.main() (line ~8) in "trouble1.c"
  [2] run_job_invoke_mfunc_once
  [3] run_my_job
  [4] slave_startup_function

(dbx) thread t@1
t@1 stopped in _$d1A7.main at line 8 in file "trouble1.c"
     8           for (i=0; i<n; i++)
(dbx) where
current thread: t@1
=>[1] _$d1A7.main() at 0x108c4 (line ~8) "trouble1.c"
  [2] run_job_invoke_mfunc_once
  [3] __mt_MasterFunction_rtc_
  [4] main() at 0x10884 (line ~7) in "trouble1.c"
```

Figure 7.26: **Call stacks for a worker and master thread** – When stopped at the breakpoint as shown in Figure 7.25, the stack trace for thread 4 contains different runtime library calls than the stack trace for thread 1, the master thread.

Besides symbolic debuggers, tools are available that help with the detection of race conditions. Examples of commercially available tools are Assure, developed by KAI [167], the Sun Studio Thread Analyzer [130], and the Intel[TM] Thread Checker [87]. These tools trace memory references during a program execution in order to detect possible data races. There is definitely a need for this kind of assistance. Recall that a data race is almost always not reproducible, so that a traditional debugger will not be of much help in finding them.

These tools have several drawbacks, however. The execution time increases noticeably, the memory requirements go up, and "false positives" may be reported.

A false positive is like a false alarm. On closer inspection (by the user) the data race is not real. Examples are user-defined synchronizations, where the tool may not be able to analyze the use of low-level primitives such as compare-and-swap (CAS) functions. Another reason for a false positive to be generated could be a memory block that is reused by various threads. There might not be any simultaneous use of the same memory location, but the tool may not be able to detect this.

These restrictions should not, however, keep one from using this kind of tool on a regular basis. Data races are easy to create, but hard to find—especially by hand.

7.5   Wrap-Up

Compared to sequential program development, writing a correct OpenMP shared memory parallel application introduces a new set of important considerations for the programmer.

Choosing which variables to make private, firstprivate, lastprivate, or shared presents major difficulties for the novice that can lead to serious problems if done incorrectly. While there are default rules for scoping these data-sharing attributes, caution must be observed because it is easy to make a mistake.

Data races must be avoided because they result in silent data corruption, and—to make matters worse—they may not be easily reproducible. Moreover, while OpenMP has several constructs to avoid a data race, knowing how to use them is critical.

Another factor to take into consideration is the memory consistency model. For performance reasons, OpenMP uses a relaxed consistency model. The downside of this choice is that the programmer needs to be aware of the place(s) in an application where a consistent view of memory is required. OpenMP provides well-chosen defaults, however, and in general there is little or no need to worry about this. In situations calling for explicit control, the `flush` directive provides a means with which the programmer can enforce a consistent view of memory.

Tools for OpenMP are a must. An often-overlooked fact is that compilers may provide support to help detect errors in an early phase of program development. Their static (compile time) as well as dynamic runtime support can greatly help in finding and fixing bugs. But sometimes, more extensive help is needed. Several parallel debuggers with support for OpenMP are available. Such tools can be very useful and save a lot of time in finding bugs. However, debuggers are not capable of finding data races. A tool to detect these should be part of the standard software development toolkit of any OpenMP programmer.

8 Under the Hood: How OpenMP Really Works

The way OpenMP is implemented has a nontrivial influence on program performance. Here we give a brief overview of the translation process, and describe some of the ways in which its actions may have an impact on the behavior of an application.

8.1 Introduction

An OpenMP compiler must recognize OpenMP directives and library routines in a program and translate both them and the source code into an explicitly multithreaded object program. In such a program, threads are started and assigned computations; individual threads may be put to sleep at different times during a program's execution, or they may busy-wait until they are permitted to continue on their work. The job of the application developer is to specify the parallelization strategy; the role of the compiler and its runtime system is to implement that strategy. The OpenMP specification was designed to make this translation to a multithreaded program a very reasonable proposition. As a result, many commercial compilers for Fortran and C/C++ have been extended to handle it.

Since an OpenMP implementation is typically built on top of a conventional compiler for Fortran, C, or C++, the programmer must usually specify an OpenMP option, or flag, on the command line to get it to recognize and translate OpenMP constructs. Otherwise, OpenMP directives, and any other code that is to be compiled by an OpenMP compiler only, will be ignored and sequential object code generated, as indicated in Figure 8.1. (In Section 3.4 of Chapter 3 we explained how the programmer can ensure that correct code results from the sequential translation.) Since there is no standard way to invoke the OpenMP translation, the application developer should consult a compiler manual for details of the option (or options) that must be given for this translation to be applied.

Most often, the target of the translation is an object program that invokes the compiler's runtime library routines to manage threads and assign work to them. Some research compilers [157, 29, 134] instead translate OpenMP code to a modified source code that makes calls to Pthreads or another thread-based library. For example, the Omni compiler [1] has two versions of its runtime library, one based on Pthreads and another based on Solaris threads. The Nanos OpenMP compiler's NthLib [120] runtime library is based on QuickThreads [99], The output can then be compiled by a native compiler that does not need to know about OpenMP. Several research compilers are freely available in addition to the vendor products (see the cOMPunity website [40] for more information).

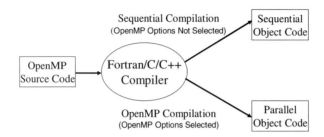

Figure 8.1: **Sequential or parallel compilation** – Depending on the compiler options chosen, a program may be translated into a single-threaded (sequential) or a multithreaded executable.

Most aspects of an OpenMP program's performance can be reasonably well understood with a little background information on the target platform, some understanding of the way the memory hierarchy works, and basic knowledge of the compilation process. However, experience with a given implementation and architecture will help in fine-tuning a program for a specific machine.

In the following section, we give a brief overview of standard compilation techniques for sequential programming languages such as Fortran and C and then explain how this process is adjusted to enable the translation of OpenMP constructs. Since each compiler is different, we can give here only a general idea of how programs are processed. To illustrate our description, we give examples that show how the OpenUH compiler [112] carries out some of the major translation steps. OpenUH is based upon the Open64 compiler infrastructure [5] and uses a runtime library derived from one developed for another Open64-based compiler [39].

8.2   The Basics of Compilation

Compilers are large, complex software packages that convert legal programs written in a given computer programming language into the corresponding object code for a particular target machine. Many compilers are able to handle multiple source languages and may also generate code for more than one target architecture. Since this process is complex, it is broken into several phases. During the first phase, known as the *front end*, an application program is read in, checked for correctness, and converted into an intermediate format suitable for further processing. The format is specific to a given compiler.

During the remainder of the compilation, often simply referred to as the *back end*, although in reality it consists of multiple steps, the intermediate code is successively modified and simplified until it is converted into machine code for the target platform. Initially, the intermediate code might look a lot like the original source. Eventually, however, it will most likely contain many simple instructions that represent operations that can be performed by the machine.

8.2.1   Optimizing the Code

Compilers have a whole range of optimizations that they may attempt to use on a program in order to reduce the overall amount of work required at run time, reduce the amount of memory needed, or make better use of the memory hierarchy. For instance, they may look for opportunities to move operations to positions where they are less frequently executed, attempt to find variables that have constant values, and detect and eliminate code that does not contribute to the result of the program. Recently, compilers have also begun to incorporate techniques to reduce the power consumed during execution of a program. Most optimizations are "local"; that is, they rely on the compiler's knowledge of short instruction sequences, of code in a loop nest or in a procedure; but some optimizations may involve analyzing and improving sequences of instructions that span multiple procedures in a program. The best opportunities for program improvement are typically to be found in loops and in long sequences of operations that do not contain branches or procedure calls. In Chapter 5 we showed how loop nests can be optimized (see Section 5.2.3). The compiler may apply the loop transformations shown to rearrange computations if it expects that they will improve performance and it can prove such transformations are safe. Such an approach may work well if the compiler is able to understand the pattern of accesses to arrays. If it cannot, however, the programmer should consider applying them manually.

Unfortunately, the optimization process can be hampered if important information is missing. For instance, if the compiler does not know what memory location a pointer will be associated with at run time, then it may not know whether a variable is modified by an instruction. Such a situation might prevent all manner of program improvements. For example, the code in Figure 8.2 updates p twice. However, the second update cannot be removed without more information. If the compiler is able to determine that procedure somestuff does not change the value of either a or p, and if it is also able to find out the memory locations to which q might point, then such an action might be possible. It is generally worthwhile to use any language features (for instance C's restrict or a noalias pragma) or compiler flags that give the compiler more information on how how pointers are being used.

```
int main(void)
{
    int a, p ;
    extern int *q ;
    . . .
    p = a + 5 ;
    somestuff ( a, &p ) ;
    *q = 13 ;
    p = a + 5 ;  /* can this be eliminated? */
    . . .
    return 0;
}
```

Figure 8.2: **A difficult program to optimize** – This program contains two identical assignment statements. However, the compiler cannot simply eliminate the second one, since it does not know whether q may point to a or p. Moreover, the function somestuff may potentially modify their values.

As part of the optimization process, the compiler may change the order of instructions in the code. There are several reasons for this action. The reordering might help reduce the amount of time spent waiting for data to be fetched from main memory or higher levels of cache, or it might lead to a more efficient use of functional units in the hardware. It could also help reduce the number of cycles wasted when setting up and executing branches in a program. As a result, the programmer cannot rely on operations being performed in precisely the order they were specified in a program (see Figure 8.3).

8.2.2   Setting Up Storage for the Program's Data

As part of its work, the compiler must also allocate space in memory for a program's code and data. It usually stores global and persistent data (for example, common blocks and SAVE variables in Fortran, static or file scope variables in C) in a specific region of memory. These objects require storage for the duration of the program's execution. It is often possible to ensure that they are accessed with great efficiency.

Variables that are dynamically allocated at run time will be stored in a different area, called the heap. Since these objects may potentially be allocated and deallocated at different times during a run, heap memory can become fragmented. Thus, some extra support is usually needed to manage it.

```
p = a * b ;
q = x * y ;
r = p + q ; /* the value of q is not yet available */
s = p + a ;
go to next ;
nop
```

may be reordered thus:

```
p = a * b ;
q = x * y ;
s = p + a ;
go to next ;
r = p + q ; /* this has been moved to fill the delay slot */
```

Figure 8.3: **Compiler reordering of instructions** – The simplified instructions generated by the compiler may be reordered to improve performance. Here, reordering reduces the likelihood that the code must wait for the value of q to become available and fills the delay slot while the branch is being set up with useful work.

Local variables (automatic variables in C, for example) are stored in another area of memory, using a special structure called the stack. New data is always put (or pushed) onto the top of a stack; and when data is removed, or "popped," it is invariably the most recent data.[1] It turns out that the stack is a convenient place to store information needed to execute an instance of a procedure in the program. At any given time, the stack will hold data, including local variables, for each instance of each procedure that has begun and has not yet terminated. The values of arguments to procedures (or their addresses) and of results are also saved on the stack. Especially in the case of C, the space needed to hold arguments could be quite large. When a procedure terminates, its data is simply popped off the top of the stack.

In Figure 8.4, we see one way in which a compiler might organize data in memory. In addition to reserving space for the object code, there is a fixed area for static and global data. Both the stack and the heap require varying amounts of space during execution. The approach shown provides maximum flexibility because it allows each of them to grow (and shrink) over time. Many good books on compilers are available [8, 138, 41], to which the interested reader is referred for further details.

---

[1]This is like putting a book on top of or taking the topmost book off a pile of books on a desk.

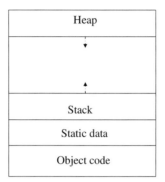

Figure 8.4: **Organizing data in memory** – This is one of several possible strategies for assigning memory to a program's objects.

8.3   OpenMP Translation

An OpenMP compiler must recognize, validate, and translate OpenMP directives according to their semantics in order to obtain the desired multithreaded object program. Of course, it must also compile the associated Fortran or C/C++ code. The process of replacing OpenMP constructs by explicitly multithreaded code and calls to runtime library routines is sometimes known as *lowering* them. The complexity of lowering is significantly reduced by the use of a compiler-specific runtime library. The library typically includes routines to start up threads, to help determine the work that each will perform, to pass this work to them, and to synchronize their actions. One of the design decisions that must be made by the compiler writer is to decide what functions to include in the runtime library. Its efficiency is critical because the object code typically makes many calls to its routines.

The overall structure of the OpenUH compiler is reproduced in Figure 8.5. It recognizes OpenMP constructs in its front ends as discussed in Section 8.3.1 and lowers OpenMP in two phases. The first of these is a preparatory phase called OMP_PRELOWER that standardizes its constructs, as described in Sections 8.3.2 and 8.3.3, and performs some semantic checks. The second phase, called LOWER_MP, performs the actual lowering. It carries out all of the other translations described in this section. OpenUH generates object code for Itanium systems. For other systems, it generates explicitly multithreaded code, where the parallelism is encapsulated in its library routines. Once this output has been translated by a native compiler, it will run in parallel on other platforms too.

Since each compiler has its own strategy for handling OpenMP, we can only give

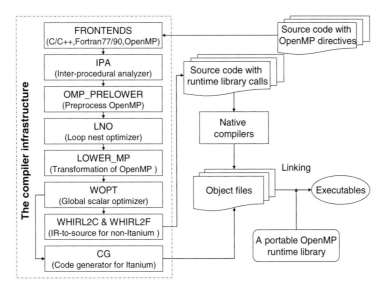

Figure 8.5: **Structure of the OpenUH compiler** – The compiler recognizes OpenMP constructs in the front end.

an idea of how it is translated here. Providing a good implementation of some features can be tricky. The compiler and runtime library writers must be careful to ensure that they do not introduce any performance problems that were not present in the original program (for example, this means that the runtime library routines should not suffer from false sharing as described in Section 5.5.2, or require large amounts of synchronization). Another challenge is to make sure that the translation does not unduly interfere with the rest of the compiler's work. The implementation strategy may depend in part on the hardware and on the operating system routines available for manipulating threads.

8.3.1   Front-End Extensions

The first step in processing OpenMP occurs in the front end. A Fortran, C, or C++ front end is extended to recognize OpenMP constructs and represent them in the compiler's intermediate code. For this to work, the compiler must be able to figure out the start and end of the region of code that an OpenMP construct (such as a parallel region or work-sharing directive) applies to. The OpenMP syntax makes it quite easy to do so. The front end will most likely also look for a variety of syntactic errors in the use of OpenMP, such as incorrect nesting of constructs, illegal constructs or directives (with the proper sentinel), or attempts to use a directive in a context where it is not permitted. For example, it should detect the improper use of a `for` directive with a loop nest that does not conform to OpenMP restrictions (see Section 4.4.1), and it may detect a barrier that has been incorrectly inserted into a `critical` region.

Some compilers will output warnings and OpenMP-specific error messages if constructs are used inappropriately or if it thinks there may be a problem. For example, the OpenUH compiler generated warnings for the code in Figure 8.6, where the developer had wrongly assumed that the iteration variables for loops inside a parallel loop were private by default. This is not the case for C or C++ programs. The code was easily fixed, as shown in Figure 8.7. This compiler also outputs messages if, for example, it detects reductions that have not been declared via the corresponding clause by the programmer.

```
#pragma omp for private(ii,jj,kk,if,kf,nf)
    for ( m = 0; m <  m_blk(myproc); m++ )
      for ( k = 0; k < nk(m); k++ )  //  k is shared by default
        for ( j = 0; j < nj(m); j++) // j is shared by default
          for ( i = 0; i < ni(m); i++) // i is shared by default
            {
            res_xi[i,j,k,m] = 0.0
            . . . . . . . . . . .
            }
```

Figure 8.6: **Error in data sharing attributes** – The programmer has assumed that the inner loop variables are private by default. Since this is a common error, the compiler emitted a warning that made the programmer aware of the default attribute.

8.3.2 Normalization of OpenMP Constructs

Compilers will usually put some program constructs into a standard format and eliminate others altogether by converting them into a different, but equivalent, construct. The purpose of this normalization is to simplify subsequent work. OpenMP work-sharing constructs are typically put into a standard form in this way. In particular, parallel `sections` are often converted into parallel `for` or `do` loops where each section corresponds to one loop iteration. The loop's schedule will be set up so that each thread executes a single iteration at a time, either statically or dynamically; the latter is beneficial if there are more sections than threads and they

```
#pragma omp for private(i, j, k, ii,jj,kk,if,kf,nf)
   for ( m = 0; m < m_blk(myproc); m++ )
      for ( k = 0; k < nk(m); k++ )  //  k is now private
         for ( j = 0; j < nj(m); j++) // j is now private
            for ( i = 0; i < ni(m); i++) // i is now private
               {
               res_xi[i,j,k,m] = 0.0
               ..........
               }
```

Figure 8.7: **Data-sharing attributes fixed** – The programmer has corrected the error in the above loop by declaring i, j, and k to be private. As explained in Chapter 3, it is safer to explicitly declare these attributes for all variables.

may take different amounts of time to complete. A **single** work-sharing directive might even be turned into a loop with just one iteration and a dynamic schedule. Directives that combine the creation of a parallel region and a work-sharing construct (such as **parallel for**) might be split into the two constructs at this stage, possibly in a specialized way to avoid multiple barriers.

```
#pragma omp sections
{
  #pragma omp section
   section1();
  #pragma omp section
   section2();
  #pragma omp section
   section3();
}
```

Figure 8.8: **Program with a parallel sections construct** – This might be converted into a parallel loop by the compiler to simplify its work.

The **sections** construct shown in Figure 8.8 is translated by the OpenUH compiler into a parallel loop with one iteration per section of the original code. In order to accomplish this, a switch has been inserted that branches to the code for a given section. The loop's iterations will be shared among the threads in chunks of one iteration. This means that each thread will be given one of the original sections to compute until there are no more remaining sections.

```
#pragma omp for
for(omp_section0 =0; omp_section0 <= 2; omp_section0 ++ )
 {
 switch( omp_section0)      {
      case 0 : section1(); break;
      case 1 : section2();  break;
      case 2 : section3();  break;
      }
 }
```

Figure 8.9: **Normalized sections construct** – The `sections` construct of Fig. 8.8 has been converted into a parallel loop by the compiler for more convenient handling.

8.3.3   Translating Array Statements

Fortran 90 array statements are converted into equivalent Fortran loops before they are further compiled. Hence, any `workshare` constructs associated with them must be turned into work-sharing directives for those loops. In Figure 8.10, we show the conversion of a `workshare` construct that relies on the default schedule for parallel loops to assign work to threads. This must be done in a coordinated manner if the loop nests are to perform well. If the Fortran 90 version of a code does not provide the expected level of performance, the compiler may have been unable to do so efficiently. Unfortunately, this situation may require the user to rewrite some array statements as loops.

8.3.4   Translating Parallel Regions

At the start of a parallel region, threads must be created (or made available) and computation assigned to them. Most compilers arrange for threads to be created when the first parallel region is encountered, by inserting appropriate calls to the compiler's runtime library into the code; then they put all but the master thread to sleep when the parallel region ends. When a new parallel region is begun, the remaining threads are woken up, a process that is much faster than creating new threads.

Routines for starting up threads typically also pass their work to them in the form of a procedure. In order to support this, the compiler must turn the code lexically contained in a parallel region into a new procedure. It will then convert the parallel directive into a call to the appropriate runtime library routine and pass the new procedure as an argument. (If one uses an OpenMP-aware debugger, one might see

```
real a(n,n), b(n,n), c(n,n), d(n,n)
...
!$omp parallel
!$omp workshare
   a = b
   c = d
!$omp end workshare
!$omp end parallel
```

is converted, prior to any further translation, to

```
real a(n,n), b(n,n), c(n,n), d(n,n)
...
!$omp parallel
!$omp do
  do j = 1, n, 1
    do i = 1, n, 1
        a(i,j) = b(i,j)
    end do
  end do

$omp do
  do j = 1, n, 1
    do i = 1, n, 1
        c(i,j) = d(i,j)
    end do
  end do
!$omp end parallel
```

Figure 8.10: **Compiler conversion of OpenMP** workshare **directive to parallel loop directives** – This conversion is needed because array statements are converted to loop nests at an early stage of compilation.

this routine in its output. It might be identified by the procedure that contained it in the original program, and possibly a line number.) This process has come to be known as *outlining*, in an analogy to the inverse strategy named inlining, where a procedure call is replaced by the body of that call. The compiler will implement a barrier, usually by inserting an appropriate function in the runtime library, at the end of a parallel region.

Some work is needed to ensure that outlined procedures are able to access the data they need. Shared data that is local to the procedure containing the parallel construct has to be passed as an argument to the outlined procedure. All threads must be given the address of any such object, so that they may access the original data and not local copies. References to the shared data in the outlined code may need to be modified to take into account the fact that it is the address that has been passed in. Private data is easily translated, as such objects simply become local variables of the outlined routine.

```
int main(void)
{
   int a,b,c;
#pragma omp parallel private(c)
   do_something(a,b,c);
   return 0;
}
```

Figure 8.11: **Program with a parallel region** – This program contains a parallel region that performs some work encapsulated within a procedure.

We illustrate the creation of parallel regions by showing the strategy implemented in the freely available Omni compiler [1]. The code fragment in Figure 8.11 shows a program with a parallel region containing the procedure do_something. Variables a and b are shared between the threads that execute the parallel region, whereas c is private.

The translated program is displayed in Figure 8.12. The outlined routine that will be executed by each thread in the team comes first. The compiler has given it the name __ompc_func_0. It has an argument that is used to pass the addresses of the shared variables a and b to the procedure. As we have already stated, each thread must be able to directly access the shared objects so we cannot simply copy them in. Their addresses are unpacked and assigned to two pointers that enable access to b and a, respectively. Then, the function do_something is invoked. Its argument list has been modified to ensure that it accesses the shared variables a and b via their addresses. Since c is private, each thread will have its own local copy. Hence, we do not need to pass in an address in this case.

The second part of the code is the modified main program. It first retrieves the addresses of the shared data to construct the argument for the outlined routine. It is then ready to begin parallel execution. In order to accomplish this, the compiler has inserted a call to the runtime library routine _ompc_do_parallel. This routine will start up the default number of threads to execute the parallel code. It has two arguments: the outlined procedure and its argument. These are used to hand off the required computation to each thread. Note that the initial thread will also be given the outlined function to execute.

```
/* Outlined function has an extra argument for passing addresses*/
static void __ompc_func_0(void **__ompc_args){
     int *_pp_b, *_pp_a, _p_c;

/* need to dereference addresses to get shared variables a and b*/
_pp_b=(int *)(*__ompc_args);
_pp_a=(int *)(*(__ompc_args+1));

/*substitute accesses for all variables*/
do_something (*_pp_a,*_pp_b,_p_c);
}

int _ompc_main(void){
     int a,b,c;
     void *__ompc_argv[2];

/*wrap addresses of shared variables*/
*(__ompc_argv)=(void *)(&b);
*(__ompc_argv+1)=(void *)(&a);

/*OpenMP runtime call must pass the addresses of shared variables*/
_ompc_do_parallel(__ompc_func_0, __ompc_argv);
  . . .
}
```

Figure 8.12: **A parallel region is outlined** – A function has been created to encapsulate the work of the parallel region. It will be passed to all the threads in the team for execution. Threads are created to execute the parallel region by a call to a runtime library routine that also passes the threads their work.

This approach incurs a few overheads that are not present in the corresponding sequential program: they include the cost of setting up the new procedure, and of passing local variables to it. It may be slightly more expensive to access the shared objects. Moreover, some optimizations may suffer as a result of the need to pass addresses rather than values. An alternative strategy [173, 39] has been developed that uses a special technique that essentially allows a block of code to be passed to the threads for execution rather than outlining the parallel region. The benefit of this approach is that the local shared data can be directly accessed and the associated overheads are at least partly avoided.

If nested parallelism is disabled or not provided by the implementation, then a parallel region may be serialized. This might also occur if the application developer has used an `if` clause along with the `parallel` directive, and the clause evaluates to false at run time. If the compiler cannot determine whether a parallel region will be executed by more than one thread, or if both single-threaded and multithreaded execution may occur, then it might generate two different code versions to enable each case to be translated as efficiently as possible. If nested parallelism is not enabled, the compiler must also insert code to test whether the executable is already within a parallel region. If it is, both the parallel region construct and any work-sharing directives it contains will be ignored.

```
#pragma omp parallel
   printf("Hello,world!\n");
```

Figure 8.13: **Implementing potential serial execution** – If this parallel region may sometimes be inactive, the compiler must ensure that both parallel and sequential execution is possible.

We illustrate this situation by showing how the parallel region in Figure 8.13 may be handled if serial execution is possible. Runtime routines are extensively used in the translation performed by OpenUH (see Figure 8.14) when nested parallelism is disabled. The compiler has given the name `__ompregion_main1` to the outlined procedure because it is the first parallel region encountered in the main program. The main program invokes the routine `__ompc_in_parallel` to find out whether this is an attempt to start a parallel region from within a parallel portion of the code: if so, the function will return a value of `true` and the subsequent test will ensure that this region is inactive. Next the compiler checks whether additional threads can be created. If these functions confirm that parallel execution is possible, the condition in the `if` statement will hold, and the `ompc_do_parallel` runtime library routine will be called to implement the parallel directive. It will ensure that each of the threads is passed the procedure `ompregion_main1` for execution. Otherwise, the `else` branch will be taken and the original, sequential code executed. This translation strategy ensures that no unnecessary overheads are incurred when the sequential version is selected.

```
{
/* outlined function generated from parallel region  */
void __ompregion_main1(  )
 {
    printf("Hello,world!\n");
    return;
 }   /* end of __ompregion_main1 */
 ..
/* Implement multithreaded model, one level of parallelism only */
  __ompv_in_parallel = __ompc_in_parallel();
  __ompv_ok_to_fork = __ompc_can_fork();
  if(((__ompv_in_parallel == 0) && (__ompv_ok_to_fork == 1)))
  {
/* Parallel version: create multiple threads, execute in parallel */
    __ompc_do_parallel(__ompregion_main1);
  }
  else
  { /* Perform sequential version */
  printf("Hello,world!\n");
  }
}
```

Figure 8.14: **A parallel region that may be executed sequentially or in parallel** – This region will be executed sequentially if the program is already in a parallel region or if the system does not support the creation of additional threads.

8.3.5 Implementing Worksharing

If a parallel region has no work-sharing constructs, then each thread will perform all of its computation (possibly skipping parts that are explicitly assigned to a thread with a given `threadid`). Typically, however, the programmer will have inserted one or more work-sharing directives to assign portions of the calculation to each participating thread. Each such directive is separately translated by the compiler. At the end of a work-sharing construct, a barrier is also inserted to ensure that the threads wait for each other to complete. Since compilers typically convert other kinds of work-sharing directives to parallel loops, we focus exclusively on loops in the following.

The compiler evaluates the loop schedule in order to determine the strategy for assigning sets of iterations to individual threads. Each kind of schedule must be translated in a manner that allows a thread to compute its own iteration set or grab its share of the work.

For example, OpenUH has different strategies for handling static schedules without a chunk size, other static schedules, dynamic, guided, and runtime schedules (see Figure 8.15), as well as their `ordered` variants. The static schedule can be implemented by getting each thread to compute its own loop bounds. The loop header (bounds and stride) is modified to ensure that only the required iterations are carried out. When the static schedule comes with a chunk size, each thread may have several sets of iterations. Since the threads must compute bounds multiple times, the overheads are slightly higher. Dynamic and guided schedules require threads to fetch chunks of iterations at run time; in the latter case, the size of the chunk also decreases. As a result, a queue of available chunks must be maintained, and chunk sizes computed via a potentially expensive algorithm, so that the overheads are higher than for static schedules. However, if the loop iterations contain varying amounts of work, it may be worthwhile to use one of these schedules.

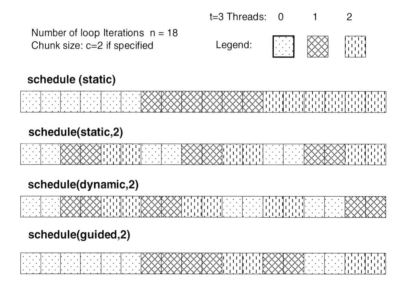

Figure 8.15: **Different kinds of loop schedules** – OpenUH has different strategies for handling static, dynamic, and guided schedules.

The programmer has not specified a schedule for the parallel loop given in Figure 8.16, so the compiler is free to choose one. In Figure 8.17 we indicate the code that will be generated by OpenUH. Like most other compilers, it uses a static

```
static double a[1000];
  int i;
#pragma omp for
  for (i=0;i<1000;i++)
   a[i]=(double)i/2.0;
```

Figure 8.16: **Loop with default schedule** – This loop nest will be translated using the compiler's implementation-dependent default schedule. Most often, this will be a static schedule with one chunk per thread.

schedule with one chunk of roughly equal size per thread in such situations. A typical strategy for computing the chunk size is

$$chunksize = \lceil loopiters/p \rceil , \qquad (8.1)$$

where *loopiters* is the total number of loop iterations and p is the number of threads. This formula computes the smallest integer greater than or equal to the expression. It ensures that all threads except possibly the last one will be assigned the same number, *chunksize*, of consecutive iterations. The last thread may receive fewer than the others. Occasionally, in fact, it may receive none at all. For example, if there are 27 iterations and 6 executing threads, then each except the last will receive 5 iterations. If there are 16 iterations and 5 executing threads, then the first 4 threads will perform 4 iterations, and the last will have none.

The code shown in Figure 8.17 will be executed by each thread in the current team. In the first statement, a thread retrieves its **threadid**. It next invokes the runtime library routine for this kind of scheduling. The routine will use the **threadid** and the loop bounds and stride to compute the set of iterations the thread must perform. Formula 8.2 shows how easy it is to determine the local lower bound for the case where the stride is 1, where *lowerbd* is the original lower bound of the loop and **mytid** is the thread's id.

$$mylower = lowerbd + chunksize * mytid \qquad (8.2)$$

Since there is just one chunk of iterations, the local bounds are immediately derived from these and the *chunksize*. The compiler has modified the loop header so that these values will be exploited. Similarly, the original loop variable i has been replaced by the new loop variable **myloci** wherever it occurs in the body of the loop. Once a thread has completed its share of the loop, it must potentially wait at a barrier for the remaining threads to complete. In order to achieve this, a call to the runtime library routine that implements a barrier synchronization is inserted after the loop body.

If a static schedule is chosen that may require a thread to execute multiple chunks, this process has to be slightly modified. In this case, when a thread has finished a chunk of iterations, it will test whether it has more work to do. If so, it will compute the bounds of its next chunk of iterations in a similar manner. The process is repeated until all of the chunks assigned to it have been completed.

```
mytid = __ompc_get_thread_num(); /* get threadid  */
   .  .  .  .
/*  invoke static scheduler  */
__ompc_static_init(mytid,  mylower, myupper,
                                       mystride );


/* execute loop body using assigned iteration space */
  for(myloci = mylower;
                  myloci<= myupper);myloci=myloci+1)
  {     a[myloci] = myloci * 2;
  }


__ompc_barrier(); /* Implicit barrier after worksharing  */
```

Figure 8.17: **Implementing static worksharing** – Here, the program has been modified so that each thread computes its schedule and then executes the appropriately modified loop. A barrier is entered at the end.

Sometimes, data created or used in a parallel loop is also accessed in the next parallel loop. Some of the corresponding values may be in the caches corresponding to different threads at the end of the first loop. With some care, it might be possible to assign work to threads in a manner that allows it to be reused.

8.3.6   Implementing Clauses on Worksharing Constructs

Some variations on the strategies introduced above are needed to implement the other clauses that may be appended to directives. It is particularly easy to implement the `nowait` clause. When it is specified at the end of a work-sharing directive, the only difference is that no code is generated for the barrier at the end.

We have already seen that shared variables in a parallel region are implemented by passing the address of the variable to the outlined procedure as an argument.

Private variables are even easier to support because they simply become local variables in the outlined routine: each thread automatically has its own copy. It is also fairly straightforward to implement `firstprivate`. If a parallel region has a `firstprivate` variable, then this private variable must be initialized using a value available prior to the parallel region. In order to achieve this, an additional argument containing this value might have to be passed to the outlined procedure. Each thread can then assign the value of that variable to the local copy of the private variable.

The translation of a `lastprivate` clause is a little more complex, because it may have to detect which value of the variable would be final in a sequential run. As noted in Section 4.5.3, the compiler will most likely have to insert code that will check for the "last" definition of the variable; this process may incur some overheads. Once this is done, this value may be assigned to a variable that is visible to the master thread.

```
static double a[1000], b[1000], k, m;
void update_a(void)
  {  int i;
#pragma omp parallel for firstprivate(k) \
        lastprivate(m)
   for (i=0;i<1000;i++) {
     m =   k * (double)i/2.0;
     a[i]= b[i] + m ;      }
  }
```

Figure 8.18: **Firstprivate and lastprivate variables** – Here, the `omp parallel for` directive in function `update_a` has two clauses, declaring k to be firstprivate and m to be lastprivate, respectively. Both of these require minor modifications to the basic translation strategy.

The parallel region in Figure 8.18 specifies that the private variable k is to be initialized with the value of the variable with the same name prior to the parallel region. Moreover, the value of m in the final iteration is required after the parallel region terminates and is therefore declared to be `lastprivate`. The corresponding code produced by the compiler is given in Figure 8.19. In this case, both k and m are static variables, which means that their values are visible to the code that will be executed by the team of threads. So here, no extra work is needed to pass the values to and from the parallel region.

```
/* outlined function generated from parallel region */
static void __ompdo_update_a1()
{
  double myloc_m, myloc_k; /* private copies of m, k */
  int mytid, mylower, myupper, myloc_i; /* private copy of i*/
  myloc_k = k; /* initialize local k with global value of k */

  mytid = __ompc_get_thread_num(); /* get threadid */
  __ompc_static_init(mytid, mylower, myupper ); /* scheduler */

  /* execute loop body using assigned iteration space */
  for(myloc_i =mylower; myloc_i <= myupper; myloc_i = myloc_i+1)
   {
     myloc_m = myloc_k*(double)myloc_i/2.0;
     a[myloc_i] = b[myloc_i] + myloc_m;
   }

  if(myloc_i > 999) /* pass the sequentially last value */
  m = myloc_m;
  __ompc_barrier(); /* Implicit barrier after worksharing */
  return;
} /* end of __ompdo_update_a1 */
```

Figure 8.19: **Implementing** `firstprivate` **and** `lastprivate` – Here, the generated outlined region has been modified to include private variables that will hold the threads' local copies of k and m. In order to implement the latter clause, it must also add code to identify the last value of m. Since m is static, the corresponding local value of myloc_m is simply assigned to it. Since k is also static, the `firstprivate` clause is implemented by a simple copy of its value to myloc_k.

Reductions are relatively common in technical computations. In order to implement them, the compiler creates and initializes a private variable as well as the shared result variable. The work of combining data according to the specified operation is then shared among the threads so that each of them independently computes a roughly equal portion of the result. The result value is created by accumulating the individual threads' partial results, for which an atomic update, critical region, or lock is required to ensure that their accesses to this memory location do not overlap. Reduction operations can be implemented in a number of different ways. They may potentially be handled very efficiently, possibly using fast hardware-specific atomic operations. We remind the programmer that, as a result, no assumptions can be made on the order in which updates are performed – and that the original order is also essentially arbitrary.

8.3.7 Dealing with Orphan Directives

OpenMP permits the use of work-sharing constructs and synchronization operations in a different procedure from the one in which the corresponding parallel region was created. This makes it easier for the application developer to create large parallel regions without unnecessary program modification. However, a procedure containing orphan directives may potentially be invoked from within multiple different parallel regions, as well as in a sequential part of the code, at run time (see the example in Figure 8.20). Consequently, the constructs may be active in some execution instances and ignored in others. The implementation must ensure that these cases are distinguished and dealt with appropriately.

```
static double a[1000], b[1000];
void update_a(void)
  { int i;
#pragma omp for
    for (i=0;i<1000;i++)
      a[i]= b[i] + (double)i/2.0;
  }

int main(void){
#pragma omp parallel
  { init_all();
    compute_b();
    update_a();
  }
}
```

Figure 8.20: **Orphan directives** – Here, the `omp for` directive in function `update_a` is an orphan directive. If this function is invoked from outside a parallel region, the `omp for` directive is ignored. Note that the use of orphan directives can help maximize the size of the parallel region.

In Figure 8.21, we show how this can be achieved. The compiler has inserted an instruction that tests whether or not it is being executed in parallel. If so, the code to implement the `for` directive is performed: each thread obtains its set of iterations and carries out its share of the work. If, however, the test shows that the instruction is in a sequential part of the code, the original loop is executed in full by the thread that encounters it. Since a routine that computes a thread's share of loop iterations should also work when only one thread is executing the loop, an alternative is to simply apply the same translation strategy for both sequential and parallel execution. This approach may have slightly higher overheads for the sequential case.

```
  .  .  .  .
  __ompv_in_parallel = __ompc_in_parallel();
  if( (__ompv_in_parallel == 1) )
  {
/* We are in parallel region: execute for loop in parallel */
 mytid = __ompc_get_thread_num(); /* get threadid  */
  /* next invoke static scheduler  */
  __ompc_static_init(mytid, STATIC,  mylower, myupper,
            mystride,);

/* execute loop body using assigned iteration space */
  for(myloci = mylower; myloci<= myupper ;myloci++ )
  {        a[myloci]= b[myloci] + (double)myloci/2.0;
  }
  __ompc_barrier(); /* Implicit BARRIER after worksharing  */
  }
  else
  { /* Perform sequential version */
   for (i=0;i<1000;i++)
     a[i]= b[i] + (double)i/2.0;
  }
```

Figure 8.21: **Implementation of orphan directive** – Here, we show how the omp for directive in function update_a has been translated by generating two versions of the code. If it is invoked from outside a parallel region, the omp for directive is ignored.

8.3.8 OpenMP Data Environment

OpenMP extends the set of data storage attributes of Fortran and C by introducing the concepts of shared and private data (as well as threadprivate, firstprivate, lastprivate, and reduction variables). In order to implement these attributes, an

OpenMP compiler must expand a sequential compiler's strategies for allocating data.

In Section 8.2.2, we discussed how a compiler sets up storage for the data of a (sequential) program. As part of this process, it uses a stack to hold the local data for different procedures while they are being executed. This does not suffice for an OpenMP program, since each thread can independently execute procedures in a parallel region. In other words, each thread in an OpenMP program will need a stack of its own. This stack is also the ideal place for it to save its own private data. Therefore, the compiler's strategy for allocating storage is modified as shown in Figure 8.22. The "main process stack" holds data for the initial thread.

Since local data in routines invoked within a parallel region are private by default, they are also stored on a thread's stack. Firstprivate and lastprivate variables are private variables for which a small amount of extra work is needed to initialize or to determine and transfer the final value, respectively. Thus they are also allocated on each thread's stack.

Note that each thread's stack has a fixed amount of space. If the programmer does not specify its size, the compiler will arrange for an implementation-dependent default amount of memory to be allocated per thread when they are started up. Since it may need to hold copies of a considerable amount of data including the private variables of all the procedures active at any given time, the stack can grow quickly and may exceed the space reserved for it. As a result, it may be necessary to increase the thread stacksize. The programmer should consult the documentation to find out how to do so.

Allocating memory on the heap is relatively expensive under OpenMP because care must be taken to ensure that two different threads do not simultaneously allocate the same space. Thus, this operation needs to be protected by a critical region. All threads must be made aware of any such allocations for shared data.

The values of threadprivate objects in an OpenMP program may persist across multiple parallel regions, so this data cannot be stored in the same place as other private variables. Some compilers implement this by reserving space for them right next to a thread's stack. Others put them on the heap, which is otherwise used to store dynamically allocated objects. Depending on its translation, the compiler may need to set up a data structure to hold the start address of threadprivate data for each thread: to access this data, a thread would then use its `threadid` and this structure to determine its location, incurring minor overheads.

OpenUH stores threadprivate data on the heap. In order to translate the code fragment illustrated in Figure 8.23, the compiler will declare an array of pointers to integers. There will be one pointer for each of the threads that executes the

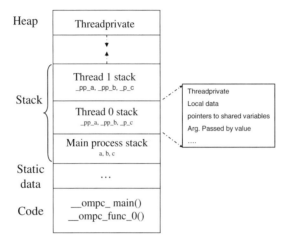

Figure 8.22: **Storing an OpenMP program's objects in memory** – Each thread has its own stack for storing its private data, including local data in procedures invoked from within parallel regions. We have indicated two places in which threadprivate data might be saved. The actual location is implementation-dependent. We indicate where objects from the program shown in Figure 8.11 will be stored.

parallel region. Inside the parallel region, memory will be dynamically allocated on the heap to store the integers pointed to by this array. Each thread will retrieve its own threadprivate variable via the corresponding pointer and its `threadid`. The address it computes is used thereafter in the code. In Figure 8.24, we give an excerpt from the translated code fragment. Recall that this construct requires that the number of threads used to execute parallel regions does not change for the duration of the program.

8.3.9   Do Idle Threads Sleep?

When threads are not working, perhaps because a parallel region has terminated or because there is an imbalance in the workload between different threads, they may need to wait. The waiting may be realized in two different ways: idle threads may busy-wait (or spin-wait) or they may be put to sleep (or be suspended). In the former case, the threads actively continue to check for new work. They will begin this work without delay when it is available. Unfortunately, however, busy-waiting threads also consume resources and may interfere with the work of other threads. The alternative strategy is to put threads to sleep. This removes the problem of

```
#include <omp.h>
static int sum0=0;
#pragma omp threadprivate (sum0)
int main()
{ int sum = 0;
  int i ;
  . . .
  for ( . . . )
#pragma omp parallel
   {
  sum0 = 0;
  #pragma omp for
    for ( i = 0; i <= 1000; i++)
       sum0 = sum0 + . . .
  #pragma omp critical
     sum = sum + sum0 ;
} /* end of parallel region */
```

Figure 8.23: **Threadprivate directive** – Here, each thread has its own copy of sum0, updated in a parallel region that is called several times. The values for sum0 from one execution of the parallel region will still be available when it is next started.

```
/* get address of threadprivate variable for current thread */
  myloc_ppthd_sum0 = thdprv_sum0 + mytid ;
/* use it as usual */
  * myloc_ppthd_sum0 = 0;
  __ompc_static_int( mytid, . . . . ) ;
  for (myloci = mylower ; myloci<= myupper ;myloci++)
     * myloc_ppthd_sum0 = * myloc_ppthd_sum0 +  . . . .
  __ompc_barrier();
  __ompc_critical ( ...) ;
     sum = *myloc_ppthd_sum0 + sum ;
  __ompc_end_critical ( ...) ;
```

Figure 8.24: **Translation of threadprivate directive** – In order to access and use its own persistent variable myloc_ppthd_sum0 in multiple parallel regions, an individual thread computes its address as an offset from the shared variable thdprv_sum0 here.

resource consumption by otherwise idle threads. However, they must be woken up and this introduces a delay before they do useful work.

The best choice may depend in part on the target platform and in part on the amount of time the threads are likely to spend waiting, which is hard for the compiler to determine. Some implementations will allow threads to busy-wait for a certain time period and then, if they are still idle, they will be put to sleep. Sometimes the user might have been able to provide a default behavior to influence this decision. Most systems provide some way for the application developer to specify whether an idle thread should be put to sleep.

8.3.10   Handling Synchronization Constructs

Many different constructs have been designed to enable thread synchronization. OpenMP provides a modest set of them. Generally the compiler can easily translate its implicit and explicit `barrier`, `atomic` and `flush` directives, since they normally have one or more equivalents in the OpenMP runtime library. Thus the compiler must simply select the desired routine and replace the directive by a call to it. Any further complexity involved is dealt with in the runtime system. For some synchronization constructs, there may be direct support in the hardware. Since the cost of different synchronization operations may vary significantly, it can be worthwhile to use microbenchmarks to evaluate their overheads ([30, 47]).

Most synchronization features can be implemented in a number of ways [15]. For instance, a straightforward way to implement a `barrier` is to use a variable as a barrier flag and have a shared counter that is initialized to reflect the number of threads in a team. When a thread reaches the barrier, it will decrement the counter atomically and wait until the counter is set to 0 by the last thread to arrive. Then the barrier flag is reset via an atomic update, and all threads can proceed. (How they are made aware of the update will depend on whether they are busy-waiting or have been suspended.) This process will deadlock if one or more threads does not encounter the barrier construct, which is, however, prohibited by the standard. Some systems provide hardware support for barriers.

The `flush` directive can usually be implemented by a single operation that commits variables to memory and fetches new values of data as required. The tricky part in dealing with this is deciding how it can be moved relative to other instructions during the instruction scheduling phase. We remind the reader that its location may move with respect to instructions that do not involve flushed data (see Chapter 7).

8.4   The OpenMP Runtime System

Most compilers have a runtime library that implements some standard operations (starting up execution, terminating a program, performing I/O, etc.). This can simplify the code generation process and reduce the size of the resulting object code.

The OpenMP compilation process can also be streamlined by using suitable runtime routines. Each compiler has its own library of supporting routines that are tailored to the translation strategy it has adopted. Its functionality and the efficiency of its individual functions will have a big impact on the performance of OpenMP code on the target platform. Indeed, the functions of the OpenMP runtime library typically play a significant role in the translation process. The example translations in this chapter include many such calls.

Typically, library routines will take care of interactions with the system, such as those required to start up and manage the system threads that execute the code. There are also routines to implement OpenMP user-level library functions such as `omp_get_num_threads`, but also including the `lock` routines. Some operations, such as determining the OpenMP `threadid`, will be frequently performed and must be made as efficient as possible. Others require a careful implementation to avoid high overheads: for example, the implementer must avoid introducing false sharing.

Extensive runtime support is needed to realize dynamic and guided loop schedules. These may require runtime routines to initialize the loop, to enable threads to request chunks of loop iterations, and to terminate the loop. Additional routines might be needed to compute the next chunk size for guided scheduling: the size chosen may depend on a number of different factors, including the thread count and number of remaining iterations. If information needs to be generated for external tools, the work of gathering it is also likely to be carried out in the runtime system. Run-time routines will also take care of a variety of book-keeping and management tasks. The compiler writer may choose to deploy library routines in other places too, in order to reduce the amount of work required of the compiler.

There is no standard way in which implementations create threads to execute the OpenMP code. As stated in Section 8.3.4, some implementations will do so when the first parallel region is encountered, setting up exactly the number the region needs. Additional threads will subsequently be created on demand. Other implementations create the maximum number of threads, or the user-specified number if this is known, at the outset and do not dynamically set up any others. There is also no standard way of dealing with threads that are idle. As we pointed out in Section 8.3.9, different schemes may be chosen to handle this situation. Other implementation-defined behavior includes the default loop schedule, and the number of threads used, if the user does not specify this.

As we described in Section 5.3.2, a cost is associated with most OpenMP constructs that is not present in the original, sequential program. These overheads are a result of the extra computation inserted by the compiler, to compute thread-specific loop bounds for instance, and the time taken by the runtime library routines used to perform the associated tasks.

8.5 Impact of OpenMP on Compiler Optimizations

One of the challenges for OpenMP compiler developers is to ensure that the translation of OpenMP does not unduly affect the compiler's ability to carry out traditional optimizations. If the OpenMP code were not optimized as well as the sequential code, this would offset some of the benefits of parallelization. But it is much trickier to analyze and optimize parallel programs than their sequential counterparts.

One reason optimization may be difficult is that the power of some optimizations lies in their ability to recognize and exploit relationships between different instructions: the longer the region of code that they may analyze and reorganize, the more opportunities they are likely to find. It is hard for compilers to optimize code across procedure boundaries. But the outlining strategy not only introduces new procedures, it may lead to an increased use of pointers, which also inhibit some optimizations. As a general rule, instructions are not moved past a synchronization point in the program (although this may be unnecessarily strict). Fortunately, OpenMP semantics otherwise permit a variety of traditional optimizations to be applied as usual to the code within parallel regions. Note, too, that a sophisticated compiler (e.g., [173]) may perform some kinds of optimization prior to the OpenMP lowering process.

Recent platforms may provide features for achieving additional levels of parallelism, such as SIMD or vector extensions. These may interact with OpenMP and may sometimes be used to improve translation of OpenMP constructs [173]. In general, however, the interactions between different kinds of parallelism is a matter to be explored.

8.6 Wrap-Up

In this chapter, we have described how a compiler is extended to enable it to turn a program with OpenMP constructs into an explicitly multithreaded program. We have presented code fragments to illustrate the kind of code that will be generated, but we remind the reader that each compiler has its own strategy and details will differ. OpenMP directives are usually translated fairly early on during compilation. The multithreaded code can be optimized: the compiler may do a considerable amount of work behind the scenes to overcome performance problems. Several OpenMP constructs, and the user-level library routines, are likely to have one or more direct equivalents in the runtime library. But most of them require some effort from the compiler. As a result, overheads are introduced into the program. The relative cost of features differs considerably. The reader is encouraged to determine them for the compiler and target systems of interest (see Section 5.3.2).

As platforms evolve, and OpenMP is used in an increasing variety of programs, research and development continues to explore alternative compilation strategies and runtime techniques. For instance, an alternative translation of OpenMP to a collection of tasks is considered in [176, 177]. This approach attempts to determine the dependences between the chunks of work executed by different threads and to remove any synchronizations that are not actually required. Wide-area privatization of shared data is proposed and evaluated in [117, 118].

A number of studies have been done on runtime systems. Researchers have designed, extended, and explored the use of runtime systems that can support languages such as OpenMP [119, 17]. Some researchers [179, 180, 45] have proposed adaptive methods for dynamically choosing an appropriate number of threads and scheduling policies according to the execution behavior of a code on multithreading platforms, which includes new kinds of hardware that enable a single processor to execute more than one thread. Run-time optimizations and overheads have been explored in [32, 33].

Energy efficiency [70, 109, 110] will need to be taken into account when translating OpenMP programs in the future, and we can expect to see more work on this. Some researchers [111, 115] have attempted to do so by dealing with the idle time caused by imbalanced barriers. Controlling the number of threads is a natural way to regulate energy efficiency on some kinds of multithreading computers [46].

Transactional memory (TM) [76], based on the concept of transactions [68] in the database community, has shown some promise as a means to reduce synchronization overheads. It could be used to provide essentially the functionality of critical regions, potentially at a lower cost in situations where different threads are unlikely to update the same data. As a result it could be interesting to explore the use of TM software [164, 73, 75, 63] or hardware [76, 153, 12, 71] in the context of OpenMP.

9 The Future of OpenMP

Many factors are likely to influence the further development of OpenMP. We discuss some of them briefly in this chapter.

9.1 Introduction

OpenMP was carefully designed to be a "lean," or minimal, shared-memory parallel API. Having relatively few features makes it easier for a programmer to learn the constructs; it also reduces the amount of work for the compiler writer.

But naturally a modest feature set has a downside. Sometimes, it is not easy to express exactly the desired parallelism; it may be necessary to modify a program in some way to enable the use of OpenMP. For example, we may parallelize only a single level of a loop nest (unless we use nested parallel regions). This can lead to load imbalance, or it might simply not provide enough exploitable parallelism. To overcome this problem, the application developer can rewrite the loop nest to turn several dimensions into a single larger one. But making such a change is not necessarily easy, and requiring it is not truly in the spirit of OpenMP.

With an increasing reliance on shared-memory parallelism in the hardware being designed and brought onto the market, the providers of OpenMP must consider whether the language requires extensions, or its implementation nontrivial adaptation, to improve its ability to target new kinds of architectures. By the same token, more and more different kinds of programs are being parallelized to run on shared-memory systems. OpenMP was primarily (although not exclusively) designed to exploit concurrency in structured loop nests. However, many applications are not based on this kind of loop. Additional directives might make it easier to exploit other kinds of parallel patterns.

Increasingly large SMPs and distributed shared-memory systems are being constructed, so that the size of problem that may be tackled by an OpenMP programmer is growing. More data may be processed by an OpenMP application; more threads may need to access shared memory simultaneously, meet at a barrier, or wait to execute a critical region; and sequential code regions and load imbalances may severely impact performance. Systems that execute programs with large numbers of threads may potentially stress all aspects of the application's parallelization as well as the performance characteristics of an OpenMP implementation. We have already seen that approaches that work well when a program is run on two or four CPUs may no longer be appropriate for larger computations. Clearly, one topic for the future of OpenMP is to make it easier to exploit large numbers of threads well.

Several efforts have been undertaken to provide OpenMP on MPPs and clusters where there is no shared memory. Success in this respect would provide a high-level API for such platforms while increasing the portability of OpenMP programs. This is a difficult problem but a desirable goal, and efforts to improve this technology are likely to continue.

One of the best features of OpenMP is that it is actively maintained and that the organizations responsible for it are concerned about these matters. In order to ensure that the language remains relevant, the OpenMP Architecture Review Board (ARB) has set up a language committee that actively debates proposals to extend OpenMP and attempts to find solutions to programming problems that are acceptable to all vendors and on all platforms. Anyone may submit a proposal by writing to the ARB (see `http://www.openmp.org`), and many of those under discussion have come from users or researchers.

Ensuring that OpenMP continues to provide the right set of features for shared-memory parallel programming in the light of so much innovation is not just a matter of getting the ARB to agree on new language and runtime library features. For example, operating system help may be needed to schedule threads appropriately across some systems, just as it can help to distribute data across the fragmented memory of a large DSM platform. Satisfying performance constraints as well as meeting security concerns is difficult on some kinds of chip multithreading platforms. It is hard to implement locks and barriers in software in a manner that scales: hardware support may be able to help. New compiler strategies may be needed to take different architectural characteristics into account, and dynamic compilers might be capable of improving some aspects of a program's performance at run time. Fortunately, a good deal of today's research and development in operating systems, compilers and other system software addresses the challenges posed by new kinds of shared-memory platforms.

All of the above—problems with expressivity, new kinds of shared-memory architectures, new kinds of algorithms that must be supported, greater emphasis on scalability, and support for distributed-memory machines and clusters—must be debated and may in some cases lead to the addition of features to the API. Yet it is not unreasonable to hope that a small set of extensions may solve many programming problems. In the remainder of this chapter, we discuss a few of these topics in more depth and consider their implications for the future of OpenMP.

9.2   The Architectural Challenge

When OpenMP was first introduced, most of its developers expected that it would be used to create programs that would run on a "flat" uniform-memory-access computer, where all threads have equal access to shared memory. It was also assumed that one thread would be executed per processor. The purveyors of DSM systems, and those engaged in building software for them, considered language and operating system support to help place the threads and data suitably across a platform that did not conform to these characteristics (see, for example, [165, 126, 26]). These features did not become part of the OpenMP API.

Recent and emerging computer platforms increasingly rely on chip multithreading (CMT) [168] to provide support for the execution of multiple threads on a single chip. In fact, CMT is now the dominant trend in general-purpose processor design. But it comes in many different forms and implies some amount of resource-sharing by threads that share the same core or same processor.

Some implementations provide a very fast context switch and replicate registers so that several threads may be ready to issue instructions at a given time. Interleaved Multithreading (for example, Intel's Montecito [125]) interleaves instructions from different threads in the pipeline in order to obtain high utilization of the processor's resources. Simultaneous MultiThreading (SMT) [175] permits several independent threads to issue instructions each cycle. If their instructions use different functional units, they will execute concurrently. If they require the same units, however, they may compete for access to them.

Chip multiprocessing (CMP, also known as multicore) [145] integrates multiple processor cores on a single chip. Each core is able to execute one or more threads independently. Here too, however, some chip-level resources will be shared, or partially shared, by multiple threads. Early designs show a variety of schema for sharing resources, including scalar and floating-point units (such as the IBM Cyclops [9]). The two cores of the Sun Microsystems UltraSPARC IV processor are almost completely independent except for the shared off-chip data paths [88], while the Power4 [172] processor has two cores with shared L2 cache to facilitate fast interchip communication between threads. Thus, CMP reduces but does not eliminate competition for access to some resources. Figure 9.1 shows the structure of a CMP processor, an SMT processor, and the combination of these technologies.

The nature of resource sharing among threads has clear implications for application performance (see, for example, [107, 45, 113]). It is fairly hard to exploit current SMT capabilities in an application ([38]). Interference between different threads can also affect program performance on a CMP platform. For instance,

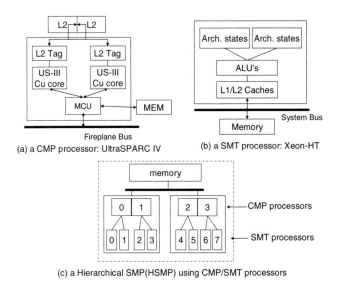

(a) a CMP processor: UltraSPARC IV

(b) a SMT processor: Xeon-HT

(c) a Hierarchical SMP(HSMP) using CMP/SMT processors

Figure 9.1: **CMP, SMT, and hierarchical SMP architectures** – Figures (a) and (b) show the difference in design between multicore and simultaneous multithreading platforms. In (c) we show the hierarchical parallelism that may be present in a system. It may lead to a complex relationship between threads as a result of the way in which they may share some resources.

Frumkin [64] showed that optimizing use of the shared L2 cache for data locality is important for scalability. Lee et al. [107] demonstrated the negative effect of the shared bandwidth to memory for memory-intensive applications.

When these technologies are combined and used in SMPs, the resulting system (such as IBM's Power5 [96]), is likely to have an even deeper memory hierarchy and a more complex relationship between threads. Cores within one chip may exchange data faster than cores crossing processor boundaries. Some threads will compete with each other for resources while others do not.

In order to better support such platforms, it may be necessary to permit the application developer to give some additional scheduling information to the implementation, for example to "spread" threads across the different cores or processors or, alternatively, keep them as closely together as possible. The operating system may be able to help by making good default choices, but finer tuning seems to rest with the application developer. If applications are not to be hard-wired to a specific machine, language support must be carefully designed.

9.3   OpenMP for Distributed-Memory Systems

Massively parallel processing systems and clusters [4] are widely used for scientific computing. Unfortunately, it is not a simple proposition to implement OpenMP on such platforms. Several research systems and one product [82] have done so by relying on software distributed shared memory (software DSM) (such as TreadMarks [11], Omni/SCASH [156], ParADE [98], NanosDSM [42], and FDSM [121]), which emulates shared memory on platforms where there is none. Under this approach, a compiler translates OpenMP constructs to the software DSM's API, possibly performing special optimizations to improve the resulting code. As there is no standard API for software DSM, most compilers work with a specific implementation. The software DSM will manage the OpenMP program's shared data at run time: it will allocate space for this data across the system, will handle read and write accesses to shared objects, and will ensure that their values are kept consistent according to the OpenMP memory model. It can be expensive to maintain data consistency, since the executing processes must share their updates with other processes at each synchronization point in the program, including (explicit and implicit) barriers, the start and end of critical regions, points where locks are acquired or released, and anywhere that the programmer has inserted a `flush` directive. Since software DSMs usually manage data in pages, the modification of a single byte on a page can cause other processes to fetch the entire page of data again at the next synchronization point. Nevertheless, programs that have been written to take data locality into consideration and that do not have too much synchronization may perform well.

Given the benefits of the shared-memory model, it is not surprising that research [42, 121, 133, 83, 157, 43] is being carried out to improve the quality of this translation, develop relevant compiler optimizations [143, 158, 116], and look for alternative strategies. One such alternative is to translate OpenMP to a distributed memory programming model. So far, MPI [137] and Global Arrays [141] have been considered. It is quite difficult to translate some kinds of code to MPI, so a translation to MPI that uses software DSM as needed has been proposed [53]. The translation to Global Arrays [84] is somewhat simpler because this API provides an abstraction of shared memory. However, tough problems remain: sequential regions must be carefully translated if they are not to be a bottleneck, and critical sections and ordered regions are likely to degrade performance significantly.

Language extensions proposed to help translate OpenMP to distributed memory include data distribution notation that could guide the compiler and software DSM in their choice of a suitable layout of data across the nodes of a cluster [156], and point-to-point synchronization features that could be used to reduce the overheads of synchronization. Another is to let the user state explicitly which data may be shared between threads on multiple nodes of the system.

9.4   Increasing the Expressivity of OpenMP

OpenMP could be enhanced in a number of ways to make it easier to obtain performance, exploit higher thread counts, or parallelize new applications. Certain extensions could further improve the ease of migrating programs to parallel platforms. We briefly consider some features that might support one or more of these desirable goals.

9.4.1   Enhancing OpenMP Features

A number of suggestions have been put forward to extend the functionality of existing features of OpenMP, improve its support for Fortran 90 and C++ [97], and achieve a greater uniformity of implementation.

Several means have been developed to allow the programmer to share the work of several loops in a nest (rather than the current single level) among threads. In its implementation of OpenMP for DSMs, SGI permits the programmer to specify which levels of a loop nest are to be parallelized by listing the corresponding loop variables in an additional clause on the `do` directive. Other ideas are to list the nesting depth of the loop levels that should be parallelized or to apply some form of `collapse` directive, which would require the implementation to transform multiple adjacent loop levels into a single loop (see Figure 9.2). This can be performed manually but is rather messy. One of the problems with providing features to share the work of multiple loops in a nest among threads is that it is difficult to implement them for arbitrary loop nests.

Since loop schedules are important for performance, it could be worthwhile to provide a more extensive set of static schedules. Suggestions on this topic include giving threads chunks of iterations that have different sizes. Another proposal would permit schedules that are provided indirectly via a list of array values. In other words, in order to determine the set of iterations for a thread, the contents of a sequence of array elements would be evaluated. Such iterations would not be consecutive, nor would they necessarily follow any other regular pattern. One option would be to let a schedule of this kind be named and reused, potentially with lower overheads on subsequent uses [142]. Another idea is to permit schedules to be used with parallel sections.

```
!$omp parallel do collapse(2) schedule (guided)
 do j = 1, n, p
   do i = m1, m2, q
      call dosomething (a, i, j)
   end do
 enddo
```

Figure 9.2: **A collapse clause might be added to a loop nest to enable parallelization of multiple loop levels** – Factors to consider include deciding whether the loop levels must be consecutive for this to work and whether loops that are not tightly nested can be parallelized. The syntax might specify the number of loop levels to be collapsed or indicate which loops are involved in some other way.

Other ideas proposed include letting threads steal iterations from other threads if they have completed their own iteration set ahead of time, and getting the implementation to choose a suitable schedule dynamically (which need not be one of the predefined ones). An advanced strategy for scheduling might permit work to be shared among a subset of the threads in a team rather than all of the threads. Then, different subteams could perform different tasks simultaneously with low programming overhead [37, 36].

One of the other places where there is scope for enhancement of the current API is in its support for nested parallelism [66]. This language feature can facilitate high levels of scalability, by enabling the specification of multiple levels of parallelism in an application [91]. It might also enable a program's structure to match hierarchical parallelism in hardware. It would be useful to allow different teams of threads to have their own runtime settings, for example for the default number of threads or runtime schedule. New runtime library routines might allow the program to test the nesting level at any given place, or to find out how many threads there are in a team at a given nesting level. More sophisticated ideas including allowing interaction between threads in different, concurrently executing parallel regions, and allowing for a predetermined mapping of the threads in different parallel regions to the system's threads.

Researchers have also expressed an interest in reducing the work of the application developer even further. One popular idea is to get the compiler to decide which variables should be shared and which should be private (or firstprivate, or lastprivate) in a parallel region. If the region contains many different variables, it can be annoying to list all of the private variables at the start of the construct (and it can be easy to forget one or more of them). It is not always straightforward for the compiler to decide which option is appropriate, and it is not clear whether this kind of support should be part of the API or could be provided in a separate tool. Nevertheless, some vendors have already implemented the idea.

9.4.2   New Features and New Kinds of Applications

Researchers have expressed the desire to have OpenMP support a wider variety of parallel program patterns [123]. OpenMP has so far been successful principally when applied to array-based computations, for which its loop parallelization features are particularly well suited. An increasing number of applications (especially those written in C or C++) rely on other kinds of data structures, however, and may have other kinds of exploitable parallelism. For them, a fresh approach is needed.

Enhancements to existing features may enable or greatly facilitate the parallelization of some kinds of problems. However, researchers have also proposed new features that might substantially improve the ability of OpenMP to support large problems and different application areas. Recurring themes are a desire to be able to express data and work locality, the need to support recursive and list-based parallelism, and the usefulness of a bigger variety of synchronization options. A possible Java binding and implementation [31, 100] have been explored.

Synchronization   Synchronization constructs that could be added to OpenMP range from condition variables and other means to enable individual threads to coordinate their work all the way to monitors and transactions. Particularly as the number of threads grows, global synchronizations such as barriers will become increasingly expensive. Despite a number of different suggestions, considering potential additions to the current set of synchronization features is a matter for future discussion.

Data Locality   Remote data accesses on large DSM platforms and clusters can be expensive. Better performance could be achieved if one could allocate most of the objects used by a thread in memory that is local to the thread. But this approach makes sense only if the data objects and array elements are primarily accessed by just one thread. The easiest way to achieve this kind of data locality in OpenMP is to declare as much data as possible to be `private`. Where this wholesale privatization is inconvenient, some way of mapping data across a distributed memory system might help. Syntax borrowed from High Performance Fortran [57] has been used to achieve this [67, 26, 156]. The merits of providing syntax for data mapping in the API itself are contentious [143], since many believe that it is best dealt with by the system. We note that on page-based systems, data mappings must suggest a strategy for spreading pages of data, rather than individual objects, across the memories. For a cluster, it may be desirable to specify the distribution of data objects precisely.

A simpler approach has been implemented that relies on storing data so that it is local to the thread that accesses it: this relies on directives that allow the programmer to mark the access to ("next_touch" of) an object that will be used to determine its storage. Other features debated in this context are means to specify a logical thread structure or even the hierarchical parallelism in a machine. The question of how best to achieve data locality in an API such as OpenMP remains an important topic.

Tasks and Queues of Tasks   OpenMP's `for` pragma can be applied to C/C++ loop nests with an integer loop counter that monotonically increases or decreases. But many more kinds of loops may be encountered in C or C++ programs. Figure 9.3 gives one such example. Here, a pointer is used to traverse a list of objects. For each of them, some work is performed on its local data. Often, each of these computations is independent of the others, implying that there is considerable parallelism in the loop. Unlike the loops that can be parallelized with today's OpenMP constructs, however, the amount of work involved is unknown at the start of the loop. Indeed, the number of individual computations will be apparent only when the last pointer is reached. Considerable rewriting of code is necessary if such loops are to be implemented in parallel in OpenMP. The same holds for most recursive algorithms. Indeed, given the variety of loops that may occur in C/C++ codes, the range of loops that the `#pragma omp for` directive may be applied to is severely limited.

To support applications with a variety of loops that traverse lists or other pointer-based structures, one OpenMP compiler has implemented a `task queue` construct [163, 170] partly inspired by the Cilk programming language and its implementation [27]. Two new `pragmas` were added to OpenMP, one to create an empty queue of tasks and one to specify the single-threaded tasks, or pieces of work, to be executed by a thread. (This is somewhat analogous to the `section` pragma within a `sections` construct, although it follows different rules.)

Various strategies have been proposed for describing and implementing such tasks, not all of which are based on the creation of task queues. We show one way in which the loop in Figure 9.3 might be described in the form of tasks in Figure 9.4. For maximum expressivity, tasks might be generated in different places

```
node *list, *p;
...
for ( p = list; p!= NULL; p = p-> next ) {
  if (p -> left)
    doworkon ( p -> left.data) ;
  if (p -> right)
    domoreworkon ( p -> right.data ) ;
}
```

Figure 9.3: **Pointer-chasing loop** – This simple loop cannot be parallelized by using an OpenMP `for` construct.

in the code, including within other tasks. In the OpenMP context, some of the questions that arise are how best to fit this into the notion of worksharing, and how flexible the rules for task execution may be. For instance, an implementation might let a thread suspend execution on one task while it works on another one. This raises the interesting question of what happens if it is then completed by another thread. In particular, this does not fit in well with the idea that threads have private variables: to permit this, some variables would have to belong to the task rather than the thread. The functionality provided by this kind of language feature would appear to be important for the future of OpenMP.

```
%node *list, *p;
%...
#pragma omp taskgroup
{
 for ( p = list; p!= NULL; p = p-> next ) {
  if (p -> left)
    #pragma omp task
    doworkon ( p -> left.data) ;
  if (p -> right)
    #pragma omp task
    domoreworkon ( p -> right.data ) ;
   }
 }
```

Figure 9.4: **Specifying tasks** – Tasks can be dynamically generated and will be executed by threads as they become available. In this example, we see a structured approach to the creation of tasks that can deal with our example in Figure 9.3.

9.5   How Might OpenMP Evolve?

Most of the existing features of OpenMP are based on features designed for small-scale SMPs in the late 1980s. They have been surprisingly useful. Larger numbers of threads are becoming the norm, however, and the range of applications being parallelized is vastly greater than that of a few decades ago. A good number of proposals for extending OpenMP have been submitted to the ARB for consideration; the examples in the preceding section are based on such proposals.

But extending OpenMP is not just a matter of technical feasibility. Compilers and their runtime libraries are large, complex software systems that are expensive to develop and maintain. Each new feature increases the complexity; its impact on optimization strategies must be considered. The more evidence there is that a given extension will meet a variety of important programming needs, the more likely are its chances of being included.

The OpenMP ARB's language committee has been actively considering a wide variety of language features, and several of these are almost certain to be included in the next revision, OpenMP 3.0, in the reasonably near future. These range from minor tweaks, such as revising the standard to allow unsigned integers to be used as parallel loop iteration variables in C/C++, to major extensions, such as adding a *task* extension to broaden the range of programs that it can support.

A couple of the other features that we have discussed in the preceding sections appear likely to make it to the next version of OpenMP. Among those is notation to allow multiple loops in a loop nest to be *collapsed*. As a result, the combined iteration spaces of the loops specified would be shared among the executing threads. Additional support for nested parallelism will probably also be provided. The features most likely to make it in this context are the ability to set different control values for different, concurrent teams of threads, and user-level routines to obtain information on the depth of nesting of parallel regions and the numbers of threads in different teams.

The ARB strives to harmonize the implementation of OpenMP wherever possible. As we saw in the preceding chapter, the implementation must set up stacks for each of the threads in a team. Since the default stack size may not be sufficient, implementations typically provide the programmer with a means to influence it. A future version of the API is likely to provide a standard means for requesting a given stack size, possibly in the form of an environment variable. Note that this would not control the size of the initial thread's stack.

In Chapter 8, we noted that it may be hard for the implementation to decide how best to deal with idle threads. In order to let the programmer influence this important aspect of runtime behavior, future versions of OpenMP are likely to allow the user to specify whether the implementation should select an *active* default policy or a *passive* one. The former would mean that threads mostly busy-wait for an opportunity to perform more work, whereas the latter would mean that they should yield resources or be put to sleep.

Another probable change is a minor modification to the rules governing the implementation of static schedules. The idea is to guarantee the uniform assignment of loop iterations to threads when the same schedule is used. It would permit the use of a `nowait` on the example in Figure 4.41.

The current language is ambiguous on a few points. One of those is the relationship between variables in sequential code and the master thread's private variables of the same name in a parallel region. Future specifications are expected to clarify this to ensure that these are kept strictly separate: implementations will probably be required to store them in distinct locations. This change also means that we might be able to continue to use the sequential object after the parallel region has terminated, in contrast to current rules.

Several other matters are receiving attention from the ARB. There is a perceived need to better handle situations when the resources required for a job are not available. It should be easier to write libraries and modular code (or to integrate components). The memory model is still hard to understand. Tools for analyzing and tuning performance [78, 79, 148, 92, 77, 136], and for debugging [54, 122, 166] exist. But more are sorely needed, as are tools to help identify possible sources of data races, and interfaces to enable tools to receive program information from the implementation. Some of these topics will undoubtedly receive focused attention by the ARB and its members and may influence future versions of the API.

9.6 In Conclusion

OpenMP was designed in an industry-wide collaboration. It is now available in most standard Fortran and C compilers, and several public-domain systems. Tools are available. In this respect, OpenMP has been a resounding success.

Providing a parallel programming API that combines expressivity and high performance with ease of use is one of the holy grails of parallel language design. The current OpenMP specification represents real progress in this respect. Among its innovations are the separation of thread creation from work distribution, introduction of orphan directives to facilitate the creation of large parallel regions, support for nested parallelism, and explicit specification of a relaxed consistency memory model.

Given the strong growth in systems that support shared-memory parallel applications, and the steady increase in the number of threads they can support, we expect similar growth in the development of algorithms that expose considerable exploitable parallelism, in compiler technology to help optimize such codes for a variety of target architectures, and in the run time and operating system support. OpenMP will need to continue to evolve to meet new user needs and will exploit new techniques to help do so.

OpenMP is relatively easy to learn. Sometimes, it is also easy to use this API to create a parallel program that provides the desired level of performance. Sometimes it is surprisingly hard, especially when an algorithm requires non-trivial interactions between threads. It can be particularly difficult to find bugs that arise as the result of race conditions or improperly implemented thread synchronization. The memory hierarchy and the operating system support for OpenMP on the target architecture may have considerable influence on the performance of an application: but this is not apparent from a study of the OpenMP specification alone.

In this book, we have therefore not simply introduced the features of OpenMP: we have explained the most important factors that influence the performance of an OpenMP program, and we have discussed some of the ways in which a programmer can deal with the problems that arise. We have given some insight into the manner in which OpenMP is implemented in the hope that this provides a deeper understanding of the factors that influence an OpenMP program's performance.

OpenMP is still under active development, and we have mentioned a few of the concerns that may shape future additions to the API. With its particular blend of simplicity and its high-level support for creating threads and exploiting shared memory, we are confident that OpenMP will be the API of choice for shared-memory parallel programming on a diverse variety of computer systems for the foreseeable future.

A Glossary

Address space The set of all legal addresses in memory for a process, it constitutes the amount of memory available to it. The OpenMP programming model assumes a shared address space for all threads in a process.

API *Application Programming Interface.* An API consists of a well-defined set of language features, library routines, annotations, or directives that may be employed by a programmer to solve a programming problem, often in a system-independent manner. An API often serves to hide lower-level implementation details from the user. OpenMP is an API for shared memory parallel programming.

Bandwidth For memory system transfer rates, the peak speed expressed in the number of bytes that can be transferred per second. There are different bandwidth rates between different parts of the memory system. For example, the transfer rate between a cache and CPU may be higher than the bandwidth between main memory and the cache. There may be multiple caches and paths to memory with different rates. The *peak memory bandwidth* quoted by vendors is usually the speed between the data cache and the memory system. However, the peak transfer rate may be encountered only in programs with highly suitable memory access patterns and then not for very long. The data rate that is actually measured over a period of code, or time, is the *sustained transfer rate* and is often much lower than the peak transfer rate. When running an OpenMP code on a system with a shared path to the memory subsystem, multiple threads may compete for the same fixed bandwidth. This could result in a performance degradation.

Barrier A synchronization point in the code where all threads in a team have to wait. No thread reaching the barrier can continue until all threads have reached the barrier. OpenMP provides explicit barriers as well as implicit barriers at the end of parallel loops, sections, single constructs, and parallel regions. The user has the option of removing barriers at the end of worksharing constructs to achieve better performance. Barriers at the end of parallel regions cannot be removed.

Cache A relatively small, very high speed memory buffer between main memory and the processor. Data is copied from main memory to cache and back in blocks of contiguous data, whose size depends on the machine. A block of data is stored in a *line* of cache and may be evicted from cache if another data block needs to be stored in the same line. The strategy for replacing data in cache is system-dependent. Since cache is usually built from very expensive memory components, it is substantially smaller than main memory. However, cache sizes are growing and on some platforms, small data sets might fit entirely into cache. Without cache, a program would spend the vast majority of its execution time waiting for the arrival of data, since CPU speeds are significantly faster than memory access times. Computers may have several levels of cache, with those closest to the CPU being smaller, faster, and more expensive than those closer to main memory. Data is copied between levels. There may be separate caches for data, instructions, and addresses (TLB).

Cache coherence The ability of a multiprocessor system to maintain the integrity of data stored in local caches of shared memory. On uniprocessor systems, data written into cache typically remains there until the cache line is replaced, at which point it is written back to main memory. Multiprocessor systems share memory and caches. Without a mechanism for maintaining coherency between memory and cache, code executing on one processor might not have access to values recently updated by other processors. With cache coherency, a processor is informed that data it needs is in a cache line that is stale or invalid, requiring a fetch of the updated value. The cache coherency mechanism is implemented in various ways on different systems.

Cache line A level of cache is subdivided into lines, each of which may be filled by a block of data from main memory. The cache line size thus determines the unit of data transfer between the cache and memory, as well between the various levels of a specific cache type. The size of the line is system dependent and may differ from one level to another. For instance, a level-1 cache line could be smaller than a level-2 cache line. There is no unique best size for a cache line. A long line, for example, increases bandwidth but also increases the chance that false sharing will occur.

cc-NUMA *Cache-coherent NUMA.* These are NUMA systems where coherence is maintained across the local caches of the individual processors. Maintaining cache coherence across shared memory is costly, but NUMA systems without this feature are extremely difficult to program. Therefore, shared memory NUMA systems available today generally provide some form of cache coherence. Note that the existence of cache coherence does not prevent the user from introducing race conditions into OpenMP programs as a result of faulty programming.

Compiler directive   A source-code comment in Fortran or pragma in C/C++ that provides the compiler with additional information and guidance. OpenMP directives identify parts of the code the compiler should parallelize, and indicate shared and private data, thread synchronization, and more.

Core   A component of a microprocessor that is able to load/store data and execute instructions. Beyond this generic description there are significant implementation differences. Depending on the architecture, hardware resources, and components may be shared among, or specific to, a core. Examples are the register file, caches (for both data and instructions), functional units, and paths to other components. In some designs, an individual core is able to execute multiple independent threads.

CPU   *Central processing unit,* also referred to as the *processor.* The circuitry within a computer that executes the instructions of a program and processes the data. Recent designs may contain multiple cores.

Deadlock   A situation where one or more threads are waiting for a resource that will never become available. There are various ways to introduce such deadlock situations into an OpenMP application. For example, a barrier inserted at a point not encountered by all threads, or improper calls to OpenMP locking routines, will result in deadlocks.

Directive sentinel   A special sequence of characters that indicates that the line is to be interpreted as a compiler directive. OpenMP directives in Fortran must begin with a directive sentinel. The format of the sentinel differs between fixed and free-form source files.

DSM   *Distributed shared memory.* A DSM system provides a shared-memory model in a physically distributed-memory system. The shared-memory abstraction may be realized via hardware, software, or a combination of the two. DSM platforms may differ in the way in which the distributed shared data is managed. By providing a shared address space, DSM systems have the potential to make the OpenMP programming model applicable to distributed memory systems.

Environment variable   A Unix shell variable that may be set by the user to influence some aspect of a program's execution behavior. The OpenMP API includes a set of environment variables to control aspects of the program's execution, including the number of threads to use, the default work schedule, and the use of nested parallelism.

False sharing   A situation where multiple threads update different values in the same cache line. Since the granularity of information used by cache coherence mechanisms is a cache line, it cannot distinguish between the individual locations updated by the threads. False sharing results in poor performance, but it is not an error.

Latency   Time spent waiting for a response. Memory latency is the time it takes for data to arrive after the initiation of a memory reference. A data path with high memory latency would be inappropriate for moving small amounts of data.

Livelock   A situation where a thread is waiting for a resource that will never become available. A livelock is similar to a deadlock, except that the state of the processes involved in the livelock constantly changes with regards to each other, none progressing. Livelock is a special case of resource starvation.

Lock   A mechanism for controlling access to a resource in an environment where there are multiple threads of execution. Locks are commonly used when multiple threads need to perform some activity, but only one at a time is allowed to do so. Initially, all threads contend for the lock. One thread gets exclusive access to the lock and performs the task. Meanwhile, the other threads wait for the lock to be released. When that happens, a next thread takes ownership of the lock, and so forth. There may be a special data type for declaring locks. In a C/C++ OpenMP program, this is the `omp_lock_t` type. In Fortran, it must be an integer variable of `kind=omp_lock_kind`.

Memory fence   A set of instructions that cause the processor to enforce an ordering constraint on memory operations issued before and after the barrier instruction. The exact nature of the ordering constraint is hardware dependent and is defined by the architecture's memory model.

Mflop/s   Million floating-point operations per second. Mflop/s is a performance metric that can be calculated if the number of floating-point operations is known. Except for certain algorithms, computing the Mflop/s for an entire application could be extremely complicated. Hardware counters on some processors can be used to measure the number of floating-point operations (flops) executed. Dividing flops by execution time in seconds and scaling by by 10^{-6} gives Mflop/s. Related metrics are Gflop/s (gigaflop/s) and Tflop/s' (teraflop/s).

MPI *Message Passing Interface.* This is a de facto standard API that was developed to facilitate programming for distributed-memory architectures. MPI consists of a collection of library routines. In an MPI program, multiple processes operate independently and communicate data via messages that are inserted by the programmer. The MPI API specifies the syntax of the functions and format of the messages. MPI is increasingly mixed with OpenMP to create a program that is tailored to exploit both the distributed memory and shared memory, as supported in a cluster of shared-memory nodes. This model can also be used to take advantage of hierarchical parallelism inherent in an application.

MPI Forum An open group with representatives from many organizations that define and maintain the MPI standard. Their official website is at `http://www.mpi-forum.org`.

MPP *Massively parallel processor.* MPPs are multiprocessing architectures that use a very large number (such as thousands) of processors.

Multicore A microprocessor design with multiple cores integrated onto a single processor die. Just as with the individual cores, there are vast differences between the various designs available on the market. Among others, there are differences in cache access and organization, system interface, and support for executing more than one independent thread per core.

NUMA *Non-uniform memory access.* Typically, individual processors in small shared memory machines can access any memory location with the same speed. This is not necessarily the case for larger systems, and is also not true for all small platforms. One way to enable many CPUs to share a large amount of memory is to connect clusters of CPUs with a fast network (for example, a shared-memory bus) to a certain chunk of memory while these clusters are connected by a less costly network. The effect of such a structure is that some memory may be *nearer to* one or more of the processors and thus accessed faster by them. The difference in memory access time may affect the performance of an OpenMP program.

OpenMP Architecture Review Board (ARB) An organization created to maintain the OpenMP specifications and keep OpenMP relevant to evolving computer architectures, programming languages, and multiprocessing paradigms. Members of the ARB are organizations, not individuals. The website is at http://www.openmp.org.

Parallel programming model   A conceptual system to express parallel processing algorithms and map them onto underlying multiprocessor systems. The model engages programming languages, compilers, libraries, communication systems, parallel I/O, and applications. One such model that is well suited for developing parallel applications on shared-memory platforms is the shared memory model realized by the OpenMP API.

Parallel scalability   The behavior of an application when an increasing number of threads are used to solve a problem of constant size. Ideally, increasing the number of threads from 1 to P would yield a parallel speed-up of P.

Parallel speedup   The ratio of the wall-clock time measured for the execution of the program by one thread to the wall-clock time measured for execution by multiple threads. Theoretically, a program run on P threads should run P times as fast as the same program executed on only one thread.

Peak performance   The maximum performance of a processor or system, often measured in Mflops/s, Gflop/s, or Tflop/s. At the processor level, this value is obtained by assuming that the maximum number of the fastest floating-point instructions (typically the multiply and add) are executed without any delay (caused by a cache miss for example). For an entire system, the single-processor, or core, peak performance is multiplied by the number of processors or cores. The actual performance observed depends on many factors, including the processor and system characteristics, the algorithm used, and the compiler.

Process   An entity created by the operating system code and data. At run time, it will have its own set of registers, address space, program counter, and stack pointer. A process can have multiple threads of control and instructions, which is the basis for the OpenMP programming model.

Processors   A physical resource that may be used to execute programs. Many different processors have been built, some of which are designed for a special purpose. A general-purpose processor is typically able to execute multiple instructions simultaneously since it has functional units that can operate independently. A conventional processor executes multiple processes via time slicing, in which each gets some share of the overall CPU time. To achieve this, the state of a program including the values in its registers, is saved and the state of another process loaded. This is known as context switching. Context switching is considerably faster for threads, as they share some of their state. The processes or threads appear to be executing in parallel. A single processor may also be able to execute multiple instruction streams simultaneously by interleaving their instructions or by permitting two or more threads to issue instructions. Machines with this capability appear to the user to be a shared memory parallel computer.

Pthreads Thread implementations that adhere to the IEEE POSIX standard. Pthreads are an effort to standardize the programming interface for the use of threads. The interface defines a set of C language programming types, procedure calls, and a thread library. As a library, the Pthreads standard does not fully address such important matters as memory consistency.

Race condition A programming fault that produces unpredictable program behavior due to unsynchronized concurrent executions. Race conditions are hard to find with conventional debugging methods and tools. Most common is the *data race condition* that occurs when two or more threads access the same shared variable simultaneously with at least one thread modifying its value. Without the appropriate synchronization to protect the update, the behavior will be indeterminate, and the results produced by the program will differ from run to run. Other, more general race conditions are also possible.

Sequential consistency Defined by Leslie Lamport [104], a (shared memory) parallel program implementation conforms to this property if it guarantees that "the result of any execution is the same as if the operations of all the processors were executed in some sequential order, and the operations of each individual processor appear in this sequence in the order specified by its program." If applied to an OpenMP program, this would require a memory update after each operation that modifies a shared variable and, potentially, before each use of a shared variable. This would obviously make if extremely difficult to write efficient code, which is the reason OpenMP does not provide a sequentially consistent memory model.

SMP A *Shared Memory Parallel* or *Symmetric MultiProcessor* system whose individual processors share memory in such a way that each of them can access any memory location in the same amount of time. While many small shared-memory machines are symmetric in this sense, larger systems do not necessarily satisfy this definition. On non-symmetric systems, the physical distance between a CPU and a memory store will determine the length of time it takes to retrieve data from memory. Memory access times do not affect the OpenMP programming model, but can have a significant impact on the performance of the application. The term can also refer to other kinds of shared-memory computers. In this book, we use the the acronym SMP broadly to refer to all platforms where multiple processes share memory.

SPMD programming   A *single program multiple data* programming style in which a number of different processes or threads perform essentially the same computation but on different sets of data. The user has to explicitly assign subdomains of the data to the threads. OpenMP can be used to write SPMD-style programs. Ideally, such a program would consist of one large parallel region, within which each thread would use its own thread ID to determine its share of the work, such as computing individual loop bounds. Explicit synchronization must be inserted by the programmer. While more cumbersome to program than simple loop-level parallelism, this approach usually achieves better scalability.

Structured block   For C/C++ programs, an executable statement with a single entry at the top and a single exit at the bottom. In Fortran code, it refers to a block of executable statements with a single entry at the top and a single exit at the bottom.

Superlinear speedup   Performance of more than a factor of P over the single thread execution when using P threads, for example, a speedup of 5 on 4 threads. One reason this might occur is that a program may have access to more cache and it is possible that less data must be fetched from main memory at run time. If each thread had its own processor or core to run on, the aggregate cache may be considerably larger than that of a single processor. For example, assume that a processor is equipped with a 1 MByte cache. If a single-threaded program updates an array that requires 4 MByte storage, 75% of the array does not fit in cache. If, however, 4 threads on 4 processors are used, where each thread operates on a subset of the array, it is possible that all accesses are satisfied directly from cache. Since this is much faster than main memory, superlinear speedup will be observed.

Synchronization   Any mechanism that coordinates the actions of multiple threads. Synchronization is generally essential in order to ensure correctness of the application. By default, an OpenMP program has barrier synchronization points at the end of parallel work-sharing constructs and parallel regions, where all threads have to wait until the last thread has finished its work. Synchronization may be expressed in many ways. OpenMP provides several constructs for explicit thread synchronization that should be used if accesses to shared data need to be ordered or if interference between multiple updates is to be avoided. These include critical regions, atomic updates, lock routines, and barriers. Memory synchronization, where thread-local shared data is made consistent with the process-wide values, is achieved via flushing.

Thread   An operating system entity that executes a stream of instructions. A process is executed by one or more threads and many of its resources (e.g., page tables, address space) are shared among these threads. However, a thread has some resources of its own, including a program counter and an associated stack. Since so few resources are involved, it is considerably faster to create a thread or to context switch between threads than it is to perform the same operation for processes. Sometimes threads are known as lightweight processes. In Unix environments, a thread is generally the smallest execution context.

Thread ID   A means to identify a thread. In OpenMP the thread IDs are consecutive integer numbers. The sequence starts at zero, which is reserved for the master thread, and ends with $P - 1$, if P threads are used. The `omp_get_thread_num()` function call enables a thread to obtain its thread ID. This can be used, for example, to compute a thread-specific workload in an SPMD type of algorithm, to determine an index into an array, or to label printed messages with a thread-specific number.

Thread safe   A property that guarantees software will execute correctly when run on multiple threads simultaneously. Programs that are not thread safe can fail due to race conditions or deadlocks when run with multiple parallel threads. Particular care has to be taken when using library calls or shared objects and methods within OpenMP parallel regions.

TLB   *Translation-lookaside buffer.* TLB is an important part of the memory system. It is a relatively small cache that maintains information on the physical pages of memory associated with a running process. If the address of data needed by a thread is loaded but not covered through the TLB, a TLB miss occurs. Setting up a new entry in the TLB is an expensive operation that should be avoided where possible.

Wall-clock time   A measure of how much actual time it takes to complete a task, in this case a program or part of a program. Wall-clock time is an important metric for parallel programs. Although the aggregate CPU time most likely goes up, the wall clock time of a parallel application should decrease when an increasing number of threads is used to execute it. Care needs to be taken when measuring this value. If there are more threads than processors or cores on the system, or if the load is such that a thread will not have a processor or core to itself, there may be little or no reduction in wall-clock time when adding a thread.

References

[1] Omni OpenMP compiler project. `http://phase.hpcc.jp/Omni/`.

[2] OpenMP website. `http://www.openmp.org`.

[3] OProfile. `http://oprofile.sourceforge.net/about/`.

[4] The Beowulf Cluster website. `http://www.beowulf.org`, 2006.

[5] The Open64 compiler. `http://open64.sourceforge.net`, 2006.

[6] S. V. Adve and K. Gharachorloo. Shared Memory Consistency Models. *IEEE Computer*, 29(12):66–76, 1996.

[7] M. J. Aftosmis. Cart3d v1.3. `http://people.nas.nasa.gov/~aftosmis/cart3d/`, 2007.

[8] Alfred V. Aho, Ravi Sethi, and Jeffrey D. Ullman. *Compilers: Principles, techniques, and tools.* Addison-Wesley Longman Publishing Co., Boston, MA, 1986.

[9] George Almasi, Calin Cascaval, Jose G. Castanos, Monty Denneau, Derek Lieber, Jose E. Moreira, and Henry S. Warren Jr. Dissecting Cyclops: A detailed analysis of a multithreaded architecture. *SIGARCH Comput. Archit. News*, 31(1):26–38, 2003.

[10] G.S. Almasi and A. Gottlieb. *Highly Parallel Computing.* Benjamin/Cummings, Menlo Park, CA, 1994.

[11] Cristinana Amza, Alan L. Cox, Sandhya Dwarkadas, Pete Keleher, Honghui Lu, Ramakrishnan Rajamony, Weimin Yu, and Willy Zwaenepoel. Treadmarks: Shared memory computing on networks of workstations. *IEEE Computer*, 29(2):18–28, Feburary 1996.

[12] C. Scott Ananian, Krste Asanovic, Bradley C. Kuszmaul, Charles E. Leiserson, and Sean Lie. Unbounded transactional memory. In *Proceedings of the Eleventh International Symposium on High-Performance Computer Architecture*, pages 316–327. Feb 2005.

[13] E. Anderson, Z. Bai, C. Bischof, S. Blackford, J. Demmel, J. Dongarra, J. Du Croz, A. Greenbaum, S. Hammarling, A. McKenney, and D. Sorensen. *LAPACK Users' Guide*. Society for Industrial and Applied Mathematics, Philadelphia, PA, third edition, 1999.

[14] E. Anderson, Z. Bai, C. Bischof, S. Blackford, J. Demmel, J. Dongarra, J. Du Croz, A. Greenbaum, S. Hammarling, A. McKenney, and D. Sorensen. LAPACK – Linear Algebra PACKage Version 3.0. `http://www.netlib.org/lapack/index.html`, 2000.

[15] G. R. Andrews. *Foundations of Multithreaded, Parallel, and Distributed Programming*. Addison-Wesley, Reading, MA, 2000.

[16] Vishal Aslot, Max J. Domeika, Rudolf Eigenmann, Greg Gaertner, Wesley B. Jones, and Bodo Parady. SPEComp: A New Benchmark Suite for Measuring Parallel Computer Performance. In *WOMPAT '01: Proceedings of the International Workshop on OpenMP Applications and Tools*, pages 1–10, London, UK, 2001. Springer-Verlag.

[17] E. Ayguadé, M. Gonzàlez, X. Martorell, J. Oliver, J. Labarta, and N. Navarro. NANOSCompiler: A research platform for OpenMP extensions. In *The First European Workshop on OpenMP*, pages 27–31, Lund, Sweden, October 1999.

[18] E. Ayguad, M. Gonzalez, X. Martorell, and G. Jost. Employing Nested OpenMP for the Parallelization of Multi-Zone Computational Fluid Dynamics Applications. In *Proceedings of the 18th International Parallel and Distributed Processing Symposium (IPDPS'2004)*, 2004.

[19] ed. B. Leasure. Parallel processing model for high level programming languages. Draft Proposed American National Standard for Information Processing Systems, 1994.

[20] D. Bailey, E. Barscz, J. Barton, D. Browning. R. Carter, L. Dagum, R. Fatoohi, S. Fineberg, P. Frederickson, T. Lasinski, R. Schreiber, H. Simon, V. Venkatakrishnan, and S. Weeratunga. The NAS Parallel Benchmarks. *NAS Technical Report RNR-94-007*, 1994.

[21] D. Bailey, T. Harris, W. C. Saphir, R. F. Van der Wijngaart, A. C. Woo, and M. Yarrow. The NAS Parallel Benchmarks 2.0. *NAS Technical Report NAS-95-020*, 1995.

[22] E. Barton, J. Cownie, and M. McLaren. Message Passing on the Meiko CS-2. *Parallel Computing*, 20(4):497–507, 1994.

[23] BBN. Butterfly Parallel Processor Overview. Technical report, BBN Laboratories Inc., 1986. BBN Report No. 6149, version 2.

[24] M. J. Berger, M. J. Aftosmis, D. D. Marshall, and S. M. Murman. Performance of a new CFD flow solver using a hybrid programming paradigm. *Journal of Parallel and Distributed Computing*, 65:414–423, 2005.

[25] A.J. Bernstein. Analysis of programs for parallel processing. *IEEE Transactions on Computers*, EC-15(5):757–762, 1966.

[26] John Bircsak, Peter Craig, RaeLyn Crowell, Zarka Cvetanovic, Jonathan Harris, C. Alexander Nelson, and Carl D. Offner. Extending OpenMP for NUMA Machines. In *Proceedings of the 2000 ACM/IEEE conference on Supercomputing (CDROM)*, Dallas, TX, November 2000. IEEE Computer Society.

[27] Robert D. Blumofe, Christopher F. Joerg, Bradley C. Kuszmaul, Charles E. Leiserson, Keith H. Randall, and Yuli Zhou. Cilk: An Efficient Multithreaded Runtime System. *Journal of Parallel and Distributed Computing*, 37(1):55–69, 1996.

[28] L. Bomans and D. Roose. Benchmarking the iPSC/2 Hypercube Multiprocessor. *Concurrency: Practice and Experience*, 1(1):3–18, 1989.

[29] Christian Brunschen and Mats Brorsson. OdinMP/CCp – a portable implementation of OpenMP for C. *Concurrency – Practice and Experience*, 12(12):1193–1203, 2000.

[30] J. M. Bull and D. O'Neill. A Microbenchmark Suite for OpenMP 2.0. In *Proceedings of the Third European Workshop on OpenMP (EWOMP'01)*, Barcelona, Spain, September 2001.

[31] J. M. Bull and M. D. Westhead. Towards OpenMP for Java. In *in Proceedings of the Second European Workshop on OpenMP*, pages 98–105, Edinburgh, UK, 2000.

[32] Mihai Burcea and Michael Voss. A runtime optimization system for OpenMP. In *WOMPAT '03*, pages 42–53, 2003.

[33] Mihai Burcea and Michael Voss. Managing Compilation Overheads in a Runtime Specializer for OpenMP. In *IASTED PDCS*, pages 181–186, 2005.

[34] K.M. Chandy and J. Misra. *Parallel Program Design: A Foundation.* Addison-Wesley, Reading, MA, 1988.

[35] B. Chapman, F. Bregier, A. Patil, and A. Prabhakar. Achieving high performance under OpenMP on ccNUMA and software distributed shared memory systems. *Concurrency and Computation Practice and Experience*, 14:1–17, 2002.

[36] Barbara M. Chapman, Lei Huang, Haoqiang Jin, Gabriele Jost, and Bronis R. de Supinski. Toward Enhancing OpenMP's Work-Sharing Directives. In *Europar 2006*, pages 645–654, 2006.

[37] Barbara M. Chapman, Lei Huang, Gabriele Jost, Haoqiang Jin, and Bronis R. de Supinski. Support for flexibility and user control of worksharing in OpenMP. Technical Report NAS-05-015, National Aeronautics and Space Administration, October 2005.

[38] Y.-K. Chen, M. Holliman, E. Debes, S. Zheltov, A. Knyazev, S. Bratanov, R. Belenov, and I. Santos. Media applications on hyperthreading technology. *Intel Technology Journal*, 1, 2002.

[39] Yongjian Chen, Jianjiang Li, Shengyuan Wang, and Dingxing Wang. ORC-OpenMP: An OpenMP compiler based on ORC. In *International Conference on Computational Science*, pages 414–423, 2004.

[40] cOMPunity – the community of OpenMP users. `http://www.compunity.org/`.

[41] Keith D. Cooper and Linda Torczon. *Engineering a Compiler.* Morgan Kaufmann Publishers, Inc., SanFrancisco, 2004.

[42] J. J. Costa, T. Cortes, X. Martorell, E. Ayguade, and J. Labarta. Running OpenMP Applications Efficiently on an Everything-Shared SDSM. In *Proceedings of the 18th International Parallel and Distributed Processing Symposium (IPDPS '04)*. IEEE, 2004.

[43] Alan L. Cox, Eyal de Lara, Charlie Hu, and Willy Zwaenepoel. A performance comparison of homeless and home-based lazy release consistency protocols in software shared memory. In *HPCA '99: Proceedings of the 5th International Symposium on High Performance Computer Architecture*, page 279, Washington, DC, 1999. IEEE Computer Society.

[44] D.E. Culler, J.P. Singh, and A. Gupta. *Parallel Computer Architecture, A Hardware/Software Approach*. Morgan Kaufmann Publishers, Inc., San Francisco, CA, 1999.

[45] Matthew Curtis-Maury, Xiaoning Ding, Christos D. Antonopoulos, and Dimitrios S. Nikolopoulos. An Evaluation of OpenMP on Current and Emerging Multithreaded/Multicore Processors. In *Proceedings of the 1st International Workshop on OpenMP (IWOMP)*, Eugene, OR, June 2005.

[46] Matthew Curtis-Maury, James Dzierwa, Christos D. Antonopoulis, and Dimitros S. Nikolopoulos. Online Strategies for High-Performance Power-Aware Thread Execution on Emerging Multiprocessors. In *Parallel and Distributed Processing Symposium, 2006 (IPDPS 2006)*, page 8, April 2006.

[47] Bronis R. de Supinski. The Sphinx Parallel Microbenchmark Suite. `http://www.llnl.gov/CASC/sphinx/sphinx.html`, 2001.

[48] J. B. Dennis and E. C. Van Horn. Programming semantics for multiprogrammed computations. *Comm. ACM*, 9(3):143–155, 1966.

[49] R. Van der Wijngaart and H. Jin. NAS Parallel Benchmarks, Multi-Zone Versions. *NAS Technical Report NAS-03-010*, 2003.

[50] E. W. Dijkstra. Cooperating sequential processes. In F. Genuys, editor, *Programming Languages*, pages 43–112. Academic Press, New York, 1968.

[51] E.W. Dijkstra. Solution of a problem in concurrent programming control. *Comm. ACM*, 8(9):569, 1965.

[52] M. Jahed Djomehri and Rupak Biswas. Performance enhancement strategies for multi-block overset grid CFD applications. *Parallel Computing*, 29:1791–1810, 2003.

[53] Rudolf Eigenmann, Jay Hoeflinger, Robert H. Kuhn, David Padua, Ayon Basumallik, Seung-Jai Min, and Jiajing Zhu. Is OpenMP for Grids? In *International Parallel and Distributed Processing Symposium (IPDPS'02)*, Fort Lauderdale, FL, April 2002.

[54] Etnus. Totalview^{TM}. http://www.etnus.com/.

[55] M. J. Flynn. Some Computer Organizations and Their Effectiveness. *IEEE Transactions on Computing*, C-21:948–960, 1972.

[56] European Center for Parallelism of Barcelona. The Paraver Performance Analysis System. http://www.cepba.upc.edu/paraver/.

[57] High Performance Fortran Forum. High Performance Fortran Language Specification. *Scientific Programming*, 2(1):1 – 270, 1993.

[58] MPI Forum. MPI-2: Extensions to the Message-Passing Interface. http://www.mpi-forum.org/docs/mpi-20-html/mpi2-report.html, 1997.

[59] Parallel Computing Forum. PCF Parallel Fortran Extensions, V5.0. *ACM Sigplan Fortran Forum*, 10(3):1–57, 1991.

[60] G. Fox, M. Johnson, G. Lyzenga, S. Otto, J. Salmon, and D. Walker. *Solving Problems on Concurrent Processors* , volume 1. Prentice Hall, Englewood Cliffs, 1988.

[61] G. C. Fox, R. D. Williams, and P. C. Messina. *Parallel Computing Works!* Morgan Kaufmann Publishers, Inc., 1994.

[62] S. Frank, H. Burkhardt, and J. Rothnie. The KSR1: Bridging the Gap between Shared Memory and MPPs. In *Proceedings of the COMPCON Digest of Papers*, pages 285–294, 1993.

[63] K. Fraser. *Practical lock-freedom.* PhD thesis, University of Cambridge, 2003.

[64] M. Frumkin. Efficiency and Scalability of an Explicit Operator on an IBM POWER4 System. Technical Report NAS-02-008, NASA Ames Research Center, August 2002.

[65] M. Galles and E. Williams E. Performance Optimizations, Implementation and Verification of the SGI Challenge Multiprocessor. In *Proceedings of the 27th Hawaii International Conference on System Sciences Vol 1: Architecture*, 1993.

[66] M. Gonzalez, E. Ayguade, X. Martorell, J. Labarta, N. Navaro, and J. Oliver. NanosCompiler: Supporting Flexible Multilevel Parallelism in OpenMP. *Concurrency: Practice and Experience, Special Issue on OpenMP*, 12(12):1205–1218, 2000.

[67] Silicon Graphics. MIPSPro 7 Fortran 90 Commands and Directives Reference Manual 007-3696-03. Reference manual, Silicon Graphics Inc., 2002.

[68] Jim Gray and Andreas Reuter. *Transaction Processing: Concepts and Techniques.* Morgan Kaufmann Publishers, Inc., San Francisco, CA, 1993.

[69] W. Gropp, E. Lusk, and A. Skjellum. *Using MPI. Portable Parallel Programming with the Message-Passing Interface.* MIT Press, Cambridge, MA, 2nd edition, 1999.

[70] S. Gunther, F. Binns, D. M. Carmean, and J. C. Hall. Managing the impact of increasing microprocessor power consumption. *Intel Technology Journal,* Q1, 2001.

[71] Lance Hammond, Vicky Wong, Mike Chen, Brian D. Carlstrom, John D. Davis, Ben Hertzberg, Manohar K. Prabhu, Honggo Wijaya, Christos Kozyrakis, and Kunle Olukotun. Transactional Memory Coherence and Consistency. In *Proceedings of the 31st Annual International Symposium on Computer Architecture,* page 102. IEEE Computer Society, Jun 2004.

[72] P. Brinch Hansen. *Studies in Computational Science.* Prentice-Hall, Englewood Cliffs, NJ, 1995.

[73] Tim Harris and Keir Fraser. Language support for lightweight transactions. In *Proceedings of the 2003 ACM SIGPLAN Conference on Object-Oriented Programming Systems, Languages and Applications, OOPSLA,* pages 388–402, 2003.

[74] J.L. Hennessy and D.A. Patterson. *Computer Architecture: A Quantitative Approach.* Morgan Kaufmann Publishers, Inc., San Francisco, CA, 2nd edition, 1996.

[75] M. Herlihy, V. Luchangco, M. Moir, and W.N. Scherer. Software transactional memory for dynamic-sized data structures. In *Twenty-Second Annual ACM SIGACT-SIGOPS Symposium on Principles of Distributed Computing,* 2003.

[76] Maurice Herlihy, J. Eliot, and B. Moss. Transactional memory: Architectural support for lock-free data structures. In *ISCA '93: Proceedings of the 20th Annual Intl. Symposium on Computer Architecture,* pages 289–300, New York, NY, 1993. ACM Press.

[77] O. Hernandez, F. Song, B. Chapman, J. Dongarra, B. Mohr, S. Moore, and F. Wolf. Performance Instrumentation and Compiler Optimizations for MPI/OpenMP Applications. In *Proceedings of the 2nd International Workshop on OpenMP (IWOMP)*, 2006.

[78] Oscar Hernandez, Chunhua Liao, and Barbara Chapman. Dragon: A static and dynamic tool for OpenMP. In *Workshop on OpenMP Applications and Tools (WOMPAT '04)*, Houston, TX, 2004. University of Houston.

[79] Oscar Hernandez, Chunhua Liao, and Barbara Chapman. A tool to display array access patterns in OpenMP programs. In *PARA'04 Workshop On State-Of-The-Art In Scientific Computing*. Springer, 2004.

[80] D. Hillis. *The Connection Machine*. MIT Press, Cambridge, MA, 1985.

[81] C.A.R. Hoare. Monitors: An operating system structuring concept. *Comm. ACM*, 17(10):549–557, 1974.

[82] Jay P. Hoeflinger. Extending OpenMP to Clusters. White paper, Intel Corporation, 2006.

[83] Y. Charlie Hu, Honghui Lu, Alan L. Cox, and Willy Zwaenepoel. OpenMP for networks of SMPs. *Journal of Parallel and Distributed Computing*, 60(12):1512–1530, 2000.

[84] Lei Huang, Barbara Chapman, and Zhenying Liu. Towards a more efficient implementation of OpenMP for clusters via translation to Global Arrays. *Parallel Computing*, 31(10-12), 2005.

[85] K. Hwang. *Advanced Computer Architecture: Parallelism, Scalability, Programmability*. McGraw-Hill, New York, 1993.

[86] IBM. Processor affinity on AIX. `http://www-128.ibm.com/developerworks/aix/library/au-processinfinity.html`.

[87] Intel. Intel^{TM} thread checker and thread profiler. `http://www.intel.com/software/products/threading`, 2003.

[88] Q. Jacobson. UltraSPARC IV processors. In *Microprocessor Forum*, 2003.

[89] H. Jin and R. Van der Wijngaart. Performance Characteristics of the multi-zone NAS Parallel Benchmarks. *Proceedings of the International Parallel and Distributed Processing Symposium (IPDPS)*, 2004.

[90] H. Jin, M. Frumkin, and J. Yan. The OpenMP Implementation of NAS Parallel Benchmarks and Its Performance. *NAS Technical Report NAS-99-011*, 1991.

[91] H. Jin, G. Jost, J. Yan, E. Ayguade, M. Gonzalez, and X. Martorell. Automatic Multilevel Parallelization using OpenMP. *Scientific Programming*, 11(2):177–190, 2003.

[92] S. P. Johnson, Emyr Evans, Haoqiang Jin, and Cos S. Ierotheou. The Para-Wise Expert Assistant – Widening Accessibility to Efficient and Scalable Tool Generated OpenMP Code. In *WOMPAT '04*, pages 67–82, 2004.

[93] Gabriele Jost, Haoqiang Jin, Dieter an Mey, and Ferhat Hatay. Comparing the OpenMP, MPI, and Hybrid Programming Paradigm on an SMP Cluster. *Proceedings of the 5th European Workshop on OpenMP*, 2003.

[94] Gabriele Jost, Jesús Labarta, and Judit Gimenez. What Multilevel Parallel Programs Do When You Are Not Watching: A Performance Analysis Case Study Comparing MPI/OpenMP, MLP, and Nested OpenMP. In *WOMPAT '04*, volume 3349 of *Lecture Notes in Computer Science*, pages 29–40. Springer, 2004.

[95] N.P. Jouppi and D. Wall. Available instruction-level parallelism for super-scalar and superpipelined machines. In *Proceedings of ASPLOS III*, pages 272–282, 1989.

[96] R. Kalla, B. Sinharoy, and J. Tendler. IBM POWER5 chip: a dualcore multithreaded processor. *IEEE Micro*, 24(2):40–47, 2004.

[97] Shi-Jung Kao. Managing C++ OpenMP Code and Its Exception Handling. In *OpenMP Shared Memory Parallel Programming: International Workshop on OpenMP Applications and Tools (WOMPAT '03)*, pages 227–243. Springer-Verlag Heidelberg, 2003.

[98] Y.-S. Kee, J.-S. Kim, and S. Ha. ParADE: An OpenMP programming environment for SMP cluster systems. November 15–21, 2003.

[99] David Keppel. Tools and Techniques for Building Fast Portable Threads Packages. Technical Report 93-05-06, Department of CS&E, University of Washington, Seattle, WA, May 1993.

[100] Michael Klemm, Ronald Veldema, Matthias Bezold, and Michael Philippsen1. A Proposal for OpenMP for Java. In *Proceedings of the 2nd International Workshop on OpenMP (IWOMP)*, 2006.

[101] C. H. Koelbel, D. B. Loveman, R. S. Schreiber, Guy L. Steele Jr., and M. E. Zosel. *The High Performance Fortran Handbook*. MIT Press, Cambridge, MA, 1993.

[102] V. Kumar, A: Grama, A. Gupta, and G. Karypis. *Introduction to Parallel Computing: Design and Analysis of Algorithms*. Benjamin/Cummings Publishing Company, 1994.

[103] Los Alamos National Laboratory. The Parallel Ocean Program (POP). `http://climate.lanl.gov/Models/POP/`, 2004.

[104] L. Lamport. How to make a multiprocessor computer that correctly executes multiprocess programs. *IEEE Trans. on Software Engineering*, C-28(9):690–691, 1979.

[105] Leslie Lamport. How to make a correct multiprocess program execute correctly on a multiprocessor. *IEEE Trans. Comput.*, 46(7):779–782, 1997.

[106] J.P. Laudon and D. Lenoski. The SGI Origin: A ccNUMA highly scalable server. In *Proceedings of the 24th Int. Symposium on Computer Architecture*, 1997.

[107] M. Lee, B. Whitney, and N. Copty. Performance and Scalability of OpenMP Programs on the Sun Fire™ E25K Throughput Computing Server. In *WOMPAT '04*, pages 19–28, Houston, TX, 2004.

[108] B. Lewis and D. Berg. *Multithreaded Programming with Pthreads*. Sun Microsystems Press, Mountain View, CA, 1998.

[109] J. Li and J. F. Martinez. Dynamic power-performance adaptation of parallel computation on chip multiprocessors. In *Intl. Symp. on High-Performance Computer Architecture*, Feb. 2006.

[110] J. Li and J. F. Martnez. Power-performance implications of thread-level parallelism in chip multiprocessors. In *Intl. Symp. on Performance Analysis of Systems and Software(ISPASS)*, 2005.

[111] Jian Li, Jose F. Martinez, and Michael C. Huang. The Thrifty Barrier: Energy-Aware Synchronization in Shared-Memory Multiprocessors. In *HPCA '04: Proceedings of the 10th International Symposium on High Performance Computer Architecture*, page 14, Washington, DC, 2004. IEEE Computer Society.

[112] Chunhua Liao, Oscar Hernandez, Barbara Chapman, Wenguang Chen, and Weimin Zheng. OpenUH: An optimizing, portable OpenMP compiler. In *12th Workshop on Compilers for Parallel Computers*, 2006.

[113] Chunhua Liao, Zhenying Liu, Lei Huang, and Barbara Chapman. Evaluating OpenMP on chip multithreading platforms. In *Proceedings of the 1st International Workshop on OpenMP (IWOMP)*, Eugene, OR, June 2005.

[114] N.R. Lincoln. Technology and design tradeoffs in the creation of a modern supercomputer. In *Supercomputers. Class VI Systems: Hardware and Software*, pages 83–111. North-Holland, Amsterdam, 1986.

[115] Chun Liu, Anand Sivasubramaniam, Mahmut Kandemir, and Mary Jane Irwin. Exploiting Barriers to Optimize Power Consumption of CMPs. In *IPDPS '05: Proceedings of the 19th IEEE International Parallel and Distributed Processing Symposium (IPDPS'05) - Papers*, page 5.1, Washington, DC, 2005. IEEE Computer Society.

[116] Zhenying Liu, Barbara Chapman, Yi Wen, Lei Huang, and Oscar Hernandez. Analyses for the translation of OpenMP codes into SPMD style with array privatization. In *OpenMP Shared Memory Parallel Programming: International Workshop on OpenMP Applications and Tools, WOMPAT '03, June 26-27, 2003. Proceedings*, volume 2716 of *Lecture Notes in Computer Science*, pages 26–41. Springer-Verlag, Heidelberg, June 2003.

[117] Zhenying Liu, Barbara Chapman, Tien-Hsiung Weng, and Oscar Hernandez. Improving the performance of OpenMP by array privatization. In *OpenMP Shared Memory Parallel Programming: International Workshop on OpenMP Applications and Tools (WOMPAT '03)*, pages 244–259. Springer-Verlag Heidelberg, 2003.

[118] Ami Marowka, Zhenying Liu, and Barbara Chapman. OpenMP-Oriented applications for distributed shared memory architectures. *Concurrency and Computation: Practice and Experience*, 16(4):371–384, April 2004.

[119] X. Martorell, J. Labarta, N. Navarro, and E. Ayguade. Nano-threads library design, implementation and evaluation. Technical Report UPC-DAC-1995-33, Universitat Politecnica de Catalunya, 1995.

[120] Xavier Martorell, Jesus Labarta, Nacho Navarro, and Eduard Ayguade. A Library Implementation of the Nano-Threads Programming Model. In *Euro-Par, Vol. II*, pages 644–649, 1996.

[121] H. Matsuba and Y. Ishikawa. OpenMP on the FDSM Software Distributed Shared Memory. In *Fifth European Workshop on OpenMP, EWOMP'03*, Aachen, Germany, September, 2003.

[122] G. Matthews, R. Hood, H. Jin, S. P. Johnson, and C. S. Ierotheou. Automatic relative debugging of OpenMP programs. In *European Workshop of OpenMP (EWOMP'03)*, 2003.

[123] Timothy G. Mattson, Berverly A. Sanders, and Berna Massingill. *Patterns for Parallel Programming*. Addison-Wesley Professional, 2004.

[124] D. J. Mavriplis, M. J. Aftosmis, and M. Berger. High Resolution Aerospace Applications Using the NASA Columbia Supercomputer. *International Journal of High Performance Computing Applications*, 21:106–126, 2007.

[125] Cameron McNairy and Rohit Bhatia. Montecito: A Dual-Core, Dual-Thread Itanium Processor. *IEEE Micro*, 25(2):10–20, 2005.

[126] J. Merlin. Distributed OpenMP: Extensions to OpenMP for SMP clusters. In *2nd European Workshop on OpenMP (EWOMP'00)*, Edinburgh, UK, September, 2000.

[127] Sun Microsystems. Solaris Memory Placement Optimization and Sun Fire Servers. `http://www.sun.com/servers/wp/docs/mpo_v7_CUSTOMER.pdf`.

[128] Sun Microsystems. Sun Studio 11 Performance Analyzer. `http://docs.sun.com/app/docs/doc/819-3687`.

[129] Sun Microsystems. Sun Studio Compilers and Tools. `http://developers.sun.com/sunstudio`.

[130] Sun Microsystems. Sun Studio Thread Analyzer. `http://developers.sun.com/sunstudio/`.

[131] Sun Microsystems. UltraSPARC® III Cu User's Manual. http://www.sun.com/processors/manuals/USIIIv2.pdf.

[132] Sun Microsystems. UltraSPARC® IV Processor User's Manual Supplement. http://www.sun.com/processors/manuals/USIV_v1.0.pdf.

[133] Seung-Jai Min, Ayon Basumallik, and Rudolf Eigenmann. Optimizing OpenMP programs on software distributed shared memory systems. *International Journal of Parallel Programming*, 31(3):225–249.

[134] Seung Jai Min, Seon Wook Kim, Michael Voss, Sang Ik Lee, and Rudolf Eigenmann. Portable compilers for OpenMP. In *WOMPAT '01: Proceedings of the International Workshop on OpenMP Applications and Tools*, pages 11 19. Springer-Verlag, 2001.

[135] K. Miura and K. Uchida. FACOM vector processor VP-100/VP-200. In J.S. Kowalik, editor, *High-Speed Computation*, volume 7 of *NATO ASI Series F: Computer and System Sciences*, pages 127–138. Springer, Berlin, 1984.

[136] B. Mohr and F Wolf. KOJAK - A Tool Set for Automatic Performance Analysis of Parallel Applications. In *Proceedings of the European Conference on Parallel Computing (EuroPar)*, pages 1301–1304, 2003.

[137] MPI Forum. MPI: A Message Passing Interface. *Int. Journal of Supercomputing Applications*, 8(3/4), 1994.

[138] Steven S. Muchnick. *Advanced compiler design and implementation*. Morgan Kaufmann Publishers, Inc., San Francisco, CA, 1997.

[139] Kengo Nakajima. Three-Level Hybrid vs. Flat MPI on the Earth Simulator: Parallel Iterative Solvers for Finite-Element Method. *RIST/Tokyo GeoFEM Report 2002-007*, 2003.

[140] J.R. Nickolls. The Design of the MasPar MP-1: A Cost-Effective massively parallel computer. In *Proceedings COMPCON Digest of Paper*, pages 25–28, 1990.

[141] J. Nieplocha, R.J. Harrison, and R.J. Littlefield. Global arrays: A non-uniform memory access programming model for high-performance computers. *The Journal of Supercomputing*, (10):197–220, 1996.

[142] D. Nikolopoulos, E. Artiaga, E. Ayguade, and J. Labarta. Scaling non-regular shared-memory codes by reusing custom loop schedules. *Scientific Programming*, 11(2):143–158, 2003.

[143] Dimitrios S. Nikolopoulos, Theodore S. Papatheodorou, Constantine D. Polychronopoulos, Jesus Labarta, and Eduard Ayguadé. Is data distribution necessary in OpenMP? In *Proceedings of Supercomputing '00*. IEEE Computer Society, 2000.

[144] M. Norden, H. Löf, J. Rantakokko, and S. Holmgren. Geographical Locality and Dynamic Data Migration for OpenMP Implementations of Adaptive PDE Solvers. In *Proceedings of the 2nd International Workshop on OpenMP (IWOMP)*, 2006.

[145] K. Olukotun. The Case for a Single-Chip Multiprocessor. In *Intl. Conf. on Architectural Support for Programming Languages and Operating Systems*, pages 2–11, 1996.

[146] A. Osterhaug, editor. *Guide to Parallel Programming on Sequent Computer Systems*. Prentice-Hall, Englewood Cliffs, NJ, 2nd edition, 1989.

[147] P. Pacheco. *Parallel Programming with MPI*. Morgan Kaufmann Publishers, Inc., San Francisco, CA, 1996.

[148] P. Petersen and S. Shah. OpenMP Support in the Intel Thread Checker. *Proceedings of WOMPAT '03 (Workshop on OpenMP Programming, Applications and Tools) 2003, Springer Lecture Notes in Computer Science*, 2716:1 – 12, 2003.

[149] G.F. Pfister, W.C. Brantley, D.A. George, S.L. Harvey, W.J. Klienfelder, K.P. McAuliffe, E.A. Melton, V.A. Norton, and J. Weiss. An introduction to the IBM research parallel processor prototype (RP3). In *Experimental Parallel Computing Architectures*, volume 1, pages 123–140. North-Holland, Amsterdam, 1987.

[150] A. Prabhakar, V. Getov, and B. Chapman. Performance comparisons of basic OpenMP constructs. *Lecture Notes in Computer Science*, 2327:413–424, 2002.

[151] The GNU Project. GDB: The GNU Project Debugger version 6.4. `http://www.gnu.org/software/gdb/`, 2004.

[152] M.J. Quinn. *Parallel Computing: Theory and Practice*. McGraw-Hill, New York, NY, 1994.

[153] Ravi Rajwar and James R. Goodman. Transactional lock-free execution of lock-based programs. In *Proceedings of the Tenth Symposium on Architectural Support for Programming Languages and Operating Systems*, pages 5–17, Oct 2002.

[154] NASA Ames research Center. NAS Parallel Benchmarks. `http://www.nas.nasa.gov/Resources/Software/npb.html`.

[155] R.M. Russell. The CRAY-1 computer system. *Comm. ACM.*, 21:63–72, 1978.

[156] M. Sato, H. Harada, A. Hasegawa, and Y. Ishikawa. Cluster-enabled OpenMP: An OpenMP compiler for the SCASH software distributed shared memory system. *Scientific Programming, Special Issue: OpenMP*, 9(2,3):123–130, 2001.

[157] Mitsuhisa Sato, Shigehisa Satoh, Kazuhiro Kusano, and Yoshio Tanaka. Design of OpenMP compiler for an SMP cluster. In *the 1st European Workshop on OpenMP(EWOMP'99)*, pages 32–39, September 1999.

[158] S. Satoh, K. Kusano, and M. Sato. Compiler optimization techniques for OpenMP programs. *Scientific Programming, Special Issue: OpenMP*, 9(2,3):131–142, 2001.

[159] Clark Scheffy. *Multi-Core Processing for Dummies*. Wiley Publishing, Hoboken, NJ, 2006.

[160] SGI. SGI Altix Family. `http://www.sgi.com/products/servers/altix`.

[161] SGI. Message Passing Toolkit (MPT) User's Guide (IRIX). `http://http://techpubs.sgi.com`, 2003.

[162] SGI. Message Passing Toolkit (MPT) User's Guide (Linux). `http://http://techpubs.sgi.com`, 2005.

[163] Sanjiv Shah, Grant Haab, Paul Petersen, and Joe Throop. Flexible control structures for parallelism in OpenMP. *Concurrency: Practice and Experience*, 12(12):1219–1239, October 2000.

[164] Nir Shavit and Dan Touitou. Software transactional memory. In *Proceedings of the 14th ACM Symposium on Principles of Distributed Computing*, pages 204–213, Aug 1995.

[165] Silicon Graphics Inc. *MIPSpro 7 FORTRAN 90 Commands and Directives Reference Manual*, 2002.

[166] Allinea Software. Distributed Debugging Tool (DDT). `http://www.allinea.com/`.

[167] KAI Software. KAP/Pro™ Toolset Reference Manual Version 4.0. `http://developer.intel.com/software/products/kappro`, 2001.

[168] Lawrence Spracklen and Santosh G. Abraham. Chip multithreading: Opportunities and challenges. In *11th International Conference on High-Performance Computer Architecture*, pages 248–252, 2005.

[169] T. L. Sterling, J. Salmon, D. J. Becker, and D. F. Savarese. *How to Build a Beowulf*. MIT Press, Cambridge, MA, 1999.

[170] Ernesto Su, Xinmin Tian, Milind Girkar, Grant Haab, Sanjiv Shah, and Paul Petersen. Compiler support of the workqueuing execution model for Intel SMP architectures. In *The Fourth European Workshop on OpenMP*, 2002.

[171] Herb Sutter. A Fundamental Turn toward Concurrency in Software. `http://www.ddj.com/dept/architect/184405990`, February 2005.

[172] Joel M. Tendler, J. Steve Dodson, J. S. Fields Jr., Hung Le, and Balaram Sinharoy. POWER4 system microarchitecture. *IBM Journal of Research and Development*, 46(1):5–26, 2002.

[173] Xinmin Tian, Aart Bik, Milind Girkar, Paul Grey, Hideki Saito, and Ernesto Su. Intel OpenMP C++/Fortran Compiler for Hyper-Threading Technology: Implementation and Performance. *Intel Technology Journal*, 6(1):36–46, 2002.

[174] Xinmin Tian, Yen-Kuang Chen, Milind Girkar, Steven Ge, Rainer Lienhart, and Sanjiv Shah. Exploring the Use of Hyper-Threading Technology for Multimedia Applications with the Intel OpenMP Compiler. *Proceedings of the International Parallel and Distributed Processing Symposium (IPDPS)*, 2003.

[175] Dean M. Tullsen, Susan Eggers, and Henry M. Levy. Simultaneous Multithreading: Maximizing On-Chip Parallelism. In *Proceedings of the 22th*

Annual International Symposium on Computer Architecture, pages 392–403, 1995.

[176] Tien-Hsiung Weng and Barbara Chapman. Implementing OpenMP using dataflow execution model for data locality and efficient parallel execution. In *Proceedings of the 7th workshop on High-Level Parallel Programming Models and Supportive Environments (HIPS-7)*. IEEE Press, 2002.

[177] Tien-Hsiung Weng and Barbara Chapman. Toward optimization of OpenMP codes for synchronization and data reuse. In *The 2nd Workshop on Hardware/Software Support for High Performane Scientific and Engineering Computing (SHPSEC-03), in conjunction with the 12th International Conference on Parallel Architectures and Compilation Techniques (PACT-03)*, 2003.

[178] Michael Wolfe. *High-Performance Compilers for Parallel Computing*. Addison-Wesley, 1995.

[179] Y. Zhang, M. Burcea, V. Cheng, R. Ho, and M. Voss. An Adaptive OpenMP loop Scheduler for Hyperthreaded SMPs. In *Proceeding of the Intl. Conf. on Parallel and Distributed Systems (PDCS-2004)*, San Francisco, CA, September 2004.

[180] Yun Zhang and Michael Voss. Runtime Empirical Selection of Loop Schedulers on Hyperthreaded SMPs. In *IPDPS*, 2005.

[181] Hans Zima and Barbara Chapman. *Supercompilers for parallel and vector computers*. ACM Press, New York, NY, 1991.

Index